D0236066

Encyclopedia
of
Vegetable Gardening

Encyclopedia
of
Vegetable Gardening

The Complete Growing,
Cooking & Freezing Guide
to Vegetables, Herbs & Fruit

OCTOPUS

Contents

First published in 1977

by Octopus Books Limited
59 Grosvenor Street, London W1

© Octopus Books Limited
ISBN 0 7064 0616 8
Printed in Czechoslovakia

Introduction

Planning the Plot

When establishing your fruit and vegetable garden you must work to a plan. It does not matter whether you are changing a mature, existing garden or fighting your way through the builders' debris for the first time—a plan is essential. Before you draw the plan, however, you must decide upon your objectives. What do you want to grow and what produce are you prepared to buy? Are you aiming for complete self-sufficiency? If you have only a limited space do you want to grow only the expensive items? How much time are you prepared to spend in the garden? When are you likely to be away on holiday? Will there be enough room in the freezer when particular crops mature? And, perhaps most important of all, what are the particular likes and dislikes of your family?

These, and no doubt other, questions must be considered with other factors such as the area of garden available, the soil type and geographical location. You will certainly have fresh produce and probably save money but, above all, you will derive a great deal of personal satisfaction from your garden provided that the initial plan is well designed and realistic. So measure the size of the plot, equip yourself with paper and pencil, settle into a comfortable chair and—having consulted the next few sections—start to draw your plan.

Area available

The usual-sized allotment, or a vegetable garden measuring approximately 30 metres (33 yds) by 10 metres (11 yds) will, if intensively and systematically cropped, be large enough to enable a family of four to be more or less self-sufficient in vegetables other than maincrop potatoes. Potatoes can take up a lot of room so you must decide if you are able to grow all your requirements. If both early and maincrop potatoes are grown, more land will be needed so that total self-sufficiency in outdoor vegetables may, therefore, require 350 or 400 square metres (380 to 440 sq yds). Protected cropping and out-of-season crop production, however, must make use of greenhouses, polythene-covered structures or frames and these features may add another 100 square metres (110 sq yds) to the plan.

Fruit plants, too, can easily occupy large areas although intensive and hedgerow systems of growing allow more efficient and profitable space utilization. Cordon, pyramid or espalier apples and pears make at-

Above: Runner beans, tomatoes, parsley, carrots and beetroot thriving in pots

tractive fruiting screens and trellises, while fan-trained plums, peaches and nectarines do well against sheltered walls. Soft fruit plants, canes and bushes can be grouped together with the permanent or semi-permanent perennial vegetables. Particular care should be taken, however, to ensure that sufficient space is left for the erection of a fruit cage to give protection against birds. Standard and half-standard fruit trees will ultimately require a great deal of room and are not suitable for the average garden. Dwarfing rootstocks, where available, allow the use of closer spacings.

A good sized fruit and vegetable garden may, therefore, occupy 1000 square metres (1100 sq yds) or more but, in this age of smaller gardens, not everyone is able or prepared to use so much land. People with smaller gardens will need to return to their list of objectives while those in town houses, flats and apartments must use their ingenuity to make maximum use of their limited facilities. Make sure however, that your ideas are practicable, otherwise failure and disappointment will follow.

Using the house and its immediate surroundings

Mustard and cress and other seedlings can certainly be raised on window sills but the unilateral light will cause them to bend over unless the containers are turned round each day. Care with watering is also necessary, particularly when you are going away for a few days. Seeds which need high temperatures for germination can be started in the airing cupboard; but do not leave them there

to become leggy, and never allow them to dry out. Herbs can easily be grown in pots or in a window box which can also be used for strawberries or dwarf forms of fruiting vegetables such as tomatoes and peppers. Balconies, too, can be used for these crops along with cucumbers, melons and climbing forms of french and runner beans. Most of these vegetables will need a support system, and protection against the wind—in the form of a clear polythene or netting screen—may also be necessary. Balcony plants will be growing in containers which can be heavy; they require careful feeding and watering. Peat-based composts are useful since they have less weight and are easier to handle. Pre-filled peat bolsters or growing-bags are also very convenient but, again, feeding and watering need to be monitored accurately.

Patios and terraces are popular features in modern gardens and they, too, can be used for fruit and vegetable culture. Dwarf growing and trailing herbs are ideal for breaking up the formal lines of the patio or terrace floor while surrounding walls can be used to support or protect tomatoes, cucumbers, melons, sweet corn, climbing beans, trained forms of soft and top fruit and, in sheltered areas, your own grape vine. Meanwhile the attractiveness of the sitting area will be enhanced by the inclusion of containerized plants of peppers, aubergines, marrows and pumpkins, globe artichokes, cape gooseberries and, of course, tubs of strawberries.

Garden layout

When planning the shape and layout of your fruit and vegetable garden it is important to remember certain basic principles. You will have decided what area you are prepared or able to use but now you must work out how that area can best be fitted into your overall garden plan. You may have different types and depths of soil but you must always put your fruit and vegetables on the deepest and most fertile sites. The continual addition of compost and manure will improve the condition of your soil but it is vital to start with as many natural advantages as possible. For the same reason try to find an unshaded site with a southerly aspect.

Since permanent and semi-permanent crops such as tree and soft fruits, rhubarb, asparagus and globe artichokes will remain undisturbed for several years, the choice of site and pre-planting preparations of the soil are particularly important. Fertility and drainage may need to be improved while sites with soil-borne pests and diseases must

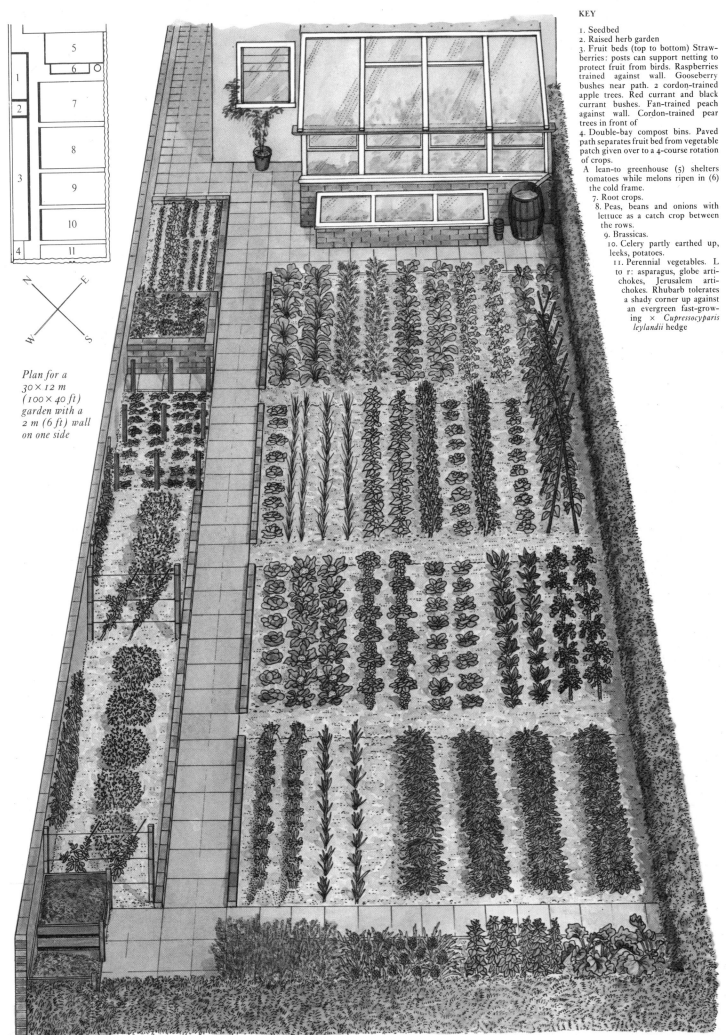

1. Seedbed
2. Raised herb garden
3. Fruit beds (top to bottom) Strawberries: posts can support netting to protect fruit from birds. Raspberries trained against wall. Gooseberry bushes near path. 2 cordon-trained apple trees. Red currant and black currant bushes. Fan-trained peach against wall. Cordon-trained pear trees in front of
4. Double-bay compost bins. Paved path separates fruit bed from vegetable patch given over to a 4-course rotation of crops.

A lean-to greenhouse (5) shelters tomatoes while melons ripen in (6) the cold frame.

7. Root crops.
8. Peas, beans and onions with lettuce as a catch crop between the rows.
9. Brassicas.
10. Celery partly earthed up, leeks, potatoes.
11. Perennial vegetables. L to r: asparagus, globe artichokes, Jerusalem artichokes. Rhubarb tolerates a shady corner up against an evergreen fast-growing × *Cupressocyparis leylandii* hedge

Plan for a 30 × 12 m (100 × 40 ft) garden with a 2 m (6 ft) wall on one side

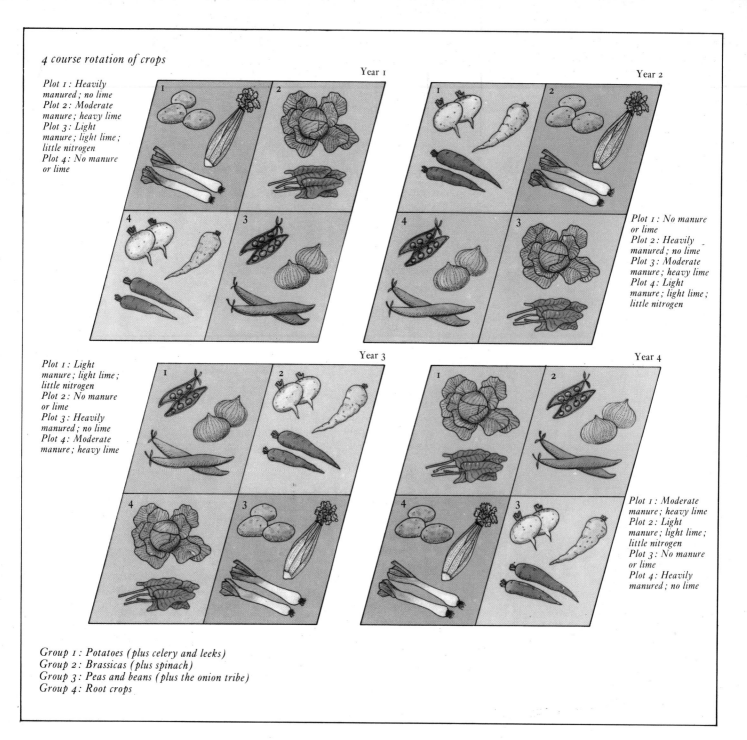

4 course rotation of crops

Year 1

Year 2

Plot 1: Heavily manured; no lime
Plot 2: Moderate manure; heavy lime
Plot 3: Light manure; light lime; little nitrogen
Plot 4: No manure or lime

Plot 1: No manure or lime
Plot 2: Heavily manured; no lime
Plot 3: Moderate manure; heavy lime
Plot 4: Light manure; light lime; little nitrogen

Year 3

Year 4

Plot 1: Light manure; light lime; little nitrogen
Plot 2: No manure or lime
Plot 3: Heavily manured; no lime
Plot 4: Moderate manure; heavy lime

Plot 1: Moderate manure; heavy lime
Plot 2: Light manure; light lime; little nitrogen
Plot 3: No manure or lime
Plot 4: Heavily manured; no lime

Group 1: Potatoes (plus celery and leeks)
Group 2: Brassicas (plus spinach)
Group 3: Peas and beans (plus the onion tribe)
Group 4: Root crops

be avoided and all perennial weeds removed. Plants grow better when they are protected from the drying and buffeting action of the wind so make full use of natural windbreaks, especially when they give protection from the prevailing wind without causing problems of shading, dripping or competition with the crops. If there are not already fences and hedges in convenient positions, space may be needed for artificial windbreaks.

Consider too, the desirability of protective cages already mentioned. Space must be set aside for the compost heaps which, if necessary, can be camouflaged with screens of climbing French or runner beans, sweet corn, Jerusalem artichokes or the more permanent blackberries, loganberries or raspberries. Similar screening may be used to hide the garden shed. If the growing of early or out of season fruit and vegetables is

part of your plan, then the site for the static protective structures—greenhouses, walk-in polythene tunnels or frames—must be allocated. Poor light, short days and low temperatures are the main reasons why plants grow more slowly in the winter.

Growing them under protection will provide shelter but you must position the structure to make maximum use of natural light and warmth. Choose an unshaded but protected site, for strong winds cause rapid heat loss from such structures. If possible build the greenhouse or polythene tunnel with the ridge running east-west; more winter light will then penetrate through the glass or polythene. Single-span frames should be sited so that they face south and thus receive more light and sunshine.

Rotations and cropping
Many crops are attacked by soil-borne pathogens which are extremely difficult to

control without a complete change of soil. The build-up of these pathogens is encouraged by continuously growing the same crop on a single site and while soil replacement may be feasible in greenhouses or other protective structures it is impracticable in the open. The pathogens concerned include eelworms of various types, club-root of brassicas, white rot of alliums and red core of strawberries. The most satisfactory method of control is to move the crops around so that those which are related do not occupy the same site in successive seasons. Before a rotational scheme can be devised the crops must be categorized into groups each of which have particular requirements and dislikes as to manure, lime and nitrogen. The usual divisions in a four-course rotation are potatoes; brassicas; peas and beans; and root crops. A suggested rotational scheme is set out above.

Lettuce, salad onions, radishes, marrows, pumpkins and outdoor tomatoes can be treated as catch crops and grown between rows of more slowly developing vegetables or sited at the end of the plot. The permanent or semi-permanent soft fruits and vegetables should be planted on a separate site and the annual vegetable plot should then be divided into four equal sized areas. The groups of crops are allocated as indicated in the first year while the order in the following year is obtained by moving root crops up to position (1) and moving all the rest down one position. This rotation is then continued each year. It is also possible to devise a three-course rotation of:

1 Potatoes
2 Brassicas
3 All other vegetables

Although pest and disease control is the main benefit of crop rotation there are other important advantages. Not all crops require the same types of soil preparation and cultivation while the manure, fertilizer and lime requirements also vary. Peas and beans, for example, have nitrogen-fixing bacteria in small nodules on their roots. These are able to convert the nitrogen gas in the soil air into a form which they and subsequent crops can use—provided that the legume roots are left in the ground. Crops such as carrots and parsnips are liable to produce 'fanged' roots if fresh organic manure is incorporated during soil cultivation so that it is best to leave the root crop plot unmanured. Brassica crops grow better and are less likely to succumb to club-root disease if they are in alkaline soil. If your site needs liming apply this in the winter to the plot intended for the brassicas. It is a simple matter to draw such a crop rotation system on a piece of paper but much more difficult to put it into practice, especially in modern gardens where plots are likely to be small.

Catch crops are those which grow rapidly to maturity between rows of slow growing plants—for example lettuces on the ridged soil between celery trenches. This process may also be called inter-cropping. Succession or follow-on crops are those which come after others while successional sowings are made—as for example in the case of peas, salad crops and spinach—to reduce the likelihood of gluts at harvest time.

Seeds and plant material
As you sit beside the fireside in mid-winter studying the latest seed and plant catalogues you will be filled with a sense of expectation and challenge but you must start with the best material available otherwise you will continually be fighting a battle. The cost of these items will be a relatively small proportion of your total costs; buying cheap or untested material is certainly a false economy. Write off for catalogues early and order seed as soon as you can. When saving your own seed be careful that the parent plants are healthy and true-to-type. Make sure that the seeds are dried and ripened properly. Never save seed from F1 hybrid cultivars.

LIKELY YIELDS OF VEGETABLES

The yields indicated are only a guide and will be influenced by soil type, situation, cultivar grown, pest and disease attack, weather, time of harvesting and many other factors.

CROP	SPACING BETWEEN PLANTS	LIKELY YIELDS PER 10m (33ft) ROW
The cabbage family		
Brussels sprouts	75–90cm (30–36in)	9–12Kg (20–26½lbs)
Cauliflower	45–90cm (18–36in)	10–20 curds of 10–15cm (4–6in) diam.
Sprouting broccoli	75–90cm (30–36in)	7–10Kg (15–22lbs)
Cabbage	35–60cm (14–24in)	1 head per plant
Peas and beans		
Peas	10–15cm (4–6in)*	5–10Kg (11–22lbs)
Broad beans	15–20cm (6–8in)	7–12Kg (15–26½lbs)
Dwarf French beans	15cm (6in)	10–15Kg (22–33lbs)
Runner beans	30cm (12in)	25–30Kg (55–66lbs)
The onion tribe		
Bulb onions	5–7cm (2–3in)	10–15Kg (22–33lbs)
Shallots	25cm (10in)	8–10Kg (17½–22lbs)
Leeks	20–30cm (8–12in)	12–15Kg (26½–33lbs)
Root vegetables		
Beetroot	10–15cm (4–6in)	15–18Kg (33–40lbs)
Carrots—bunching	5cm (2in)	8–10 bunches of 0.45Kg (1lb)
Carrots—maincrop	10–15cm (4–6in)	12–15Kg (26½–33lbs)
Parsnips	15–20cm (6–8in)	10–15Kg (22–33lbs)
Celeriac	30–40cm (12–16in)	15–20Kg (33–44lbs)
Swedes	30cm (12in)	13–16Kg (28½–35lbs)
Turnips	15–30cm (6–12in)	7–10Kg (15–22lbs)
Fruiting vegetables		
Tomatoes—outdoor	45cm (18in)	2–2½Kg per plant (4½–5½lbs)
Sweet corn	45–60cm (18–24in)	25–30 cobs
Leaves, stalks and stems		
Asparagus	40cm (16in)	20–25 bundles of 0.2Kg (½lb)
Celery	25cm (10in)	40 sticks of 0.45–0.6Kg (1–1½lbs)
Rhubarb	1 metre (39in)	15–20Kg (33–44lbs)
Spinach	15cm (6in)	7–10Kg (15–22lbs)
Leaf beets	20cm (8in)	15–20Kg (33–44lbs)
Potatoes		
Earlies		10–14Kg (22–31lbs)
Second earlies	30–40cm (12–16in)	13–18Kg (28½–40lbs)
Maincrop		15–20Kg (33–44lbs)
	*Width of drill	

Catch cropping

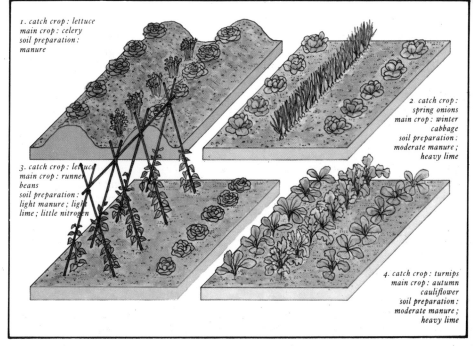

1. catch crop: lettuce
main crop: celery
soil preparation: manure

2. catch crop: spring onions
main crop: winter cabbage
soil preparation: moderate manure; heavy lime

3. catch crop: lettuce
main crop: runner beans
soil preparation: light manure; light lime; little nitrogen

4. catch crop: turnips
main crop: autumn cauliflower
soil preparation: moderate manure; heavy lime

Care of the Soil

It is a major theme of this book that good food comes from good gardens but only if the soil is maintained in good health.

Soils vary considerably. The nature of the differences depends on a number of related factors, including the size of the particles which make up the soil, the manner in which these particles are grouped together, the amount of organic matter present, the natural drainage, the pH reaction and the levels of essential nutrients.

Texture, structure and drainage

An ideal soil would be deep enough for good rooting and one in which the particles were so mixed and compounded to ensure both drainage and adequate aeration, with a large proportion of organic matter and humus to enable water and nutrients to be retained without waterlogging; and it would also be well supplied with the essential nutrients and possess sufficient lime to give a pH reaction of around 6.5.

We usually buy or rent houses without much regard to the type of soil in the garden and then have to make the most of what we have. Heavy, sticky clay soils can be improved by drainage, by deep digging, by the addition of large quantities of bulky organic matter, by the incorporation of sand or grit and, usually but not always, by liming. At the other extreme the coarse particled sand or gravel soils can also be much improved by the liberal addition of bulky organic materials, by minimal cultivations, by irrigation and by liming if the soil is acid. In some of these soils a hard pan occurs at 30cm (1ft) or so below the surface, brought about by constant ploughing at the same depth in times gone by, or by the cavorting of builders' trucks, or by chemical reactions. If a hard pan is present it must be broken to obtain the best results.

We cannot do much to alter the structure, which is determined by the particle size—very small in clays and very large in gravels—but we can do something to improve the texture, in that we can open the pores, so to speak, by working into it organic matter in the form of farmyard manure, composted vegetation, peat, green crops and similar bulky materials.

Humus

Organic matter, and the humus which results from its decomposition, not only helps to keep the soil open and at the same time to achieve the apparent paradox of retaining moisture for the roots to extract, but those soils which are high in organic matter are warmer, richer in nutrients and generally more fertile than soils not so well endowed.

All soils contain life in the form of millions upon millions of bacteria and other micro-organisms. Most of these organisms are beneficial to the soil and the plants growing in them; and soils that are rich in humus contain much more beneficial biological activity than do their hungry opposites.

Some rich soils may become acid but that is easily remedied by the application of lime, about which more is said below.

Because of the continuous process of decomposition brought about by this biological activity, it is necessary to replace organic matter in all but the most fertile of soils. This presents a problem to farmers, growers and gardeners. The farmer, lucky man, may keep livestock, or use surplus straw, or can plough-in the occasional grass ley; but the gardener is not so fortunate. Sometimes farmyard manure, preferably well-rotted, can be bought and delivered at a reasonable price. It can be dug in to assist such crops as potatoes, cabbages, sprouts, leeks, onions, celery and strawberries; or it can be used in the initial soil preparations for planting bush and tree fruits; or it can with great benefit provide a surface mulch for perennial plants. Or it can be added to the compost heap to assist the breakdown of vegetation—perhaps in many ways the best use to which the gardener can put scarce supplies of dung. The benefits are, after all, merely delayed.

The compost heap

The term 'heap' suggests a pile of miscellaneous garden rubbish dumped in an out-of-the-way corner of the garden. Such a heap is highly convenient, indeed necessary, but it is not composting in the proper sense. This is best described as the controlled but rapid decomposition of vegetation. The rotting process is brought about by the action of micro-organisms. To function efficiently bacteria and fungi require a supply of suitable vegetable material, warmth, air, nitrogen, and an environment which is not excessively acid.

The garden compost heap is often disappointing in that a small bulk of material is difficult to keep moist in summer and is slow to generate heat. A minimum size is 2m × 2m (6ft 6in square), with a completed height of 1.5m (5ft); 3m × 3m (10ft square) is to be preferred. Obviously it is impossible for a small garden to produce enough waste material for successful composting on the scale suggested, so that the garden waste should be supplemented by suitable household scraps and other bits and pieces of vegetable origin, and by material from outside. Neighbours, not so compost minded, may be glad to help and sometimes farmyard manure, waste straw or hay, mushroom compost, shoddy or spent hops can be obtained locally at low cost. In some districts fallen tree leaves can be had for nothing in the autumn. All is grist to the mill.

Not all garden material is suitable for composting. Plants suffering from those diseases and pests which produce long lasting resting bodies are best burned. It is unlikely that sufficient heat can be generated in a small compost heap to kill such persistent organisms. On the other hand, the tops of potatoes can be safely composted because potato blight does not produce resting spores on the aerial parts. Equally, the roots of strong perennial weeds are much better burned or consigned to the corporation tip.

Tough, woody material such as fruit tree prunings and Brussels sprout stems take a long time to rot down unless chopped or shredded into small pieces, which is a tiresome undertaking. Such materials, in reasonable quantities, do, however, have the advantage of keeping the heap open and preventing degeneration into a wet, soggy, airless mass. All materials should be evenly mixed—for example, soft rubbish, such as lawn mowings, with harder stemmed plants—to ensure quick and even decomposition.

The beneficial micro-organisms need a supply of nitrogen. Farmyard and other animal manures are excellent sources and the remains of the last compost heap can also assist to start the process. If these organic starters and activators are lacking, a nitrogenous fertilizer can be used. The addition of a little garden soil also helps.

The rapid breakdown of vegetation sometimes produces an acid medium but this can readily be counteracted by adding lime.

Constructing the heap

Mark out a suitable level but well-drained site and fork over the ground. Prepare a drainage channel, or create a sump if the natural drainage is not good.

Neatness is a great help to orderly procedures. The heap should be confined so that it forms, in effect, a bin which can easily be loaded and unloaded. Coarse mesh wire-netting, supported on stakes, makes for a trim, well-aerated heap but drying out is apt to occur. Straw bales make excellent compost heap walls and can also form the basis of the next heap. Wooden railway sleepers are also very suitable but rather heavy for hauling. Generally, walls formed from straw or wood are best, but the newer plastic proprietary bins have much to commend them and are certainly neat and tidy.

The heap should be built up in layers about 15cm (6in) deep, each one consisting ideally of pre-mixed material. Each layer should be reasonably firmed (if loose, open waste is being used) and well-watered.

The farmyard manure, or nitrogenous fertilizer (ammonium nitrate at 18g per m^2 ($\frac{1}{2}$oz per sq yd) for example) is added by sprinkling over every second layer. Lime, as hydrated lime or chalk, should be sprinkled over each alternate layer at 100g per m^2 (3oz per sq yd) thus keeping the manure and lime initially separate. The lime can with advantage be mixed with enough soil to form a thin layer over the surface. The heap should wherever possible be completed in one filling, the top domed and finished with a layer of soil or a plastic cover, and then left to decay at a merry rate. Most of us have to build the heap in stages over a period but the principle holds good—the larger the initial charge and the sooner the heap is completed, the better will be the eventual reward. It will be seen that ideally there should be two heaps or bins, one rotting and the other in the process of preparation.

The completed heap will sink alarmingly and if all goes well will be less than half its original size after six weeks. If, then, you are particularly energetic, after this period you can turn the heap, placing outsides to insides in the process. By introducing oxygen to the heap in this way the pace of decomposition will be accelerated. Most composters however, will be content to wait for some four to six months, according to the weather, the materials and the skill used in construction.

The final product is a dark brown, friable material, pleasant to handle and, as one enthusiast has described it, 'almost fit to eat'.

Application

Compost should be used in the same way as well-rotted farmyard manure, that is, dug in or applied as a surface mulch for the worms to incorporate in their own good time.

Green manuring

Growing the organic material on the spot clearly makes sense but the opportunities for the owner of the small garden are limited. Ground newly cleared of rubbish and rubble can be improved by sowing a green manure crop such as mustard or rape at 33g per m^2 (1oz per sq yd) and turning in the whole crop just before flowering. Mustard and rape are both members of the cabbage family and should not be used if club-root is present. Grass mown regularly in the orchard is a form of green manuring and soil improvement of great merit, but it has the disadvantage of competing with the fruit trees.

Fertilizers and lime

Plants require a supply of twelve, or possibly more, nutrient elements in addition to water, air and sunlight.

Most of the essential nutrients are needed only in very small quantities and are present naturally in soils; or they may be added in the normal way of good gardening as bulky manures and composts.

If we could obtain enough farmyard manure we could probably manage in nature's way without added fertilizers. There is however, simply not enough to go round and for the best results we must use fertilizers for those essential nutrients needed by the plant in large quantities.

In practice we need to add to most garden soils fertilizers containing nitrogen, phosphorus, potassium, calcium and magnesium, especially the first three.

There are exceptions. On soils which have a high chalk content there is obviously no need to add calcium, as chemically chalk is calcium carbonate. The presence of chalk in excess, however, may lead to the locking-up of iron and manganese with consequent deficiencies of these two elements for the plant concerned. Some soils are naturally rich in phosphates and some in potash; it is a waste of money to add phosphatic and potassic fertilizers to such soils.

It is safe to say that most soils will benefit from the addition of the three major nutrients. These can be added singly or in compound mixtures. Straight fertilizers, that is those supplying one major nutrient, include in the nitrogen group sulphate of ammonia (21% N), ammonium nitrate (35% N) and nitrate of soda (16% N). The nitrate fertilizers act very quickly and are best used in spring as top dressings for vegetables such as over-wintered spring cabbage, or in the late summer to assist bud completion in fruit trees. Phosphate is best added as superphosphate (18% P) and potash as sulphate of potash (48% K).

Fertilizers are also derived from organic sources, such as dried blood, bone meal and hoof-and-horn meal, but these, valuable though they are, tend to be expensive. Moreover, although longer lasting, they are no more effective than the inorganic materials. Organic manures depend on the quantity of nitrogen, potassium and phosphate they contain for their value as fertilizers in the same way that inorganic preparations do, but generally the proportions found in organic substances are lower than those in chemical compounds. Dried blood, hoof and horn meal and shoddy are sources of nitrogen; steamed bone flour provides phosphate, while fish guano provides about equal quantities of both at around 10%. Farmyard manure offers equal, but tiny proportions, of all three major nutrients, its chief value for use as a fertilizer being in its bulk.

For most purposes the amateur is best served by compound fertilizers, which are very convenient and effective even if the approach is of a somewhat hit-and-miss character. Two examples will suffice from a wide choice of excellent compounds. 'Growmore', containing 7% nitrogen, 7% phosphates and 7% potash, is a good general fertilizer used at, say, 100g per m^2 (3oz per sq yd). John Innes Base fertilizer, 5.1% nitrogen, 6.4% phosphorus and 9.7% potassium, more expensive because the nitrogen is derived from hoof-and-horn meal, is excellent for glasshouse plants or where it is desirable to obtain a relatively slower release of nitrogen over a longer period of time than occurs with Growmore.

Speed of response

Even the quickest acting nitrate fertilizer may be delayed when applied to the soil because it has still to be absorbed in solution by the roots; if either or both water and roots are lacking the nutrient cannot enter. Spraying nutrients on to the foliage is an efficient way to solve this problem. Most proprietary foliar sprays are based on urea but some are compounded to produce other ingredients as well as nitrogen.

Foliar spraying is not confined to the major elements. Indeed, iron chelates (sequestrenes) or magnesium sulphate can also be used in this way to overcome the inhibiting effect of chalky soils.

Foliar sprays are best applied to young leaves in the spring, but occasionally there are special cases justifying their use at other times to give a boost to growth.

Liquid fertilizers

These are usually concentrated materials offered in proprietary form. One such fertilizer is designed for plants with relatively high nitrogen needs and has an analysis of 29.5% nitrogen, 10% phosphorus and 14.5% potassium. Sometimes a different balance of nutrients is desirable; this can be met by a high potash liquid feed particularly suitable for tomatoes and containing 17% nitrogen, 8.5% phosphorus and 33.5% potassium.

Liming

The rule is to apply lime only if the soil is acid. Lime-testing kits can be bought cheaply and many county agricultural colleges will test soils for a small fee. The latter service can also be used to check levels of soil phosphate and potash.

Lime status is expressed in terms of pH values. A pH of 6.5 is about right for most food crops. If the reading is lower the soil is acid and lime may be needed. Generally speaking, a reading of pH 6 would call for a dressing of hydrated lime at 0.25kg per m^2 ($\frac{1}{2}$lb per sq yd). Lime used on acid clay soils may improve the structure by causing the tiny particles to group together.

Other sources of nutrients

Assuming reasonable supplies of bulky organic manures and the sensible use of fertilizers in the various forms suggested above there are not many other sources which need concern you.

We should, however, mention the bonfire. Some districts are bonfire free by law but where it is allowed, burn garden rubbish such as woody prunings and diseased plants. Large branches should be chopped up first. The ash yields valuable potash. Ashes should be collected as soon as they are cool enough to handle and either spread evenly over vacant ground or stored in the dry for later use. Coal ashes are of no value as sources of plant food; they are best used for making paths or, in extreme cases only, used on very stiff clay soil as an opening agent.

Summary

1) Use bulky organic matter as freely as you can.

2) Supplement bulky organic materials with highly efficient inorganic fertilizers, foliar sprays and liquid feeds.

3) 'Lime and time without manure makes both land and farmer poor.' And only use lime if the soil is acid.

4) Soil is a precious, living material. Treat it as such. For example, never work on clay soils when they are wet: there is no quicker way to ruin the structure.

5) Digging, forking, hoeing and all soil cultivations must be carried out at the right time and serve a practical purpose —not merely provide exercise.

Unless it is necessary to deepen the root range, incorporate muck, prepare a tilth, destroy weeds or lift crops, you may be losing moisture, burning humus, and generally wasting time and energy by unnecessary and unproductive cultivations.

Cultivating vegetables

Digging

Outdoor vegetables are grown in the soil which most gardeners cultivate before sowing or planting. Greenhouse soils are also usually cultivated. There are, however, a number of growing techniques where natural soil is not used. Tomatoes, peppers, aubergines and melons can be grown in pots, growing-bags or in a ring-culture system while cucumbers and mushrooms are grown in special beds built on the surface of the soil. 'Non-cultivation' systems of growing may also be used and these depend on regular application of large quantities of organic compost to the soil surface.

While, therefore, there may be reasons for not cultivating the soil such a situation is the exception rather than the norm. Digging is the most common method of tilling the garden soil and, provided that you are physically fit, it can be a very satisfying gardening operation. Your objectives when digging are the same as those of the farmer when he is winter ploughing—to bury the weeds and rubbish, to incorporate organic manure or compost, to improve drainage by breaking up 'hard pan' layers, to aerate the soil and to leave a rough and broken surface which the winter conditions of freezing and thawing, wetting and drying will turn into a reasonable tilth. If possible you should dig your garden in the autumn and winter, not only to achieve these objectives but because there is then more time available. Most vegetable crops produce roots in the depth range of 30 to 60cm (1 to 2ft). Better growth will result if a large amount of soil is available to the plants, especially where valuable soil-conditioning and moisture-holding organic matter has been dug in. Spades and forks usually have blades or tines between 25 and 30cm (10 and 12in) in length. Turning over one depth or spit of soil constitutes single-spit digging. Better soil utilization and root development —and thus plant growth—is likely if the second spit below the surface is also cultivated; hence double-spit digging. Most people dig with a spade but some use a fork. This is particularly suitable in heavy soils and when removing the roots of perennial weeds. Digging will be much more enjoyable if you have a well-balanced and comfortable spade or fork.

Good digging should leave the soil with an even surface and not with ridges and dips. This is a skill that cannot be learned from a book. The accompanying diagrams illustrate different techniques and methods of approach. You must then develop your own expertise while taking care not to attempt too much at a time.

Seed sowing

Most vegetable crops are raised from seeds, which should always be obtained from a reputable seedsman. Buying cheap, untested seed is a false economy.

Seed catalogues usually contain a wealth of useful information. Study them carefully during the dark winter evenings while you are compiling your seed list. When seed is harvested from the mother plant and then merely cleaned and purified before packeting, it is called natural seed. This is what we normally buy although it may have been chemically treated against pests or diseases. Seeds of plants such as lettuce, carrots, parsnips and celery are small, irregularly shaped and therefore difficult to handle. This problem can be overcome by coating the individual seeds with a clay-like material to produce a pellet. This so-called pelleted seed is much easier to handle and to space sow; but it also requires more soil moisture to break down the pellet and release the seed for germination. Natural seed is usually sown dry but there are advantages in pregermination or 'chitting' as a more certain plant stand can then be obtained. This is useful for large seeds such as those of cucumber, marrow and sweet corn. Careful handling after 'chitting' is most important. A recent development has been the technique of fluid drilling where pre-germinated seed is mixed with a protective gel and then 'sown' into a drill in a similar way to the piping of icing on to a cake. The age of the seed is important as the germination percentage is likely to fall as age increases unless carefully controlled storage conditions are provided. It is rarely worth keeping seeds for more than two seasons; even then it is essential that they are kept at a cool, even temperature.

Vegetable cultivars can be categorized as 'open-pollinated' or 'F1 hybrids' and the differences between these two groups may influence your choice. F1 hybrids are uniform and tend to mature all at the same time; this is ideal if you want the crop for the freezer. Open-pollinated types are more

Sowing Outdoors

Rake the seed bed over evenly. The fineness of the seed bed should vary with seed size and soil type

Take out shallow drills by drawing a hoe alongside a taut line

Sow thinly by allowing the seeds to run slowly out of your hand

Use the back of the rake to draw soil back over the seeds after sowing

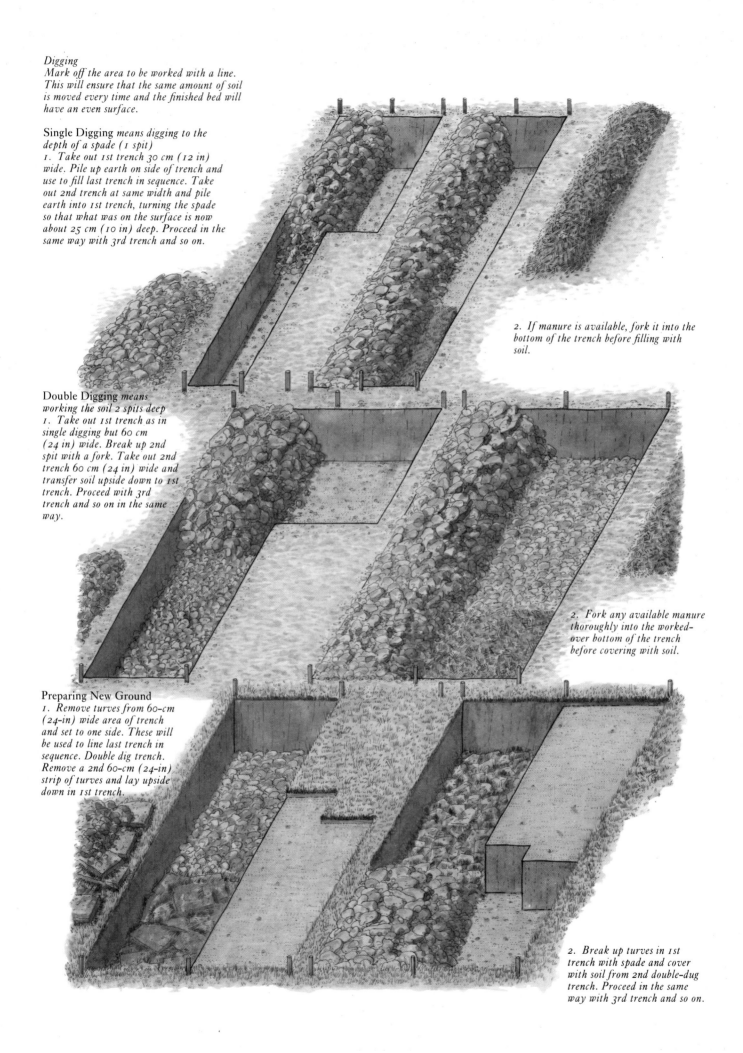

Digging

Mark off the area to be worked with a line. This will ensure that the same amount of soil is moved every time and the finished bed will have an even surface.

Single Digging *means digging to the depth of a spade (1 spit)*
1. Take out 1st trench 30 cm (12 in) wide. Pile up earth on side of trench and use to fill last trench in sequence. Take out 2nd trench at same width and pile earth into 1st trench, turning the spade so that what was on the surface is now about 25 cm (10 in) deep. Proceed in the same way with 3rd trench and so on.

2. If manure is available, fork it into the bottom of the trench before filling with soil.

Double Digging *means working the soil 2 spits deep*
1. Take out 1st trench as in single digging but 60 cm (24 in) wide. Break up 2nd spit with a fork. Take out 2nd trench 60 cm (24 in) wide and transfer soil upside down to 1st trench. Proceed with 3rd trench and so on in the same way.

2. Fork any available manure thoroughly into the worked-over bottom of the trench before covering with soil.

Preparing New Ground

1. Remove turves from 60-cm (24-in) wide area of trench and set to one side. These will be used to line last trench in sequence. Double dig trench. Remove a 2nd 60-cm (24-in) strip of turves and lay upside down in 1st trench.

2. Break up turves in 1st trench with spade and cover with soil from 2nd double-dug trench. Proceed in the same way with 3rd trench and so on.

variable, mature over a longer period and are particularly suited to gradual and selective harvesting. Never save seed from F1 hybrids because the progeny will show considerable variation from the parent.

a) Sowing under protection

Early crops of summer vegetables such as cauliflower, cabbage and lettuce are frequently sown under glass in January or February while greenhouse or frame crops such as tomato, cucumber, pepper, aubergine and melon are also raised in heated structures. If seedlings are to be pricked out then it is sufficient to make garden-scale sowings into seed trays or seed pans. Sow the seed thinly and give water sparingly as damping-off diseases are more likely to attack wet, overcrowded seedlings. Seed which is very fine, such as celery, can be bulked up with sand to facilitate easy and even sowing. Sow on to compost which has been gently firmed and moistened. Most vegetable seed should be covered with a layer of compost equivalent to the seed thickness but some—notably celery and celeriac—can be left uncovered provided that they are not allowed to dry out. Seeds can usually be germinated in dark places such as airing cupboards but must then be removed immediately into a well-lit area. Poor light will cause weak seedlings to develop while those which are raised on window sills grow towards the light and must be turned round each day. Prick out seedlings—holding them gently by the leaves—as soon as they are large enough to handle. Marrow, melon, cucumber and sweet corn seeds can be sown singly and directly into containers such as 9cm (3½in) pots, possibly after 'chitting', while smaller seed such as lettuce (whether natural or pelleted) can be sown two or three to a 4cm

sowing and good light; you must also be prepared to pay constant care and attention to detail. Look every day at the seeds or seedlings and, if you go away for a while, make arrangements for them to be tended in your absence.

b) Outdoor sowings

Outside sowings are usually made in drills. These are normally V-shaped, made with a draw hoe, but may be flat-bottomed for peas. Straight rows are most important and you should always use the drill against a tightly stretched line. Depth is important and may require a very delicate touch. Soil type and preparation will influence drill-making but the fineness of the seed bed tilth should correspond with seed size. In dry weather water the bottom of the drill before sowing. Sow the seed thinly but not too thinly. Do not oversow and cause unnecessary competition. Space sowing two or three seeds at

Thin out seedlings as soon as they can be handled. Do not leave the discarded seedlings on the ground where they may spread disease

Hoe carefully to destroy weeds without damaging plants or disturbing the soil.

Use a Dutch hoe between rows and a hand hoe close to young plants.

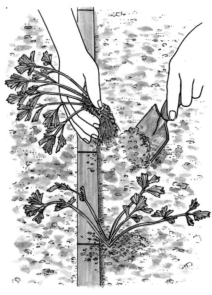

Planting celery raised under glass. Use a trowel and place plants 15 cm (6 in) apart. A measuring rod will ensure straight lines.

(1½in) peat pot or block. This is a useful way of raising lettuce for the garden as there are usually periods in the summer when we produce far too many for our needs. It is much better to sow three or four containers each week as described, thinning to one seedling per pot or block as necessary and planting them outside when they have three or four true leaves.

Seeds can also be sown under cold frames or cloches. Early summer cauliflower can be over-wintered from a late September sowing, while early spring sowings of lettuce, leek, cabbage, cauliflower and Brussels sprouts will provide plants for transplanting in early summer. Thin sowing is again essential in order to produce strong, sturdy, disease-resistant plants. Cloches and polythene tunnels may be used to protect the earliest sowings of crops such as peas, French beans, runner beans, carrots and radishes.

Vegetable seeds tolerate a wide range of germination conditions provided that common sense rules are followed. Reference has already been made to careful watering, thin

the intervals finally required is a useful technique if seeds are large enough to handle. Fine seed such as carrots may be mixed with sand to allow more even sowing. Draw the soil back into the drills after sowing and lightly firm it over the seeds. Do not pack the soil down tightly: compaction, 'capping' and poor emergence may result. Regular watering is particularly important until the seedlings emerge and strands of cotton stretched over the rows will give protection against birds.

Thinning

Even after the most careful efforts, seeds are usually sown too thickly and crops such as carrots, parsnips, beetroot, spring greens and lettuce will require thinning to the desired spacing. Do this as early as possible in order to minimize both competition and disturbance.

Planting and transplanting

Transplants may be raised in open ground or in a protected seedbed—brassicas, leeks, lettuce; or they may be sown in seed trays or individual containers under glass—onions, celery, celeriac, tomatoes, marrows, sweet corn. Thin sowing should ensure that strong, sturdy seedlings develop but they need careful handling when transplanting. Give the plants a thorough soaking before lifting them from the seedbed or removing them from their containers. Grade the plants according to size and keep together those of similar size. Transplant as soon as possible after lifting the plants from the seedbed otherwise establishment will be slower. Regrowth will be most rapid if plants are not damaged although it may be necessary to trim the leaves and roots of large leek or brassica plants, particularly in hot weather. Delayed establishment and growth checks to cauliflower will lead to premature heading or 'buttoning'.

Row crops should be planted to a line, preferably with a trowel, although a dibber, which may cause more soil compaction and smearing, is also useful. Make sure that the plants are planted firmly and always water them afterwards. Careful watering in the first few days after transplanting will help rapid establishment. Plant survival and growth continues even in very dry seasons if transplants are well watered both before and after setting out. If some of the plants do not grow the rows should be 'gapped-up' as soon as possible with plants which have been kept back especially for this purpose. Birds, too, may sometimes pull out the plants; be prepared to protect the newly planted area with strands of cotton.

Weed control
This is one of the most important post-sowing or post-planting operations. Although chemical weedkillers are available they can cause problems when used in small, intensively-cropped gardens. The potential dangers of persistence, spray drift and crop damage from herbicides are avoided by carrying out weed control with a hoe.

Over-frequent and deep hoeing will increase moisture loss by bringing up wet soil to the surface and it may also damage the plant root systems. Hoeing done correctly and at the right time with a sharp-bladed hoe should cause very little soil disturbance and leave the severed weed seedlings on the surface to desiccate. Care is needed especially with root crops such as carrots and beetroot which are easily damaged by sharp tools. Weeds may also be controlled by mulching either with organic materials, such as grass cuttings, straw or peat, or with inert inorganic materials such as black polythene sheeting. These materials form a barrier against the weeds and may not only protect the soil surface but also add organic matter, reduce moisture loss and maintain a more even soil temperature.

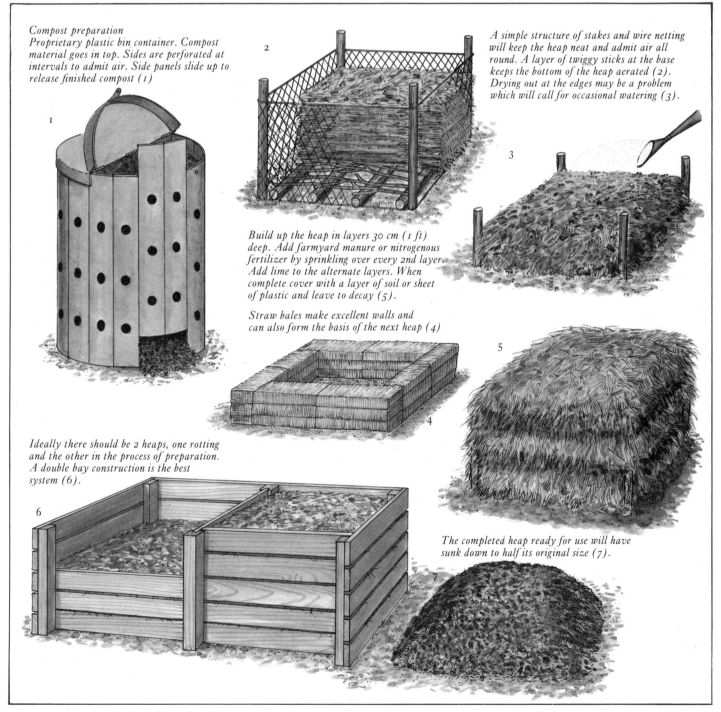

Compost preparation
Proprietary plastic bin container. Compost material goes in top. Sides are perforated at intervals to admit air. Side panels slide up to release finished compost (1)

A simple structure of stakes and wire netting will keep the heap neat and admit air all round. A layer of twiggy sticks at the base keeps the bottom of the heap aerated (2). Drying out at the edges may be a problem which will call for occasional watering (3).

Build up the heap in layers 30 cm (1 ft) deep. Add farmyard manure or nitrogenous fertilizer by sprinkling over every 2nd layer. Add lime to the alternate layers. When complete cover with a layer of soil or sheet of plastic and leave to decay (5).

Straw bales make excellent walls and can also form the basis of the next heap (4)

Ideally there should be 2 heaps, one rotting and the other in the process of preparation. A double bay construction is the best system (6).

The completed heap ready for use will have sunk down to half its original size (7).

Fruit training and propagation

Why prune at all?

Left to themselves fruit trees become over-crowded, diseased and pest-ridden, carrying small fruits on exhausted branches. On the other hand, excessive pruning can lead to too much growth and to light crops of poor quality.

All pruning must have a purpose. There is nothing magical about the process. Experts tend to complicate what should be an essentially common-sense sequence of events. Let us start with objectives:

A fruit tree should be pruned to:

a admit light and air
b train the tree to an acceptable shape and size
c increase the size of the fruit
d encourage or control growth, whichever the tree demands
e assist establishment after transplanting
f remove diseased and broken parts
g strengthen the branch structure

Information on pruning is given in the chapters on individual fruits because each differs somewhat in its requirements.

Let us take the apple tree for our illustration, knowing that other tree fruits may call for rather different treatment.

The young tree

The most common form is the open-centre bush tree. Let us start with a one-year-old maiden tree without side shoots to be pruned in the winter on planting. Roots will have been lost in transplanting. Compensate by pruning severely, leaving some 60cm (2ft). This will encourage the tree to produce strong branches. Four branches, growing at wide angles and evenly spaced round the tree, will be a proper reward in the next season.

At the end of the first growing season these primary branches may be about 45 to 60cm (18 to 24in) in length. In the winter months these should be pruned back by one third, each to an outward pointing bud. This may seem wasteful but it is necessary in order to direct, strengthen and increase the numbers of the branches and their side shoots.

During the next season you will, of course, water, manure, spray and secure the young tree, with the result that the head will have taken shape with perhaps six to eight strong and well-placed branches with a number of side shoots.

The following winter brings a problem. At the end of each primary branch there will be shoots called leaders. Should you prune these? They should be pruned only if it is necessary to achieve one or more of the following objectives:

a to strengthen the branch
b to change its direction
c to provide it with new side shoots
d to remove diseased or over-crowded branches

If it is necessary to do so for any of these purposes the leaders should be shortened again by some one third, each to an outward pointing bud.

The side shoots are called laterals. Those growing to the outside may be left unpruned to form fruit buds. Those growing inwards should be pruned back to about 8cm (3in) or removed entirely if there is overcrowding.

At the end of the third growing season look again at the leaders. Use your previous experience about the extent of cutting back, knowing that weak shoots should be pruned harder than strong shoots.

Follow similar procedures with maiden laterals—leave alone those which are well placed and shorten or remove the others. You must also deal with last year's maidens, now burgeoning two-year-olds. Leave alone those which are well placed and not competing with the primary branches. Those for which there is no room for further extension should be cut back to the top-most fruit bud. Two-year budded laterals should fruit in the following summer.

The cut-back laterals of an earlier year may be pruned to any obvious fruit bud; if no fruit bud has appeared the extension shoots should be pruned to 2.5cm (1in).

Simple rules for straightforward growing

Although there are more complicated procedures undertaken by experts, the amateur can content himself with the simple rules mentioned on leaders and laterals. These will suffice amply for apples, pears, plums and Morello cherries as well as for gooseberries and red currants, with only minor variations of scale.

The pruning of raspberries, blackberries and loganberries is straightforward. Remove the fruited canes and the weak tips of the new canes each spring.

Black currants, too, fruit best on the two year wood, but a larger crop can be obtained if some of the older healthy shoots are left.

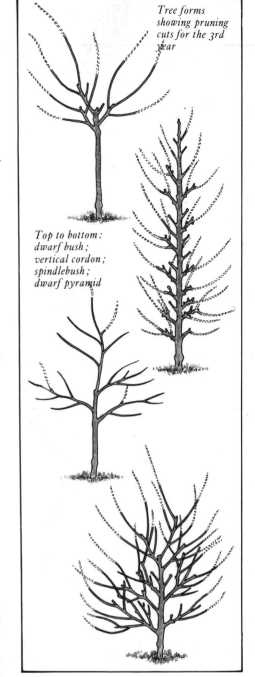

Tree forms showing pruning cuts for the 3rd year

Top to bottom: dwarf bush; vertical cordon; spindlebush; dwarf pyramid

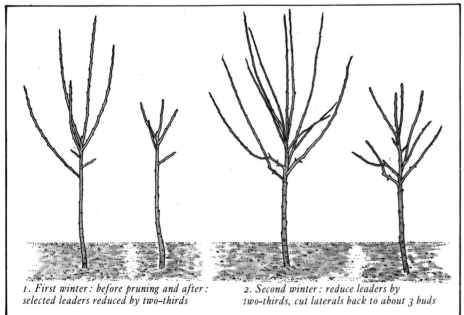

1. First winter: before pruning and after: selected leaders reduced by two-thirds

2. Second winter: reduce leaders by two-thirds, cut laterals back to about 3 buds

Training

Generally, the most convenient and successful form of tree is the open-centre bush or the open-centre half-standard or full standard. There is no essential difference between these other than in the length of the stem and the size of the tree.

There is, however, an interesting variant, now popular with the commercial grower, called the central leader tree. The main stem is carried upwards as a central axis for some 2m (6ft 6in) or so. Leader pruning is necessary but care is taken to keep the central stem for a series of central growths. The fruiting branches develop at regular intervals from this central leader instead of originating from a small region of the cutback stem as with the open centre tree. This allows trees to be more closely planted without loss of fruiting wood and is one reason for the popularity of the pyramid, spindle-bush and vertical cordon forms.

The fan-shaped tree, with the branch system trained in two dimensions rather than three, is an effective and attractive means of covering wall space. In the open the palmette shape, adapted from Italian practice, is similar in appearance.

The espalier is a multiple cordon shape, forming horizontal arms in series on either side of a central axis. There are some splendid examples to be seen in older gardens, but growing branches horizontally in this way is contrary to nature and takes a long time to achieve. The strong vertical shoots which push out from the horizontal arms in response to nature's dictates tend to be discordant. On the whole the training of espaliers is a task for professionals and dedicated amateurs.

Propagation

There is no reason why the amateur gardener should not propagate his own black currants, red currants and gooseberry bushes from hard-wood cuttings; equally there is no reason why strawberry runners should not be taken, blackberry and loganberry tips layered and raspberry suckers lifted for increase, providing always that the parent plants are healthy. Details are given in the appropriate chapters.

Much more tricky is the propagation of tree fruits. In the main these are grown on specially selected rootstocks to which the cultivated varieties (scions) are united by budding or grafting. Occasionally the opportunity arises for the amateur to practise budding or grafting and in any case it is interesting to know something about the techniques involved.

Budding is a form of grafting carried out in July using only a single scion bud. The dormant bud is detached from the maiden shoot, after removing the leaf, by making a shallow slicing cut to produce a shield some 4cm (1½in) in length. Make sure the hard wood at the back of the shield is removed carefully to reveal the bud 'germ' before the thin shield is inserted into the bark of the stock by means of a T-shaped cut. The bud,

once snugly home in a manner roughly comparable to its original position, is secured by a tie. This is to keep the bud close to the healing cambium tissue so that the scion and stock unite. In the spring the stem of the stock is cut back to the bud, usually in two stages.

For grafting young trees the nurseryman normally uses the whip and tongue graft, involving a scion shoot 15cm (6in) or so in length, which is united to the cut end of the stock in the spring. The tongue is a device to keep the two elements in place. The whole business is no more than a simple piece of joinery designed to bring the cambium layer, the tissue under the bark, into contact so that stock and scion unite, after tying and waxing to aid the process. Plastic strips can be used instead of tie and wax.

The graft inserted in April will start to grow immediately, giving a maiden tree by the end of the summer.

Clever controls

Pruning, training and propagation are based on a simple knowledge of plant behaviour and response and using that knowledge to control the growth and cropping of trees.

You have probably met the tree which produces vast quantities of useless timber and little fruit. This may be due to a variety of causes including the following:

a The rootstock may be too vigorous
b The variety may naturally be energetic
c The pruning may have been too severe, the manuring extravagant, or the soil inherently rich

The remedies include the following:

a reducing the level of manuring, and especially the nitrogen content
b grassing down, if feasible
c confining the winter pruning to the removal of diseased, damaged and overcrowded branches
d pruning the unwanted laterals in August
e transplanting, if the tree is young enough
f bark-ringing

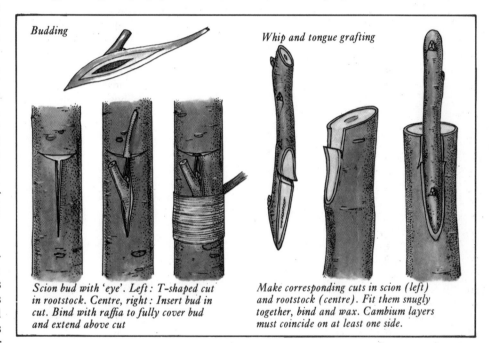

Budding

Scion bud with 'eye'. Left: T-shaped cut in rootstock. Centre, right: Insert bud in cut. Bind with raffia to fully cover bud and extend above cut

Whip and tongue grafting

Make corresponding cuts in scion (left) and rootstock (centre). Fit them snugly together, bind and wax. Cambium layers must coincide on at least one side.

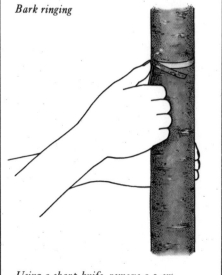

Bark ringing

Using a sharp knife, remove a 1-cm (¼-in) strip of bark. Cover cut area completely with masking tape.

The last is a subtle, beautiful use of applied science. All that is required is the removal in April of a ring of bark, about 1cm (¼in) wide, around the main trunk, covering the wound immediately with masking tape to exclude air. This causes the sudden but temporary suspension of the downward flow of sugars from the green parts of the tree to the roots which, thus deprived of foodstuff, cease their rampant growth. Correspondingly, more sugars are retained in the fruiting parts, helping to induce blossom buds.

The stunted, depressed tree which has ceased to grow calls for different remedies. The owner should:

a increase the manuring, particularly the nitrogen applications in spring
b mulch and water liberally
c remove competitive grass and weeds
d shorten the leaders and remove any unwanted shoots and suckers
e stake and tie, to prevent wind rocking.

Pest Control

Definitions

A *pest* is a member of the animal kingdom harmful to cultivated plants. This definition embraces a wide range, from tiny organisms invisible to the human eye, such as some mites and eelworms, to the only too obvious rabbits, deer, horses and other mammals. Some birds are pests, although many are beneficial. Most damage to crops is caused by a group of pests known loosely as insects, and often that damage is caused at only one stage of the life cycle, for example, the larva or caterpillar.

Generally speaking the specifics employed against pests are called *insecticides*, an adequate even if not a strictly accurate term.

Diseases are caused in the main by the invasion of vegetable and related parasites, including fungi and bacteria. Many troubles are caused by viruses, against which there are no chemical controls. As most diseases are nevertheless caused by fungi it is reasonable to refer to the materials used to control them as *fungicides*. It is difficult to kill one plant, a fungus, living on another plant, and this is one reason why there are fewer fungicides than insecticides.

Much ill-health in plants is caused not by insect attack or fungal invasion but by faults in the environment, or bad nutrition, or poor cultivation—in other words, by bad gardening. As we have to use names to distinguish we call these non-parasitical states of ill-health *disorders*.

The wrong site, too much or too little water, failure to ensure that the soil is maintained in a fertile state—all these cause more distress to plants in gardens than do pests and diseases. The first step in pest and disease control must be to grow good plants.

We should not overlook *weeds*, which can be defined as plants in the wrong place. A rose in a potato field is a weed; so is a potato plant in the rose garden. Grasses are splendid in lawns but undesirable among the onions. Materials used to control weeds are called *herbicides*.

Why not let nature have her way?

There is a school of thought which holds that nature, left alone, produces a balance in which predators and parasites keep insect and similar pests in check. One never sees the same argument applied to weeds, which only too readily overcome our cultivated plants if left alone. It is not really possible under the artificial conditions in which we live to leave the safeguarding of our crops entirely to nature. It is necessary for the gardener to work with nature if he wishes to obtain the best results.

Good husbandry

Emphasis must always be placed on growing a good plant and accepting that good cultivation, proper manuring and all that is involved in the splendid term 'good husbandry' form the proper foundations for success. And never forget that good husbandry includes the prevention and control of pests, diseases and weeds.

Making a good start

The gardener should never skimp on seeds but always go to a reputable seedsman. This will ensure the best varieties (cultivars) and strains and avoid some of those troubles which can be carried by seeds. So, too, buy plants from a well-known source, especially fruit plants and perennial vegetables. In the chapters on fruit stress is again laid on the wisdom of purchasing certified plants.

Beware of kind friends who offer largesse in the shape of cabbage plants, leek seedlings and the like. There is no better way of spreading the spores of clubroot or the cysts of eelworm from infected to clean ground than through soil attached to plant roots. Be wary of those old, long established allotments as sources of plants. Many such sites, perhaps most, are infected with potato root-eelworm and acid soils in particular are rife with club-root. Both these troubles remain in the soil almost indefinitely and cannot readily be cured.

Crop rotations

Because of the problem of persistent soil borne pests and diseases it is advisable to stick to a rotational cropping plan whenever possible. This means that related crops, such as cabbages, cauliflowers, Brussels sprouts, turnips and swedes, should be grouped together and the site for the group moved each year. This will reduce the risk of diseases, such as club-root, which attack only these crops. Similar considerations apply to potatoes and root crops, to peas and beans and to salads and bulb crops.

The large scale grower with plenty of land can, of course, switch his crops around without difficulty; the smaller grower is, however, limited. He will not gain much by moving the cabbage patch or the potatoes a few yards down the garden; and he will find himself further restricted if the family has a passion for a particular vegetable which is occupying a disproportionately large area. Nevertheless he should make what changes he reasonably can.

Feathered friends

Unfortunately birds cause a lot of damage, particularly to fruit buds in winter and to ripe fruits in season. In some districts seedlings of vegetables may be attacked to the point at which it is not worth the attempt to grow lettuce or peas.

The traditional reply is to scare the birds, which simply means that they are moved on to someone else's crops. Strips of fluttering plastic, cotton threads, stuffed owls and cats and deterrent sprays have all proved to have their value. But none is completely effective.

The best method, if it is at all practicable, is to enclose the crops concerned in a netted enclosure or cage. Materials for temporary structures can be bought but a permanent cage, although expensive, is clearly the more effective. Pears, plums, red currants, gooseberries and strawberries are always at risk. Bird damage to vegetables varies, but in most districts peas, lettuce, sweet corn and the choicer brassicas deserve protection.

Specifics

A modern development is the introduction of chemicals within the plant itself to give added and longer protection. These insecticides and fungicides are called systemic. Some sprays which can be employed safely by farmers and commercial growers using special equipment should not be used in gardens because of the risks involved. There is much to be said for insecticides derived from natural sources, including derris and pyrethrum. Experience shows, however, that the natural products are not always efficient against some pests, and some, such as nicotine, are highly poisonous when concentrated. Whatever is used the application should be thorough — on a calm day and preferably in the evening when the bees are safely at home.

The gardener's medicine chest

All garden spray materials should be kept in a dry safe place out of the reach of children. Most plant protection materials are dangerous if wrongly used; herbicides as well as pesticides must be kept under lock and key and the maker's instructions closely followed.

Occasionally some spray materials produce slight taints in fruit and vegetables. Take special care if you want to freeze or to preserve the produce.

Weeds

Herbicides can be divided into two categories. There is the herbicide which will scorch any foliage on which it is deposited or which will kill any plant indiscriminately when absorbed by its roots. This is a non-selective weed killer.

The other category will selectively affect some plants but be harmless to others, because some plants possess the capacity to neutralize the chemicals while others do not and therefore succumb.

Also in use are weedkillers which are held fast in the surface soil. This is thereby rendered temporarily toxic to seedlings while existing plants with root systems exploring the deeper soil are free from harm.

Finally, there are those materials which are translocated within the plant, so that if one part is touched the whole weed is ultimately affected.

Herbicides can be of considerable use even though they have a limited function in a vegetable garden. Take, as an appropriate start, the new or grossly neglected garden, covered with weeds of every description. A spraying with paraquat/diquat will kill all save the deep rooted vagabonds. Cultivation will be much easier and the soil will not be contaminated. An alternative approach is to use sodium chlorate, which kills all the plants but as it persists for several months planting will have to be delayed. Paraquat, carefully applied, will kill grass and weeds growing close to the stems of established fruit trees and so reduce competition; casoron can be employed similarly. Simazine can be used to prevent the growth of annual weeds among black currants and sweet corn and propachlor granules can also control annuals among some vegetables.

Biological control

Man has practised the biological control of pests since time immemorial. Modern developments are highly sophisticated.

It is now possible for the amateur gardener to control white fly attacking plants grown in a glasshouse by introducing deliberately a parasite, *Encarsia formosa*. Similarly another serious pest, the glasshouse red spider mite, can be reduced considerably by the introduction of a predatory mite with the awkward name of *Phytoseiulus persimmilis*. Both these organisms are bred by specialists and can be placed in the glasshouse at exactly the right stage.

Another form of biological control is represented by what may be called negative action. For example, the spraying of fruit trees can be reduced to a minimum so that the natural enemies of the fruit tree red spider mite are left to carry out unhampered their gruesome but desirable activities.

The use of traps is another form of control, with man as the predator. For instance, loose bands of sacking or corrugated cardboard tied around the trunks of fruit trees in July and removed for burning in October will reduce the number of codling moth larvae which will survive the winter. Similarly, greasebands placed on the trunks in autumn will trap the wingless females of the winter moth on their way up to lay eggs.

A summary of advice

It is perhaps appropriate to conclude with a summary of the approach to the control of pests, diseases, disorders and weeds in the garden.

1 Do not spray open blossoms with insecticides; remember the busy bees.
2 Burn the remains of any plants affected with persistent troubles such as clubroot or onion eelworm; the compost heap is no place for these.
3 Equally, perennial weeds of the nature of couch grass, ground elder and bellbine (bindweed) should be consigned to the bonfire
4 Be thorough when destroying weeds; 'one year's seeding may mean seven years' weeding'.
5 'Prevention is better than cure'. Spray well in advance against such inevitable troubles as apple scab, peach leaf curl, blight on potatoes and tomatoes, and grey mould on strawberries.
6 Follow the maker's instructions—always.
7 Prune as soon as you see shoots affected with mildew or silver leaf; remove immediately any diseased fruits, pare away cankers and paint all large wounds.
8 Rotate crops as much as space permits.
9 Remember the beneficial insects and allow them to work on your behalf.
10 The battle is half won before it starts if the soil is kept in good condition.

Specifics	Aphids etc.	*Control of Pests and Diseases*			Comments
		Biting pests	Fungus diseases	Glasshouse troubles	
Pyrethrum	×			×	For use especially
Resmethrin	×			×	against white fly
Derris	×	×			Good against raspberry beetle
Malathion	×	×		×	Used against a wide range of sucking and biting pests
Rogor	×	×			For fruit pests
Tar oil	×				Overwintering eggs of aphis
Diazinon		×			Particularly useful against pests of vegetables—pea moth, leaf miner, flea beetles, carrot fly and cabbage root fly
Metaldehyde		×			Both specific to slug
Methiocarb		×			control
Lime-sulphur	×		×		Controls big bud mite on black currants
Captan			×		No control of mildews See note 2
Dinocap			×		'Karathane'—particularly effective against mildews
Benomyl			×	×	'Benlate', for scab, grey mould, leaf mould and mildews
Thiophanate-methyl			×	×	'systemic fungicide', for scab, mildews, leaf spot, grey mould on fruits, vegetables and glasshouse plants
Sulphur dust			×	×	Useful as a dust against mildew. See note 2

Herbicide	Total control	Fruit plants	*Herbicides* Vegetables	Comments
Sodium chlorate	×			Inflammable when dry
Dalapon	×			Useful against couch grass
Paraquat/ diquat	×	×	×	Non-selective, but can be directed to achieve contact killing of active weeds
Simazine	×	×		Excellent for control of annual weeds
Dichlobenil (Casoran G)	×	×		Granules for spot treatment
Propachlor (Ramrod)			×	Selective control of germinating annual weeds
Chloroxuron			×	Also gives selective control of germinating annuals in vegetable crops

Note 1: Plant protection materials and herbicides are dangerous if used incorrectly. Keep them under lock and key, out of the reach of children, and follow strictly the maker's instructions.

Note 2: Some materials—captan for example—may produce occasional slight taints in fruits and vegetables used for processing.

Tools and Equipment

The essential gardening operations can be carried out with a small number of tools such as spade, fork, rake, trowel and Dutch hoe with a draw-hoe for taking out drills and earthing up potatoes. Nevertheless you will undoubtedly accumulate a well filled tool-shed over the years with regular additions taking place at birthdays and Christmas. Good tools and equipment are not cheap but it is a wise investment always to buy the best; cheap or shoddily-made items will soon break and have to be replaced. Take your time and examine all models available when buying the basic items such as a spade and a fork. Handle them and determine if their weight and balance are suitable for you. Do not be hoodwinked by gimmicky features but look for those which are of practical use. Be prepared to spend a lot of money on your garden tools and equipment but don't expect your involvement with them to come to an abrupt halt. Tools must be cleaned and oiled after use in order to keep them in first class condition. Soil can be removed with a piece of wood or a stiff brush while there should be an oil-can and rag ready for use in every toolshed.

Spades

The spade will be the most used tool which you must buy and, with careful attention, will last you for a lifetime. Make your choice very carefully because there are many types available. The size of the blade can range from the digging spade at 30 × 20cm (12 × 8 in) to the small border spade at 22 × 14cm (8 × 6in). The shaft is frequently made from a durable wood such as ash but there are spades with plastic covered shafts which are easier to handle and clean. Handles are either T-shaped, or more usually D-shaped, which are stronger. Choose a spade with a tread along the top of the blade as this will minimize damage to the soles of your boots when digging. There is a so-called automatic spade which turns over the soil with the aid of a lever and a spring-operated blade which is interchangeable with a fork head. There is much to be said for a stainless steel spade which is light and easy to clean; it is, however, expensive.

Forks

Some people prefer to dig with a fork and this method is useful on heavy soil. The fork will also be used for breaking down winter digging into a tilth in the spring, for 'forking-over' around over-wintered and perennial fruit and vegetable crops, for aerating grassed areas and for lifting root crops such as potatoes and carrots. A good, general-purpose fork will have four prongs or tines which can be either square, round or flat in cross-section. Flat-tined forks are useful for root lifting—when they cause less crop

Above, left to right: draw hoe, lawn rake, triple-edged hoe, long-handled fork, rake and Dutch hoe

Left: Border spade and fork (at rear). The larger spade and fork are for general digging and lifting work

damage—as well as for digging. Again, several sizes and weights are available so that it is important to choose one with which you are happy. The small hand fork, while not an essential item in your equipment, is a useful tool particularly when you are planting and cultivating around small, closely spaced plants.

Rakes

The metal-headed rake with a long wooden handle is essential for seedbed preparation. Make sure that the head is robust, sturdy and light, while the teeth must not bend easily. In large gardens and on stony soils a rake with a wooden head will also be useful for rubbish clearance.

Hoes

There are various types of hoes but all of them are basically cultivating tools. The draw hoe has a rectangular or semi-circular blade which is attached more or less at right angles to the handle. It should be pulled towards you with a chopping action as you walk forwards over the hoed ground. Draw hoes are particularly useful on hard-surfaced ground and where there are large weeds. They are also used for taking out seed-drills and for earthing up crops such as potatoes and celery. When the blade is joined to the handle with a hook-like shaft the hoe is described as swan-necked. The handles are usually about 1.5m (5ft) in length. There are also swan-necked hoes with short handles; these are called onion hoes and are ideal for delicate thinning and weeding. Dutch hoes, of which there are various patterns and designs, have the blade in the same plane as the handle. Dutch or push hoes are pushed along only just beneath the soil surface in order to break the surface and cut off the weeds. You must, of course, walk backwards to avoid re-firming the soil and the severed weeds. With all hoes it is most important to keep the blades sharp so that weeds are cut off cleanly and not dragged out.

Trowels and dibbers
Transplanting is often done with a trowel of which the design and weight are important features. Lightweight aluminium alloy blades are best with a handle which is comfortable and which doesn't give you blisters. A dibber is required for sowing large seeds such as broad beans or for transplanting crops such as leeks. You can make your own dibber by trimming the broken shaft of an old spade. Cut and sharpen the shaft to leave 25cm (10in) of dibbing handle.

Lines and measuring rods
You will use space in your garden more efficiently if your crops are sown or planted in straight lines. For this purpose you will need a strong and durable garden line which should be 20–30m (22–33yd) in length. Tarred string, polythene cord or electrical wire all make suitable lines when attached either to wooden pegs or to a metal peg and reel. It is desirable to clean the line after use by wiping it with a damp cloth. If you wish to mark a straight line of some length it will be necessary to pin down the string or wire with crossed sticks or a fork mid-way along its length to prevent it moving. When taking out a drill you should place one foot on the line so that it remains still. When transplanting it is best to set the plants in front of, but close against the line. Correct and regular in-the-row spacing is as important as straight lines if optimum crop growth and size are to be achieved. A measuring rod 2m (6ft 6in) in length with marks at 10cm (4in) intervals is useful for this purpose.

Knives and pruning equipment
All gardeners should own a good knife with a strong handle and blade. Keep it well sharpened and resist the temptation to use it for cleaning your spade or gardening shoes! You will need a heavy-bladed knife for pruning and grafting fruit trees and, if you intend to do any budding, another special knife will be necessary. A pruning saw is an optional extra. A good pair of secateurs, however, is essential; both double-

bladed and single-bladed types are available.

Grass cutting equipment
When your fruit and vegetables form part of a larger garden which also has ornamental grass areas it may be possible to use the lawn mower to cut the orchard grass and the dividing pathways in the vegetable plot. Cylinder mowers are not ideal for cutting 'rough' grass although they can be used on a small scale. Rotary mowers do not produce such a good lawn finish but are better general-purpose machines. They are of simple construction with the cutting blades rotating under a protective shield. Various types of cutting blades are available, some of which need regular sharpening. The power is usually provided by a two-stroke engine which requires regular routine maintenance and cleaning. Choose an easy-to-handle and compact-to-store model.

Spraying equipment
Although some pesticides are available as

Above: Useful small tools include (l to r) a fine point and trowel, hand trowel and fork, and dibber. On the step, a trug holds gardening twine and raffia

Below: Of the many excellent cutting tools available, secateurs are essential

dusts, granules or in aerosol cans, a garden sprayer will still be a useful part of your pest, disease and weed control armoury. A range of knapsack and pressurized cylinder sprayers is available with capacities in the range of 10 to 15 litres (2 to 3 Imp gal). Double-action lance sprayers are used in conjunction with a bucket or can of pesticide while you will find that a small garden syringe is very useful in the greenhouse and for crops under frames and cloches. All spraying equipment should be carefully washed out with clean water after use and must never be put away for the winter while still containing water or pesticide.

Watering equipment
Buckets and watering cans—with a range of roses—are adequate for small gardens but a hosepipe is a big advantage for larger areas. Remember that you will need a licence if you intend to use a hose. Rubber or plastic hoses are available in a variety of internal diameters and lengths. They usually develop kinks and ultimately split but reinforced hoses are now on the market. The most tidy way of storing hoses between use is to wind them on to a reel which also allows them to be moved more easily. Different nozzles produce different spray patterns while an on/off connection is a very useful fitting at the open end.

Wheelbarrows, ladders and other equipment
You will certainly need means of moving materials—ranging from soil and farmyard manure to young seedlings and harvested crops—from one part of the garden to another. Choose a light, wooden or rust-proof metal wheelbarrow, preferably with an inflatable rubber tyre to allow easier handling. Always clean your wheelbarrow out after use. Fruit picking ladders may be needed in a large fruit garden. You should make a practice of labelling all crops clearly and concisely. Plastic or wooden labels, both of which can be re-used, are to be preferred. Write with a water-proof lead pencil which will remain legible on the label even after being outside for a long, wet winter.

Mechanical cultivators
The use of these cultivators may be justified on medium or large sized gardens. They can be very useful aids but they rarely do such an efficient job as you will achieve by hand digging or hoeing. It is important to choose a machine with a power capacity in excess of that required for operating in absolutely ideal conditions. Most mechanical cultivators have a motor which drives a rotor to which are attached a number of blades or tines. As the rotor spins round at high speed the cultivator is pushed or driven forward and produces a fine tilth; blade (tine) shape and rotor speed determine the type of tilth. Care must be taken not to ruin the soil structure or induce the formation of hard pans. Easy manoeuvrability is very important in a garden, together with lightness and ease of handling. Some mechanical cultivators can be fitted with spraying equipment for pesticide application.

Crops under Glass

This chapter is concerned with some of the general principles underlying protected cultivation. With the aid of some form of protective structure it is possible to extend the production season for a number of fruits and vegetables. These structures include greenhouses both heated and cold, walk-in polythene tunnels, cloches, low polythene coverings, cold frames and bell jars. The extension of the season may be caused by earlier growth in the spring or by protection later into the autumn.

Special chapters are devoted elsewhere to the production of out-of-season strawberries, grapes and peaches.

Greenhouses

Various designs of garden greenhouses are available but most have either a wooden or an extruded alloy framework. The latter type is probably easier to put up and has better light transmission but it looks less attractive than the wooden variety. The size will be influenced by the space available and you must be careful to erect your greenhouse in a sheltered but un-shaded part of the garden. If you can align its ridge so that it runs as near as possible to east/west, you will get more winter light on to your plants. The amount and quality of light has an important effect on crop growth. Clean the glass regularly, for dirty glass reduces light transmission and therefore growth. The other design feature to which you should pay great attention is the ventilation. Many small greenhouses have insufficient ridge and side ventilation capacity so that occasionally the door must be left open to reduce both temperature and humidity. This is often inconvenient and it is better to provide adequate ventilation from the outset. When all vents are fully open the apertures should be equivalent to about one sixth of the floor area of the greenhouse. Heat loss can be very rapid from greenhouses so make sure that there are no cracked or broken panes and consider putting up a polythene inner skin during the winter.

How can you best use your greenhouse? If it is heated, a wide range of crops can be grown. It is worth while partitioning off one end as a propagation area for plants for the greenhouse itself or for early outdoor planting. You may prefer to use a purpose built propagator where the temperature is controlled thermostatically. Early tomatoes, cucumbers, melons, sweet peppers and aubergines will all do well in heated houses. Be careful, however, not to mix too many crops together, especially if they have different environmental requirements as in the case of tomatoes and cucumbers. During the autumn and winter the heated greenhouse may be used for crops of lettuce and for forcing chicory and rhubarb, provided that black out facilities are available. Early crops of dwarf French beans can also be produced in heated houses by sowing six to seven seeds in 22cm (9in) pots during February; picking should begin in May. The cropping potential of an unheated greenhouse is more limited but tomatoes, cucumbers, sweet peppers and aubergines will still do well, particularly in southern districts. It is seldom worth planting tomatoes in unheated greenhouses before late April, while the other crops mentioned should wait another three or four weeks. Planting too early can cause a severe check to the plants and greatly reduce overall production. Spring-maturing lettuce is a useful crop for a cold greenhouse, grown either from a planting in November or February. January sowings of radish or carrots will produce roots in about eight and 14 weeks respectively; plantings of potatoes made at the same time — whether in ridged border soil, in large containers or under black polythene — will produce early tubers.

Walk-in polythene tunnels

The expense of glass covered structures— and the ease with which breakages occur— may deter you from buying a glasshouse. An alternative protected structure is a walk-in polythene tunnel. This consists of a framework of semi-circular metal hoops joined together at the apex with another metal tube. The tubing should be of 1.5cm (0.5in) internal diameter. The ends of the semi-circular hoops are pushed into foundation tubes which have been driven into the ground. These tubes should be 60cm (24in) in length with an internal diameter of 2.5cm (1in); they should be 1.5m (5ft) apart and in two parallel rows about 4m (13ft) apart. If the hooped tubes have an area of between 2.0 and 2.5m (7ft) radius, the structure framework will have a basic width of about 4m (13ft). This framework should be covered with a sheet of 500 gauge ultra-violet inhibited clear polythene which, for a 4m (13ft) wide structure, will need to be 7.0 to 7.5m (24ft) wide. The sheet must be tightly stretched over the framework and this can best be done in warm, still weather conditions. The edges of the sheet are buried in a 15cm (6in) deep trench on the outsides of the two rows of foundation tubes. Roll-up or hinged doors made out of the same polythene sheet and attached to a wooden framework are satisfactory for polythene tunnels. Polythene sheet of the type indica-

Above: A frame with Dutch lights can be put to many practical uses throughout the gardening year

Left: A small lean-to fully glazed greenhouse will be of enormous value to the enthusiastic vegetable gardener

ted will last for about three growing seasons by which time it will probably have become brittle and should be replaced.

Crop production in polythene-covered structures is generally similar to that in greenhouses but there are a number of different considerations. The framework of a walk-in tunnel is less substantial than that of a greenhouse and this may present problems with crops like tomatoes, cucumbers and melons which need vertical supports. Polythene and glass have different heat transmission and retention properties which will affect crops. Both materials allow

radiant heat to enter during the daytime but polythene allows the heat to pass out again at night so that on a clear starlit night very little heat indeed is retained by the structure. Radiation frosts are most likely to occur in the late spring, when particular care must be taken. Polythene-covered structures are more difficult to ventilate than greenhouses which have ridge or side ventilators but the humidity and temperature can be controlled by opening the doors.

Frames

Garden frames can, for many purposes, be used instead of a greenhouse or polythene tunnel. Again, maximum light transmission is vital and your frame should, therefore, be built on a sunny, southerly site. The base may be constructed of bricks or wood and the covering may either be old English lights or the more versatile and less heavy Dutch lights. Dutch lights allow more light into the frame and can also be used for protecting tender vegetables which are planted on patios or against walls. It is possible to buy frames with an aluminium skeleton which is glazed right down to the soil and which, therefore, admits more light. Cold frames are most commonly used but thermostatically controlled soil-warming cables may be incorporated to provide some heating.

Frames can be used to raise vegetable plants for transplanting. Early summer cauliflowers may be sown in late September and over-wintered prior to planting in the spring. Early plants of spring lettuce may be raised in the same way. Summer planted vegetables such as cabbage, cauliflower, Brussels sprouts, calabrese and leeks can also be raised in your cold frame for transplanting. Another valuable use is hardening off heated greenhouse raised plants before they are planted outside.

Cold glass lettuce can be planted in your frame in November or February and will mature at about Easter time. Radish and carrots sown in January will produce very early roots. During the summer use the frames to start off early crops of marrows or courgettes, removing the glass after the danger of frost has passed. Melons are a useful summer frame crop but they will need protecting throughout their life.

Finally, frames can be used for drying off and ripening potatoes, bulb onions or root crops which have been harvested while wet and which are to be stored.

Cloches and low polythene coverings

Several varieties of cloche are available. They may be constructed either of glass or plastic but are more draughty than frames. They are easily moved and invaluable for warming up the soil prior to sowing or planting, raising seedlings, extending the growing season, producing low-growing crops during the summer and drying off harvested crops. If you draw up a cropping programme beforehand you will be surprised at the amount of produce which can be raised from efficiently used cloches.

The earliest outdoor sowings or plantings of peas, French beans, runner beans, carrots, radishes, lettuce, marrows, courgettes and sweet corn can be protected by cloches, while late maturing crops of peas, dwarf

Below left: Clear plastic cloches are quickly assembled and easy to move

Below: A double row of spring-maturing lettuces under a barn cloche, next to flat-topped cloches sheltering an early sowing of peas

French beans and endive can also be protected well into the autumn.

Melons must be covered throughout the growing season. Other fruiting vegetables, such as tomatoes, peppers and aubergines, can be protected by surrounding them with barn cloches stood on end.

Low polythene coverings are constructed by stretching thin gauge clear polythene film over semi-circular metal hoops covering a 60cm (2ft) wide strip of ground. The polythene is held on to the hoops by lengths of string or wires over the top. The ends of the tunnels are formed by burying the polythene in the ground or securing it around wooden stakes. The polythene will degrade rapidly and can be used only for one season. These tunnels are useful for strawberries, spring-planted lettuce and early sowings or plantings of peas, dwarf or runner beans. Ventilation is particularly necessary on warm, sunny days for, unlike glass or plastic-covered cloches, the polythene film produces an airtight seal. Lifting up the polythene between the metal hoops and the retaining strings will allow sufficient air movement.

Cropping details have been set out under the descriptions for cultivating particular fruits and vegetables.

Growing your own
Vegetables

The Cabbage Family

Brassicas are an essential feature of any vegetable garden. They provide green leafy vegetables and other edible plant parts over a large part of the year. Many of the plants are derived from the wild cabbage—*Brassica oleracea*—which is native to the coastal cliffs of Britain and explains why the plants grow so readily under our climatic and soil conditions. Selection and adaptation from the original parent have produced widely differing, and apparently unrelated, cultivated races, such as cabbage, Brussels sprout, cauliflower, broccoli and kale. Their common ancestry becomes apparent, however, if the plants are allowed to 'bolt' when the familiar pale yellow, cross-like flowers are seen. All of the members of the cabbage family are biennials; most of them are hardy under British winter conditions. We grow them as annuals, however, since we are interested in the edible vegetative parts. A typical vegetable garden will probably have up to a third of the space devoted to crops of the cabbage family. Many of them are ideal subjects for deep freezing.

Brussels sprouts
Brassica oleracea var. *gemmifera*

This plant is grown for its crisp, tasty buds which, resembling miniature cabbages, are produced in the leaf axils during the autumn and winter months. As the name suggests the plant originated in Belgium, but Britain is now accepted as the most important and climatically suitable centre of production in the world. It is a hardy plant and withstands severe cold weather. The individual sprouts develop on the stems gradually from the bottom upwards and each cultivar produces sprouts over a long period. Many of the numerous cultivars now available have been specially bred for their freezing qualities.

Soil requirements

Brussels sprouts prefer fertile, deeply worked soils which have been firmly prepared. Since the plants may be in their final positions for 8 or 9 months, the roots will need considerable depth to support such a long season of growth. None of the brassicas should be grown on acid soils, where the danger of attack by the club root fungus will be increased. Counteract this by applying lime to an acid soil in the autumn/winter before planting. Since so many other related crops are also prone to this fungus it is important to keep Brussels sprouts off ground which has just grown a brassica. The

earliest crops—from which picking can begin in August/September—should be grown on light, open soil which allows early planting. Beware, however, of producing an open, fluffy planting bed since open sprouts, or 'blowers' at the base of the stem will undoubtedly result. Crops which are intended to go on into the New Year must be grown on well-drained soils to avoid the problem of waterlogging. If the previous crop has been well manured so much the better: the application of fresh organic manure or compost just before planting sprouts may again produce 'blowers'.

Suitable fertilizers

The yield of sprouts will largely be determined by the length of stem and the number of leaves on it. Consequently you should get more sprouts from a long stem with closely arranged leaves than from a short, sparsely-leaved stem. To achieve this you will need to give reasonable amounts of inorganic

'Early Half Tall' is a compact cultivar with sprouts ready from late August

fertilizer, particularly nitrogen. A base dressing of 50g per m² (2 oz per sq yd) of a general purpose fertilizer supplying nitrogen, phosphorus and potassium should be worked into the soil immediately before transplanting. If plant growth is slow in the summer you may find it beneficial to give a top dressing of 25 to 50g per m² (1 to 2 oz per sq yd) of a nitrogenous fertilizer such as Nitro Chalk. There are, however, real dangers in giving too much nitrogenous fertilizer to late-maturing Brussels sprouts which are going to be most productive after Christmas. In a wet autumn, when the soil is still warm after a fine summer, the plants may take up too much nitrogen and become very soft. The stems may then bend over and the lower sprouts will become soiled and rotten.

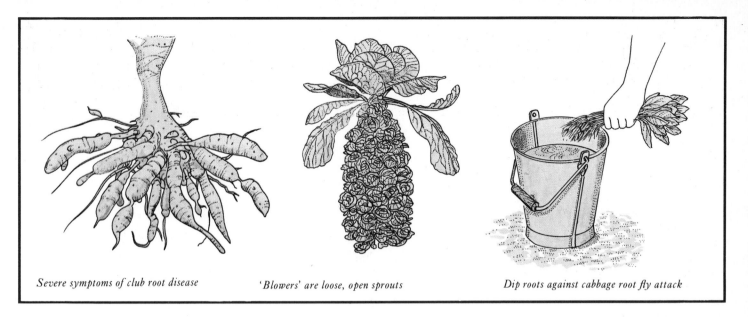

Severe symptoms of club root disease   *'Blowers' are loose, open sprouts*   *Dip roots against cabbage root fly attack*

Plant raising

Although many commercial growers now direct drill their Brussels sprouts it is better, on a small scale, to transplant. Depending on what facilities you have available a number of plant raising techniques are possible.

To produce early sprout plants, sow seed in trays in a slightly heated greenhouse (7°C/45°F) in mid-March. Prick out at 5.0cm × 2.5cm (2in × 1in) into other trays when the first pair of leaves appears. Harden off in a cold frame before transplanting in mid to late May. This method is more laborious and requires protected facilities, but gives the longer growing period on which sprout plants will flourish.

If cloches or polythene tunnels are available, rather than a greenhouse, you can raise the plants from a sowing made in the middle of March. Seed should be sown thinly, in order to produce strong, sturdy plants, in drills 1.5cm (¾in) deep and 25 to 30 cm (10 to 12in) apart. The more usual method of raising plants is to sow the seed, at the spacings indicated, in an outdoor seedbed situated in a sheltered part of the garden. Be careful to choose a site that did not have brassicas recently or the young sprout plants may be infected with club root even before they are transplanted. The earliest outdoor sowings will be made in the middle of March while any time up until mid-April is suitable in northerly or more exposed areas. Plants will normally be ready for transplanting to their permanent positions approximately 8 to 10 weeks after the date of sowing.

Transplanting

Between the middle of May and the middle of June is the best time to transplant Brussels sprouts into their final quarters. Careful programming of the sowing date is necessary if your plants are to be the right size for putting out at that time. They should be about 15cm (6in) tall and be graded for size before planting. Small plants are not necessarily useless but more uniform growth will occur if you separate them from the large plants. Make sure that you thoroughly soak the seedbed before gently easing the young plants out with a fork. Reducing root damage at this stage will minimize the check in growth that occurs at transplanting and help to ensure that the plants grow away rapidly. Discard any damaged or diseased plants or any which do not have a growing point. Transplanting is best carried out during showery weather; otherwise be certain to give the young plants a good ball watering immediately after putting them out. The traditional distance for planting Brussels sprouts is 90cm × 90cm (36in × 36in) but modern cultivars are often grown closer than this. To produce small, button sprouts for freezing, spacings of 60cm × 60cm (24in × 24in) are often used. 75cm × 75cm (30in × 30in) is probably more suitable in your garden. Individual sprout size is influenced by spacing, growing conditions and the cultivar being used. If you want small sprouts for freezing put the plants closer together; you will get a lower total yield than if a wider spacing is used. At the time of transplanting precautions must be taken against one of the most important

Uniform sprouts on the early F1 hybrid cultivar 'Peer Gynt'

pests of all brassicas—namely cabbage root fly. The roots of the young plants must be dipped in a protective chemical such as Trichlorphon before transplanting so that the fly larvae do not eat them and cause the plants to collapse.

Crop management

Once the plants have settled down after transplanting, they should grow rapidly. Until the leaves meet between the rows you will need to keep weeds down by hoeing. Top dressing with a nitrogenous fertilizer may be necessary in August, depending on crop growth. In very dry seasons the plants will respond to the application of water around the base of the stems. Although the sprout buttons normally develop gradually from the bottom of the plant upwards it is possible to induce them to develop more uniformly. Remove the growing point—a piece of tissue about the size of a table tennis ball—when the lower sprouts on the stem are between 1.5cm and 2cm (about ¾in) in diameter. This will effectively stop the plants growing upwards and encourage the uppermost sprouts on the stem to fill out in time for harvesting 4 to 6 weeks later. If you want large numbers of sprouts for freezing at one time this technique of 'stopping' is useful but it is probably not worth doing after the end of October. One drawback to 'stopping' the plants is that you have removed the most tender parts of the sprout tops which provide such useful and well-flavoured 'greens' in severe winters when nothing else can be harvested.

Harvesting

You may feel that the flavour of sprouts will be improved if you delay picking until after the first frosts. This is a nice thought, but there is no scientific evidence to support the theory. Regular picking of sprouts is essential unless they are all to be removed at one time following 'stopping'. Dead and decaying leaves and poor quality sprouts should also be removed as they appear. If mature sprouts are left unpicked for any length of time the outer leaves may go yellow and the likelihood of a condition known as internal

F1 hybrids such as 'Sigmund' produce sprouts which are ideal for freezing

browning will increase. The canopy of leaves at the top of the plant should be retained since it is this which protects the developing sprouts and may itself be eaten as 'greens' in severe weather.

Pests and diseases

Aphids can be a great nuisance on Brussels sprouts, particularly if the attack comes in late summer when it is difficult to spray the insecticide chemicals right into the growing points and developing sprouts where the aphids feed. These grey, mealy aphids carry on feeding all winter so be certain to spray when the first ones are seen.

In warm, dry summers plants may also be attacked by glasshouse white fly. These are very difficult to control but at least they stop feeding when, and if, the cold weather comes!

Cabbage root flies can have as many as three generations in a year but the first, which appears in late May, will usually cause the most trouble. Flies lay their eggs round the plants and the ensuing larvae are attracted to their feeding zone by chemicals given off by the brassica roots. Here they eat the young rootlets and tunnel into the larger root system, causing the plant to wilt—particularly in warm weather. The only method of control is to protect the root system by dipping it in a protective chemical before transplanting.

The seedling leaves of Brussels sprouts and other brassicas may be attacked by flea beetles whose feeding will produce tiny holes and pitted marks. Attack from this pest is rarely serious since the young plants usually continue to grow rapidly.

A number of caterpillars—which are the larvae of cabbage white butterflies and cabbage moths—attack sprouts and may cause severe damage. Watch out in mid-summer for tell-tale symptoms such as eggs laid under the leaves, droppings left by feeding caterpillars, or the tattered appearance of leaves after feeding.

Birds, particularly wood pigeons, may also attack your sprouts especially during severe winters when other food is in short supply. The presence of human beings usually deters them so grow the sprouts close to where people are moving about.

Club root is the most important fungal disease of sprouts and other brassicas. It causes the roots to become thick and swollen while the aerial parts of the plant are distorted and turn blue. Removal of the plants often reveals a foul-smelling mass of rotting roots. The disease, which is soil-borne, is most likely to occur in wet, acid soils which have grown continuous crops of brassicas without adequate rotational breaks.

Internal browning is a physiological disorder which, as the name suggests, causes the inside of sprouts to go brown and, ultimately, rotten.

Suitable Cultivars

The many cultivars available can be divided into two main groups—F1 hybrids and open pollinated types. The hybrids have been bred for uniformity and are particularly useful for a single harvest of freezing sprouts, although they can also be used for successional pickings. Seed of these cultivars is much more expensive and you will want to take great care with plant raising to make sure all the seeds produce healthy plants. As seed costs continually rise you may be tempted to save a few choice plants after all the sprouts have been picked and allow them to go up to seed in the spring. This is a dubious practice for the amateur, since complete isolation is required against cross pollination with other brassicas (isolation distances of hundreds of metres may be necessary). Never be tempted to save seed from F1 hybrid sprouts: the resultant plants will show considerable variation from the uniform parents which you originally selected. Some cultivars produce sprouts continually throughout autumn and winter but it is better to choose separate early, mid-season and late cultivars in order to cover the whole period.

* indicates suitability for freezing.

Early (September/October) 'Early Half Tall': dwarf open pollinated type; very early. 'Peer Gynt'*: good, even F1 hybrid.

Midseason (October/November) 'Irish Elegance': tall, high yielding under good conditions. 'King Arthur'*: F1 hybrid; fairly tall; smooth sprouts.

Late (December/post Christmas) 'Market Rearguard': open pollinated; dark green sprouts from Christmas until March. 'Citadel': F1 hybrid; stands well; small, solid dark green buttons.

Cauliflower

Brassical oleracea var. *botrytis cauliflora*

This very important member of the Cabbage family has cultivars which mature at different times of the year and, if a careful choice is made, it is possible for you to have cauliflowers ready almost all the year round. It is difficult to maintain continuity in early summer and mid-winter due to the weather conditions prevailing at those times. In commercial horticulture the cultivars which mature in summer and autumn are termed 'cauliflowers' while those which mature in the winter are confusingly called 'broccoli'. The former types are not frost hardy and have a more tender and delicate flavour than the hardier winter types. Complete success with winter cauliflower is only likely in mild coastal areas where frost damage rarely occurs. The single stem of cauliflower culminates in a large, swollen, domed flower head comprising a mass of white or creamy-white undeveloped flower buds. This structure is known as the 'curd' and nestles snugly within the leaves. In the case of summer and autumn cauliflower the leaves

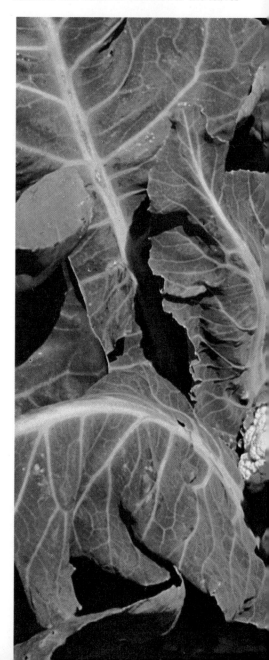

are usually upright or spreading whereas they tend to be wrapped over winter cauliflower as protection.

Soil requirements

While the general soil requirements for all cauliflowers are similar there are slight variations depending on whether you are growing summer/autumn or winter types. As with all brassicas you should go for an alkaline soil which has not recently grown a related crop. It may be necessary to add lime but it is much better if club root can be kept out of the garden altogether. Summer and autumn crops must be grown without any form of check, otherwise small, immature curds will form. To avoid this condition, known as 'buttoning', the soil must be open, fertile and able to sustain un-interrupted growth. The previous crop should have been well-manured, since the well-rotted organic matter will help retain water—an essential ingredient for successful cauliflower growing. The very earliest crops which are planted in March or April to provide snowy white curds in early June need very light, open soils which drain and warm up quickly in the spring. Attempts to grow this early crop on anything but ideal soils in well-favoured districts will almost certainly end in the condition known as 'buttoning'.

Suitable fertilizers

Summer and autumn cauliflower also need inorganic fertilizers, particularly nitrogen, if they are to produce large, good quality curds. A suitable programme would be a base dressing of 50g per m² (2 oz per sq yd) of a general purpose fertilizer followed by a top dressing of 25 to 50g per m² (1 to 2 oz per sq yd) of a nitrogenous fertilizer if required. The formula for success with summer and autumn cauliflower is, therefore, to grow them rapidly in soils which are well supplied with nitrogenous fertilizer and water. Winter cauliflower are somewhat different in that they are in their final positions during the winter period. Choose soils and fertilizer programmes which discourage lush, sappy growth developing in the autumn since this kind of plant is likely to be damaged by cold weather. Good soil drainage is important, however, along with plenty of body and depth so that a strong root system can develop. This will hold the

'All The Year Round' is useful for summer and autumn cutting

Earth up cauliflowers to prevent plants blowing over in the wind

Container-raised cauliflowers are planted with a trowel

plants steady during the winter winds and storms. When the plants start to grow again in February give them a top dressing of 50g per m² (2 oz per sq yd) of Nitro-Chalk applied carefully around the base of the plants and hoed in. They may respond to another application in March.

Plant raising

The earliest summer cauliflowers require very careful plant raising. Seed may be sown in a cold frame in late September and the developing seedlings either potted into 9-cm (3½-in) pots or pricked out into the frame soil at a spacing of 4cm × 6cm (1½in × 2½in). The soil/compost in which the cauliflowers are overwintered should be well-drained and low in nitrogen so that sturdy young plants are produced by March/April. No heating is given but the frames must be ventilated on warm, sunny days. An alternative method of raising this group of cauliflowers is to sow seed in

January in seed trays which are kept in a greenhouse with a temperature of 13°C/55°F. The seedlings are pricked out when they are large enough to handle into other seed trays at a spacing of 5cm × 2.5cm (2in × 1in). A proprietary potting compost should be used for the pricked out seedlings. The January sowing will produce plants which are ready for planting a little after those from the September sowing, but is likely to be a more successful method. Later summer and autumn cauliflowers can be raised in an outdoor seedbed. Depending on your location and soil type sow the seed from mid-March onwards in drills 1cm (½in) deep and 20 to 30cm (8in to 12in) apart. Further sowings can be made until the end of May to produce plants which are transplanted in mid–late July. Winter cauliflower plants are produced by sowing seed in an outdoor seedbed in April or May as described for the late summer/autumn types. Sow the cultivars which mature latest before those which mature first. Make sure that outdoor seedbed areas have not grown brassica plants recently and that club root fungus is not present.

Transplanting and crop management
Early summer cauliflowers are planted in March or April depending on weather and location. Spacings of between 45cm × 45cm (18in × 18in) and 55cm × 55cm (21in × 21in) are best. Planting too early into cold soil will cause checking and induce 'buttoning'. Hoeing will be necessary to keep down weeds and growth must be maintained with top dressings of nitrogen and regular waterings. Cabbage root fly larvae may attack the plants in late May as they approach readiness for cutting and you should water on a protectant chemical beforehand.

Summer/autumn cauliflowers are probably the easiest group to grow and your plants should be ready for planting about 8 to 10 weeks after sowing. The mature plants are larger than early summer types so wider spacings—up to 60cm × 60cm (24in × 24in) are used. Continuous, unchecked growth is important if you are to get top quality curds. Protection against cabbage root fly is likely to be necessary both in the seedbed and in the final position. Winter cauliflowers which are planted in July produce the largest plants of all and must, therefore, be spaced 75cm × 75cm (30in × 30in) and 90cm × 90cm (36in × 36in). Short, sturdy plants are essential, so thin the plants out in the seedbed if they come up too close together. A spacing of 1.5cm (¾in) between seedlings in the seedbed row will ensure sturdy development. When the rate of growth slows down during the autumn months, guard against weeds. If you live in a windy area earth up the soil around the base of the stems to prevent the plants being damaged by rocking. After topdressing in the spring the fertilizer should be worked in with a hoe to encourage rapid uptake by the plants.

Harvesting
Cauliflowers should be cut early in the day

Australian cultivars like 'South Pacific' form superb curds in the autumn

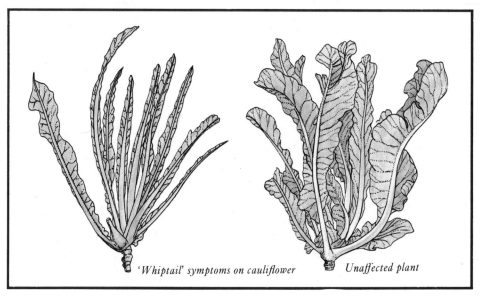

'Whiptail' symptoms on cauliflower   *Unaffected plant*

before the curds become over-heated. Inspect the plants regularly as they approach maturity to make sure that curds are cut as soon as they are ready. Some cultivars have leaves which curl over the tender curd and protect it from the sun's rays. Most have upright leaves, however, and in this case break a leaf over the young curd to prevent it yellowing. Curd quality rapidly deteriorates in warm weather so regular cutting is essential.

Pests and diseases
Many of the pests and diseases which attack Brussels sprouts can also be a problem on cauliflowers—namely aphids, whitefly, cabbage root fly, flea beetles, caterpillars, birds and club root. There are no other common pests to worry you, but mention must be made of a few additional diseases and disorders. All cauliflowers are liable to develop symptoms of 'whiptail'—a condition caused by deficiency of the micronutrient molybdenum. In severe cases the area of leaf blade is so reduced that the leaves become strap-like in appearance. Often the real reason for this condition is that acidity in the soil prevents the plants absorbing molybdenum. Water the plants with a molybdate solution before planting

if your soil is likely to induce 'whiptail'.

There is always a chance of frost damage on late autumn and winter crops. In the case of frost it is more likely that a secondary infection, such as grey mould (botrytis), will invade the damaged tissues and be more obvious. Cauliflower seedlings are particularly prone to downy mildew infection. Be especially vigilant with early summer types which are raised from an autumn sowing. The upper surfaces of the young leaves show yellow patches while white fungal growth can be seen on the undersides.

Damping off of the seedlings is caused by a number of soil-borne fungi while wirestem, which causes a brown, corky constriction of the young stem at ground level, is also a soil-borne disease.

Curd peculiarities and deformities are not usually caused by disease organisms but are often a reaction to weather conditions or the absence of micro-nutrients. Brown spots on the curds can be caused by boron deficiency or by very dry growing conditions. Projections from the surface of the curd giving an uneven appearance—a condition known as 'riciness'—are often caused by very warm weather while the curd is developing. Wide fluctuations in temperature may cause small leaves to appear in the curds when they are referred to as 'bracted'.

Suitable cultivars
All the following may be frozen.
Early Summer cauliflowers: 'Alpha': large, early pure white heads. 'Snow King': F1 hybrid; very fast growing. 'Snowball': reliable heads until the end of June.
Summer/Autumn cauliflower 'All the Year Round': aptly named, general purpose. 'South Pacific': good heads in early autumn. 'Brisbane': protected heads mature in October/November. 'Beacon': high quality heads in September.
Winter cauliflower: 'Early White': heads in January/February. 'Snow White': usually ready in March/April. 'English Winter Leamington': reliable heads in April. 'Late Enterprise': heads at the end of May.

Broccoli
Brassica oleracea var. *botrytis cymosa*

Sprouting broccoli is very similar to cauliflower but instead of culminating in a single, terminal curd the plants produce a more branched and loose collection of flower heads, many of which are in leaf axils lower down the stem. Purple sprouting broccoli—which goes green during cooking—is most popular, but there is a lesser known white form. Both mature in the winter and are hardy in most areas, providing a useful continuity and variation of winter greens. Green sprouting broccoli is better known as calabrese and is becoming increasingly popular. It is much-liked in Italy but is not winter hardy in Britain and must be harvested in August and September. Calabrese is a superb vegetable for your freezer. There is also a perennial sprouting broccoli which will go on producing for several years.

Soil and fertilizer requirements
Overwintering purple and white forms of broccoli have the same needs as winter cauliflower. They do best after well-manured crops such as early potatoes and, of course, need well-drained soils. Once again there is a danger of high winds blowing plants over during the winter so it is worthwhile earthing up around the stems. Calabrese is a summer-grown brassica which must be grown rapidly if you are to get young tender shoots or 'spears'. This means that summer/autumn cauliflower conditions are needed. Soils must be fertile and well-drained but also moisture-retentive. Constant supplies of water and nitrogenous fertilizer are needed if the necessary strong plant framework is to be produced.

Plant raising
Sow the seed of purple and white sprouting forms in an outside seedbed in mid-April. Sturdy plants are required which means that the seedlings must develop at a spacing of 1.5cm (¾in) apart—in drills 1cm (½in) deep and 20cm to 30cm (8in to 12in) apart. The tender calabrese requires an earlier start to plant raising. Seed can be sown in an outside seedbed during late March or early April—as described above—in very sheltered areas with light well-drained soil. Better results will be obtained if the plants are raised in a cold frame or under cloches. Having put the frames/cloches over the soil well in advance to warm it up, you can sow the seed in the same way as for purple and white sprouting forms, in early April. Plants of perennial broccoli are best raised in the same way as purple and white sprouting forms.

Transplanting and crop management
Winter and perennial broccoli are transplanted in June or July—the former at 75cm (30in) square and the latter at 90cm (36in) square. Purple and white sprouting forms will probably respond to a worked-in top dressing of 50g per m² (2 oz per sq yd) of Nitro-Chalk in early spring. Calabrese

should also be planted out in June at 75cm (30in) square and grown rapidly through the summer months. It is necessary to look out for the common brassica pests such as aphids, caterpillars and cabbage root fly.

Harvesting
Remove sprouting side shoots when they are mature so that more will be produced further down. Snap them off as close to the main stem as possible. A number of purple/white cultivars are available to spread the season from January until April or May. Perennial broccoli produces a large central head surrounded by half-a-dozen or so smaller axillary heads. In order to keep the perennial habit of the plant these heads must all be cut off at the end of the season before going to seed. Calabrese plants also produce a central head of terminal shoots initially but when these are cut side branches quickly develop. The increased popularity of this vegetable has led to the recent introduction of new cultivars—including a number of very uniform and high yielding F1 hybrids —which allow you to extend the season from August until October.

Pests and diseases
Sprouting broccoli are liable to be attacked by the same pests and diseases as cauli-

The young 'spears' of calabrese are produced in late summer

flowers. Reduce the destructive effects of aphids as soon as they become evident with sprays of malathion. Cabbage root fly, the pest common to all members of the brassica family, is resistant to many insecticides. The only effective defence against infestation by this pest is to apply a root chemical such as triclorphon to the seedlings before transplanting. Malathion, triclorphon and derris may also be used against caterpillars.

Suitable cultivars
* indicates suitability for freezing
Purple/white Sprouting broccoli 'Early Purple Sprouting': February/March. 'Late Purple Sprouting': April.
N.B.—there are White Sprouting forms of both cultivars.
Green Sprouting broccoli/Calabrese 'Express Corona'*: F1 hybrid; heavy crop in August/September. 'Green Comet'*: F1 hybrid; large, early heads. 'Italian Sprouting': September onwards.
Perennial broccoli 'Nine Star': late spring. 'Hen and chickens': produces small white heads in May.

Cabbage

Brassica oleracea var. *bullata* (Savoys)
Brassica oleracea var. *capitata* (other
cabbage)

Plants in this group are characterized by the
large terminal bud which forms the familiar
cabbage. Careful management and choice of
cultivars allows the gardener to have mature
cabbages available throughout the year. All
are biennials which we treat as annuals and
the large number of cultivars may be
divided into two groups: those which are
sown in the spring to mature in the summer,
autumn or winter, and those which are sown
in the autumn to mature in the spring.
Spring sown types may go to seed or 'bolt'
if sown too early and exposed to cold winter
weather, while autumn sown types may fail
to heart if sown in the spring. In each group
there are round-headed (ball-headed) and
pointed types, while F1 hybrid and open-
pollinated cultivars of each are now available. Cabbages may also be classified
according to their season of maturity. Spring
cabbage may be cut either before a heart
forms—spring 'greens' or 'collards'—or
when hearted; Summer/Autumn cabbages
are cut from late May until October;
Savoy cabbage—frost resistant types with
wrinkled leaves—are mature from September until March; Red cabbage—traditionally used for pickling; and Winter cabbage,

*Right : Ball-headed cabbages such as
'Higusta' are cut in summer*

*Below : 'Offenham' is a crisp
spring-maturing cabbage*

which may either be cut and used from the garden or cut in the autumn and used from store. Some late maturing cabbages have distinctly flattened heads and are referred to as Drumheads.

Soil requirements

All cabbages prefer rich, deep soils which are moisture-retentive—but well drained—and which have had plenty of well-rotted organic manure. They should not be grown in soil that grew brassicas the previous year, but the danger of club root can be reduced by liming if necessary.

Suitable fertilizers

Spring-sown crops which are to mature before early autumn, and which must bulk up rapidly, need readily available supplies of nitrogenous fertilizer and water, while those which are in season during the colder autumn and winter periods will need to be more hardy and receive fertilizers where the nitrogen is balanced by potassium. Fertilizer programmes depend largely on soil analysis but assuming a reasonably fertile soil, well-supplied with organic matter, you can expect to give a base dressing of 50g per m² (2 oz per sq yd) of a general fertilizer, such as fish and bone meal, immediately before transplanting. The difference in nitrogen requirement between early and later maturing types can then be given in the form of top dressings with fertilizers such as Nitro-Chalk at 25 to 50g per m² (1 to 2 oz per sq yd) as needed. Autumn sown cabbages will probably follow a crop such as potatoes, peas or beans and may not require any fertilizer before planting. They over-winter as relatively small plants and must be encouraged to grow rapidly in the spring by applying, and hoeing in, nitrogenous top dressings (see above). Freely drained soils are essential for these crops to ensure that plant roots do not become waterlogged over winter and in order that new growth may begin early in the spring.

Plant raising

In January or February you can make the very earliest spring sowings in cold or slightly heated greenhouses or frames (10°C/50°F). Cabbages from these plants will be ready for cutting in late May or June. Either sow thinly directly into the frame or greenhouse soil—in drills 1cm (½in) deep and 20cm (8in) apart—or sow into seedtrays. In the latter method, prick out the young seedlings into other seedtrays—containing a proprietary potting compost—when they are large enough to handle. Space them at 5cm × 2.5cm (2in × 1in). The seedlings will be ready for planting outside at the end of March or in early April. Planting too early in a cold spring may cause the cabbages to run directly to seed. Other summer and autumn cabbages along with Red cabbages and Savoys are sown in outdoor seedbeds during April or May and planted out in June and July. Once again sow thinly in drills 1cm (½in) deep and 20 to 30cm (8 to 12 in) apart.

Late July and early August is the time for autumn sowings of hearting spring cabbage with the plants being put out in September and October. Use the seedbed technique described for summer and autumn cabbages. Spring 'greens' are best sown in late July in their final positions with the shallow 1-cm (½-in) drills spaced 30cm (12in) apart. Once the seedlings have one or two true leaves, thin them to 8 to 12cm (3 to 5in) apart in the rows. If a general purpose cultivar is grown—that is one which can be used either for spring 'greens' or cabbage—then the thinnings from the 'greens' rows may be used as the transplants for the cabbage crop.

Transplanting and crop management

Water the plants well in their seedtrays/seedbeds before lifting. They should then be removed with as little root damage as possible and, having removed any diseased and otherwise unacceptable plants, the re-

mainder should be size graded before planting. Suitable distances for the various types of cabbages are as follows:—

Spring sown cabbages	Between plants in the rows	Between rows
Early summer types*	45cm (18in)	45cm
Summer/ autumn types*	45–60cm (18–24in)	45–60cm
Savoy cabbage	45–60cm (18–24in)	45–60cm
Winter cabbage	60cm (24in)	60cm
Red cabbage	90cm (36in)	90cm

* pointed cultivars can be grown at 30cm × 30cm (12in × 12in)

Autumn sown cabbages		
Spring cabbage (large hearts)	35cm (14in)	45cm (18in)
(small hearts)	30cm (12in)	45cm (18in)
Spring 'greens'	8–12cm (3–4in)	30cm (12in)

Left: As the name suggests, the cabbage 'Derby Day' is ready for cutting in early June

Below: Savoys such as 'Ice Queen' are frost resistant and have crinkled leaves

Water the plants in immediately after planting to get them off to a good start. Early maturing types must be encouraged to grow rapidly by top dressings and frequent waterings in dry weather. Hoe between the plants to keep weeds down until the rosette leaves of the cabbages meet together. The soil around spring maturing types will tend to become compacted during the winter and this should be broken up when the fertilizer top dressing is hoed in during the spring. You may have to deal with cabbage root fly in late May, while caterpillars and aphids will almost certainly attack the plants in August/September.

Harvesting and storage

You can cut most cabbages whenever you need them. They will taste all the better if picked when fresh and crisp. Summer types will soon get past their best if not harvested regularly, but autumn and winter types have been bred for their long-standing qualities. Red cabbage is best harvested in the autumn while the white, winter cabbage types should be cut in November or December and stored in a cool, dry, frost-free shed. Before storing the cabbage, trim the heads

This perfectly round and solid head is just ready for cutting

neatly to resemble a football; all traces of rotten or damaged leaves should be cut off with a sharp knife. The heads can be stacked pyramid fashion and should be inspected regularly for rotting leaves. Peel them off and throw them away. This method of storing white cabbage—or Dutch white cabbage as it is sometimes called—is widely practised in the Netherlands where it is grown in large quantities. Its importance has increased in Britain recently, not only as a cooked vegetable but also as an ingredient in winter salads and cole slaw.

Pests and diseases

The main pests and diseases, which have been previously mentioned under Brussels sprouts and cauliflower, are aphids, cabbage root fly, caterpillars, flea beetles, birds, whitefly and club root, damping off, wire stem and frost damage.

Above: 'Niggerhead' and other red cultivars produce large, drumhead cabbage

Left: In spite of its name 'January King' is ready from October until March

Suitable cultivars

Early summer cabbage 'May Star': very early F1 hybrid. 'Golden Acre': solid, medium sized heads. 'Greyhound': pointed and compact. 'Hispi': earliest pointed cultivar, F1 hybrid.

Summer/autumn cabbage 'Golden Acre'; 'Greyhound'; 'Hispi' as well as 'Primo': summer, round headed type. 'Delicatesse': small, compact heads in September. 'Winnigstadt': traditional, compact; August–October.

Kales

Brassica oleracea var. *acephala* (curly kales/borecole), *Brassica napus* (plain-leaved, fodder or rape kales)

Kales are hardy winter greens and will withstand very severe weather indeed. In Britain they are, therefore, particularly useful in northern districts. Plants may be classified into two groups according to their leaf shape. Plain-leaved, Fodder or Rape Kales have large, simple leaves with a strong flavour and are mainly used for feeding livestock although some may be used for culinary purposes. Curly Kales or Borecole have curled, crimped leaves not unlike those of parsley and are more popular for human consumption. There are also a number of ornamental kales with red or variegated leaves.

Soil and fertilizer requirements

Kales do best if they follow well-manured crops such as early potatoes or peas. Soils should be well-drained and fertilizer levels should be kept low to start with but increased by giving nitrogenous fertilizer topdressings after Christmas.

Plant raising

Sow curly kale seed in an outdoor seedbed in April or May to provide plants for putting out in July or early August. Drills should be 1cm (½in) deep and 30cm (12in) apart with seed sown thinly to produce sturdy plants. Plain-leaved types are best sown in situ during July and thinned to the required spacing later. Rows should be 60cm (24in) apart and plants thinned to 45 to 60cm (18 to 24in). Transplanting these types may cause them to be killed off in severe winters.

Transplanting and crop management

Transplant curly types in July to give a final spacing of 60cm (24in) square for tall cultivars and 45cm (18in) for dwarf ones.

Harvesting

Pick the young leaves off the plants from Christmas onwards. Regular picking will encourage sideshoots to develop which will produce more tender shoots in March and April.

Pests and diseases

The usual brassica pests and diseases are liable to attack this crop.

Suitable cultivars

Curly Kales: 'Dwarf Green Curled': dwarf habit, intensely curled. 'Extra Curled Scotch': dark green, particularly hardy. 'Fribor': newly introduced F1 hybrid. 'Pentland Brig': produces leaves followed by broccoli-like stems.

Plain leaved Kales 'Thousand Headed': very hardy with strong flavour.

Curly Kale is very winter hardy and particularly useful in northern areas

Savoy cabbage 'Best of All': produces large heads in September. 'Ormskirk-Rearguard': dark colour, good in severe weather and in colder districts.

Winter cabbage 'January King': hardy drumhead; November–March. 'Christmas Drumhead': dwarf, compact heads. 'Winter Salad': solid white heads, stores well in a cool, airy place.

Red cabbage 'Ruby Ball': F1 hybrid, heads stand well, November. 'Large Blood Red': large solid heads.

Spring cabbage 'April': a compact cultivar, resistant to 'bolting'. 'Durham Early': early maturing, medium size. 'Harbinger': very early, small hearts.

Spring 'greens' 'April'; 'Durham Early'; 'Harbinger': may all successfully be used for spring 'greens' as well as 'First Early Market': general purpose cultivar.

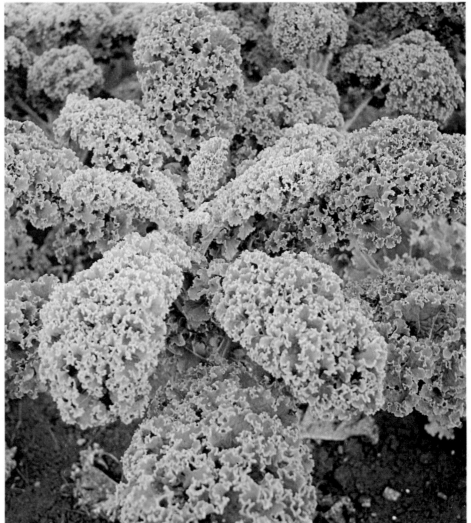

Some members of this family provide fresh vegetables throughout the summer and early autumn, while there are others—such as haricot beans, navy beans and lentils (none of which are grown much in Britain) whose seeds we can use during the winter months. Most of the subjects are true annual plants but, strictly speaking, the runner bean is a perennial which we just treat as an annual. In common with many other legumes, peas and beans have nodules on their roots which contain bacteria capable of converting the nitrogen gas in the air into a form in which it can be used by plants. Sometimes this means that you need to give less nitrogenous fertilizer to legumes than you do to other vegetables. This benefit of nitrogen fixation can be passed on to the following crops if the roots of healthy legumes are dug into the soil when the rest of the plant is removed. For culinary purposes we are interested in the fruits which, in the case of the pea and bean family, are called pods. In some cases the whole pod, complete with the young, immature seeds, is prepared and cooked in the fresh state as with dwarf and climbing French beans, runner beans, sugar peas, and asparagus peas. Alternatively the pods are opened and the seeds shelled out before cooking as with green peas, petit pois, broad beans—all of which are used fresh—and haricot or flageolet beans, navy beans and lentils which are used in the dry or semi-dry state.

The classification is not quite as clear-cut as indicated since many people enjoy the

These long, even pods of the French bean 'Remus' are ready for picking

Runner beans may be supported or grown as a bushy, 'pinched' plant

young complete pods of broad beans either cooked whole or after slicing.

The growing of peas and beans is a must for vegetable gardeners who have a deep-freeze, especially now that cultivars which have been bred for commercial freezing and food processing companies are slowly becoming available to the amateur. It is possible for the amateur to save seed from peas and beans with more certainty than from other crops such as brassicas. Great care is required, however, to ensure that the selected pods contain healthy seeds which are then properly dried and ripened. Another danger is that pods will be selected at the end of the crop which means that you select for lateness—it would be better to choose typical pods in the middle of the picking period for their seed.

Garden peas

Pisum sativum hortense—Green pea
Pisum sativum macrocarpum—Sugar pea
Tetragonolobus purpureus—Asparagus pea

Green peas, sugar peas (Mangetout or Edible—podded peas) and petit pois—all of which have been developed from the same basic ancestor—are dealt with here along with the reddish flowered asparagus pea (not a true pea at all).

The exact origins of the pea are unknown but it probably comes from the Near East. The crop was certainly known to the Greeks and Romans who ate peas dried—green peas were not eaten until the sixteenth century. The early types were round-seeded but

subsequent breeding and selection has led to the introduction of the sweeter, but less hardy, wrinkle-seeded or marrowfat types. The marrowfat types are now the most important group for freezing, canning and also for fresh, green peas. Over 100,000 acres (40,000 hectares) of peas are currently grown in Britain for the various types of processing—quick-freezing being the most important outlet. Consequently there has been a considerable reduction in the area of peas grown for fresh market work so that, in some seasons, green peas may not be seen in your local greengrocers at all.

The two main groups of peas still exist although round-seeded or 'blues' are now mainly used for winter and early spring sowings because of their greater hardiness. Wrinkle-seeded peas have a much higher sugar content, and, as a result, a better flavour. Peas are also classified according to the time taken from outdoor sowing until picking. Thus first early cultivars are usually ready 11 to 13 weeks after sowing; second earlies after 13 to 14 weeks and maincrop/late cultivars after 14 to 16 weeks. Peas climb by means of leaf tendrils with cultivars ranging in height from 40 to 150cm (16 to 60in). The tallest cultivars are usually the latest to mature but dwarf ones are not always the earliest. All types will grow better and yield more prolifically if they are given supports up which they climb.

Sugar peas and petit pois are grown in the same way as the marrowfat group of garden peas. Both must be harvested at just the right time if their full flavour is to be obtained and neither are particularly suitable for freezing. A novelty pea, with purple pods,

is also available and has peas which are green with an excellent flavour when cooked.

The asparagus pea is a half-hardy annual and, therefore, must not be sown until the danger of frost is almost past. They are grown for their light green edible pods which have 4 wavy outgrowths or ribs. This plant, too, is grown more as a novelty than for its economic food value.

Soil and fertilizer requirements

All peas grow best in deep, rich soils which are moisture-retentive. It is most important that the roots are always able to obtain enough water since peas and beans are particularly susceptible to drought conditions. Early sowings must be made on 'warm', open textured soils—any excess of water may cause the newly sown seed to rot. Deep cultivations are best done in the autumn when well-rotted organic matter should be incorporated. It is worth testing the soil to find if it is acid or alkaline because peas will not do at all well in very acid conditions. They prefer soils which are neutral to alkaline. Fertilizer should be worked in during the final preparations before sowing, but be sure to use materials which are low in nitrogen for this purpose.

Below left: Well-filled, blunt pods of the second early 'Canice'

Below: 'Hurst Green Shaft' has long pods with peas which are ideal for freezing

Seed sowing

In very favourable areas such as the south west it may be worthwhile making a sowing with a round-seeded cultivar in November. This will then be ready for harvesting in early to mid-May. Success with early peas is more likely in other areas, however, if the first sowings are made under cloches or polythene tunnels. This can be done from mid-February onwards when picking will again be possible at the end of May. Main sowings of early cultivars should begin in early March when the soil begins to dry out and warm up. If first early, second early and maincrop peas are sown at intervals during March and April there will be crops maturing through June and July. If you want a supply of peas throughout the summer then further sowings should be made during May and June while a sowing of one of the first early, round-seeded cultivars made in early July will often provide a very welcome crop of late peas in mid to late September. Asparagus peas should be sown in late April or May—about two weeks before the last killing frosts in your area.

Seeds should be sown in flat bottomed drills which are 10 to 15cm (4 to 6in) wide and 5 to 7cm (2 to 3in) deep. Scatter the peas evenly in the bottom of the drill to leave the individual seeds 5 to 7cm apart.

The asparagus pea with its low growing, bushy habit should be grown in a single, narrow drill with seeds sown 10 to 15cm

(4 to 6in) apart and 1 to 2cm ($\frac{1}{2}$ to $\frac{3}{4}$in) deep. In dry weather the bottom of the drill should be well watered and then allowed to drain before sowing. Birds and mice may cause damage by eating or removing the germinating seeds, but they can be deterred by treating/soaking the seed in red lead/ paraffin before sowing. Be certain to wash the poisonous red lead off your hands afterwards. After sowing rake the soil back over

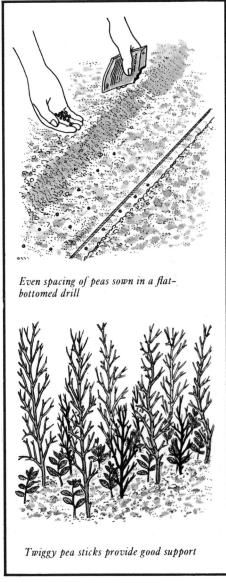

Even spacing of peas sown in a flat-bottomed drill

Twiggy pea sticks provide good support

the seeds. At this stage it is worthwhile covering the rows with close meshed wire netting or strands of black cotton further to deter birds and vermin from disturbing the seeds. Distances between rows will vary from 60 to 120cm (2 to 4ft) and should be roughly equivalent to the expected height of the cultivars being grown. If you have ample space available, however, it is better to err on the wide side between rows as the areas of protection so formed (when the peas have been supported) are ideal for growing such catch crops as radishes, lettuce and early turnips.

Crop management

When the seedlings are 5 to 7cm (2 to 3in) high, remove the wire netting and put in the supports. It would be much too time-consuming to support commercially grown

crops of peas but growth and productivity are certainly improved when the plants are allowed to climb. Traditionally the support is provided by well-branched and twiggy pea sticks—hazel trimmings are very good—which have been cut from local hedges or woods. It is now easier to use wire or nylon netting which is stretched between posts at either end of the rows. Whatever you use for supports make certain that they are sufficiently thin for the tendrils to grasp and that they are as tall as the expected height of the cultivar being grown. As well as getting the plants off the ground the supports should, ideally, encourage the peas to grow outwards so that air and light can get into the middle of the rows. There are certain stages in the life of a pea plant when it is very susceptible to moisture stress. If water is given at these times in a dry season then the yield and quality of peas will be improved. The critical times are at the start of flowering and, even more important, at the beginning of pod swelling. In most seasons—but particularly when water is in short supply—it is just as important to prevent moisture loss as it is to replenish supplies. Mulching the plants with such materials as grass cuttings will help to cut down moisture loss from the surface of the soil. It will also protect the soil surface, encourage root growth (which will mean better shoot growth) and help to keep down weeds. Even so you will probably need to do some hoeing around the rows to keep down weeds, particularly in the early stages. Your crop should be ready for picking to start about 3 weeks after flowering.

Harvesting

Green peas must be picked when they are young and tender if you are to enjoy them at their best. This is particularly true if they are to be frozen. Commercially the maturity of peas for freezing and canning is assessed with an instrument called a tenderometer which indicates the amount of fibre in the sample. Pick only the juiciest peas with the lowest fibre content (test this by chewing a few of the peas) for freezing and, once they are ready, they must be harvested and frozen as quickly as possible to ensure that they stay tender. The pods should, of course, be well filled. The tender peas of yesterday can be as hard as bullets tomorrow especially in the hot, dry days of midsummer, so regular harvesting is needed at 2 to 3 day intervals. Removing the mature pods will also allow the young, developing pods to fill out.

It is equally important to pick petit pois and sugar peas at the right stage. Many people—but particularly the French—consider that petit pois are the finest flavoured peas especially if they are picked when young and eaten fresh. Pick the pods of sugar peas while flat and immature—before you can see the seeds from the outside. When these are 'topped and tailed' and cooked whole they have a delightful flavour. Asparagus peas also have edible pods which must be picked when no more than 3cm (about 1in) long or they will become stringy. This plant is something of a misnomer since there is little resemblance to asparagus either in appearance or flavour. Regular picking encourages the plants to go on cropping over a period of several weeks.

Pests and diseases

Aphids attack peas but are only a severe problem in warm, dry summers. The damage caused to germinating seeds by birds and mice has already been mentioned. Irregular, silvery markings which appear on leaves and pods are caused by the feeding of pea thrips (thunderflies) but probably the most serious pest is the pea moth. Eggs are laid in the flowers, and the resultant larvae tunnel into the developing pods to feed on the young peas. You do not see the larvae until they—and their trails of destruction—are exposed when the peas are podded. Peas are self-fertile and pollination usually takes place before the flowers are fully open. Consequently you can spray the open flowers to kill the pea moth larvae as they emerge from the eggs but choose your chemicals carefully otherwise there may still be a residue left at picking time.

Damping-off diseases are in the soil and will cause the seeds to rot especially if the conditions are wet. Fusarium wilt, foot rot and several root rot fungi also occur more frequently in damp soil conditions. The leaves go yellow, the stem bases develop brown or black marks, root nodule development is poor and the plants wilt and eventually collapse and die. Unfortunately many of these diseases can remain in the soil for a number of years so you must be absolutely certain not to grow peas where infections have occurred in previous seasons. Again the practice of rotating crops from plot to plot will help prevent a build-up of disease.

Grey mould fungus (Botrytis) will infect previously damaged pods and stems especially in damp weather. Dark, rusty red spots

First early peas like 'Kelvedon Wonder' may also be used for summer sowings

are sometimes seen inside individual peas when they are split open even though no discoloration is seen on the outer surface. This condition, known as marsh spot, is caused by a deficiency of the micronutrient manganese and is more likely to occur on acid soils. Late sowings may be infected by downy mildew but a number of disease-resistant cultivars are now available. Finally peas may become infected with a number of virus diseases—mostly spread by aphids or thrips—which induce mottling, stunting and dead patches on leaves.

Suitable cultivars

Most green pea cultivars may be used for freezing but the particularly suitable ones are marked *. Round seeded types are marked (R)

First earlies, all growing to 45cm (18in) 'Feltham First' (R): good for very early crops. 'Meteor' (R): the most hardy cultivar. 'Little Marvel'*: dwarf, well flavoured, suitable for cloches. 'Kelvedon Wonder'*: very good early and late. 'Hurst Beagle'*: early and long podded.

Second earlies, all growing to 75cm (30in). 'Onward'*: well known, wilt resistant. 'Kelvedon Monarch'*: long podded all round cultivar. 'Hurst Green Shaft'*: long podded, disease resistant.

Maincrop/Lates 'Recette'*: 3 long pods per stem, 60cm (24in). 'Lord Chancellor'*: dark green pods, good flavour, 90–100cm (3ft to 3ft 6in).

Sugar pea (Mangetout) 'Caronby de Maussane' 150cm (5ft). 'Oregon Sugar pod' 90 to 120cm (3 to 4ft).

Petit pois 'Gullivert' 90cm (3ft).

Novelties 'Purple podded' attractive, green and tasty peas. 150cm (5ft).

Asparagus pea Interesting vegetable with a long season. 30 to 45cm (12 to 18in).

Broad beans

Vicia faba

This vegetable was well known to the Egyptians and Romans while broad bean seeds have been found associated with Iron Age relics. It was certainly introduced to Britain as a cultivated plant well before the seventeenth century. Broad beans are usually shelled from the pods when they are almost fully grown although young, 8 to 10cm (3 to 4in) long pods may be cooked whole or sliced like French or runner beans.

Broad beans are the hardiest of the legumes that we grow. In many parts of the country sowings can be made in the autumn to mature in early June, while sowings made between January and April are ready for picking throughout July. Early growth in the spring can be encouraged by covering the first sowings with cloches or polythene tunnels. Cultivars can be classified into two main groups—'Windsors' and 'Longpods'—although some with intermediate characteristics are now available. 'Windsors' have short pods with 4 or 5 almost circular seeds in each, whereas 'Longpods' have larger, more slender pods each with about 8 kidney-shaped seeds. Broad beans may also be classified according to seed colour—white or green—the green seeded cultivars being especially suitable for freezing.

Soil requirements

Autumn sown crops are best grown in a sheltered position with well-drained soil. In no circumstances must overwintered beans become waterlogged as seeds/young plants soon rot. Broad beans generally appreciate rich soils which have been deeply worked but they will tolerate heavier soils than many other vegetables. The earliest of the successional sowings in the spring will need to be made into light, open textured soils. All crops respond to the digging in of organic manures or composts which help to improve

An early crop of spring sown Tozer's 'May Express'

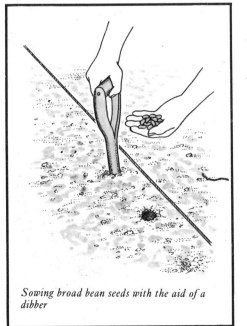

Sowing broad bean seeds with the aid of a dibber

soil structure as well as retaining moisture. In common with many other legumes, broad beans do not grow well in acid soils. If you have such conditions you must lime the soil well before sowing.

Base fertilizers which have too much nitrogen will prevent satisfactory plant establishment and, particularly in over-wintered crops, cause vigorous and unwanted growth of the young plants. On soils which are reasonably fertile and have had organic material worked into them it should be possible to apply base fertilizers which just provide phosphate and potassium. These two nutrients will balance the nitrogen and ensure sturdy growth which is less likely to fall over when the plants eventually reach their cropping height of 60 to 90cm (2 to 3ft). Nitrogenous top dressings can be given to overwintered broad beans to replenish supplies which have been leached away and to encourage early growth in the spring. Apply nitro-chalk at 25 to 50g per m² (1–2 oz per sq yd) and hoe in lightly during mid-February.

Seed sowing

You can grow broad beans in double rows allowing 15 to 20cm (6 to 8in) between the two lines and from 60 to 90cm (2 to 3ft), according to cultivar, between the double rows. Alternatively they can be grown in single rows spaced 60cm (2ft) apart. Put each individual seed into 6 to 8-cm (2 to 3-in) deep holes made with a dibber. Leave 15 to 20cm (6 to 8in) between the seeds within the row. Overwintered crops are sown in late October or early November according to district while maincrop sowings are made in March. Not all cultivars are recommended for autumn sowing so be sure to choose one which is suitable.

Crop management

You may need to apply top dressings in the spring. Keep a stringent check on weeds, especially during the early stages. Black bean aphids (blackfly) may attack from May onwards but the damage can be reduced by pinching out the tops of the plants when they are in full flower. This applies especially to autumn sown crops when the pinching out will also encourage an earlier crop of well-filled pods. Taller growing cultivars may need supporting particularly in exposed areas. This can be done cheaply and easily by knocking in stakes at the ends of the rows—also at intervals if the rows are very long—and stretching a piece of string around one side of the plants and back up the other.

Harvesting

Beans for slicing or cooking whole should be picked when they are 8 to 10cm (max. 4in) long. Those for shelling are ready when the seeds are about 2cm (under an inch) across with the scar of attachment to the pod remaining green. The beans are over-mature when this scar is brown or black. When all the beans have been picked, cut off and take away the stems and leaves (haulm) but leave the roots in the soil: they contain valuable nitrogen which will benefit subsequent crops.

Pests and diseases
Your main enemy is the black bean aphid, which commonly lays its eggs during the early autumn on Viburnum shrubs where

Above: The longpod 'Gillit Imperial' supported by horizontal wires

they overwinter. They hatch during the following spring/early summer and the aphids soon migrate to broad beans—and other crops—which are the summer hosts. Some control will be achieved by eliminating the winter host plants but, of course, there are likely to be others nearby which you cannot remove. Pinching out the shoot tops—where aphids usually prefer to feed—during flowering will reduce the damage but it may still be necessary to do some spraying. In this case be careful not to spray when the flowers are being worked by bees and other pollinating insects. It is preferable to spray relatively non-toxic chemicals on warm, still evenings when the insects have finished work for the day. You may also notice scalloped edges on the broad bean leaves. This condition, which rarely causes significant crop losses, is caused by the feeding of pea and bean weevils on the leaves.

Chocolate spot is the most common disease of broad beans and is caused by the Botrytis fungus. Some signs of the disease are almost certain to appear every year but very severe attacks are less likely. The tell-tale brown spots first appear on the leaves but can, under adverse conditions, spread to the stems, pods and even through into the beans themselves. Initial attack and subsequent spread are more likely on plants which are damaged or not growing well, and as with other botrytis-type fungi the best method of control is to grow strong healthy crops in a well-prepared site that is carefully maintained.

Suitable cultivars
Those which can be sown in the autumn are marked (A) while (*) indicates good freezing qualities.
'Aquadulce' (A) gives early crops from autumn sowings. 'Colossal': white seeded; good for exhibition. 'Masterpiece'*: Long-pod type of excellent quality. 'Green Windsor'*: heavy cropper; ideal for late crops. 'The Sutton': dwarf 30cm (12in); useful in limited space and for cloche work.

French beans
Phaseolus vulgaris

This plant, which originated in South America, has been grown in Britain since the mid-sixteenth century. This type of bean is most popular in France—hence its common name. It is sometimes known as kidney bean because of the shape of the seeds. There are dwarf forms, climbing forms and purple podded forms—all of which are grown for their edible pods which are usually sliced before cooking. Flageolet and haricot beans are grown for their seeds which are used either semi-dry or completely dry. Recently there has been a big increase in the area of french beans grown for quick-freezing. Plant breeders have produced cultivars which produce all the beans at the top of the plant, can be mechanically harvested and which remain stringless for long periods. A number of these new

Below: The novelty purple-podded bean which has a superb flavour when cooked

introductions are slowly becoming available to the amateur. French beans are half-hardy annuals which cannot be sown in the open until all danger of frost has passed. Protected crops, which are grown in heated greenhouses or under cloches, will produce beans in May and June respectively whereas the first open-ground sowings will be ready in July. Successional sowings produce beans until well into the autumn.

Soil and fertilizer requirements

Light, well drained soils are required while it helps if organic manure/compost has been worked in during the autumn preparations. Acid soils will not be tolerated. Incorporate a good general base fertilizer dressing during the final preparations before sowing. 25 to 50g per m² (1 to 2oz per sq yd) of something like fish and bone meal will be suitable provided that soft growth is not induced by too much nitrogen.

Seed sowing

If you have a greenhouse with a temperature of 15°C/60°F from February onwards a very early crop of french beans can be obtained. Sow 6 or 7 dwarf french bean seeds 4 to 5cm (1½ to 2in) deep in a 22-cm (8-in) pot which

Growth habits of climbing and dwarf french beans

contains a well-drained potting compost. If kept in the greenhouse these plants will produce beans by May. Outdoor sowings can begin with dwarf cultivars in mid-March. After sowing cover the rows with cloches or polythene tunnels until mid-May. Plants should be fully ventilated in warm weather. Open-ground sowings of all types of french beans can be made from late April onwards with successional sowings at monthly intervals giving continuity of picking from July onwards. You can make further sowings of dwarf cultivars in mid to late July to produce beans at the end of the season in October. The onset of cold, wet autumnal conditions will kill off the plants but protection with cloches will allow picking to continue into November.

Seeds are sown in single rows which are spaced 45cm to 60cm (18 to 24in) apart for dwarf types and up to 90cm (3ft) apart for climbing and purple podded types. Sow seeds 8cm (3in) apart and 4 to 5cm (1½ to 2in) deep, but thin to 15cm (6in) apart in the

rows after the first leaves emerge.

Crop management

Dwarf french beans need little attention during the growing season apart from weeding and pest and disease control. You will need to give supports to climbing and purple podded types, as they will reach 150 to 180cm (up to 6ft). Tall pea sticks, bamboo canes or strings may be used but take care to grow these taller types in sheltered areas as they are easily damaged by wind buffeting.

Harvesting

Pick the beans when they are young and tender. Any delay will tend to cause stringiness even though 'stringless' cultivars are now available. Regular picking will also encourage more pods to develop. Purple podded beans are also stringless and remain tender longer than other types. They lose the purple colour during cooking and compare well with other beans for flavour. The traditional french bean cultivars produce flat pods but cylindrical or 'pencil'-podded cultivars are now available. The beans are in prime picking condition when the pods can be snapped cleanly. Yellow-podded or 'wax-pod' beans can also be grown. Again they are stringless and have a very delicate flavour. Only the seeds of flageolet and haricot beans are eaten—harvested soft and green in the case of flageolets and white or light brown in the case of haricots.

At the end of the crop remove the visible parts of the plants and dig in the roots to provide valuable nitrogen. It is safe to keep your own seed from french beans but you must be careful to choose healthy, true-to-type plants. The seeds must be carefully dried and ripened before they are stored.

Pests and diseases

Apart from the seemingly ever-present

'Brittlewax' is one of the best stringless, wax-pod beans

aphids and the possibility of red spider mite attack (they produce yellow speckles on the leaves which then become bronzed and brittle), french and other types of bean may be attacked by the larvae of the bean seed fly. These legless larvae eat germinating seeds and are more likely to occur on heavily manured soils.

Grey mould (Botrytis) attacks any damaged tissues and you should be particularly watchful in wet seasons. The same conditions favour a seed-borne fungus which causes anthracnose of french, broad or runner beans. Sunken black spots develop on leaves, stems and, eventually, pods. The seeds ultimately become infected with a brownish/black discoloration. On no account save these seeds for next season's crop.

Suitable cultivars
Dwarf french beans
Most are suitable for freezing.

Green pods (flat-podded) 'The Prince': early; suitable for cloche work. 'Masterpiece': good yields over long periods (round or pencil podded.) 'Sprite': stringless, continental type. 'Tendergreen': early but also long seasoned variety.

Yellow pods 'Kinghorn Waxpod': golden pods with white seeds.

Climbing french beans 'Blue Lake': very popular and high yielding. 'Earliest of All': green beans during summer, ripened as haricots in autumn.

Purple podded beans 'Blue Coco'.

Haricot/Flageolet beans 'Chevrier Vert': general purpose. Used for green beans, flageolets or haricots. 'Comtesse de Chambourd': traditional haricot.

frame or greenhouse until planting time in mid-May. You may still need to protect the plants so have cloches ready. Seed can be sown outside in mid-April on a site where the soil has been covered by cloches for about a month. Leave the cloches over the plants until they touch the glass when, for early beans, the tops should be pinched out. Maincrop runner beans are sown outside from early May onwards depending on the district. If late frosts are forecast after they

Left: Runner bean 'Enorma' is ideal for freezing or exhibition work

Below: White flowered runner beans go stringy less quickly

Scarlet runner bean

Phaseolus multiflorus

When this well known and popular vegetable was introduced into Britain in 1633 it was for the ornamental value of its beautiful scarlet flowers. It is now grown for the edible pods, which are often over 30cm (12in) long and 2cm ($\frac{3}{4}$in) wide, and which are usually sliced before cooking. In its native South America it is a perennial but we grow it annually from seed. By the end of the growing season a small tuberous root system has usually developed and this can be stored in frost-free conditions and then used to start the crop in the following year. The scarlet runner bean is a very tender plant and will be killed by very slight frosts either at the beginning or end of the season. By nature it is a climber and most crops attain a height of 150 to 180cm (5 to 6ft) when grown on supports. A bushy habit can be induced, however, by pinching out the growing points in which case pods are produced slightly earlier. With the aid of cloches to protect the young plants during April and May it is possible to pick beans in mid-July from the earliest sowings. Picking should then continue from open ground sowings until the first killing frost in the autumn. The runner bean is yet another legume which has been grown increasingly for quick-freezing in

recent years. It is important, however, to pick the pods before they become stringy. As the name suggests most cultivars have scarlet flowers but both white and pink flowered introductions—which go stringy less quickly—are also available. As well as producing quantities of beans both for fresh consumption and freezing, runner beans plants form very attractive living screens in summer.

Soil and fertilizer requirements

Any good garden soil will grow runner beans but the best results are obtained if you use fertile, well-drained land which has been deeply dug in the autumn and had liberal dressings of organic manure incorporated. The benefits of deep cultivations and incorporation of organic manure are most apparent in a dry season. Although they, in common with other legumes, have root nodules which contain nitrogen-fixing bacteria runner beans respond to base dressings of fertilizers which contain nitrogen. Fish and bone meal—or an equivalent general purpose material—at 25 to 50g per m² (1 to 2oz per sq yd) should be adequate.

Seed sowing and crop support systems

Never expose runner bean plants to frosts: they will turn black and die. Choosing a sowing date for the crop in your area must always take account of this. For a very early crop sow seeds in seedtrays (space the seeds 5cm × 5cm (2in) or in individual pots during April and keep them in a frost-free

have appeared you can earth soil very gently over the plants to give protection.

There are a number of ways of growing and supporting runner beans—with each one requiring a particular seed spacing. Early cloche and pinched crops are best grown in single rows with the seeds sown 5cm (2in) deep and 15cm (6in) apart. Allow 60cm (2ft) between rows. Maincrops are most usually grown in double rows and supported by 2.5-m (9-ft) long poles or bamboo canes. Leave 60cm (2ft) between the two lines of plants with seeds sown at the depth and spacing as for pinched crops. Allow 100cm (3ft 6in) between each double row. Put the supports in as soon as the young plants emerge. Less root damage is done at this stage and valuable protection against wind is also provided. Push canes or poles firmly into the ground at 30-cm (12-in) intervals; cross them over and join tightly together 30cm (12in) from the top. Another pole/cane laid crossways along the junction and tied to the uprights will add rigidity to the framework. If all the seeds come up you will need to train two plants up each support but this will not lead to overcrowding. The importance of constructing a firm, rigid support framework cannot be over-emphasized. Many badly supported rows are blown down later in the season when the plants have formed a wind-resistant canopy on the poles/canes.

Runner beans can also be grown on a

wigwam framework constructed from four 2.5-m (9-ft) long poles/canes which are pushed firmly into the ground at the corners of a 75 to 90cm (3ft) square and then tied tightly together 30cm (12in) from their tops. Two seeds are then sown to each support. If they both germinate let both of them continue to grow. Finally, the crop may be grown up strings which are tied to a post and wire framework. In this case sow the seeds in single rows as for the pinched crop but leave 100cm (3ft 6in) between rows. Stretch three strands of wire between the uprights at 15cm, 1m and 2m (6in, 3ft 6in and 7ft).

Crop management

When the plants are tall enough, train them on to the support poles, canes or strings. Runner bean stems spiral upwards in an anti-clockwise direction around the supports. Allow about 14 to 16 weeks from open-ground sowing until the start of picking of climbing beans. During this time keep the plants well-supplied with water particularly during the flowering and pod swelling period. Setting of the flowers is often poor in hot, dry weather when the pollen is less viable and the plant roots are under moisture stress. Spraying the flowers and watering the plants will improve setting, while mulching from an early stage will reduce water loss from the soil. Runner beans must be pollinated by insects; bees are the most useful. Do not discourage them by spraying against aphids and red spider mites while bees are present. It is best to spray on warm still evenings when the bees have returned to their hives. Use relatively non-toxic chemicals which quickly disappear. Since strong winds will not only blow down rows of beans but will also damage flowers and young pods by buffeting (and thus reduce yield), runner beans must be grown in sheltered positions. Stop the plants by removing the growing tips when the stems reach the top of the supports. This will ensure that all the lower beans develop quickly and be of better flavour.

Harvesting

Cloche and pinched crops will provide the first beans. The induced bushy habit of the plants (there are no true dwarf cultivars) means that the pods hang close to the ground and may be soiled and rain splashed in wet weather. Pick when the pods are young and tender—before the seeds become obvious through the pod wall. Regular picking will ensure continuous flowering and fruiting. Make sure that any pods which you save for seed are true-to-type and disease-free. Dry them thoroughly before storage.

Pests and diseases

Aphids, bean seed fly and red spider mites will all attack runner beans. The disease known as anthracnose can also be a problem as can fusarium wilt and foot and root rots caused by fungi such as Rhizoctonia. All are

'Streamline' a popular and reliable runner bean

more likely to occur in badly drained soil. Do not grow runner beans where fusarium wilt has attacked recently.

Halo blight is a bacterial disease which causes yellow rings and water soaked areas on leaves, and pods. It is favoured by warm, wet weather but doesn't usually occur in Britain. Seeds from infected plants will carry the disease from one year to the next so be careful when sowing your own. Remember that your seedsman will be much better equipped to supply seeds which have been tested against disease.

Suitable cultivars

All climbing cultivars (*) are suitable for freezing.
'Kelvedon Marvel': early; good under cloches. 'Enorma'*: long beans of excellent flavour. 'Streamline'*: popular and reliable. 'Sunset'*: early bean with pink flowers. 'White Achievement'*: white flowered.

Mulching runner bean plants with grass cuttings

Early runner beans can be raised in pots and then transplanted

The Onion Tribe

The genus *Allium* contains several species which have been grown as food crops for centuries. The Egyptians were known to eat onions and garlic while there is reference to the Israelites eating leeks during their time in Egypt.

Members of the onion tribe are widely used either as separate vegetables or as flavourings for other dishes. They are biennial or perennial plants which we mainly grow as annuals in our gardens. The biennials—onions and leeks—will flower if they are allowed to grow on into a second year and may even 'bolt' if the young plants are put out—in an attempt to produce bigger or earlier crops—at a date when prolonged cold weather may still occur.

For culinary purposes we are interested in the modified leaves of the plants. They are concentrically wrapped to form a cylindrical 'bulb', which we blanch, in the case of leeks, while the familiar bulbs or bulbils of onion, shallot and garlic are made up of swollen leaf bases which contain the plant's stored food. Like all members of the *Alliaceae* the onion tribe contain pungent and aromatic materials which give them their familiar taste and smell. The British climate is well-suited to growing these vegetables but the drying and ripening of onion bulbs is sometimes hampered by wet conditions in late summer and early autumn.

Bulb and salad onions
Allium cepa

This group, which includes dry bulb onions, salad (or spring) onions and pickling onions, can be grown anywhere in Britain but uncertain weather can make harvesting difficult. Every year Britain imports over 100,000 tons of bulb onions from all over the world. With modern cultivars and an understanding of storage requirements there is no reason, however, why you cannot have your own bulb onions in all but the early to mid-summer period. Most commercial crops of bulb onions in this country are grown from seed which is sown directly outside in the early spring. Small, partially developed bulbs or sets are used on a limited scale and are particularly useful in the colder, wetter areas. Seed may also be sown under protection in the New Year and the resultant plants transplanted in the spring. Sowing onions outdoors in the autumn—to produce an earlier maturing and ripening crop of bulbs the following summer—is an established practice. The danger here however, is that, after the winter cold, the young plants will immediately flower rather than grow on to produce a bulb. Cultivars of Japanese onions have recently become available which can safely be sown in the autumn and which then produce an early crop of good quality bulbs in July.

Closely-spaced sowings of special, quick growing cultivars should be made in the spring if you wish to grow your own pickling onions. Other cultivars have been developed for use as salad—or spring—onions. Once again these are grown very close together to restrict bulb development. If pickling and salad onion cultivars are grown at bulb onion spacings then good sized bulbs will develop but they will not keep in store.

The growth of spring sown bulb onions in this country is largely influenced by daylength. The young plants continue to produce leaves until the daylength reaches about 15 hours, when the bases of those leaves begin to swell to form the familiar bulb. To produce large bulbs you must, therefore, make sure that the plants have as many leaves as possible at this 'switch-over' point in their growth. This will occur, depending on location and cultivar, in late

Japanese F1 hybrids such as 'Express Yellow' are only for autumn sowing

May or early June and final bulb size will then depend on the plant's ability to produce food and store it in the leaf bases.

Soil requirements

In traditional kitchen gardens the onions usually had a permanent site and this onion bed was heavily manured each year in attempts to maintain healthy bulb growth. There are considerable dangers in this non-rotational practice—mainly from soil-borne pests and diseases. Onions must have a long leaf-producing season so choose your site with this in mind. Onions, in common with other Alliums, do not tolerate acid soil conditions. Those crops (bulb or salad onions) which are sown in the autumn and over-wintered must be grown on well-drained, 'warm' soils so that winter losses are minimized. For the same reason it is better to grow these crops after a well-manured summer vegetable, such as a brassica or potatoes, and to withhold dressings of inorganic fertilizer until growth begins again in the spring. Too much soft, lush growth in the autumn can lead to considerable crop losses if severe weather follows. Prepare the ground for spring-sown

which should be fine, level and firm. Onion seedlings take a long time to emerge after sowing. During this time fine-textured soils—like silts and clays—may develop a crust, or 'cap'. Emergence of the seedling then becomes more difficult so don't prepare an ultra-fine tilth on soils which 'cap'.

Seed sowing and plant raising

Open-ground sowings of Japanese cultivars should be made from the middle to the end

are large enough. Gradually harden the plants off from late March onwards prior to planting outside in mid-April. Space the plants 7cm (3in) apart in rows which are 30 to 40cm (12 to 15in) apart. Outdoor sowings in the spring should be made as soon as a seedbed can be prepared. Mid-February is the ideal time, the spacings being similar to those used in the autumn. Seed can be sown more thinly in the rows, however, since the

Left: 'Stuttgarter Giant' onions grown from sets in peat-filled growing bags

Below: Space salad onions like 'White Lisbon' closely together

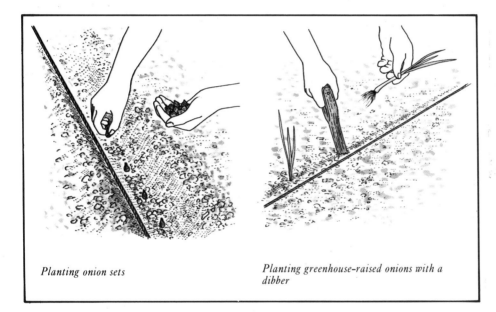

Planting onion sets

Planting greenhouse-raised onions with a dibber

or planted (sets or plants) crops in the autumn and leave it in a roughly dug condition over winter for a crumbly tilth to develop. Rich textured soils are ideal for this purpose but even the heaviest soils can be used if you prepare them carefully.

Suitable fertilizers

All the fertilizer for spring sown/planted onions is applied in the base dressing. Work it into the soil during the preparation of the seedbed. Fertilizers with too much nitrogen will encourage soft, sappy growth and the production of bulbs which do not store well. Try to use a material with nitrogen and potassium in the ratio of 1:2 and apply it at the rate of 50 to 70g per m² (2 to 3oz per sq yd). Pickling and successional crops of summer salad onions are not for storing so use an equally balanced fertilizer to encourage crisp, rapid growth. The final operation before sowing is to prepare the seedbed

of August. This will ensure that the plants are the right size to overwinter because if they are too large they are more likely to 'bolt' and to be damaged by frost. When growth begins again in the spring the plants should be 5 to 7cm (2 to 3in) apart in the row but the initial sowing will have to be closer than this to allow for germination losses and winter die-back. The drills should be 1.0 to 1.5cm ($\frac{1}{2}$ to $\frac{3}{4}$in) deep with the rows 35 to 40cm (12 to 15in) apart. Overwintered bulb onions will be ready for harvesting 6 to 8 weeks before spring sown crops. On no account sow Japanese cultivars in the spring.

A sowing of bulb onions can be made under slightly heated glass (10°C/50°F) in January. Sow the seed in seedpans or trays and prick out into seedtrays or into individual containers—allowing 25cm² (10 sq in) per plant—as soon as the seedlings

danger of winter loss does not apply. Thinnings from autumn or spring sown bulb onion crops can be eaten in salads.

Onion sets are bulbs which have been partially grown in the previous season, then lifted and dried, and finally kept in temperature controlled stores so that the small bulb continues to grow vegetatively when it is replanted rather than running to seed. Growing onions from sets allows less suitable soils to be used and, since some of the growing has been done already, they are good for districts with shorter growing periods. Sets are planted 5 to 7cm (2 to 3in) apart in drills, which are themselves 30 to 40cm (12 to 15in) apart, with only the necks of the small bulbs protruding above the soil. Plant them firmly; even then some will be disturbed by birds, earthworms or frost. Replant them immediately. March or April is the best time for planting onion sets.

If you want your own salad onions at Easter then sow the seed in late August in much the same way as for overwintered bulb onions. This time, however, we require young, immature plants with no bulb so space the rows very closely. If the seed is sown less than half an inch apart no thinning will be needed in the spring. Salad onions in the summer are obtained from successional sowings made outside from February or March onwards. The overwintered crop will probably carry on until late May. The earliest spring sowings be ready in June.

Silverskin onion cultivars for pickling should be sown outside in April and grown rapidly to produce small, crisp and succulent bulbs. Seed may either be broadcast or drilled in rows which are 15 to 20cm (6 to 8in) apart. Sow very closely to make sure that the individual bulbs remain small.

Crop management

There must be no check to the growth of onion plants. Weeds are a major form of competition especially when the onions are small so hoe them out with a short-handled onion hoe. Be careful not to damage the developing bulbs or to pull soil up around them as this will slow down ripening. It is not usual to water bulb onions but it may be necessary in dry seasons until ripening begins. Salad onions may need watering to keep them growing rapidly.

In August (June for autumn sown crops; July for picklers) the leaves of bulb onions will turn yellow and topple over. This marks

Thick-necked onions (right) produce bulbs which rot during storage

Typical distortion (above) caused by eelworms feeding on young onion plant

the start of the ripening process which will be hastened if the leaves are folded over neatly. The leaves of thick-necked ('bull-necked') onions remain standing and the bulbs from these plants must be separated from the rest since they do not store well.

Harvesting, ripening and storage

The condition of the bulbs at harvest time and the efficiency of the ripening process will largely determine how effectively they will be stored. When the leaves have become brittle choose a warm, sunny day on which carefully to lift the bulbs. Lay them out in the sun to continue drying and turn them frequently to prevent damp patches developing. Warm conditions are needed to ripen the outer scales of the bulb, seal the neck and produce a rich skin colour and finish. In wet autumns it means that onions will have to be ripened under protection. It may

Above: 'Conquest' is a bulb onion that crops and keeps well

Japanese Onion 'Matsumoto Long White'

Pests and diseases

Onion crops need to be rotated to prevent a build-up of stem eelworm in the onion bed. These microscopic pests can remain in the soil for many years and will not be content only to attack the onion family. Infested plants take on a 'bloated', twisted appearance and produce bulbs which quickly go rotten in store. Make sure that you follow a carefully programmed crop rotation and don't buy untested seed.

Onion fly is the other major pest of onions. Like cabbage rootfly on brassicas, its eggs are laid near to the onion plants—particularly those growing on light land—and the resultant larvae tunnel into the young plants and, eventually, into mature bulbs.

White rot is a serious disease of onion and related crops since it, too, is soil-borne and remains viable for several years. The leaves go yellow, the roots rot and the base of the plant becomes covered with a white fungal growth. Crop rotation is the only satisfactory control. Downy mildew will cause the leaves to go grey and topple over while they develop a purple coloration in wet weather. Onion smut fungus produces black, streak-like pustules on the leaves which split open to release clouds of soot-like spores. Fortunately smut is not very common, and grey mould (Botrytis) only infects previously damaged tissues. It sometimes appears on overwintered crops following frost damage. Neck rot—caused by another species of Botrytis—causes bulbs to rot in store. The fungal spores are taken into store in the necks of onions which are badly sealed. This fungus is often on the seed at sowing time so—once again—clean, reliable seed must be used. A number of other rots may occur in store, caused by bacteria taken in on the bulbs. Damaged bulbs are attacked and quickly degenerate into a soft, evil-smelling mass which acts as a centre of infection for other bulbs.

Suitable cultivars
Dry bulb
(*Autumn sown*) 'Express Yellow': F1 hybrid, Japanese; flattish bulbs. 'Imai Yellow': Japanese; pale yellow and globular. 'Reliance': flat bulbs; keeps well. 'Solidity': large flat bulbs; less likely to 'bolt'.
(*Spring sown*) 'Hygro': F1 hybrid; Dutch type which keeps well. 'Wijbo': Golden brown; ball-shaped; heavy cropper. 'Bedfordshire Champion': popular; mild flavour. 'Ailsa Craig': well known for exhibition work.
Onion sets 'Stuttgarter Giant': resists 'bolting', keeps well. 'Sturon': new earlier cultivar.
Salad onions 'White Lisbon': best known. 'Winter Hardy': hardier strain of 'White Lisbon'.
Pickling onions 'Paris Silverskin': ripens early. 'The Queen' small, very early cultivar.

take 4 weeks to ripen the bulbs fully. Unless you do this carefully they may rot during storage or 'sprout' early in the spring. Use 'bull-necked' onions immediately and do not attempt to store damaged or soft bulbs. For storage they can be made into ropes or, alternatively, can be kept in wire-bottomed, wooden trays with corner posts to allow air to circulate. Keep bulbs in a cool, dry, frost-free place and inspect them regularly. All being well they can be kept until the following Spring.

Pull salad onions as needed. Remember that large-bulbed plants are usually very hot! Pickling onions will be ready in July. Pull them up when the tops begin to shrivel and pickle them as soon as possible.

Although seed can be saved from non-F1 hybrid cultivars of onion it is often difficult to dry and ripen in Britain.

Unusual onions

A number of other onions can be grown in British gardens and, while they are not of great culinary value, they do add considerable interest.

Egyptian onion
Allium cepa aggregatum

This perennial, clustering onion can be grown for its shallot-like clusters of bulbils which, in this case, are produced at the top of 20-cm (8-in) high stems. The bulbils are small and of little value but the young plants may be used as a substitute for salad onions. The plant is vegetatively propagated either from bulbils or by division. The former are planted in August or September on well-drained soil at a spacing of 30cm (12in) square. More bulbils will then be ready in the following summer/autumn. Established clumps can be divided and replanted in March.

Below: The Welsh or 'Ever-Ready' onion is a useful hardy perennial

Potato onion
Allium cepa aggregatum

Another form of the ordinary bulb onion. It produces a collection of small, shallot-like bulbs just below the soil surface.

Welsh onion
Allium fistulosum—Ever ready onion

This onion has no connection with Wales—in fact it is the major onion of importance in Japan and China—but can easily be grown in Britain. It is a perfectly hardy, multi-stemmed perennial which can be used either as a substitute for salad onions or for flavouring purposes in winter. Plants grow as clumps and reach a height of up to 30cm (12in). Propagation is by division with the pieces planted 25cm (10in) apart in each direction.

Shallots
Allium ascalonicum

Not all botanists accept that the shallot is a distinct Allium species—many regard it as another type of bulb onion (*Allium cepa aggregatum*). It is an ancient, hardy perennial native to the near East. The small bulbs (3 to 5cm (1 to 2in) diameter) which have a milder flavour than onions, are produced in clump and are commonly used either as pickling onions or to give flavouring. Shallots are usually propagated vegetatively by saving the best bulbs from the previous season's crop. The old saying—'Plant on the shortest day to lift on the longest day'—provides a useful guide to growing shallots.

Soil and fertilizer requirements
Shallots require the same soil conditions as bulb onions. If they follow a well-manured crop no fertilizer need be given unless very large bulbs are wanted.

Planting and crop management
It is rarely possible strictly to follow the old saying but shallots should at least be planted as early as possible in February since the bulbs go soft if they are stored much longer. Plant in the same way as onion sets with the bulbs 25cm (10in) apart in rows spaced 30cm (12in) apart. Shallot bulbs, too, may be pushed or pulled out of the soil and will need replanting. Only plant firm, undamaged bulbs and make sure that weeds are kept down by constant hoeing. Be very careful, however, not to damage the developing bulbs during hoeing. As the bulbs begin to dry off in June or July it will help if you gently remove the soil from around the clumps of bulbs.

Harvesting, ripening and storage
Shallots are usually easier to ripen than bulb onions since they mature in the warmer, sunnier conditions of June or July. The leaves will turn yellow and wither when growth has finished. At this point, lift the

Bulb onions and shallots require similar growing conditions

shallots carefully and spread them out in the sun to dry for a few days. If the weather is wet then dry the bulbs under protection. When required for pickling the shallots will be used immediately but if they are to be stored for winter use then follow the same rules as for bulb onions. The best bulbs should be saved and planted for next year's crop of shallots.

Pests and diseases
These are exactly the same as described above for bulb onions.

Suitable cultivars
Both yellow and red-skinned forms are available: 'Long Keeping Yellow', 'Dutch Yellow', 'Red Dutch', 'Hative de Niort'.

Leek
Allium porrum

This totally hardy biennial plant is grown in Britain as an annual from seed. It is probably derived from *Allium ampeloprasum* —which is native around the Mediterranean —and has been cultivated in Europe since the middle ages. We grow leeks for their stem-like structure which is, in fact, a collection of concentrically wrapped, elongated leaves. The familiar white base is produced by drawing up soil around the plants to exclude light. Although the leaf bases are blanched the tops—or 'flags'— remain green and strap-like. This vegetable, which has a mild but distinct onion flavour, is particularly useful in the mid to late winter period and may still be available when the last of the stored onion bulbs have been used. By careful choice of cultivars and sowing date, however, it is possible to have leeks available from September until April. The leek is a popular vegetable for exhibition in local shows and competitions particularly in parts of north-east England.

Soil and fertilizer requirements
Since leeks are generally harvested in winter from a summer planting, once again, take care that growth is not so soft and lush that damage occurs in cold weather. The soil should be rich, deep and well-worked in the previous autumn. Maincrop leeks are planted at the end of June or beginning of July so they can follow early peas or salad crops. A base dressing of a well-balanced, general purpose fertilizer such as fish and bone meal should be applied at the rate of 50 to 70g per m² (2 to 3oz per sq yd) and worked in before planting.

The leek 'Lyon – Prizetaker' is popular for both culinary and exhibition purposes

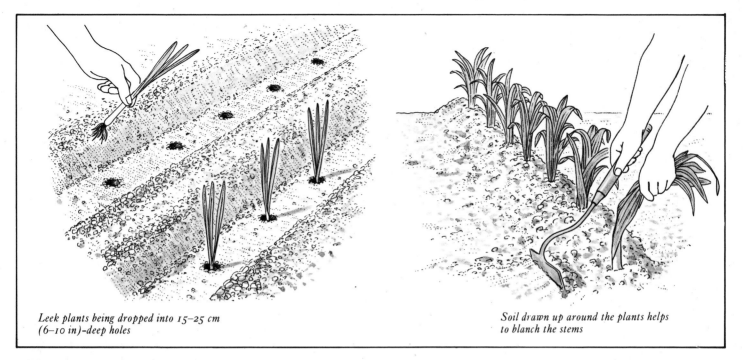

Leek plants being dropped into 15–25 cm (6–10 in)-deep holes

Soil drawn up around the plants helps to blanch the stems

A good bed of the late leek 'Royal Favourite'

Plant raising

Early, autumn-maturing leeks and those required for exhibition purposes must be raised from sowings made in gentle heat (10°C/50°F) in greenhouses during January or February. Sow the seed thinly into seed trays/pans and when the seedlings are large enough prick them out—either into other seed trays or individual containers—allowing 15 to 20 square cm (6 to 8 sq in) of space per plant. Initially the growth and development is very slow but, following a gradual hardening off before planting, the leeks will be ready to transplant in early May.

Maincrop leeks are sown in an open-ground seedbed as early in March as possible. The seedlings will appear sooner and the plants develop more quickly if you can cover the seedbed with frames/cloches during the early stages. Choose light, well-drained soils for the seedbed and sow the seed thinly in 1 to 1.5-cm (½-in) deep drills which are spaced 20 to 30cm (8 to 12in) apart. The leek plants should eventually be grown at a spacing of 1 to 2cm (about ¾in) apart in the rows. The emerging seedlings have a delicate, grass-like appearance and can easily be swamped by weeds. Make sure that the seedbed is hoed regularly but take care not to damage the young leeks. You may need to water the plants to ensure that they are big enough to plant out in late June.

Transplanting and crop management

Leeks can be grown either 'on the flat' or in trenches. Remove the young plants from the seedtray/seedbed, having given them a good watering beforehand. Grade the plants for size—keeping the large and small ones separate at planting time—and trim the roots and leaves before planting if they are too long.

It is easier to grow leeks 'on the flat' but bigger plants with larger blanched areas are produced if the crop is grown in trenches. In the former method, rows of 15 to 25-cm (6 to 10-in) deep holes are made with a 4 to 6-cm (about 2-in) diameter dibber. The holes should be 20 to 30cm (8 to 12in) apart while a 45-cm (18-in) path is left between rows. Drop one plant in each hole and then fill it with water. This will firm the plants by washing some soil over the roots and prevent birds from pulling the plants out of the holes. During the season the holes gradually fill up and further blanching can be done by drawing up soil around the plants in late summer and early autumn. Less soil movement is done with 'on the flat' growing so make sure that weeds are regularly hoed.

Prepare leek trenches well before planting. They should be 30cm (12in) deep and wide with a 45-cm (18-in) path between them. Heap the soil from the trenches neatly in the pathways. Well rotted organic manure or compost should then be dug into the bottom of each trench. At planting time set the leeks 3cm (1¼in) deep and 20cm (8in) apart in a single row down the middle of each trench. Water them in well and watch for plants which are pulled out by birds—they will need replanting. At monthly intervals through the growing season put soil from the pathways around the plants until, eventually, the trenches are completely filled in. Any additional blanching is then done by earthing up soil around the plants. The plants can be kept clean and soil-free by wrapping them round with a collar of corrugated cardboard before blanching begins.

Harvesting

Leeks are hardy enough to be left in the soil and lifted as needed. If the ground is needed for another crop after February or March, any unused plants can be lifted and heeled in elsewhere in the garden for subsequent use. The crop must be used before May, however, when leeks start to re-grow prior to producing flowers and seed. It is possible to save your own seed from leeks but, as with bulb onions, there are often problems with drying and ripening.

Pests and diseases

Like bulb onions, leeks are attacked by stem eelworm, onion fly, white rot, mildew and grey mould. Leek moth larvae may feed in the centre of the plants during the summer months and cause the leaves to become tattered. This pest is more prevalent in southern districts and the damaged leaves may quickly be attacked by a secondary infection such as botrytis.

Suitable cultivars

Early types (September–November) 'Early Market': only for early crops. 'Lyon-Prize-taker': well known and popular for exhibition and eating. 'Marble Pillar': large, heavy leeks.

Midseason types (November–January) 'Musselburgh': hardy with good length of blanched leaves. 'Walton Mammoth': popular and reliable cultivar.

Late types (January onwards) 'Winter Crop': dark green foliage; stands until late April. 'Royal Favourite': a hardy leek from Royal garden origins. 'Empire': one of the best late leeks available.

Root Vegetables

Vegetables from four plant families are dealt with in this group under the general heading of 'roots'. In strictly botanical terms this is inaccurate since turnip, swede and celeriac have swollen parts of the hypocotyl and/or stem included within the familiar storage organ.

These root vegetables are mainly biennials which we grow as annuals. They usually flower in their second year after being subjected to a winter cold period. Occasionally they flower in the first year, however, as a result of being sown too early in the spring, and subsequently being chilled. The so-called roots of some of these crops have a dual-purpose role in cooking as they are eaten either in salads or as a cooked winter vegetable. Beetroot, turnip, carrot and celeriac are in this category. Radishes are most commonly used in salads although there are firm-rooted winter radishes which can be used either raw or cooked. Parsnips, swedes, scorzonera and salsify are usually cooked, although if roots of the latter are left in the ground over winter tender young leaves, which make a palatable salad, are produced in the spring.

All the crops are easy to grow in Britain. Although you can save seed from any of them it is not usual, since cross-pollination with other brassicas is likely to occur with turnip and swede, while drying and ripening can be a problem with the remainder.

Beetroot
Beta vulgaris

Garden or red beet is a hardy biennial which is thought to have developed from the wild *Beta vulgaris maritima* which is native on sea shores in much of Europe, North Africa and Asia Minor. In Roman times it seems that only the leaves were eaten rather than the roots which we now relish. Their high sugar content gives them a distinctive flavour particularly suitable to salads, whether freshly cooked or after pickling. The roots can also be boiled and used as a hot vegetable in a variety of ways. A purée of cooked beetroot is a major ingredient of borshch, the famous Russian soup served with cream.

The two main types of beetroot are 'globe' and 'long'. The former have small, globular roots and are particularly useful for early use and processing. Long beet have larger, tapering roots which are usually lifted in the autumn and put into store for winter usage.

Nearly all garden beet cultivars are multi-germ rather than mono-germ. That means that the 'seed' which we sow is not a true seed at all but a collection of two or three single-seeded fruits. Consequently more than one seedling is likely to come up from each 'seed'. Mono-germ cultivars—which have one seed only—are slowly becoming available and make the job of thinning the crop considerably easier.

There are a number of ornamental beets, such as the Dracaena-leaved beet with reddish leaves and the Brazilian beet, which has fleshy green leaves with multicoloured midribs.

Soil and fertilizer requirements
Beetroot grow best on light, sandy soils in a sunny, open site. Avoid stony or flinty land as the roots will become mis-shapen. Any well-cultivated, fertile soil will do, however, and even heavy soils can be used provided that they have been lightened by the addition of peat or organic compost. Deep digging should be done in the autumn to leave the surface rough and cloddy over winter so that a fine tilth can develop naturally. Prepare a final tilth just before sowing when a base dressing of 50g per m² (2oz per sq yd) of a general purpose fertilizer such as meat and bone meal should be worked in.

Seed sowing and crop management
Plants from sowings made too early in the spring—in attempts to get very early roots—may 'bolt' even though specially selected, 'bolting'-resistant cultivars are now available. Make the first sowings of globe beets in early April and continue with successional sowings until mid to late July. Maincrop long beets should be sown in late May. Sow thinly in 2-cm (¾-in) deep drills which are spaced 30cm (12in) apart for globe beets and 45cm (18in) apart for long types. Two

The long roots of 'Cheltenham Green Top' beet are best for winter use

Beetroot seed is large enough to space sow to prevent overcrowding

Twist the tops off beetroot before storage

Mangold fly larvae cause irregular blisters on beetroot leaves

Store the trimmed beetroot in boxes of slightly damp sand

be squashed between the fingers. Another remedy is to give the plants a top dressing of nitrogenous fertilizer which makes them grow away from the attack.

Swift moth larvae also eat the leaves of older plants. Seedlings may be damaged by a number of damping-off fungi while leaf spot diseases cause marks or blotches on leaves. In cases of severe attack the leaves will drop off.

Beetroot react to deficiencies of a number of micronutrients by developing obvious and damaging symptoms. Boron deficiency causes heart rot with the crown of the root going brown; lack of magnesium causes yellowing between the leaf veins while

Early globe beetroot cultivars are ready from June onwards

to three weeks after the seedlings emerge thin them to 12cm (5in) or 20cm (8in) apart in the rows respectively. An alternative to thinning the crop in this way is to put 2 or 3 'seeds' at each required station at sowing time. Thinning is then done in the same way as before but weeds, which develop within the plant rows and compete with the early growth of the beet seedlings, are more easily hoed out. Continue to hoe throughout the season, being careful not to damage the roots since they 'bleed' and cannot be stored. Beetroot crops are not usually watered but irrigation can be given in very dry years to prevent the roots becoming woody.

Harvesting and storage
Pull globe beet as required throughout the summer when the roots become large enough—probably from June onwards. Long beet may either be left in the ground until required—in which case they should be strawed over to give protection against the severest frosts—or the roots can be lifted, cleaned and stored in a shed or outdoor clamp. Lift the roots carefully in

November before they go woody. If possible use a flat-tined fork, which is less likely to cause damage, and gently ease the roots out using the leaves as a handle. Remove the leaves either by twisting or by cutting neatly with a knife. Don't cut too close to the crown or 'bleeding' will occur. Damaged or diseased beetroot must not be stored as they will rot and affect adjacent roots. If you have large quantities of beetroot store them in an outdoor clamp; smaller, domestic quantities, are best stored in boxes with sand or peat around the roots. Keep the boxes in an airy, frost-free place and remember to inspect the roots at regular intervals.

Pests and diseases
Aphids (greenfly) attack beetroot and must be controlled quickly since they can spread virus diseases. Mangold fly larvae tunnel into the leaves forming irregular, blister-like tunnels and causing less efficient growth. The female flies lay eggs on the underside of the leaves and once they are inside the tissues, the larvae are difficult to control. They are easy to see in the leaves and can

manganese shortage causes marked yellow patches to develop on the leaves. These deficiencies can occur even when there is sufficient micronutrient present in the ground but, because of the acidity or alkalinity of the soil, the plant cannot make use of them. In these circumstances the deficiency is most likely to be cured by watering a dilute solution of salt containing the missing micronutrient on to the plants. The roots of beetroot may be attacked by violet root rot. The leaves become stunted and yellow while the roots are covered with a web of purple fungus.

Suitable cultivars
* indicates suitability for freezing.
Globe 'Boltardy': early cultivar selected for 'bolting' resistance. 'Detroit-Little Ball'*: very useful for successional summer sowings. 'Mono King Explorer': mono-germ type with intense red roots.
Long 'Cheltenham Green Top': longest keeping cultivar of excellent quality. 'Dobbie's Purple'; best for exhibition work.

Radishes

Raphinus sativus

Radishes were already being grown in Egypt over 2000 years ago and many forms are still widely cultivated. This is, again, a hardy biennial which we cultivate as an annual for the white-fleshed, edible roots. Those with red or red-and-white roots are most popular but white-skinned summer radishes and pink or black-skinned winter types are also available. The most popular use for radishes is in spring and summer salads when small-rooted cultivars are grown rapidly—to give a crisp, fresh texture with a peppery flavour —and eaten raw. Salad radishes can be pro- duced virtually throughout the year—from outdoor sowings during the spring and early summer and from protected crops during the autumn, winter and early spring. When grown outside they grow rapidly enough to be a useful catch crop using land which has been recently vacated—or not yet used— or fitting well between rows of other crops such as peas or beans. Winter radishes, which are not commonly grown in Britain, have large solid roots which can be lifted and stored without becoming hollow.

Soil and fertilizer requirements

Rapid growth is essential to produce crisp tender roots. Those which are grown slowly are likely to be woody, and hot. Conse- quently you should grow radishes on rich

The popular 'Scarlet Globe' radish is quick growing and has pure white flesh

soils which have sufficient organic matter to retain the necessary moisture, but do not dig in fresh manure immediately prior to this crop. Always sow into a deep, fine seedbed.

Seed sowing and crop management

Make the first sowings under frames or cloches in early January using short-topped, forcing cultivars. Begin outdoor sowings as soon as the ground is workable in February

Early radishes from a cold frame.

or March using warm, protected sites if possible. Seed can be broadcast evenly at the rate of 8g per m² (¼oz per sq yd) and lightly raked into the top 1cm (½in). Alternatively sow the seed in 1-cm (½-in) deep drills spaced 15cm (6in) apart with approximately 3cm (1in) between individual seeds. Water the seedbeds generously after sowing and continue to give further water- ings as necessary during growth. Protected crops must be given plenty of air on bright days so that excessive leaf growth is avoided. It will take up to 8 weeks for January sow- ings to mature but summer crops will be ready for pulling 3 to 4 weeks after sowing. Large rooted winter radish should be sown thinly in drills 20cm (8in) apart during July and August. Once they are big enough thin the plants to 20cm (8in) apart in the rows. This crop must be grown very rapidly to produce firm, crisp roots.

Harvesting

Salad radishes must be pulled as soon as they are mature. Young roots have the best flavour. Winter radishes can be lifted in the autumn and stored in boxes—as for beet- root—or left in the ground, strawed over if necessary, and lifted as needed.

Pests and diseases

Radishes are cruciferous plants and suffer from similar pests and diseases to brassica crops. Flea beetle and club root may be troublesome, while damping-off damage is particularly likely in thickly sown crops. Scab disease is due to another fungus which causes sunken areas on the roots.

Suitable cultivars

Early, forcing types 'Red Forcing': the earliest round radish. 'Saxerre': globular roots with little top. Wood's Early Frame. Long radish, bright rose.
Maincrop types 'French Breakfast': red and white. 'Cherry Belle': rapid growing; bright scarlet roots. 'Scarlet Globe': globular roots; scarlet colour. 'Icicle': 7-cm (3-in) long white roots produced very quickly.
Winter radishes 'Black Spanish': black skin; white flesh; round or long available. 'China Rose': rose-pink; white flesh; oval shape.

Carrot

Daucus carota sativus

This hardy biennial, which we treat as an annual, is grown for its orange/red tap roots. While they are generally eaten cooked, the Vitamin A and high sugar content of carrots makes them specially valuable for use raw in salads. Our cultivated carrots have been derived from the thin and pale-rooted wild plant which is native to much of Europe— including Britain—and the Mediterranean. Detailed plant breeding and selection have produced the familiar carrot root colour and size along with the range of root shapes which is sometimes used as a basis for classifying cultivars. Thus there are short- horns; stump-rooted; intermediate and

maincrop types which mature in that order. Choice of the correct cultivar coupled with careful management—including the use of protection such as frames or cloches—will enable you to have carrots available throughout the year. Young tender carrots of long, cylindrical-rooted cultivars should be used for freezing.

Soil and fertilizer requirements

Carrots do best in light, open textured and fertile soils provided that there is sufficient moisture to allow good sized roots to develop. The soil type is particularly important for early crops which must grow rapidly; maincrops can be grown on heavier soils if absolutely necessary. If heavy soils are used, however, you should use short-rooted cultivars and never leave them in the ground for winter storage. Carrot soils should be deeply dug in the autumn and left over winter for a tilth to develop. Don't dig in organic manure since this may cause 'fanging' or forking of the roots. If you feel, for some other reason, that manure must be incorporated then dig it in very deeply, but more reliable results will be obtained if the previous crop received the organic manure in the way recommended for planned crop rotations. Carrots do respond, however, to generous applications of inorganic base fertilizer. It is advisable to use a well-balanced, general fertilizer, raking in 75 to 100g per m² (3 to 4oz per sq yd) during the final preparations of the seedbed which, ideally, for this crop, should be fairly fine.

Maincrop carrots such as 'St Valery' prefer deep, stone-free soils

Seed sowing and crop management

If you have a slightly heated greenhouse it is possible to make a sowing in November using a stump-rooted cultivar. It is more likely that you will make the first sowings under cold frames or cloches in January. Soil type is very important and a fine tilth must be prepared before the seed is broadcast or drilled. If the seed is broadcast allow each one 3 to 4 square cm (1½ sq in) of space, while drilled crops should be sown thinly in 0.5-cm (¼-in) deep drills which are 15 to 20cm (6 to 8in) apart. Use a stump-rooted, forcing cultivar and very lightly rake the seed in after sowing. This early crop must never receive a check so apply water

Stump-rooted carrots like 'Amsterdam forcing' are best for early crops

whenever necessary. Give full ventilation to growing crops on warm, sunny days in order to keep leaf growth to a minimum. Remove the frames/cloches in mid-April. The roots will be ready for pulling between then and early May—about 14 weeks after sowing.

The first outdoor sowings can be made in early March or as soon afterwards as the ground is workable. It is possible to warm up the soil by covering it with cloches/polythene tunnels, before sowing. Seedlings emergence will also be encouraged if the area is re-covered until the carrots appear. Sow thinly in 1-cm (½-in) deep drills which are 20 to 30cm (8 to 12in) apart. As soon as the seedlings are large enough to handle, thin them to 5cm (2in) apart. A further thinning may be necessary to produce really large roots. These early sowings should also be with stump-rooted cultivars which, if sown successionally at fortnightly intervals from early March until late April, will produce carrots continuously through the summer.

For maincrop carrots use intermediate or long-rooted cultivars and sow successionally from April until mid-July. One of the worst pest problems is carrot fly which first attacks during May or early June. Carrot fly is difficult to control but one remedy is to avoid attack by delaying sowings until late May or early June. In this way the seedlings do not emerge until the flies have finished laying their eggs. Maincrop sowings are also made in 1-cm (½-in) deep drills which, this time,

The maincrop 'Chantenay red cored' carrot yields well even in shallow soils

are spaced 30 to 40cm (12 to 16in) apart. Gradually thin the carrots out until finally they are 15cm (6in) apart. These thinnings will, of course, be useful carrots for summer purposes. Severe carrot fly attack is most likely to follow crop thinning. It seems that handling and removing plants releases chemicals which attract the female flies. Consequently it is better to do the thinning late in the evening and to scatter soil over the holes from which carrots have already been removed.

Late sowings can be made on well-drained soils in July or August to produce fresh roots for harvesting from October onwards. Use stump-rooted carrots and be prepared to cover the August sowings with cloches during frosts to avoid damage.

Carrots need hoeing to keep down weeds but be careful not to damage the developing roots. Outdoor crops are not usually watered after they have emerged but they will benefit from it in very dry years. There is a danger in watering after a prolonged dry spell late in the season—regrowth of the roots may occur, leading to splitting and poor storage.

Harvesting and storage
Pull carrots for summer use as soon as the roots reach the required size. Maincrops can either be left in the ground and dug up as needed—in which case they will need

protecting with straw during severe weather —or they can be carefully lifted in October and stored indoors in boxes or outdoors in a clamp. After lifting, diseased, damaged and split roots are put to one side for immediate use since they are unsuitable for storage. Trim the remainder so that 1cm ($\frac{1}{2}$in) of leaf stalk remains above the crown. Clean off excess soil—but do not wash the roots— and store. For box storage put the roots in sand or peat and stand the boxes in an airy, frost-free place. The carrots should keep until March or April.

Pests and diseases
Aphids mainly attack carrot leaves causing weakening of the growth. They also transmit virus diseases which further reduce growth.

Carrot fly can cause serious problems. The females lay their eggs around the young carrot seedlings and they soon hatch into larvae which are chemically attracted to the root zone. The first indication of an attack is a reddening of the young leaves. The larvae feed on the roots and will kill young seedlings. Later, or less severe, attacks produce roots with tunnels just under the surface. These quickly become infected with secondary rotting diseases and so cannot be stored.

Slugs and cutworms cause severe damage by eating mature roots, especially in the autumn. Stunting and yellowing of the leaves may be caused by the aphid-transmitted carrot motley dwarf virus. Examination of the roots reveals very poor growth

indeed. Sclerotinia disease also attacks roots covering them with a white fungal growth within which may be found the black resting spore bodies of this dangerous, soil-borne fungus. Root splitting is usually due to fluctuations in water availability. Violet root rot is a commonly occurring disease, producing purple fungal threads on the roots, while bacterial soft rot will spread in stored roots that have either been damaged or are in a wet condition.

Suitable cultivars
Short-horn/stump-rooted 'Amsterdam forcing': cylindrical; long stump roots; ideal for forcing. 'Nantes': early maturing; outdoors or forced. 'Paris forcing': ball-shaped roots useful on shallow soils.
Intermediate 'Chantenay red cored': stump-rooted maincrop, little core. 'Pride of Denmark': tapering roots with smooth skin. 'Autumn King': long, large, cylindrical roots.
Maincrop 'St. Valery': heavy yielding with tapering roots. 'Scarlet Perfection': long roots which keep well.

Parsnip
Pastinaca sativa

Another hardy biennial cultivated as an annual for the long, tapering, yellowish-white roots. Parsnips have been grown at least since Roman times and the wild form is fairly common in Britain. The sweet-tasting flesh of the roots contains significant quantities of sugar and starch which help to make it an important cooked vegetable in winter. This crop must have a long growing season if good sized roots are to be produced and, on many occasions, parsnips occupy the ground for a full twelve month period. The roots are ready during autumn and winter but tradition has it that the flavour is not fully developed until they have been frosted.

Soil and fertilizer requirements
Parsnips have similar needs to carrots. Deep, rich, open-textured soils which are stone-free produce the best crops of well shaped roots. You will need to sow early to get good sized roots and sunny situations give the best results. Parsnip roots, too, will be 'fanged' if there is fresh organic manure in the root zone. A base dressing of 75 to 100g per m² (3 to 4oz per sq yd) of a well balanced fertilizer should be spread and worked in before sowing.

Seed sowing and crop management
Sow as early as possible to get the maximum length of growing season. Late February or early March is ideal or as soon afterwards as possible.

Germination can be erratic so it is best to be fairly liberal with the seed and thin the seedlings later if necessary. The drills should be 2cm (1in) deep and 45cm (18in) apart. Thin the plants to 15 to 20cm (6 to 8in) apart in the rows. An alternative method is to sow 4 or 5 seeds at each station where a plant is finally required. After emergence the strongest seedling is retained and the remainder pulled out. Keep the weeds down by regular hoeing.

Harvesting

The leaves will go yellow and begin to die down from early November onwards. The roots can then be lifted as required. Since parsnips will withstand quite severe weather it is best to leave them in the ground until you want them. Lifted and stored roots quickly soften and deteriorate. Regrowth prior to flowering will start again in March and parsnips must be used before then.

Pests and diseases

Carrot fly and aphids attack parsnips in the the same way as carrots. Larvae of the celery fly tunnel in the leaves producing blister-like chambers. Severe infestations cause reduced growth and plants must be well cultivated to withstand and grow away from the attacks. Moisture fluctuations will lead to root splitting but the most important disease is parsnip canker. This fungus causes a black/brown rot to develop from the crown of the root. Secondary infection by other fungi and bacteria soon follows, rendering the roots totally useless. Canker-resistant cultivars are now available.

Suitable cultivars

'Avonresister': small roots; grow at 10cm (4in) spacings; resistant to canker. 'Improved Hollow Crown': long, tapering roots. 'Offenham': intermediate sized roots; useful on shallow soils. 'Leda': new cultivar; tapering roots.

Celeriac

Apium graveolens var. *rapaceum*—Turnip rooted celery.

This close relative of celery (*Apium graveolens* var. *dulce*) is grown for the swollen base of the stem only while the leaf stalks are not important. Thus, contrary to the popular name, celeriac is not a true root crop. It has a similar flavour to celery and deserves to be more widely grown since the 'root' has many possible uses. Used raw, it provides a welcome and unusual base for salads, whether used alone or chopped with other vegetables. It also makes a delicious purée, and can be eaten as a separate vegetable after boiling and creaming. Celeriac is also a very useful ingredient in soups and stews for it adds bulk as well as flavour. This is a crop which is widely grown in Germany, France and Holland where ordinary celery is rarely seen.

Soil and fertilizer requirements

Celeriac thrives on deep, fertile and well-drained soils which have had liberal dressings of organic manure dug in during the winter cultivations. Soils which are able to retain moisture will produce the best 'roots' particularly if a generous amount of nitrogenous fertilizer is incorporated in the base dressing. 75 to 100g per m² (3 to 4oz per sq yd) of a general fertilizer with a high nitrogen component is ideal.

Plant raising

This crop requires a long growing season and the best results are obtained by raising plants in heated greenhouses and transplanting them. Sow the seed thinly on the surface of compost in seedtray/seedpans in the middle of March. Do not cover the seed with compost. Keep the temperature at 16°C/61°F until hardening off and never allow the seed or seedlings to dry out. Four to five weeks after sowing, the seedlings will be large enough to prick out either into other seedtrays or individual containers when you should allow between 3cm × 3cm (1¼in) and 5cm × 5cm (2in) of space per plant. After another 4 to 5 weeks the plants will be ready to plant outside following a period of hardening off.

Transplanting and crop management

Plant in late May or early June with the plants spaced 30 to 40cm (12 to 16in) apart in each direction. Thoroughly water them in and give generous amounts of water during the season. If growth slows down it may be helpful to give a top dressing of 25 to 50g per m² (1 to 2 oz per sq yd) of nitro-chalk which should be watered in. Hoe carefully between the plants to control weed growth.

Harvesting

Celeriac may be left in the ground to be lifted when they are needed in which case you may find it necessary to cover them with protective straw in severe weather. Otherwise the 'roots' are lifted and stored in peat or sand in a frost-free place. If conditions permit, the former method is preferable. The crop will be ready from September onwards —although for salad purposes even earlier liftings may be made—but good sized 'roots' have not usually developed until November.

Pests and diseases

Celeriac suffers from the same pests and diseases as celery (q.v.) but some cultivars develop brown markings inside the 'roots' during bad growing seasons.

Suitable cultivars

Celeriac is not a good subject for freezing. 'Globus' good, reliable cultivar. 'Alabaster' new with smooth-skinned roots.

Above: The compact roots of 'Avonresister' are resistant to canker

Below: Celeriac has many culinary uses and deserves to be more widely grown

Swede

Brassica napus

Swedes are biennials grown as annuals for their swollen 'roots' which are used as winter vegetables either boiled and mashed or in stews. The swollen part is, in botanical terms, slightly different from the turnip, being made up of the hypocotyl and the base of the stem (hence the swollen neck with leaf scars). The 'roots' may have purple, white or yellow skin. The flesh is usually yellow, sometimes white. Fodder swedes, normally grown as cattle food are a useful winter vegetable having a more distinct flavour.

Far right: Salsify is grown for the tapering, fleshy, white roots

Right: Swedes are winter hardy and may be lifted as needed

Soil and fertilizer requirements
All fertile soils are suitable provided they are not acid. Don't dig in fresh manure before the swede crop as forked roots may form. It is better if the ground has been well manured for the previous crop. 25 to 50g per m² (1 to 2 oz per sq yd) of a well-balanced base fertilizer should be worked into the seedbed before sowing.

Seed sowing and crop management
Sow the seed in May or June depending on your location. Drills should be 1 to 2cm (½ to ¾in) deep and 45cm (18in) apart. Thin the seedlings to 30cm (12in) apart in the rows. Treat the crop as for turnips.

Harvesting
Swedes are quite hardy enough to be left in the ground and lifted, as required, during the autumn and winter. They store in clamps better than turnips; a good idea if frozen ground conditions are likely.

Pests and diseases
The same pests and diseases that attack turnips are liable to be a problem on swedes. Among these are flea beetle damage, downy mildew, boron deficiency and violet root rot. These will be described in the turnip section.

Suitable cultivars
'Chignecto': club root resistant; purple-topped 'roots'. 'Purple Top': medium size, good quality, matures early. 'Bronze Top': excellent keeper with hard, yellow flesh.

Salsify

Tragopogon porrifolius—Vegetable Oyster

A hardy biennial which is grown as an annual for the fleshy white roots which are ready from October onwards. It is not much grown in Britain but it can be a useful winter vegetable with roots which are said to taste like oysters. If roots are left in the ground until the spring they will send up new shoots (chards) which are quite tasty when cooked like asparagus.

Soil and fertilizer requirements
Salsify grows best on ideal 'root crop' soils which are deeply cultivated and moisture retentive.

Seed sowing and crop management
When the soil has dried out in April sow the seed thinly into 2-cm (¾-in) deep drills 40cm (16in) apart. Thin the seedlings out to 20cm (8in) apart when they are large enough to handle. Weeds must be kept down by hoeing but take care not to damage the roots as the delicate flavour is impaired if the roots 'bleed'. Plants may 'bolt' in dry seasons so be prepared to water them.

Harvesting
Roots will be ready from October onwards. Ideally they should be 5cm (2in) wide at the crown and 25cm (10in) long. They can be left *in situ* and lifted as required or they can all be lifted in the autumn and stored in boxes in the same way as carrots.

Pests and diseases
Few pests and diseases attack salsify but white blister is caused by a fungus and develops as pustules on the leaves.

Suitable cultivar
'Mammoth' may be boiled, baked or used in soups.

'Laurentian' is a fine quality swede with yellow flesh and a purple top

Scorzonera

Scorzonera hispanica—Black salsify

Like salsify this vegetable is rarely grown in Britain. It is a hardy perennial, treated as an annual for the black-skinned, white-fleshed edible roots. It has the same culinary uses as salsify, but was formerly grown also for medicinal purposes. The flesh contains inulin which may contribute towards its delicate flavour.

Soil and fertilizer requirements
Fertile, well-drained soils are necessary and cultivations should be deep enough to allow un-checked root growth. Organic manure should not be dug in just before this crop otherwise 'fanged' and fibrous roots may form.

Seed sowing and crop management
Sow the seed in April in 2-cm (¾-in) deep drills 40cm (16in) apart. The seedlings should be thinned to 30cm (12in) apart as soon as they are large enough to handle. Hoe the crop regularly to control weeds but do not allow the roots to dry out since 'bolting' of scorzonera is thought to be encouraged if the roots are hot and dry. Mulching around the plants with straw or grass cuttings will help to reduce this particular problem.

Harvesting
Scorzonera roots are ready for use from October onwards. Leave in place or lift and store in boxes of sand in a frost-free place. Only disease-free specimens should be used for storage.

Pests and diseases
Like salsify, scorzonera is relatively trouble-free apart from the possibility of white blister appearing.

Suitable cultivars
'Russian Giant' black skinned roots with delicate flavour.

Turnip

Brassica rapa

This biennial 'root' vegetable—it is mainly swollen hypocotyl (the zone between the true root and the seed leaves or cotyledons)—has been known since prehistoric times. It is grown primarily for the faintly mustard-flavoured 'root' which normally has white flesh.

The usual time of use is in the winter but cultivars are available which produce young, tender roots during the summer. The very earliest summer crops are raised under frames or cloches. Roots which are left in the ground over the winter will re-grow in the spring and the new young tops can be eaten as 'spring greens'.

Soil and fertilizer requirements

Fertile, well-drained and yet moisture retentive soils are ideal for turnips. Summer crops particularly must grow rapidly to produce tender roots and they can, therefore, be grown as catch crops. Don't grow turnips on soil which has been freshly manured as the roots will be mis-shapen. Fertilizers for turnips should be low in nitrogen and rich in phosphates. Too much nitrogen for summer crops usually results in excessive leaf growth at the expense of the 'roots' while winter crops will also be less hardy if they are soft.

Seed sowing and crop management

Make the earliest sowings under protection in February, using special short-top forcing cultivars. Mark out the seedbed into a network of 12-cm (5-in) squares. At the points where the lines cross sow 3 or 4 seeds in 1 to 2-cm (about ¾-in) deep holes. Cover the seeds over and thoroughly soak the seedbed before covering with the frames or cloches. When the seedlings emerge, thin to one at each station. Water generously as required and give full ventilation on warm, sunny days. If the turnips are grown rapidly the leaves will quickly cover the ground and weeds will not be a problem.

Outdoor summer crops can be sown from March onwards in 2-cm (¾-in) deep drills which are 30cm (12in) apart. Thin the seedlings to 15cm (6in) apart as soon as possible.

Winter turnips are grown from sowings made from mid-July until mid-August. These larger rooted types should be grown at 30cm (12in) or even 40cm (16in) square.

Harvesting

Pull summer turnips once they reach 5 to 8cm (2 to 3in) in diameter which should be in May from March sowings. Any delay in pulling mature roots will cause the loss of the crisp texture and flavour. Winter turnips are lifted as needed.

Pests and diseases

Turnips and swedes not only suffer from

'Early Snowball' turnip is particularly useful for early, protected sowings

some of the pests and diseases which attack other brassicas, but also from some of the problems of root crops. Consequently flea beetle damage may occur on the young seedlings while club root, damping-off and downy mildew can also cause trouble. Discoloured areas within the roots are often due to boron deficiency while root splitting is caused by fluctuating water supplies. Violet root rot fungus appears as purple threads in and on the roots whereas soft bacterial rots cause damaged or badly stored roots to break down into a watery, evil-smelling mass.

Suitable cultivars

There is considerable variation in the 'root' form of cultivated turnips. Some are round, others flattened; many are white-skinned but others are yellow and either may have a green or purple shoulder.

Summer crops 'Tokyo Cross': F1—quick growing; globe shaped; pure white. 'Early Snowball': sweet flavoured globular roots. 'Jersey Navet': white cylindrical roots; forcing type.

Winter crops 'Golden Ball': very hardy with yellow skin and flesh. 'Green-top white': half green, half white roots with white flesh. 'Manchester Market': good, winter-hardy.

Salad Plants

Nearly all the leafy salad vegetables which we grow are members of the Daisy family or *Compositae*. Their cabbage-like appearance is misleading and the true identity is only confirmed when they run up to flower. Lettuce, endive and chicory are the best known, and most used, salading plants but corn salad—or lamb's lettuce—is also well-worth growing. They are all treated as either hardy or half-hardy annuals which are mainly grown for their green leaves. Endive and chicory are usually blanched, however, to give white or pale yellow leaves that are less bitter. Chicory may also be forced during the winter months to produce blanched hearts which are known as 'chicons'. Lettuce is the main source of salad leaves during the summer but, with the aid of a cold greenhouse, frame or cloches it is possible to extend the season to include the spring and autumn. Endive, chicory and—to a lesser extent—corn salad are of greatest value during the autumn, winter and early spring. All the salad plants except lettuce are more popular on the Continent than in Britain but they deserve to be grown more extensively for winter use.

Lettuce

Lactuca sativa

Although the exact origins of the lettuce are unknown it was certainly known to the Greeks and Romans, and has been grown in Britain since at least the middle of the sixteenth century. It is now the most important leafy salad vegetable. Lettuces are made up of over 95 per cent water, but contribute other essential components of our diet such as Vitamin A.

The lettuce is a hardy or half-hardy annual. Different cultivars can be grown outside during the summer and under protection during the winter.

The majority of lettuce cultivars produce a heart although a few leaf-lettuce/chicken-lettuce cultivars are available. Hearted lettuces are divided into two main groups—cabbage types and cos types. Many of the cabbage types have smooth, flattened leaves of a 'buttery' texture and are referred to as butterhead types. Others have large, curled, crisp leaves which wilt more rapidly after

The sweet, crisp leaves of 'Lobjoits Green Cos' make an ideal base for salads

cutting and are called crisphead types. Cos lettuce have longer, crisper leaves which have a sweeter flavour but the plants, which withstand drought more readily, take longer to reach maturity. The less popular leaf lettuce does not have a compact head but is just a collection of leaves which can be gradually removed. This 'cut-and-come-again' approach is useful and allows space to be used for other crops.

Soil requirements

Lettuce grows best on light, rich soils that are able to retain moisture but will do well on any fertile, well-drained soil. Continuity of supply after outdoor crops have finished can be achieved by growing plants under protection during the autumn, winter and early spring. Soils for the protected crops should, again, be fertile, well-drained and moisture retentive. Watering lettuce during periods of dull, cold winter weather can bring a host of associated problems so it is best to have a soil which contains adequate amounts of well-rotted organic manure or compost which will retain moisture.

Suitable fertilizers

For summer crops, apply a base dressing of a general-purpose fertilizer such as fish and bone meal before sowing and/or transplanting at the rate of 50g per m² (2 oz per square yard). Be wary of applying fertilizers with too much nitrogen before sowing since this might retard seed germination and the emergence of seedlings. For overwintered crops it is best to apply the fertilizer, in the form of a top dressing, just as growth re-commences in the spring since too much fertilizer applied while the plants are estab-

Cabbage lettuce such as 'Diana' are very popular for summer crops

lishing themselves may lead to soft, lush growth which is easily damaged by severe winter weather.

Seed sowing and plant raising

Continuous supplies of lettuce from June onwards can be assured by sowing in the open at fortnightly intervals from early April until early August. Seeds should be sown thinly in 1.5-cm (¾-in) deep drills which are 30cm (12in) apart. Thin out the seedlings as soon as they can be handled to 30cm (12in) apart in the rows. These distances apply to cabbage lettuce and the larger cos cultivars. Dwarf cos types can be grown in rows which are 25cm (10in) apart with 15cm (6in) between the plants. Outdoor summer lettuce can be harvested about 8 to 12 weeks after sowing, but the exact time depends on the sowing date. The time that the crop occupies the ground can be reduced by 3 to 4 weeks if you raise plants in seedpans—either in a greenhouse, a frame or even on a light, airy windowsill—and then transplant the seedlings once they have three true leaves. Seed of many lettuce cultivars has a very low germination percentage at temperatures above 21°C/70°F so be careful to keep the seedbed or seedpan cool until the seedlings have emerged. Cover them with a sheet of white polystyrene about 4cm (1½in) thick to insulate against increasing temperature.

Lettuce may also be overwintered outside as young plants which will then mature in May. The easiest way of starting the crop is from seed which should be sown in September, at the spacings indicated for summer crops, and subsequently thinned. Alternatively you could sow the seed in a seedbed/seedpan and plant out during November in sheltered southern and western districts or during February/March in more exposed areas. Special winter hardy cultivars must be used for this purpose.

Protected crops can be grown in greenhouses, frames or cloches (either glass or polythene). In all cases it is best to raise seedlings and transplant. The two main periods for planting are autumn and early spring. Plantings made in mid-September into unheated protection from a mid-August sowing should produce mature lettuce in December while mid-October plantings will be ready in March. Spring plantings—made in mid-February from a mid-January sowing—grow more quickly in the lengthening days and will be ready for cutting in April or May. Heated forms of protection will allow crops to be grown more quickly but it is only necessary to maintain minimum temperatures of 10°C/50°F. Plants for all protected crops can be raised by sowing thinly in seedpans/seedtrays which are kept in a heated greenhouse or the kitchen until the young seedlings are large enough to handle.

Transplanting and crop management

Protected crops are transplanted with the plants spaced 20 to 25cm (8 to 10in) apart in each direction. Great care must be taken

Lettuce plants run to seed or 'bolt' in high temperatures and long days.

Above: The non-hearting 'Salad Bowl' produces leaves throughout the summer

when you are handling the plants during transplanting since bruising of the stem or damage to the root system will allow secondary infections such as grey mould (Botrytis) to enter. Always hold the young seedlings lightly by the leaves. Slugs can be a particular problem on protected lettuce so sprinkle pellets around the plants immediately after planting. Ventilation must be given freely on bright, sunny days so that soft growth can be avoided, but on no account should air be given during damp, foggy weather. Growth of autumn-planted, spring-maturing, protected lettuce should be slow in the pre-Christmas period. Ideally only a rosette of leaves will have developed by the turn of the year. Plants will then begin to grow rapidly—as will spring-planted crops—provided no checks or competition are encountered. Carefully hoe out weeds from around plants, using an onion hoe. Once the outer leaves cover the ground other weed development will be smothered.

Weed control is also of great importance on outdoor crops. Not only do they compete with the lettuce for light, water, plant nutrients and the like but they also act as overwintering hosts for aphids (greenfly).

In order to obtain crisp, well-hearted lettuce the growth—once it begins—must be quick and unchecked. It is at this stage of development that plants need the most water and the importance of moisture-retentive soils and careful irrigation when necessary cannot be over-emphasized.

Lettuce will quickly run to seed or 'bolt' in warm weather and any delay in harvesting the mature heads will increase this likelihood.

Below: Crisphead lettuce like 'Pennlake' are at their best during summer and autumn

Harvesting

Since lettuce contain such a high percentage of water they wilt rapidly after cutting. Freshness can be maintained for the maximum period by harvesting heads early in the morning before the plants begin to heat up. If you must pick the plants when warm, freshness will be improved by immediately immersing the lettuce in ice-cold water for 15 minutes. Then shake off all the water and put the lettuce into a refrigerator until needed.

Pests and diseases

Aphids are the most common pest of lettuce. Usually the leaves are infested, causing distortion. Root aphids may also occur.

Slugs can be a persistent nuisance.

Seedlings are liable to be attacked by damping off fungi of which pythium and rhizoctonia are the most common. Downy mildew produces yellow blotches on the upper surface of leaves with patches of white fungal growth below. Cold, wet weather favours this disease. Grey mould (botrytis) is a secondary infection. Previously damaged plants develop areas of

Butterhead lettuce 'Fortune' makes large firm hearts

grey, velvety fungal growth. Wilting and complete plant collapse soon follow, accompanied by the production of innumerable spores which may infect other damaged plants. The best method of control is to prevent the primary damage being caused. Occasional plants may develop symptoms of yellowing, dwarfing or distortion which can be caused by aphid-transmitted virus diseases.

Suitable cultivars
Summer types

Cabbage—Butterheads 'Cobham Green', 'Suzan', 'Fortune'. *Crispheads* 'Webb's Wonderful', 'Great Lakes', 'Windermere', 'Avoncrisp'. *Cos* 'Lobjoits Green Cos', 'Little Gem' (smaller cultivar), 'Winter Density'. *Leaf Lettuce* 'Salad Bowl'.
Overwintered outdoor types (all hardy butterhead cultivars) 'Arctic King', 'Imperial Winter', 'Valdor'.
Protected types 'Delta', 'Knap', 'Kwiek'.

60

Endive

Cichorium endiva

This half-hardy annual, which is a native of southern Asia, has been cultivated in England for salad purposes since the early sixteenth century. The pale green, crisp leaves are usually deeply dissected and curled. Few people enjoy their very bitter taste, however, and they are normally blanched before use. Endive is particularly useful as an alternative to lettuce.

Soil and fertilizer requirements

As with most salad crops light, well-drained, fertile soils are best for endive. The early crops may require a base dressing of 25 to 50g per m² (1 to 2 oz per square yard) of a general, balanced fertilizer before sowing. Later sowings, which produce plants for blanching in the autumn and winter, do well after early potatoes or peas when no fertilizer is usually required.

Seed sowing and crop management

Endive does best when direct sown into its final position. Transplanting the seedlings can easily damage the tap root and cause a considerable check to growth. The first sowings can be made in April and May to provide plants which are ready for blanching in August and September. Plants from late June sowings will be ready for blanching in late September while those from early August sowings will need protection in October when frost threatens. It is from this latter sowing that winter endive is produced and two possible methods of giving protection are available. The seed can be sown directly into a site where cloches or frames can be put over when necessary. Alternatively the mature plants are dug up and transplanted into a frame or cold greenhouse when severe weather is imminent.

Sow the seed in 1-cm (½-in) deep drills spaced 40cm (15in) apart. When the seedlings are 5 to 7cm (2 to 3in) high thin them out to 30cm (12in) apart in the rows. Growth must be rapid and unchecked if crisp leaves are to be produced for subsequent blanching. Hoe out any weeds and water whenever necessary during dry periods.

Blanching

Endive plants are usually ready for blanching about 3 months after sowing and it may be done in one of two ways. The leaves can be gathered together when dry (damp plants may rot during blanching) and tied round with raffia or string. This keeps the light away from all but the outer leaves. Alternatively the plants can be completely covered with containers. Blanching takes 7 to 10 days in early autumn but up to 3 weeks in the winter. Don't treat too many plants at a time because endive will not keep very long after blanching.

Pests and diseases

Watch out for aphids (green fly) during the summer months.

Suitable cultivars

Curled-leaved (Staghorns) or plain-leaved (Batavians) types are available. The former are most popular since they blanch more rapidly and are ideal for general summer use. The Batavians are used more for winter blanching and have a very fine flavour.
Curled-leaved 'Moss curled': good for early sowings. 'Exquisite curled': general purpose type.
Batavian 'Broad-leafed Batavian': excellent for mid-winter salads.

Below: Endive 'Green Curled' is a good flavoured and productive cultivar

*Left: The blanched chicons of chicory
may be chopped in salads or braised in butter*

before covering them up for forcing. Unless chicory is forced in absolute darkness the hearts or 'chicons' will be yellow and bitter. The containers must, therefore, be covered to exclude all light. As the hearts grow they should be inspected regularly to make sure that slugs and swift moth caterpillars are not present. Water the plants periodically to make sure that growth is clean and crisp.

Harvesting

The hearts are ready for cutting when they are 12 to 15cm (4 to 6in) long. This will take about 8 weeks at 10°C/50°F or half that time at 16°C/60°F. After the hearts have been harvested the roots should be discarded and the process started again with some more from the store.

Pests and diseases

Apart from slugs and caterpillars chicory is a remarkably trouble-free crop.

Suitable cultivars

'Witloof' or 'Large Brussels': the most popular 'White leaf' chicory; used for forcing to give 'chicons'.
'Sugar Loaf' (Pain de Sucre): similar to cos lettuce; stands well.

Corn salad

Valerianella eriocarpa

A hardy annual plant whose tender lettuce-like leaves make a tasty winter salad.

Soil and fertilizer requirements

Corn salad grows overwinter and needs a well-drained soil and a sunny, sheltered site. Ideally it should follow a well-manured summer vegetable in which case no fertilizer will be needed. It can also be grown during the summer months on deep, rich soils.

Sowing and crop management

For winter crops, sow at 14-day intervals from early August until the end of September. Further sowings in March and April will provide leaves in summer.

The plant grows to 15 to 20cm (6 to 8in). Seed should be sown thinly in 1-cm ($\frac{1}{2}$-in) deep drills 15cm (6in) apart. Thin the seedlings to 10cm (4in) apart as soon as possible. Late autumn and early winter crops can be produced by sowing 3 or 4 rows close together—10cm (4in) apart—in September and then covering with a cloche in mid-October. Be very careful when weeding the young seedlings.

Harvesting

In summer you can pick the whole plant, but in the winter and early spring cut 3 or 4 leaves from each plant at a time. Provided this is done carefully, corn salad will be a 'cut-and-come-again' source of green salad for a long period in the winter.

Suitable cultivars

'Broad leaved English': good, general purpose type.

Chicory

Cichorium intybus

Chicory is native to Britain—where it thrives on chalky soil—and throughout most of Europe and western Asia. It is grown as annual and, like endive, usually blanched to make the leaves less bitter. The blanched hearts or 'chicons' are also served as a cooked vegetable. In some countries the roots are used as a substitute or additive for coffee.

Soil and fertilizer requirements

Deep, fertile soil which has been well manured for the previous crop is necessary to produce large, healthy tap roots. These are then forced and blanched to produce the familiar chicory leaves and hearts.

Seed sowing and crop management

Sow during late April or early May in 1-cm ($\frac{1}{2}$-in) deep drills 40cm (15in) apart. Thin the seedlings to 25cm (10in) apart when they reach the third leaf stage. Keep the plants weed-free by regular hoeing. There is a cultivar called 'Sugar loaf' (Pain de Sucre) which can be sown in June or July to produce a heart, similar to a cos lettuce in appearance, which will stand in a fresh condition for a long time.

Lifting and storage of the roots

By October or November the roots will be fully grown and the majority of leaves will have died down. Carefully lift the long parsnip-like roots and trim all the foliage back to 2cm (1in) above the crown. The ideal roots will have a diameter of 5 to 7cm (about 2$\frac{1}{2}$in) at the top and be up to 30cm (12in) in length. All thin, damaged or forked roots should be thrown away. Store the roots on their sides in boxes in a cool, frost-free building. A covering of sand or peat will prevent them from drying out too much.

Forcing and blanching

Remove the roots, a few at a time, from the storage box. Stand the roots upright, 5 to 7cm (about 2$\frac{1}{2}$in) apart, in deep boxes or pots containing sand or light soil. The crowns should protrude 2cm (1in) above the surface and the roots should be gently watered

Fruiting Vegetables

All the vegetables in this chapter—with the exception of sweet corn—are either Cucurbits or Solanaceous plants and are grown solely for their fruits. Cucumber, gherkins, vegetable marrow, courgettes, vegetable spaghetti, melon, pumpkin and squashes make up the first group while tomato, aubergine and peppers are in the second family. Sweet corn is, of course, a member of the grass family—*Gramineae*—and is cultivated for the seed head or cob.

Many of these crops are best grown under some form of protection in Britain and outdoor cultivation is only likely to succeed in sheltered southern and western districts. Sweet corn, vegetable marrows and spaghetti, courgettes, pumpkins and squashes usually produce mature fruits outside however, even if the young plants require protection during the plant raising stages. Many of the plants have—or can be given— a climbing habit and may be trained up supports. This makes them useful plants for growing on such features as patios where ground space is usually a limiting factor to vegetable production. Sweet corn is also a decorative plant in its own right and forms a very useful living screen as well as producing cobs.

Once again with the exception of sweet corn—which is an ideal subject—most of the fruiting vegetables are not particularly suitable for freezing but tomatoes, aubergines and peppers can be frozen in a number of ways. The fruits are generally used either raw in salads or as a separate cooked vegetable, although melons and pumpkins may be cooked or eaten raw as desserts.

Tomato
Lycopersicon esculentum

The tomato is a tender, half-hardy plant which we grow as an annual but which—in its native South America—is perennial in habit. When first introduced into this country, over 300 years ago, it was known as the 'Love Apple' because of the decorative appearance of the fruits, but now it is grown simply because it is good to eat. The natural habit of the tomato is bushy but most modern cultivars are encouraged to produce a single, trailing stem which is trained up some form of support. Bushy cultivars are available, however, and are particularly useful outdoors.

Tomatoes can be grown outside in many countries of the world but the most reliable

results in Britain are obtained from plants grown in heated or unheated greenhouses or polythene-covered structures. Temperatures in the range 13–24°C/55–75°F will be needed, especially at night, if early or late season crops are to be grown. Tomatoes also need long days with high light intensities for optimum growth and so early development in Britain is often poor or retarded. Fruit ripening slows down in the shortening days of autumn—even under glass—and unless heat can be provided to hasten the process green tomatoes must be picked and ripened indoors.

There are many possible growing systems for greenhouse tomatoes and it is not possible to detail them all in the limited space available but a general account will be given, along with references to the major variations currently in use.

'Tanja' is a greenhouse tomato from Sweden which has T.M.V. resistance

Tomatoes are an important and colourful component of salads but can also be cooked in a number of ways and are used in sauces and chutneys. They contain well over 90 per cent water but are sweet tasting and provide a useful source of vitamins A and C. The flavour of tomatoes is largely due to the interaction of sugars and plant acids and, while different cultivars undoubtedly have different flavours, growing conditions and crop management have an equally important contribution to make to success in growing this much discussed subject.

Soil requirements

If tomatoes are grown directly into the soil— either under glass or outside—care must be taken to ensure that no pests or diseases

Tomatoes can do well outside but greenhouse types prefer some protection

are present. Protected crops run the greatest risk since the tomatoes are probably grown in the same soil every year. The most important soil-borne pathogens are root knot and potato cyst eelworms, verticillium and fusarium wilt fungi and tobacco mosaic virus. Commercially they are controlled—to a greater or lesser extent—by partially sterilizing the greenhouse soil. This involves using steam or chemicals—some of which are highly toxic—and is unlikely to be a very practical approach for the home producer. Complete soil changing is possible but, since replacement to a depth of 45 to 60cm (18 to 24in) is necessary, this is a laborious task. The most suitable alternative to growing tomatoes in the soil is to grow them in isolated containers such as 25-cm (10-in) clay or whalehide pots, peat-filled growing bags or even to use a system such as ring-culture. Soil-borne pathogens can be avoided with outdoor tomatoes by using

Outdoor bush tomatoes can be supported by a simple post and wire framework

Removal of the lower leaves improves air movement and hastens ripening

Bush tomatoes grown in 25 cm (10 in) pots are ideal for a balcony or patio

a sufficiently long rotational system.

Any soils which are used for tomatoes must be both well-drained and moisture-retentive, a medium, fertile loam being ideal. Dig generous quantities of well-rotted organic manure or compost into the greenhouse borders and outdoor soils during the winter. If soil, or soil-based composts, are used in container grown systems then they, too, should have the properties already described. Proprietary composts may be purchased, or fibrous, loamy garden soil can be used—provided it is pathogen free—as the basis for a home-made compost. Mix the soil with peat and coarse sand in the ratio of 7 soil : 3 peat : 2 sand and add a special purpose tomato base fertilizer at the same time according to the instructions. This compost must not be stored once it has been mixed so prepare it immediately before

filling and planting the containers. Proprietary composts should be used according to the instructions and may not require base fertilizer to be added. If you have worked in heavy dressings of organic materials for greenhouse border or outdoor crops it is safest to withhold base fertilizer. Liquid feed the plants throughout their life.

If previous crops grown in the greenhouse soil received large dressings of fertilizer—either as a base dressing or as liquid feed—there will probably have been an accumulation of nutrient salts. This will lead to slow, uneven growth of a newly planted crop and the salts must be washed out by flooding the soil about 3 weeks before planting.

Suitable fertilizers

Tomato nutrition is a subject which has received considerable research attention and which varies in detail according to the

growing system used. The principles are the same, however, and are most easily followed if liquid feeding is done. From planting until the third and fourth trusses are showing feed with a low-nitrogen solution (nitrogen : potassium = 1 : 3). Then change to a medium-nitrogen solution (nitrogen : potassium = 1 : 2) until the fruits on the fifth truss are swelling. During June and July use a high-nitrogen feed (nitrogen : potassium = 1 : 1) before gradually weaning the plants on to plain water for the last 2 or 3 weeks before they are pulled out. This feeding programme applies to tomatoes grown in a heated greenhouse from a February planting. Later and outside crops should be given a medium-nitrogen feed initially and moved on to a high-nitrogen feed when the plants are carrying fruit on the first 2 or 3 trusses.

Plant raising

Tomato plants must be raised in heated conditions—even those which are intended for outdoor cultivation. A minimum temperature of 15–17°C/60–65°F is required for raising tomato plants but do not let it rise too much above 25°C/75°F otherwise weak, leggy plants will result. Bright light is also essential and dark, shaded propagation places must be avoided. A heated greenhouse in a sunny position is ideal because anything less than the best plant raising conditions will markedly reduce essential plant growth and yield. If you cannot provide the necessary heat and light you should buy plants from a local nurseryman. Sow tomato seeds thinly into seedtrays/seedpans and cover them lightly with compost. When they have two leaves pot them singly into 9-cm (3½-in) pots using a proprietary potting compost. The very earliest plants, which are intended for planting in heated greenhouses in February, can subsequently be re-potted into 12-cm (4½-in) pots if necessary. Give the plants plenty of room and light and always space them so that they do not shade each other.

Sow early tomatoes in early December to produce plants for setting out—in heated greenhouses—in February. Sowings made at the turn of the year will produce plants for a March planting—again in a heated house. Plants for unheated houses will come from a late January or early February sowing while outdoor crops—which cannot be planted until late May or early June after the risk of frost has passed—can be sown as late as the middle of March. Sow in late June to raise plants for transplanting into heated houses during early September in order to produce tomatoes during the autumn. The autumn crop is not an easy one to manage and should only be attempted in good light areas. Plants which are intended for cold house or outdoor purposes must be hardened off before planting.

Planting

The optimum time for planting tomatoes is when the first flower on the first truss is open, but you should only use this as a guide. Do not keep the plants in small pots until they are pot bound and starved—it is much better to plant them a week or so before the 'first flower open' stage. The planting distances will obviously depend on your system of growing. Plants grown in the border soil should be arranged in single or double rows with 45 to 55cm (18 to 22in) between plants in each direction. Double rows should be spaced at 1.5-metre (5-ft) centres. Similar spacings should be used when plants are grown in individual containers—either standing on the soil surface or in a ring culture system. This latter method involves the use of compost-filled, bottomless 25-cm (10-in) pots standing on a 7 to 10-cm (3 to 4-in) thick bed of either thoroughly weathered and washed clinker or a porous mixture of coarse sand and gravel. Liquid feed is watered into the pots

The small fruits of 'Gardeners' Delight' have an excellent flavour

and plain water is applied to the porous bed. If growing bags are used you should follow the manufacturer's instructions for planting. Outdoor crops which are planted directly into the soil—it may, however, be more convenient to plant them in containers and stand these on paths, patios or the soil—should be spaced 45cm (18in) apart for cordon training and 60cm (2ft) apart for bush culture. Planting times are referred to under *Plant raising*. Always give the plants a good ball-watering after planting.

Crop management

Heated greenhouse tomatoes should be grown, after planting, at a minimum night temperature of 16.5°C/62°F and a minimum day temperature of 17°C/65°F. Lower temperatures will cause slower growth and fruit development.

All but the outdoor tomato bush cultivars will need supporting and training. For greenhouse plants the easiest way is to tie one end of a length of string loosely around the stem of each plant—about 10cm (4in) above the soil surface—and to secure the other end to an overhead, horizontal wire running the length of the tomato row and attached to the roof glazing bars. As the plants grow twist them around their strings, taking care not to damage the stems and flower trusses. When long stemmed cultivars are grown outside it is better to stake each plant with a 1.5 to 2-metre (about 6-ft) cane to which the stems are then tied.

All long stemmed tomato cultivars produce unwanted side-shoots in the axils of the leaves. These must be carefully removed by snapping them off when they are small. The removal of large, fleshy side-shoots is likely to leave scars which are readily colonized by fungi such as botrytis. Outdoor bush types do not need sideshooting. As the fruits on the bottom trusses begin to ripen it will be beneficial to remove the leaves up to the truss in question. This allows better light penetration and air circulation in the bottom of the plant. Do not remove too

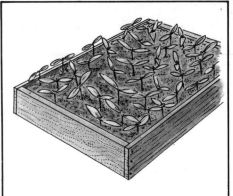

A box of tomato seedlings which are ready for pricking out

Seedlings must be handled carefully and pricked out singly into 9 cm (3½ in) pots

Side shoots must be removed when small. Snap them off cleanly between thumb and forefinger

Layering of tomatoes allows long term crops to be grown even in low houses

many leaves at a time otherwise growth will slow down. All but the very earliest greenhouse crops should be 'stopped' (the growing point removed) when they touch the roof and have 7 to 10 trusses. February-planted tomatoes can be layered (that is the stems are laid on a bed of peat or straw which is spread alongside the crop row) by first untying the original string from the top wire, then tying on to it another 1 metre (3ft) length and finally re-tying the lengthened piece of string further along the wire. This must be done very carefully so that the stems do not break and the fruits are not damaged. All the plants must be layered at the same time, otherwise a woven jungle of tomato plants is formed! Plants at the ends of the rows must be carefully bent round through 180° and laid down in the other direction. There are other methods of layering tomatoes but this one works well provided care and attention is taken at all times. Outdoor tomatoes should also be 'stopped' but it is unlikely that more than 4 or 5 trusses of fruit can be ripened on any one plant.

Most modern tomatoes are self-pollinated but fruit set is often poor both in low light and in hot, dry conditions. Gently shaking the plants will help pollination while spraying them over regularly with water in hot weather will increase humidity and improve fruit set. Damp over the floor of the greenhouse regularly in hot weather. Tomatoes should be liquid fed according to the recommendations made under *Soil and fertilizer requirements*. It is impossible to make absolute recommendations for watering tomato crops but it is very important to ensure that plants are given the right quantity. Both over-watering and under-watering will cause all kinds of plant and fruit defects. In the months between May and September it is likely, in very broad terms, that February-planted tomatoes should be receiving 4 to 8 litres (7 to 12 pints) per plant per week. Late planted and outdoor crops will reach this requirement in June or July and water, when required, should be given each day rather than once a week. Regular watering is particularly important when tomatoes are grown in individual containers or growing bags.

Outdoor crops will benefit from protection against winds or sudden cold wet spells. A useful technique is to plant—or stand—the tomatoes close to a wall—45cm (18in) away—and then suspend a clear polythene sheet along the open side of the row. Weeds may be a problem with outdoor tomatoes—protected crops should be troubled less—but they can be carefully hoed out or the plants can be mulched round with straw, peat or grass mowings.

Harvesting

As red-fruited tomato cultivars ripen they pass through various colour shades very quickly. The transition from pale green, through orange and orange-pink, to a gradually deepening red will take about

5 days at normal summer greenhouse temperatures. The time required will obviously be longer for outdoor tomatoes and the stage of picking will depend on when the fruits are to be used. Pick the tomatoes with the calyx on and do not squeeze the fruits since they bruise very easily. At the end of the season you are likely to be left with a lot of green fruit which can be picked and ripened indoors. Ethylene gas—which is given off in considerable quantities by ripening apples and pears—hastens the ripening of tomatoes and good results are obtained if green tomatoes are put in a drawer with some top fruit.

Pests and diseases

Tomatoes may be attacked by a wide range of pathogens and nutritional or other disorders. Root knot and potato cyst eelworm are the most important soil-borne pests and are most likely to appear in non-sterilized soils which are used for tomatoes or potatoes each year. Wireworms—the larvae of click beetles—can also be a problem, particularly if the crops are grown where grass has recently been dug up or if growing composts are prepared with loam which comes from a turf stack. Glasshouse red spider mite and glasshouse whitefly are very likely to attack the aerial part of the tomato plant. The tiny red spider mites feed under the leaves causing them to develop a stippled appearance. In severe attacks the leaves become bronzed and dry up. This pest can still be

'Golden Queen' may be grown under glass or outdoors

controlled by certain sprays or fumigant smokes but glasshouse whitefly is resistant to almost all chemicals. The small, but obvious, flies suck the sap from plants and leave a sticky deposit which quickly becomes colonized by smuts and moulds. Biological control is likely to be the best method against whitefly using the parasitic wasp *encarsia formosa*.

Tomato plants may suddenly wilt for no apparent reason and the cause may well be an attack by the soil-borne verticillum or fusarium wilt diseases. Root rots are caused by a number of fungi and, once again, the problem lies in the soil as it does with damping-off diseases of tomato seedlings. Stem canker causes brown or black areas usually near a cut, or where a side-shoot or leaf has been removed. This disease can spread from year to year if infected plants are composted rather than burned. Stem Botrytis also attacks tomatoes, causing grey, velvety patches of fungal growth, usually where leaves are dying, or large, untidy wounds exist. Leaf mould fungus causes brown/grey lesions on the underside of leaves especially in still, humid conditions, but many modern cultivars are resistant to the disease. Cold greenhouse and outdoor crops may be attacked by potato blight late in the summer when moist, warm weather conditions and infected potatoes in the vicinity increase the likelihood of an attack on tomatoes. Ghost spotting of tomato fruit is also caused by the grey mould fungus—Botrytis—and may be recognized by the small white rings or halo marks. Tobacco mosaic virus (T.M.V.) is a very common and infectious virus of tomatoes causing low yields and poor fruit quality. The most common symptoms are leaf mottling, stunted

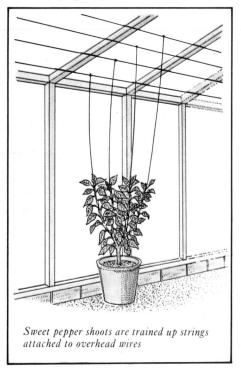

Sweet pepper shoots are trained up strings attached to overhead wires

'Amateur' has a bushy habit, requires no staking and is ideal for cloches

growth and bronzed fruits. Infected plant debris is one means by which the virus is carried over from year to year but it can also remain in the soil or be carried on tomato seed coats. Be very careful, therefore, when saving seed from tomatoes to make sure that the parent plant was not infected with tobacco mosaic virus.

Nutritional disorders of tomato are more likely to occur when plants are grown in non-soil media such as peat. The presence of soil in the growing medium provides a useful buffer of nutrient reserves. Magnesium deficiency is the most common nutritional problem and is often an induced condition on alkaline soils. An interveinal yellowing develops on the leaves starting at the bottom of the plant. Spraying the plants regularly with a solution of Epsom salts (9gm per litre/1.5oz per gallon) will usually cure the condition. Blossom end rot—a sunken dark brown scar at the base of the fruit—is caused by dry soil conditions or an excessive concentration of nutrient salts. Blotchy ripening of the fruit is a complex disorder and may be caused by any, or a combination, of the following: potassium deficiency; very high temperatures; or too much sunshine falling on ripening fruit as a result of over-zealous de-leafing. 'Greenback'—a hard, green area around the calyx and shoulder of the fruit—is encouraged by very high temperatures but some cultivars are said to be resistant.

Suitable cultivars

Tomatoes can be classified according to a number of fruit characteristics. Red, yellow or striped cultivars are available with the *yellow fruited types* often having a very good flavour and disease resistance. The shape may be round, irregular, pear-like or plum-like. Modern commercial cultivars have round fruits which average 60 to 70gm (2 to 2.5oz) in weight, while the large, irregular-shaped fruit of marmande tomatoes may each weigh over 450gm (1lb). Plant breeders have, in recent years, introduced a large number of heated greenhouse tomato cultivars. Many are F1 hybrids—and are chosen for their uniform growth and fruit—while most of the new introductions have some disease resistance qualities. Several of these cultivars are available to the amateur but are only likely to perform to their full potential if grown in heated greenhouses. Nevertheless there is a long list from which to choose your cold greenhouse cultivars. Outdoor tomatoes will have a considerably shorter growing season and quick maturing cultivars should, therefore, be chosen. Bush tomatoes are particularly useful in small gardens.

You may be tempted to save seed from your favourite cultivar especially if it has qualities which you particularly appreciate. Choose absolutely typical disease-free fully ripe fruits. Slice them in half and squeeze out the mucilage-covered seeds. 10 per cent

washing soda solution will break down the mucilage. Add sufficient to double the volume of liquid and leave the mixture for 24 hours in a moderately warm place (68°F/20°C). A 10 per cent solution contains 100g per litre or 2 oz per pint of washing soda. Wash the slurry through a household sieve under a strong jet of water. Spread the seed thinly on a sheet of glass to dry and then package it in a carefully labelled envelope. Make sure that you never attempt to save seed from F1 hybrid cultivars.

Greenhouse cultivars

'Eurocross B.B.': heavy cropper in heated houses; leaf mould resistant; F1 hybrid. 'Cura': early fruit; trusses close together, T.M.V. resistant; F1 hybrid. 'Money-maker': heavy crops of medium sized fruit; heated or cold greenhouses.

Outdoor cultivars

'The Amateur': dwarf and popular bush tomato. 'Gardener's Delight': small fruits but excellent flavour. 'Sleaford Abundance': F1 hybrid; very dwarf (45cm or 18in) but early fruit.

Yellow/unusual cultivars

'Yellow Perfection': tall habit but early fruited; does well outdoors. 'Tigerella': red fruits with yellow stripes; under glass or outdoors. 'Marmande': continental outdoor type with large, irregular shaped fruits.

Annual peppers

Capsicum annuum

Of the several species of Capsicum grown for their fruits, *C. annuum* is the most likely to succeed in Britain. It has a relatively dwarf and branched habit—reaching a height of 0.5 to 1m (18in to 3ft)—and the fruits develop from white flowers in the leaf axils. This species contains the large fruited peppers which vary in length from 5 to 25cm (2 to 10in), and in shape from round and 'blocky' to long and thin. The flavour of the fruits also varies. In many of the larger fruited types it is very mild and they are frequently termed 'sweet peppers' although the terms 'bell pepper' and 'bull-nose pepper' may also be used. As more

people travel around Mediterranean Europe so peppers have become more popular in recent years. Although plants may be grown outdoors in southern and western districts, peppers are best grown in heated or cold greenhouses or polythene structures.

Capsicum fruits are green initially and may be picked in that condition for use in salads or as a cooked vegetable. If left on the plant the fruits will eventually turn red. They can be frozen but most pepper dishes

are best if fresh fruits are used.

Soil and fertilizer requirements

Peppers have similar soil and fertilizer requirements to tomatoes. They tend to grow more slowly in the early stages and care must be taken to ensure that the plants do not become 'hard'. They respond to the incorporation of large amounts of well-rotted organic manure into the soil and should never be planted into 'cold' land. Growing peppers in containers such as 25-cm (10-in) pots has the big advantage that the soil will warm up quickly and the whole plant can be moved outside if conditions become suitable. Soil-borne pests and diseases which attack tomatoes may also cause problems on peppers.

This crop has a greater demand for nitrogenous fertilizers than tomatoes and, al-though liquid feeding is still the most convenient method, medium and high-nitrogen feeds should be used.

Plant raising

Pre-Christmas sowings of peppers, unlike tomatoes, are not made. The usual time to sow is February, or even March for later crops. Plant raising techniques and temperatures are similar to those used for tomatoes but you will find it takes longer to grow peppers to the planting stage. It is unlikely

that plants will be ready for planting until late April or May.

Planting

Peppers may, like tomatoes, be grown in a number of ways but they are usually planted either in the greenhouse soil or in individual containers. The plants have a bushy habit and should be given more space than tomatoes. Space the plants/containers 60cm (2ft) apart in each direction. It is important to plant before the peppers become root-bound in the propagation pots. Do not plant outside until early June and then only on very sheltered sites.

Crop management

The optimum conditions for growing peppers are high temperatures along with adequate supplies of nitrogenous fertilizer and water. Minimum temperatures of 18°C/64°F should ensure uninterrupted growth. Because of their branched, bushy habit peppers need supporting to give all the shoots a chance to develop. When the plants are about 30cm (12in) tall they will terminate in a flower which may either be allowed to develop into a fruit or pinched out. If they are retained then a flush of early peppers will result but there will then be a delay before the next fruits are ready. Removal of the terminal flowers will cause a later, but more continuous, fruiting pattern. If three or four shoots on each plant can be

The fruits of 'Bell Boy' peppers are thick-walled with a fine flavour

Ring culture of greenhouse plants, such as tomatoes and peppers. Place bottomless pots full of growing compost on trays of porous aggregate. Train plants on strings suspended from overhead wires

separately supported with canes or strings then light and air will be able to penetrate and fruit development will be better.

Harvesting

Pepper fruits are most commonly picked green but waiting another 3 weeks will allow them to turn red. Regular picking is essential to ensure that subsequent fruits continue to grow. The secret with most fruiting vegetables is to regulate plant growth so that vegetative development and fruit production can go on at the same time. If plants are carrying too much fruit at a particular time then vegetative growth—and future fruiting—will slow down. Remove the fruits with a sharp knife.

Pests and diseases
Peppers are subject to most tomato disorders but the most important are glasshouse red spider mite, glasshouse whitefly, tobacco mosaic virus and blossom end rot. Aphids (greenfly) are likely to be a much greater problem on peppers and care must be taken to eradicate them at an early stage.

Suitable cultivars
'New Ace': F1 hybrid: early and high yielding; best under protection. 'Canape': F1 hybrid; early but may also be grown outdoors. 'Outdoor': suitable for outdoor culture under cloches; yellow fruits.

Sweet peppers may also be grown in individual containers such as pots

Soil and fertilizer requirements
Aubergines have very similar requirements to tomatoes and peppers. Like the latter they may either be grown in the greenhouse soil or in individual containers. If they are planted outdoors a very sunny, sheltered site must be used.

Seed sowing, planting and crop management
Sow seed during February in the same way as for tomatoes and germinate at a temperature of 21°C/70°F. When they are large enough to handle, prick the seedlings out into individual 9-cm (3½-in) pots and grow them on in the same way as tomato plants. They will be ready for planting in May when they should be spaced 60cm (2ft) apart in each direction. Lateral branches will be encouraged if the growing plant is pinched out when the plants are 15cm (6in) tall. Aubergines prefer high temperatures and humidity so be prepared to spray the plants regularly with water. Use the same feeding regime as for peppers and stake the

plants in order to allow 3 or 4 shoots to develop on each. In good growing seasons it may be necessary to limit each plant to 4 to 6 fruits only. From a May planting in heated greenhouses it should be possible to pick fruits in mid-July. Space outdoor aubergines 60cm (2ft) apart in each direction. Plants can be grown under protection in containers in early summer and then moved outside on to pathways or patios when the weather is warm enough.

Harvesting
Cut off the fruits with a sharp knife.

Pests and diseases
The major pests are aphids—which can have devastating effects if not controlled—glasshouse whitefly and glasshouse red spider mite.

Suitable cultivars
'Moneymaker': F1 hybrid; early cultivar with purple fruits. 'Long Purple': large oval fruits with superb flavour. 'Short Tom': F1 hybrid; early maturing and heavy yielding.

Aubergine
Solanum melongena ovigerum

This tropical or sub-tropical perennial is grown for the fruits which are often egg-shaped—hence the common name of 'egg-plant'. It is very popular both in southern Europe and the United States where plants are grown outside, but the fickle nature of the British climate means that we must grow aubergines under protected cultivation. They have a similar bushy growth habit to sweet peppers. The purple flowers usually develop into purple coloured fruits although white-fruited cultivars are also available. Fruits range from 10cm to 25cm (4 to 10in) in length and may be cooked in a variety of delicious ways.

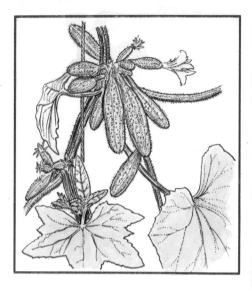

Below: These beautiful aubergine fruits have many culinary uses. Grow them in the greenhouse. If in individual pots they can be moved outside on warm sunny days.

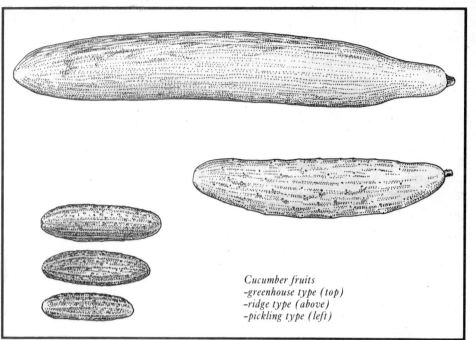

Cucumber fruits
-greenhouse type (top)
-ridge type (above)
-pickling type (left)

Cucumbers & gherkins

Cucumis sativus

These half-hardy trailing or climbing plants are natives of parts of Asia, Africa and sub-tropical America. They are cultivated for their green-skinned fruits which are used raw in salads, cooked in soups and other dishes or pickled either whole or sliced. Cucumbers may be classified as either greenhouse types or outdoor (ridge) types, while gherkins are similar to the second category. Greenhouse cucumbers usually require temperatures in excess of 21°C/70°F and high humidity although some cultivars can be grown in cold greenhouses or frames. The fruits of this group are 30 to 40cm (12 to 16in) long. Ridge cucumbers and gherkins are easier to grow and produce fruits which are up to 20cm (8in) in length although gherkins for pickling are used when 5cm (2in) long.

Most cucumbers, like other cucurbits, have separate, yellow male and female flowers which arise in the leaf axils. Greenhouse cultivars have recently been introduced which are 'all-female' and have no male flowers. The crisp, succulent fruits develop from female flowers and are mainly flesh but also have a central core of seeds. The fruits of greenhouse cucumbers must develop parthenocarpically—without fertilization—otherwise they become swollen at the end and have a bitter taste. With cultivars which have both male and female flowers it is necessary to prevent fertilization by removing all the male flowers—and thus the source of pollen—and by insect-proofing the greenhouses. This is obviously a time-consuming and laborious procedure so 'all-female' cultivars have an distinct advantage for gardeners with limited time at their disposal. Ridge cucumber fruits are produced in large numbers after fertilization.

Soil requirements

Greenhouse cucumbers should be grown in specially prepared beds made up on the greenhouse floor. Plants need a rooting medium which is well-drained and spongy but which retains sufficient water to permit rapid, uninterrupted growth and to help maintain the high humidity. Make the cucumber beds of well-rotted organic manure mixed with peat or loam. Thoroughly mix the ingredients in the proportions of 2 parts manure and 1 part peat/loam. Build the beds 60cm (2ft) wide and 45cm (18in) high with slightly sloping sides and a domed top which should be covered with a 10 to 15-cm (4 to 6-in) deep planting medium of peat or loam. Get the beds ready about 3 weeks before planting and then water copiously so that they begin to ferment and develop the required consistency. Keep the greenhouse temperature at 21°–25°C/70°–75°F during this time to encourage bed development.

Similar preparations are needed for cold greenhouse crops but, of course, it is much more difficult to provide the optimum environmental conditions of temperature and humidity. Greenhouse cultivars can be grown in frames but again a special bed must be prepared. The easiest method is to take out a hole which is one spit deep and 30cm (12in) square at the back of the frame. Fill the hole with well-rotted manure and replace the soil over the top to leave a mound which is 15 to 20cm (6 to 8in) above the soil surface. Water the bed, cover the frame and allow the temperature and humidity to build up.

Ridge cucumbers and gherkins are grown outside and prefer a light, well-drained soil in a sunny position. Dig the land deeply and thoroughly in the autumn and leave it rough for over-winter weathering. Plants may be planted into individual beds which are prepared just beforehand as for frame cucumbers. The beds should be spaced 60cm (2ft) apart in each direction. Alternatively a long bed can be prepared by taking out a trench—30cm (12in) deep and 45cm (18in) wide—half filling it with manure and then replacing the soil to form a ridge.

Suitable fertilizers

Frame and ridge cucumbers are unlikely to require any base fertilizer before planting. An application of 50g per m^2 (2 oz per sq yd) of a general purpose material should, however, be worked into the peat or loam casing just before planting greenhouse crops.

All cucumbers produce a lot of vegetative growth very quickly but as we want them to produce fruits at the same time, they must be fed in order to maintain the necessary balance. They are gross nitrogen users and liquid feeds should, therefore, have a high proportion of this material. It is impossible to give absolute recommendations for amounts and regularity of feeding, but you must judge the state of the plants and feed them accordingly.

Plant raising

Cucumbers for heated greenhouses should be sown in late February or early March. Sow the seeds singly in 9-cm (3½-in) pots at a temperature of 21°–25°C/70°–75°F when germination will be rapid. The seedlings must then be given maximum light and a slightly reduced temperature— 18°–21°C/65°–70°F—in order to produce strong, sturdy plants. Pot the plants on into 12 to 14-cm (4½ to 5½-in) pots when they have 2 or 3 true leaves. They will be growing very rapidly at the temperatures indicated and must not be allowed to become pot bound. Stake each plant with a 50-cm (20-in) cane and tie them in carefully. Copious

watering and spraying of the plants will help to maintain the high humidity. They should be ready for planting in about 4 weeks from sowing and it is most important that the bed preparations have been programmed so that they are ready to receive the plants.

Plants for cold greenhouses and frames are also propagated in heated greenhouses using the method indicated above. Provided the beds are ready to receive them the plants can be planted directly from 9-cm (3½-in) pots. These crops will be planted at the end of May or beginning of June and, at the temperatures indicated, you should allow 2 to 3 weeks from sowing to planting.

Ridge cucumbers are grown outside and must not be planted until all danger of frost has gone. Plants can, again, be raised in heated greenhouses and planted in early June. Alternatively you may sow seeds directly into the ridges and then cover them

with bell-jars, cloches or jam-jars. Sow 2 seeds at each station at the end of May and remove one of them if they both germinate. A final spacing of 60cm (2ft) apart is required.

Planting, training and crop management
Greenhouse—heated or cold—cucumbers are trained as cordons and should be planted into the compost casing on top of the beds. Plant about 3 to 4 weeks after seed sowing. Ideally the bed temperature should be between 18°–21°C/65°–70°F and the cucumbers planted with 1 to 2cm (½ to 1in) of the rootball protruding above the surface in order to encourage water to drain away from the stem base. Set the plants 90cm (3ft) apart along the bed and thoroughly firm and water them in afterwards. Frame and ridge crops should be similarly planted into the centre of the mounds or ridges. Allow 1 plant to every 90cm (3ft) length of frame.

Cordon cucumbers are trained more or less vertically and either tied in to a series of

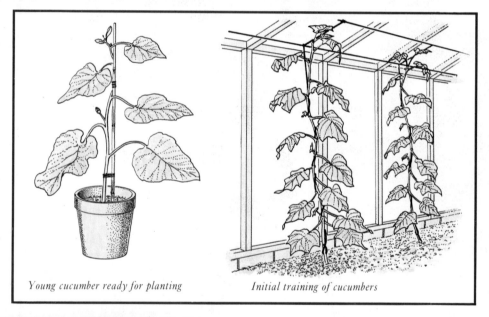

Young cucumber ready for planting   *Initial training of cucumbers*

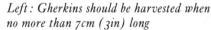

Left: Gherkins should be harvested when no more than 7cm (3in) long

horizontal wires which run the length of the rows or, alternatively, twisted around vertical strings tied to the plant stems and then to overhead wires. Stop the main stem when it reaches the top wire and allow the cucumbers to develop on lateral branches. These laterals should be stopped after the second leaf and any secondary laterals should only be allowed one leaf. Always trim cucumbers carefully and neatly with a sharp knife. Female flowers have a tiny immature cucumber behind the petals and only two should be allowed to develop on each lateral. All male flowers must be pinched out immediately to reduce the chance of fertilization. Frame cucumbers trail on the soil surface but the training system must restrict growth so that the fruits achieve a reasonable size. The objective is to train sufficient laterals to fill the frame space. Stop the plants after 4 or 5 leaves and train 3 or 4 laterals to the corners of the frame. Stop laterals at three leaves and sub-laterals at two, leaving only one or two fruits on each lateral. Remove all male flowers and trim the plants to keep a balance between vegetative and fruit growth.

Ridge cucumbers and gherkins are also grown on the flat after planting on mounds or ridges. Stop the plants after the sixth leaf and only train sufficient laterals to fill the space available. Male and female flowers must be retained as fertilization is necessary for fruit production in these crops.

After planting greenhouse cucumbers it is vital that high temperatures—preferably a minimum of 18°–21°C/65°–70°F—high humidity and correct watering and feeding are maintained. Damp down the plants and the pathways to keep the required humidity but be prepared to ventilate on very hot days, otherwise the plants will scorch and wilt. Shade the plants by whitening the glass in very bright conditions. Cucumber roots decay rapidly and are continually

Planting cucumbers in a frame
Fill a hole 1-spade deep near the back of the frame with well-rotted farmyard manure. Replace the soil in a mound on top

being replaced by others. You can encourage the development of adventitious roots by mulching the plants around the base of the stems with a mixture of organic manure and loam. Cucumbers need large quantities of water which must be applied regularly to prevent crop damage. Frame cucumbers require similar crop management but conditions of high temperature and humidity are more difficult to achieve. Only ventilate on hot days and close the frames well before nightfall so that the temperature and humidity are built up again. Outdoor crops must be well watered and feeding, if necessary at all, should not begin until fruits have begun to set.

Harvesting

Young fruits are the most succulent and tasty and regular cutting allows more to develop. Pick greenhouse and frame cucumbers when they reach 30 to 40cm (12 to 16in) long. Ridge cucumbers are at their best when 15 to 20cm (6 to 8in) in length but if you want to use them for gherkins they should only be allowed to grow 5 to 7cm (2 to 3in) long.

Pests and diseases

Cucumbers require much higher temperatures and humidities than most other greenhouse vegetables. There are likely to be considerable crop management problems if cucumbers, tomatoes and peppers are grown in the same house. If you want all three, you can grow an outdoor cultivar of tomatoes and devote a sunny windowsill to peppers. Some of the problems will be associated with pest and disease control because cucurbitaceous plants are damaged by certain protective chemicals used on other crops.

Glasshouse red spider mite and glasshouse whitefly attack in the same way as on tomatoes but the red spiders will be less of a problem in high humidity conditions—they prefer a dry atmosphere. Root rot fungi and wilt diseases, such as verticillium, cause leaves to go yellow and wilt and eventually bring about collapse of the plant. Grey mould (Botrytis) causes a grey, velvety

growth on cut and damaged parts of leaves and stems while gummosis may develop on greenhouse cultivars and cause sunken spots which turn into a sticky mass. Symptoms of cucumber mosaic virus include mottled leaves and fruits and stunted plants. The most common fungal disease is powdery mildew which produces a carpet of white growth on the leaves. It can now be controlled by watering a systemic fungicide on to the roots of the plant.

Suitable cultivars

Greenhouse/frame types

'Telegraph': can be grown in heated or cold houses or frames; long smooth fruits. 'Femdam': all female flowers; F1 hybrid; heavy yields in heated greenhouses. 'Pepi-

Firm in the young plant with the root ball slightly clear of the bed to allow water to drain away. Water in and replace frame lights

Above: Cucumbers grown in the greenhouse are very productive. One or two plants may be enough

nex': all female flowers; F1 hybrid; disease resistant; best in heated houses. 'Conqueror': heavy cropper suitable for cold greenhouses or frames.

Ridge types

'Burpee Hybrid': F1 hybrid; dark green fruits; suitable for all areas. 'Burpless': F1 hybrid; Japanese cultivar of high quality. 'Perfection': good sized fruits; crops well into the autumn.

Gherkins

'Venlo Pickling': very heavy cropper if fruits harvested when small. 'Prolific': uniform, dark green fruits ideal for pickling.

71

Marrows, courgettes, vegetable spaghetti

Cucurbita pepo ovifera

These half-hardy members of the cucumber family are also grown for their fruits which are usually ovoid and cylindrical. There are two types of true vegetable marrows—trailing type and bush type. The former produces long, sprawling stems which are difficult to train while bush marrows have a more compact habit, are more suited to small gardens and produce mature fruits about two weeks earlier. The fruit colour is either green, whitish/yellow or striped and the marrows are at least 30cm (12in) long when mature. They may be harvested fresh in summer and autumn and eaten as a boiled vegetable or may be stuffed with meat and spices before baking. They can also be stored for winter use. Courgettes are really baby marrows although special cultivars—such as the Italian Zucchini—have been developed. There are a number of courgette dishes which use 15 to 20-cm (6 to 8-in) long fruits which, if they are left on the plant, will eventually grow into full-

Male and female flowers of marrows are necessary in order to set fruit

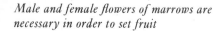

'Cobham Bush Green' marrow is excellent for the table or for exhibition

sized marrows. Custard marrows have a bush habit and dumpy, round fruits with a scalloped edge. Vegetable spaghetti is trailing and has fruits about 20cm (8in) long which are cooked whole and then sliced open to reveal the spaghetti-like flesh.

Soil and fertilizer requirements

Marrows and courgettes need fertile, well-drained soils. They grow rapidly and require large quantities of water and plant nutrients. The best soils are those which have received generous dressings of organic manure or compost while the preparations used for ridge cucumbers can also be used for these crops. Prepare the ridges or mounds in late spring—siting them in sheltered positions—

in order to plant in late May or early June. Do not apply base fertilizers, otherwise you will find yourself with a lot of leaves concealing disappointingly little fruit.

Plant raising and planting

Marrow and courgette seed sometimes has poor or erratic germination but if it is 'chitted' before sowing plant raising will be more certain. Seed should be sown under protection in late April or early May for planting a month later. Lay two or three layers of blotting paper or kitchen towel on a plate or dish and soak them with water. Scatter the seeds evenly on the surface and keep the container at 18°C/65°F while ensuring that the paper/towel remains moist.

Within a day or two the young roots will appear from some of the seeds; push them carefully to a depth of 3 to 4cm (about 1½in) into a 9-cm (8½-in) pot full of compost. Directly the seeds begin to germinate they must be transferred to individual containers. Keep the temperature between 15°–18°C/ 60°–65°F and never allow the plants to dry out. Harden the plants off in a cold frame for a few days before planting. Marrow or courgette seed—dry or 'chitted'—can also be sown directly outside into the mounds or ridges in mid to late May. Sow one chitted or two dry seeds at each station. Treat as ridge cucumbers. Do not plant outside until all danger of frost has passed, although early protection can be given by cloches or polythene tunnels. Plant bush marrows—including custards—and cour-

Assist marrow seeds to germinate by 'chitting' them on moist paper at 18°C

Immediately after germination, transfer the seeds to individual containers

Usually insects will transfer the pollen, but if cold or very dry weather has discouraged the bees, you may need to hand-pollinate the flowers. Remove a male flower, peel back the petals and push it into—and leave it inside—a female flower. Alternatively pollen can be transferred on a camel hair brush.

Weeds must be removed until the marrow/courgette leaves meet across the rows. If too much vegetative growth develops it will be necessary to remove some of the leaves.

Harvesting

Cut courgettes when they are 15 to 20cm (6 to 8in) long. This will encourage others to develop. Harvest custard marrows when young to keep the maximum flavour. Pick marrows and vegetable spaghetti as required at 30cm (12in) long. They are best when eaten young and the flesh will be over-mature if your fingernail will not penetrate the outer skin. Harvesting should be possible from July onwards if plants were transplanted in late May. Marrows which are left on the plant until the end of September will have a well-ripened skin and can be stored in an airy, frost-free place for winter use.

Pests and diseases

These crops are liable to be attacked by the same pests and diseases as cucumbers.

Right : Courgette fruits must be cut before they grow too large

gettes, 60 to 80cm (2ft to 2ft 6in) apart with trailing types and vegetable spaghetti 1.5 metres (about 5ft) apart, making sure that plants are well firmed and watered in.

Crop management

Once marrows/courgettes are established there are likely to be very few problems. Water them generously all around the root zone and conserve moisture by mulching round the stems with organic manure, peat or grass cuttings. Bush and custard marrows and courgettes require no training. Stop the stems of trailing plants when 45cm (18in) long to encourage laterals to develop.

Both male and female flowers must be retained since fertilization is necessary.

Fruit colour of marrow and courgette cultivars ranges from dark green, through light green to bright or creamy yellow. Many cultivars have patterned fruits but the flesh is not influenced by skin colour.

'Long Green Trailing': dark green with lighter stripes. 'Golden Delicious': yellow skins and flesh; good keeper.

Bush

'Smallpak': high yields of smallish fruits. 'Early Gem': F1 hybrid; early and reliable. 'Prokor': F1 hybrid; early prolific cropper. *Courgettes* Bush marrow fruits can be harvested young as courgettes. Otherwise use the following special cultivars. 'Zucchini': F1 hybrid; early, dark green fruits. 'Golden Zucchini': F1 hybrid; yellow form of 'Zucchini'. 'True French': very heavy yields; must be harvested young. *Custard marrows* 'Custard Pie': scalloped, white fruits, 15cm (6in) in diameter. *Vegetable spaghetti* No named varieties. Fruits are about 20cm long; boil whole.

Right: The marrow-like fruits of vegetable spaghetti are boiled whole

Melons
Cucumis melo

This tender, trailing plant originated in Africa and is now cultivated for the delicious edible fruits. In warmer lands melons can be grown outside, but in Britain they must be grown either in heated greenhouses—when year round production is possible—or under frames or cloches for early autumn use. When grown in heated greenhouses melons are treated like cucumbers but they must have a drier, more ventilated atmosphere. Melons come in different shapes and sizes and with different skin colours. The best known types in this country are the Musk melons or 'Netted melons', which must be grown in heated houses, and Cantaloupe or Ogen melons—which can be grown indoors but which are also suitable for frame and cloche production. Melons also have separate male and female flowers, pollination and fertilization being necessary for fruit production. Hand pollination may be necessary particularly if grown in greenhouses.

Soil and fertilizer requirements

Heated greenhouse melons are usually grown on beds like those made up for cucumbers. They may also be planted in individual containers—such as 25-cm (10-in) pots—which are filled with a rich compost. Frame melons should be planted into a previously prepared bed like the ones prepared for frame cucumbers.

Plant raising

All melons are transplanted and the young plants must be raised in heated protection. Sow the seed approximately 6 or 7 weeks before the scheduled planting time. 'Chit' the seeds (cf. marrows) and sow them in individual 9-cm (3½-in) pots. Keep the temperature at 18°C/65°F until the first true leaf has developed and then gradually reduce the temperature to 15°C/60°F. Frame or cloche plants must be hardened off for a few days before planting.

Planting

Heated greenhouse melons are, like cucumbers, grown as cordons. They can either be trained up a wire network or round a vertical string. If you decide on a bed system of growing space the plants 60 to 90cm (2 to 3ft) apart down the bed. Individual pots should be placed the same distance apart on the glasshouse floor. Planting can take place any time provided a minimum night temperature of 15°C/60°F can be maintained. Frame or cloche melons are planted into their mounded beds with the rootball

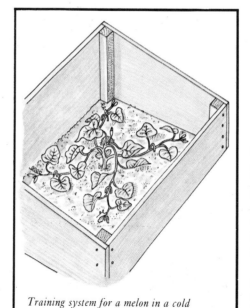

Training system for a melon in a cold frame

standing 1 to 2cm (about ¾in) above the soil surface to encourage water to run away from the base of the stem. Do not plant until late May when all danger of frost has passed.

Water the plants well in and encourage a humid atmosphere by spraying regularly until they are established. Frame crops should only be ventilated in very hot weather.

Training and crop management

The main stem of cordon melons is trained up to the top wire of the network and then stopped. Lateral branches are either trained horizontally along the lower wires or allowed to hang down by the side of the cordon stem. Stop the primary laterals when they have 4 or 5 leaves. Secondary laterals will then develop and carry the clusters of male flowers and solitary female flowers. Hand-pollinate 8 to 10 female flowers which are well spread out on each plant. If they all begin to swell then only retain 4 or 5 and stop the secondary laterals beyond the developing fruits. Take care to select fruits which are evenly spaced on the plant so that no laterals have more than one melon. Hand pollination is done by removing the petals from a mature male flower and then pushing the centre into a female flower.

Train frame and cloche melons to fill the area available. Stop the plants after 3 or 4 leaves and then again after another 4 or 5. Train and peg 3 or 4 laterals into the corners of the frame/cloche and stop them when they reach the edges. Male and female flowers will then develop. Hand pollination may not be needed if there are bees or insects around, but keep a careful watch.

Melons require a drier atmosphere than cucumbers especially once the flowers have opened. Until that time the humidity should be maintained by spraying the plants but during pollination and early fruit swelling care must be taken not to cause fruit drop. Withhold water completely from frame/cloche crops after the time of flowering until the fruits are the size of a golf ball. Watering can then be resumed and both frame and greenhouse crops should be fed regularly from that time until the fruits begin to ripen. Greenhouse melons may need to be supported in nets which are suspended from the glazing bars while frame/cloche melons should have a piece of glass or tile placed underneath them to keep them off the soil surface and reduce rotting. It is particularly important that plants are given a dry atmosphere while the fruits are ripening. Melons grow well in bright light conditions so do not shade the houses/frames/cloches in anything but very hot conditions.

Harvesting

The time taken from seed sowing to harvesting in heated greenhouses will be between 3 and 4 months while frame or cloche crops will take one month longer. Thus seed sown in mid-January will produce melon plants for transplanting in late February–early March and picking will begin in early May. Frame or cloche melons which are planted in late May will not be ripe until early September. Fruits must not be cut until they are fully ripe. At this point they will yield to a little pressure from your hands and will give off a typical sweet, heavy aroma. If absolutely necessary the fruits can be ripened indoors on the window sill.

Pests and diseases

Melons are subject to the same troubles as cucumbers and marrows but, because of the drier atmosphere, glasshouse red spider mite is likely to be more of a problem.

Suitable cultivars

Greenhouse cultivars

'Blenheim Orange': large fruits with orange flesh. 'Hero of Lockinge': green skinned with white flesh.

Frame cultivars

'Sweetheart': F1 hybrid; light green skin, orange flesh. 'Charentais': small fruits with orange flesh of fine flavour. 'Cantaloupe Dutch net': orange flesh of good quality.

Above: 'Springback' melons can be grown like cordon cucumbers

Below: Frame-grown 'Charentais' melons produce small fruits with a delicious flavour

Pumpkins & squashes

Cucurbita maxima Pumpkin
Cucurbita moschata Squashes

There are few botanical differences between pumpkins, squashes and marrows since there are trailing and bush types of each. Squashes and pumpkins can be grown in Britain but both are more popular in North America. They have similar uses to marrows, both summer and stored winter types being available.

Soil and fertilizer requirements

Treat exactly as marrows but be particularly careful to choose a full-sun site.

Below: 'Patty Pan' is a kind of custard marrow best cooked whole

Above: 'Baby Crookneck' is an easily grown cultivar of summer squash

Plant raising and planting

Pumpkin and squash plants can, like marrows, be raised under glass. They need a lower temperature—10–13°C/50–55°F—and are then transplanted. Alternatively sow either dry or 'chitted' seeds directly outside in the final positions at the end of May. They must be covered by jars or cloches until they have germinated. The spacings are the same as for bush or trailing marrow cultivars. Transplanted pumpkins and squashes should be put out, after hardening off, in early June.

Crop management

Again, follow the pattern for marrows. Stop trailing types at 45cm (18in) to encourage laterals which carry the flowers. Some people —in their attempts to produce bigger pumpkins—cover the fruit bearing laterals with soil to encourage adventitious roots which permit greater nutrient and water uptake. Only leave 1 or 2 fruits per plant if you want really large pumpkins.

Harvesting

Pumpkins are usually eaten as they mature—often in pumpkin pie—but they can also be stored in frost-free conditions for winter use. Squashes are sometimes classified into 'summer' or 'winter' types but this is confusing since they are all better to eat when they are young.

Suitable cultivars

Pumpkins 'Hundredweight': really large fruits for summer and winter use. 'Mammoth': orange skinned cultivar; can weigh over 50kg (110lb).
Squashes 'Gold Summer Crookneck': orange/yellow warty skin; use fresh or from store. 'Sweet Dumpling': tender and sweet; summer or winter use.

Sweet corn

Zea mays

Columbus brought maize, of which sweet corn is a specially selected form, to Europe from America at the end of the fifteenth century. It is a half-hardy annual in Britain with the stems growing to a height of 2 to 2.5 metres (about 7ft). Sweet corn is grown for the yellow, sweet tasting grains which are produced collectively as 'cobs'. The plant has separate male and female inflorescences with male flowers forming the familiar 'tassel' at the top of the plant and female flowers or 'silks' arising in the axils of leaves further down. Pollen is then transferred by wind. Selections from maize have produced sweet corn cultivars with grains which have a higher sugar content while special rapidly maturing types have been developed for growing in this country.

This is an ideal vegetable to grow for your domestic deep freeze—either on or off the cob—but the flavour of freshly gathered sweet corn is best. Sweet corn is also a very graceful plant and may be used singly in annual borders or to form a summer screen.

Soil and fertilizer requirements

Sweet corn must be given as long a growing period as possible if good yields of high quality cobs are to be produced in Britain. This means early sowing or planting which, in turn, requires a well-drained, open-textured and fertile soil preferably on a

Sweet corn plant showing male (top) and female (below) inflorescences

sunny, sheltered site. Vegetative growth is considerable and must be rapid in order that plants are large enough to carry two good cobs each. This type of growth needs continually available supplies of water and fertilizer—particularly nitrogen—so incorporate well-rotted organic manure or compost during the winter and rake in 50 to 100g per m² (2 to 4oz per sq yd) of a base fertilizer before sowing or planting. If mid-season growth is slow then you may need to apply another 25 to 50g per m² (1 to 2oz per sq yd) of top-dressing fertilizer around the base of the plants and water it in well.

Plant raising

The best growth and earliest cobs come from planted crops which are raised from seed sown, in slight heat—10°–13°C/50°–55°F—about four weeks before the projected planting date. In southern England sow the seed in mid-April. This is another vegetable where pre-germinating or 'chitting' the seed makes for more successful plant raising. Place the seeds on constantly damp blotting paper or kitchen towel until the young roots appear and then immediately put them 1cm (½in) deep into potting compost in individual containers such as 9-cm (3½-in) pots. The plants grow rapidly and must be given full light and complete ventilation on warm days, so that they develop sturdily. They cannot be planted in the open until all danger of frost has passed, before which time the plants must have been thoroughly hardened off. Slightly earlier planting is possible if cloches/tunnels are available to protect the plants for the first two or three weeks. Seed can also be direct sown outside from mid-May onwards depending on districts. Sow 2 or 3 seeds 2 to 3cm (about 1in) deep at each station and thin out later if necessary. The required spacing is between 45 and 60cm (18 to 24in) square while, once again, earlier sowings and quicker emergence are possible if you cover the rows with cloches or tunnels. Sown and planted crops are often plagued by large birds—such as crows—which dig up the seeds or plants but are easily deterred by strands of black thread suspended and stretched above the rows.

Planting and crop management

Sweet corn is wind pollinated and the best cobs are obtained if plants are set out in blocks rather than in long, one-plant wide rows. Transplant at the spacings indicated and water the plants well afterwards. It is most important that sweet corn is never short of water or fertilizer and that no competition arises. Hoe the weeds out at least until the plants are 50 to 60cm (up to 2ft) tall. After that they will shade out any further weed growth. Hoeing must be done carefully since any damage to the main stem will induce the development of side stems, or 'tillers', which bear later cobs. 'Tassels' and 'silks' appear from mid-July onwards.

Harvesting

The very best results with sweet corn—like green peas—are only achieved if they are harvested at just the right stage, about 4 weeks after the 'silks' begin to wither. Peel away the protective leaves around the cob and press your thumb nail into one of the developing grains. The ideal time for harvesting is when the contents shoot out as a milky white fluid. At this stage the grains are at their sweetest but very rapidly become more starchy and floury. Use the corn immediately either for fresh consumption or for deep freezing as any storage delay—particularly in warm weather—will impair the flavour and texture. Twist the complete cobs from the plant. Don't expect to get more than two—often only one—per plant.

Pests and diseases

The problem of birds has been mentioned and the only other serious pest is the frit fly, which lays its eggs around the base of the young plants in June. The developing larvae tunnel into the main stem causing it to collapse. 'Tillering' is a frequent indication of frit fly damage.

Suitable cultivars

Many sweet corn cultivars are F1 hybrids and in no circumstances should seed be saved from them for next season's crop. 'Earli King': F1 hybrid; the earliest cultivar, good sized cobs. 'North Star': F1 hybrid; does well even in northern districts and wet seasons. 'Kelvedon Glory': F1 hybrid; vigorous grower; produces quality cobs. 'Northern Belle': F1 hybrid; reliable.

Above: Plants of sweet corn 'Kelvedon Glory' in midsummer, the tassels and silks well forward

Below: Each plant will produce one or perhaps two cobs, which are ready for harvesting in August

Stalks & Stems

This group of largely unrelated vegetables comes from various plant families and is grown for a number of culinary purposes. They range from the various kinds of spinach, which are grown for the leaves; to asparagus, which is grown for the young tender stems. Also included are Umbelliferous crops such as celery and florence fennel which are grown for their elongated and swollen petioles (the stalk attaching leaves to the stem) respectively. Rhubarb and Seakale are also grown for their long petioles, early crops of which can be obtained by forcing. Finally there are the leaf beets—including spinach or perpetual beet and the seakale beets or chards—which are grown for their leaves and, in the latter case, also for the sake of their petioles.

The culinary uses are just as varied. It is possible to have fresh spinach for cooking all through the year and large quantities are canned and frozen. Asparagus is processed in the same ways to extend the season when the fresh crop—available from early May until mid-June—is over. Fresh celery for salads and as a cooked vegetable can be produced from August until well into the winter while florence fennel is also used during the autumn and winter period. Rhubarb crowns can be forced in the winter to produce earlier sticks than from outside crops which are available from March until mid summer. Seakale is blanched to produce crisp, tender petioles—which are cooked like asparagus—during the winter and early spring. The leaf beets, which are cooked like spinach, can be sown in the spring for harvesting in summer and autumn, or in late summer for harvesting in the winter and spring.

Spinach

Spinacea oleracea annual spinach
Tetragonia expansa New Zealand spinach

Both these vegetables are grown for their edible leaves. Annual spinach is a hardy, quick-growing plant, the leaves of which contain large amounts of protein and Vitamin A. The rapid growth habit allows us to use this type of spinach as a catch crop between slower growing crops. There are two types of annual spinach: round-seeded and prickly-seeded. Round-seeded cultivars are sown in the spring and summer to produce continuous supplies throughout the summer. It was formerly thought that prickly-seeded cultivars were hardier and they were therefore sown in late summer to produce winter crops. This theory has now been disproved and both round and prickly seeded types are used in the winter period. By careful planning and crop management annual spinach can be picked all the year round.

New Zealand spinach is less hardy than the annual type and is a much larger plant—producing fleshy, triangular shaped leaves on branched, spreading stems which are 60 to 90cm (2 to 3ft) long. It provides good ground cover if watered freely.

Soil and fertilizer requirements

Summer crops of annual spinach prefer deep, rich, moisture-retentive soils. Double dig the spinach land and incorporate liberal amounts of well-rotted manure. The crop must be grown as quickly as possible in order to produce large succulent leaves, so dry, infertile soils must be avoided. Spinach runs to seed in hot summer weather so try to choose a cool, shaded site. Rake 100g per m^2 (4 oz per sq yd) of high nitrogen fertilizer into the seedbed just before sowing. Winter crops of spinach have similar requirements but a well-drained soil is vital and the site can be sunnier to give more winter protection. New Zealand spinach does best in hot summers so choose a site in full sun with a light, well-drained soil.

Seed sowing and crop management

Don't sow large quantities of summer spinach at one time unless it is for the freezer. It goes to seed very quickly. The first sowing should be made sometime in March—it depends on your location—to produce leaves for picking in May. Successive sowings made at fortnightly intervals until the

Left: A bed of New Zealand spinach with the typical triangular shaped leaves

end of June will allow picking to continue until October. Sow the seed thinly in 2-cm (1-in) deep drills spaced 30cm (12in) apart. Water the bottom of the drill before sowing in dry weather (some people even soak the seed for 24 hours before sowing). Thin the seedlings to 15cm (6in) apart to allow reasonable sized plants to develop and to prevent excessive moisture loss and hence also 'bolting'.

Winter spinach should be sown from early July until late September as for summer crops. In this case, however, growth rate and the danger of 'bolting' will be less so the seedlings can be thinned, if necessary, to 8 to 15cm (3 to 6in) apart. Leaves will be ready from October onwards but plants will need protecting against frost, either with cloches, polythene tunnels or thick wads of straw placed between the rows, from mid-November onwards.

New Zealand spinach is only half-hardy and should not be sown outside until the likelihood of frost has passed. Early plants can be produced, however, by sowing seeds individually into small 5-cm (2-in) pots in late March using a proprietary potting compost. Germinate them in a temperature of 14–15°C/57–60°F and gradually harden them off before planting outside in late May at 90cm × 60cm (3ft × 2ft). Sow maincrop New Zealand spinach outdoors in early May at the spacings indicated. Seeds have a very hard coat to soak them overnight before sowing. Pinch out the tips of the leading shoots to encourage lateral branching.

All spinach will respond to applications of water in dry weather while weeds must be controlled by regular hoeing.

Harvesting
Pick the leaves from summer spinach as soon as they are ready. Quite a lot can be taken from each plant at a time because replacement plant growth should be rapid. Only the largest leaves should be taken from winter and New Zealand spinach, however, otherwise—since replacement growth is

'Elsoms 24' is a widely grown, mildew-resistant spinach cultivar

much slower—harvesting is likely to be spasmodic.

Pests and diseases
Mangold fly larvae tunnel in the leaves of annual spinach as they do in beetroot. Aphids are a continual problem especially on summer crops. Cucumber mosaic causes a blight of spinach with leaves curling at the edges and then turning yellow before finally dying. Downy mildew is the worst disease of spinach and produces the typical yellow blotches on the top of the leaves accompanied by white fungal patches below. Leaf spot fungus causes grey-brown sunken areas to develop on leaves. These areas usually develop into holes in the leaves.

Suitable cultivars
'Long standing round': very quick growing summer cultivar. 'Greenmarket': winter hardy and heavy yielding. 'Mammoth long standing'*: excellent round seeded type. 'New Zealand': good in dry conditions.
* Indicates suitability for freezing.

Celery
Apium graveolens var. *dulce*

This more or less hardy biennial, which is grown as an annual, has developed from wild celery but has only been in cultivation in Britain for about 300 years. It is grown for the U-shaped, swollen petioles which are collected together in heads or 'sticks'. The usual maturity period for home-produced celery is from late summer until mid-winter and it can be used raw in salads, cooked slowly in butter as a separate vegetable or included in a variety of dishes and sauces as a flavouring agent. Celery seed is also used for flavouring purposes.

Two types of celery can be grown in this country. The traditional kind is 'trench' celery which is winter hardy and is grown in trenches to allow soil to be drawn up around the developing 'sticks' in order to blanch them. Cultivars with white petioles are most popular and pink and red types are also available but they mature later. Trench crops are ready to use from October onwards but earlier celery is obtained from 'self-blanching' cultivars. These do not need blanching and are grown on the flat. They are not frost hardy, however, and their season of maturity stretches from late July

Earthing up trench celery
I—First earthing required

Earthing up trench celery
II—Sticks completely earthed up

Hand thinning of spinach seedlings to the required spacing

Catch cropping of spinach on ridges adjoining a celery trench

until the onset of frosts. Blanching of the so-called self-blanching celeries is achieved by planting them close together in blocks and thus excluding the light. American Green celery has green petioles with a strong flavour and is also grown on the flat.

Soil and fertilizer requirements

Wild celery is a marsh plant so, not surprisingly, its derivatives grow best when well supplied with water. Rapid growth is particularly important for the self-blanching types if 'stringless' sticks are to be grown, but trench celery, too, prefers a fertile, free draining and yet moisture-retentive soil. Celery is one of the few crops which prefer slightly acid conditions but cloddy or stony soils must obviously be avoided if trench types are grown. Prepare the trenches in early spring by taking out the soil to a depth of 30cm (12in) in trenches 40cm (16in) wide. Leave a gap of 90cm (3ft) before the next trench. The soil you remove should be formed into neat flat-topped ridges, between the trenches, on which quick-growing catch crops such as radish, turnips and lettuce may be grown. Fork over the bottom of the trench and work in liberal amounts of well-rotted organic manure or compost. The land for self-blanching celery should also have organic material incorporated. Apply a base dressing of a general purpose fertilizer at the rate of 50 to 100g per m^2 (2 to 4 oz per sq yd) and take it in just before planting.

Plant raising

You may be able to buy plants but much more choice is possible if you raise them yourself. This preferably requires some kind of heated protection although later crops can be raised under cold frames or cloches. Sow the seed thinly in a seedpan/seedtray in the middle of March. Make sure you use seed which has been treated against the seed-borne celery leaf spot fungus. Do not cover the seed with compost after sowing but make sure that it never dries out during germination. A greenhouse temperature of 18°C/65°F is ideal but, if nowhere else is available, you can use the windowsill provided the seedlings can be given enough light subsequently. Prick out the seedlings into other seedtrays or individual containers after about 5 weeks allowing them between 9 and 25 cm^2 (3 and 10 sq in) each. Keep the temperature in the range 15–18°C/60–65°F so that the celery will be ready, after a few days hardening off in a cold frame, for planting in late May or early June.

An open-ground sowing cannot be made until early April and even that should be into soil which has been warmed by a cloche or frame beforehand. Broadcast the seed thinly and water it in. Growth will be very slow and seedlings could easily be smothered by weeds unless these are removed at an early stage.

Transplanting and crop management

Celery plants are ready for planting when they are 10 to 12cm (4 to 5in) tall. Plant firmly but carefully and always water generously afterwards. Rapid establishment

Above: Harvested heads of celery 'Lathom's Self-Blanching', a reliable cultivar

Right: Celery grown in trenches is frost-hardy and is available throughout the winter

is very important. Trench celery plants should be spaced 25cm (10in) apart in a single row down the middle of the trench, while self-blanching types should be planted in a block with 25cm (10in) between the plants in each direction. The important factors of crop management are watering, feeding, hoeing, pest and disease control and, for trench celery, earthing up. Self-blanching types must be grown very rapidly so regular waterings and a top dressing of 50g per m^2 (2 oz per sq yd) of nitro-chalk—given in early to mid-July—are vital. It should not be necessary to top dress the trench celery. Regular hoeing carefully around the plants will keep weeds down. Earthing up involves the gradual replacement of the soil from the ridges back into the trenches and around the developing plants. Light will be kept away from the sticks and the mature petioles should be crisp and tender. The first earthing up should be done when the plants are 30 to 40cm (12 to 16in) tall, and soil should be drawn half way up the sticks. Choose a day when the soil is dry and put a loose tie round the tops of the sticks to prevent soil getting into the heart. Two more earthings will be needed at three-weekly intervals so that, finally, only the tops of the leaves are protruding. The soil must slope away from the celery plants so that water is carried away and is not allowed to run into the hearts.

Harvesting

Self-blanching celery will be ready from the end of July onwards while trench celery is dug up, as required, during the autumn and winter months.

Pests and diseases

Carrot fly larvae may attack celery, causing damage to roots and petioles (cf. carrots) while celery fly larvae tunnel in the leaves, making irregular shaped blisters. Slugs may get into the sticks of celery during earthing up and feed there until lifting time, so scatter slug pellets around the celery plants before each earthing. Celery leaf spot disease is seed borne and infected plants develop brown spots (on leaves and petioles) which can cause defoliation in warm, damp seasons. Spray with Bordeaux mixture from August onwards. Damping-off is a seedling problem but boron deficiency causes yellowing of the leaves and brown cracks in the petioles. The centres of trench celery, particularly, may rot after earthing up due to heart rot disease if badly constructed trenches have allowed water to enter.

Suitable cultivars
Self-blanching
'Golden self-blanching': the earliest celery to mature in summer. 'American Green': green stalks of superb flavour.
Trenching types
'Giant White': one of the earlier winter types; good flavour. 'Prizetaker': also good for exhibition purposes. 'Giant Pink': very heavy sticks with delicate colour. 'Giant Red': the hardiest winter type; dark red.

Florence fennel

Foeniculum vulgare var. *dulce* (Finnochio)

The swollen leaf bases, for which this plant is cultivated, look rather like bulbs. It originates in Italy where the warm, sunny climate allows much more certain growth than in this country. We also grow this perennial plant as an annual and it resembles common fennel (*Foeniculum vulgare*) in general appearance but is somewhat smaller

—only growing to 60cm (2ft). Florence fennel has a mild, sweet, aniseed flavour and has a range of culinary uses. The leaf bases can be sliced and used raw in salads or the whole 'bulb' can be cooked either in soups and stews or served alone with a butter sauce. After using the leaf bases you can use the leaves of Florence fennel for flavouring in the same way as the common form.

Soil and fertilizer requirements
Florence fennel will grow on any reasonably fertile garden soil which is well-drained but the best results are obtained on light, sandy soils in a sunny position. The stem bases are blanched by earthing them up, so an easily worked, stone-free soil is essential. Rapid growth is required before the leaf bases begin to swell and this will be encouraged by incorporating a base dressing of 25 to 50g per m^2 (1 to 2 oz per sq yd) of a general fertilizer before sowing.

Seed sowing
Sow the seed thinly in 1-cm ($\frac{1}{2}$-in) deep drills during April. Leave 45cm (18in) between rows and thin the seedlings to 25 to 30cm (10 to 12in) apart in the rows as soon as possible.

Crop management
Water liberally in dry weather to encourage vegetative growth at the beginning of the season. Keep weeds under control by regular

The swollen 'bulbs' of Florence Fennel are blanched to improve the flavour

The attractive leaves of Florence Fennel can be used as a garnish

hoeing. When the stem bases begin to swell they must be blanched. This can either be done by putting paper collars round the 'bulbs'—and holding them on with rubber bands—or by slightly earthing the plants up with soil.

Harvesting
Use the plants as required during the late summer and autumn, once the 'bulbs' have swollen. Harvest by cutting the plant just below the swollen leaf bases.

Pests and diseases
There are no particular problems besetting the cultivation of this crop.

Suitable cultivars
No named varieties.

Rhubarb

Rheum rhaponticum

The exact origin of this fleshy rooted perennial is not clear but it appears to have arrived in Britain sometime in the late 1700s. It is cultivated for the long, fleshy petioles which are usually red but sometimes green. The earliest supplies come from crops which are forced in heated sheds or houses in the winter months. For this purpose the roots are lifted and, after exposure to frost to break their dormancy, taken inside where they are kept in the dark. Forced rhubarb petioles are much paler than those from outside while the leaves are yellow and insignificant. Outdoor forcing is also possible by covering the plants in December with tubs

Above: Dustbins may be used to cover rhubarb in order to get earlier crops

Below: Rhubarb is one of the most attractive plants in the vegetable garden

or boxes which contain straw or leaves. Rhubarb from open ground crops is available, according to the cultivar, from February until mid-summer. Large quantities are grown for processing—particularly canning. Although the petioles of rhubarb are eaten the leaves are poisonous since they contain oxalic acid. For culinary purposes rhubarb is treated like a fruit, being stewed with sugar or used in pies and preserves.

Soil and fertilizer requirements

Like most perennial crops, rhubarb occupies the ground for several seasons and it is likely to be between 5 and 10 years from planting to lifting and dividing the crowns. You will therefore need to make thorough preparations, by incorporating organic manure or compost deeply, and removing all perennial

weeds carefully. Any ordinary garden soil will do but if you want really early crops then choose a light soil in full sun.

Propagation

It is possible to raise rhubarb from seed but it takes several years before cropping begins. The best method is to propagate the plants vegetatively by division. Large, healthy and actively growing roots are lifted in the autumn and cut up into 'sets' with a sharp knife. Make sure that there is at least one bud to each piece of root. Always choose true-to-type and desirable plants as your source of propagation material. If you do not have existing roots to divide then material can be bought from a reliable stockist or obtained from friends. When you are lifting rhubarb make certain that all the roots are

removed—otherwise growth will continue the following year.

Planting

Plant the 'sets' firmly in November or March. Allow a metre (about a yard) between plants in each direction and bury the crown just below the soil surface. Never let the newly planted crowns dry out during the establishment period.

Crop management

Remove weeds from amongst the plants and cut off flowering stems as they develop. Top dress with 50 to 75g per m² (2 to 3 oz per sq yd) of a general purpose fertilizer if growth seems slow and weak. Remove dead leaves and stalks and fork round the plants in the autumn. At this time organic manure or compost can be dug in.

Forcing

Rhubarb can be forced *in situ* by covering the crowns with straw-filled (or other suitable material) tubs or boxes in December. The best results are obtained if early maturing cultivars are used. Treatment in this way should produce sticks for pulling in February. If crowns are covered for much of the winter then they should not be forced in the following year. Really early rhubarb can be produced by simulating the forcing shed conditions used in Yorkshire. Roots are lifted in the autumn and left on the soil surface until they have been frosted several times to break their dormancy. They are then taken into heated sheds where they are planted either in the soil or in boxes. After a thorough watering the crowns are then forced into growth—in absolute darkness—at temperatures varying from 13°–18°C/ 55°–65°F. Regular watering is necessary and the forced rhubarb is ready for pulling, at the higher temperature, in about 4 weeks. Home forcing should follow the same pattern but smaller containers will be used for the crowns. If tubs, pots or boxes are used then it should be possible to provide absolute darkness by inverting a similar sized container over the top. After forcing in this way the crowns will be exhausted and should be thrown away.

Harvesting

Do not pull rhubarb from newly planted sets in the first year and be moderate in your demands in the second. Sticks are harvested by removing them from the plant with a twisting, pulling action—gripping the petiole close to the crown. Always leave a reasonable number of sticks on each plant in order that food reserves can be replenished.

Pests and diseases

Rhubarb is relatively trouble free but stem eelworm causes reduced vigour and bacterial crown rot causes plants to die from the centre outwards. Crowns showing signs of this disease should be destroyed. Leaves frequently develop those spots and blotches which are typical virus symptoms.

Suitable cultivars

'Timperley Early': several strains exist—some very early. 'Victoria'. 'Prince Albert'.

Seakale
Crambe maritima

This Cruciferous perennial is a British native which is grown for the petioles which, after blanching, are white and succulent; unblanched they have a bitter taste. It is, sadly, little grown today in comparison with its former popularity.

The principle of cultivation is to grow a good, strong crown which can then be forced in the winter and spring in the open or in heated sheds or houses, to produce the 12 to 20-cm (5 to 8-in) long blanched leaf-stalks. Seakale is boiled like asparagus and has a crisp, nutty flavour.

Soil and fertilizer requirements
The pre-planting preparations for seakale should be similar to those made for rhubarb. Well-drained, sandy loams are best, however, if the crowns are to be lifted in the winter for indoor forcing. This crop does not like acid soils so liming may be necessary but this will also help to reduce the likelihood of club root attack.

Propagation
Like rhubarb, seakale can be propagated from seed but it takes at least two years before forcing-sized crowns are produced. Seedling variation also occurs and not all plants are identically suited to forcing. It is better, therefore, to propagate the crop vegetatively either by division of existing

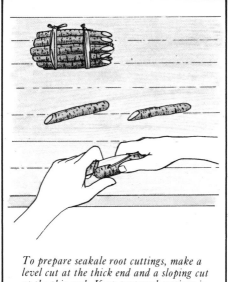

To prepare seakale root cuttings, make a level cut at the thick end and a sloping cut at the thin end. Keep prepared cuttings in bundles.

crowns or by root cuttings (thongs). Buy crowns from a reliable stockist or from a known source. Root cuttings are taken from the main root mass when it is lifted for forcing. Pieces of lateral root which are 0.5cm (¼in) thick and 15cm (6in) long are ideal for this purpose. Trim the end which was nearest the crown with a horizontal cut and the other end with a slope. Bundle the cuttings together and heel them in under a cold frame during the winter. By the spring

a number of adventitious buds will have formed on the flat tops of the cuttings. Remove all but the strongest before planting. One year is needed before the crowns will be large enough to force.

Planting and crop management
Grow seakale at a spacing of 60cm × 60cm (2ft square) and plant the divided crowns or root cuttings about 5cm (2in) below the soil surface. The management of seakale during the vegetative growth stages is, once again, very like that of rhubarb. Weed control; flower stem removal; watering (where necessary); top dressing and mulching are all required if strong crowns are to be built up.

Forcing
This, too, is similar to rhubarb and can be done either *in situ* or in heated buildings. In the former method pots or boxes are placed over the seakale crowns in late winter. Light must be excluded and the temperature inside can be raised by covering the forcing container with fermenting organic manure. For forcing inside the roots must not be lifted until they have received about a month of cold weather to meet the dormancy-breaking requirement. This means that the first forcing will not begin until late November. Lift and trim the roots sufficiently for 2 or 3 to fit into a reasonable sized tub or box. Work compost around the roots and settle them in with a thorough watering. Stand the containers in a heated shed or greenhouse with a temperature of 10°–13°C/50°–55°F. Much higher temperatures cause thin, weak petioles to develop. Cover the containers with tubs, pots, boxes or black polythene to exclude all light. Water as needed. More roots should be lifted and brought inside for forcing until February. Forcing will take up to 6 weeks—at the temperatures mentioned—for the earliest liftings but considerably less time in the spring. Roots which have been forced inside are of no further use and should be thrown away. Complete destruction is difficult as they are so easily propagated from root cuttings. Crowns which have been forced *in situ* should be cleaned up, mulched and top dressed through the next growing season ready for forcing again next year. Strong, healthy crowns may be forced for at least five consecutive seasons.

Harvesting
Cut the blanched petioles when they are 15 to 20cm (6 to 8in) long.

Pests and diseases
Pests are rarely a problem but club root—the same fungus which attacks brassicas—can cause problems especially on acid soils. The presence of violet root rot is indicated by purple fungal threads on the roots while black rot causes the centre of the crowns to rot thus making them useless for forcing.

Suitable cultivars
There are no named varieties of seakale.

Left: The stems of seakale are blanched in order to provide their distinctive flavour

Leaf beets

Beta vulgaris Spinach beet; Seakale beet or Chard

Both spinach beet and seakale beet belong to the same family as garden beetroots. Spinach beet is sometimes called perpetual spinach and is grown for the leaves which, along with the green petioles, are eaten whole for the spinach-like flavour. This crop is said to tolerate temperature fluctuations better than annual spinach. Seakale beet or Chard is very similar but has wide, flat petioles which are white in the case of Swiss Chard and red in Ruby Chard. For culinary purposes the leaves and petioles of seakale beets can be used as separate vegetables when the leaf-stalks of Swiss Chard can be substituted for seakale itself. The leaves of spinach and seakale beets have a milder flavour than those of true spinach.

Soil and fertilizer requirements
Any well-drained, fertile garden soil is suitable for leaf beets. They should be given similar fertilizers to annual spinach to encourage succulent leaf growth. In other respects their requirements are similar to those of beetroot.

Seed sowing and crop management
Leaf beets can either be sown in the spring—for harvesting in the summer or autumn—or in late summer for harvesting in winter and early spring. The best results are obtained from spring sown crops. Sow the seed thinly in 1-cm ($\frac{1}{2}$-in) deep drills during April. Leave 40cm (16in) between rows and thin the seedlings to 20cm (8in) apart when they are large enough. Weed control is particularly necessary during the early stages of these crops and regular watering is very useful in hot, dry summers.

Harvesting
Cut the entire leaves—petioles and leaf blades—from the plants as they become ready. Regular harvesting encourages more leaves to develop.

Pests and diseases
Similar problems to those found on spinach are likely to be encountered.

Suitable cultivars
Use the foliage of 'Swiss Chard' as spinach and the petioles as seakale. 'Ruby Chard' is useful as a vegetable and as an ornamental plant. 'Perpetual spinach' is an excellent substitute for annual spinach.

Above left: The wide, flat petioles of Ruby Chard have a nutty taste

Above: Seakale Beet, or Swiss Chard, has white stalks and spinach-like leaves

Asparagus

Asparagus officinale

Garden asparagus has been derived from the wild plant of the same name and is recorded as a cultivated plant in Britain from the early seventeenth century. It is a hardy perennial which is grown for the young, tender shoots or 'spears' which are cut when they are 15 to 25cm (6 to 10in) long. These green shoots have either a green or, more usually, a purple tip and a white base where the light has been excluded by the soil. Asparagus, when grown traditionally, is blanched. Soil from the pathways is continually thrown over the developing shoots to produce a long tender white area at the base. This is laborious and, more recently, crops have been grown 'on the flat'.

Asparagus beds can have a productive life lasting many years provided they are managed correctly and grown on a suitable site.

Asparagus is not difficult to grow if you follow the recommendations and the rewards are great. The 'spears' are ready for cutting from late April until mid-June. They are tied in bundles and then cooked standing upright in a little boiling water or steamed and served with melted butter. It is quite suitable for freezing as long as over-mature 'spears' are not used.

Soil and fertilizer requirements
Pre-planting preparations for asparagus, as for all other perennial vegetables, must be thorough since the crop will, it is to be hoped, be with you for up to 40 years. Deep digging and incorporation of well-rotted organic manure or compost are essential in the autumn before planting and, at the same time, all traces of perennial weed must be removed. The ideal soil is a light, easily worked and well-drained loam but heavier soils can be used if they are lightened before planting—by adding peat or compost—and used with the raised bed system of culture. Quite a large area of asparagus bed will be needed to meet the requirements of an average family so careful planning is necessary to determine if, and where, it is to be sited. Apply a general purpose fertilizer at 100g per m² (4 oz per sq yd) and rake it in during the final pre-planting preparations in the spring.

Plant raising
Asparagus can either be started from seed—which is a cheap method but takes 2 or 3 years before crops can be harvested—or from 1 to 4-year-old crowns which is more expensive but less time consuming and more instantly rewarding. Leave plants raised from seed in the seedbed for 2 years—during which time the less productive female, fruit-bearing plants should be rogued out—before the young crowns are transferred to the permanent bed. Sow the black seeds, from the red berries, thinly during April in a well prepared seedbed. Drills should be 1.5 to 2cm (about $\frac{3}{4}$in) deep and 30cm (12in) apart. The young seedlings will need plenty of room if they are to develop into strong crowns so thin them to 30cm (12in) apart in the rows. Weeding, watering in dry periods and top dressing with a general purpose fertilizer will all encourage leaf growth which will, in turn, lead to the

production of well developed crowns.

Asparagus crowns are available from a number of stockists. A uniform bed will be established more quickly from one-year rather than older material. You may get a number of female plants, which are less productive than males, but they can be rogued out later if their performance is poor.

Planting

If you grow asparagus 'on the flat' no earthing up will be needed but the 'spears' will have very little blanching. Plant the crowns 40cm (16in) apart in single rows with 60-cm (2-ft) pathways between rows. On heavy soils raised beds should be made before planting. Make them 15 to 30cm (6 to 12in) high and

The fern stage of the asparagus bed is an attractive feature of the kitchen garden

45cm (18in) wide by taking soil from the pathway areas. Again, leave 60-cm (2-ft) wide pathways between raised beds. Asparagus is then grown on the flat tops of these beds without further earthing. Earthing up asparagus—in order to produce blanched stems—is possible on light, easily worked soils and crowns should then be planted in double rows. Space the two rows 60cm (2ft) apart and leave a 1.5-metre (5-ft) path before the next double row. Once again the crowns should be 40cm (16in) apart within the rows. Plant the crowns so that the tops are 5 to 10cm (2 to 4in) below the soil surface. Make the holes large enough to take all the roots when they are spread out and work loose soil around them during planting. Leave a slightly ridged surface over the crowns to prevent water settling into their centres. Do not expose the thick, fleshy asparagus roots for too long at planting time or they may dry out. Plant in March or early April when the soil can be easily worked.

Crop management

Weed control is very important but particularly if you grow asparagus 'on the flat'. Cultivations prior to and during earthing up will help to keep down weeds but when soil is not put over the plants the weeds must be pulled out by hand. Damage can be caused to emerging 'spears' if hoeing is done before harvesting finishes. Apply a top dressing of a general purpose fertilizer at 50g per m² (2 oz per sq yd) in the spring before growth is obvious. Begin earthing up blanched crops as soon as the shoots appear through the ground. Cultivate the soil in the pathways and carefully build up vertical-sided beds over the double rows. The beds should be 1.25 metres (4ft) wide and earthing up should allow 25-cm (10-in) long 'spears' to be harvested.

Left : The richly coloured tips of asparagus 'Connover's Colossal'

Leave the shoots that emerge last to develop into the 1 to 1.5-metre (up to 5-ft) tall branched stems of fern. These produce the plant food which goes to build up the strength of the crowns. Pieces of fern can be used in decoration and flower arranging provided not too much is removed. Draw away the soil from the earthed-up plants at the end of the season and cut back the stems, when they turn yellow, to within 2cm (¾in) of ground level. Apply a mulch of rotted organic manure or compost in autumn.

Harvesting

Newly planted beds should only be sparingly cropped in the first year but once they are fully established—after 2 or 3 years— cutting can continue from late April until mid-June. Cut the 'spears' from flat beds when they are 15 to 20cm (6 to 8in) tall. Use a sharp knife and cut 5 to 7cm (about 3in) below the soil surface taking care not to damage the crown or other 'spears'. Earthed-up crops are more difficult to harvest since the knife must be pushed in from the side of the bed. The tip of the 'spear' will just be visible through the top of the bed. Hold this with the fingers of one hand while carefully pushing the knife with the other. You will feel the 'spear' move when you touch it with the knife and it can then be cut—about 25cm (10in) from the tip. Be very careful not to cut other— concealed—developing 'spears'. A very sensitive touch is required! Stop cutting in mid-June to allow sufficient vegetative growth during the rest of the summer.

Pests and diseases

Adult and larval forms of the asparagus beetle feed on developing shoots and emerged foliage. The beetles have a black cross on an orange background on the back. Violet root rot fungus produces the tell-tale purple threads on the roots.

Suitable cultivars

'Perfection', 'Connovers' Colossal' and 'K.F.B.' are long established cultivars while 'Purple Argenteuil' is the traditional French asparagus. 'White Cap' is an early cultivar with a white, rather than purple, tip.

Trench for asparagus growing, 30 cm (12 m) wide and 20 cm (8 in) deep, with a slightly mounded bottom

Plant the crowns on the mounded bed 40 cm (16 in) apart and cover with soil

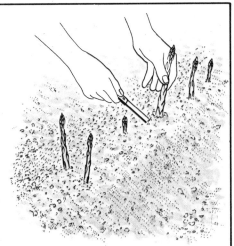

Cut the spears below the surface of the soil with a sharp knife

There are many wild edible fungi but the true mushroom is more commonly grown as a commercial crop. The common, or wild mushroom—*Psalliota campestris*—has an underground network of hyphae (mycelium) from which the familiar fruiting bodies (mushrooms) arise. During late August and September they appear in established grassland particularly during damp but bright autumnal weather. When the 'buttons' first appear the spore-bearing gills are covered by a white membrane which ruptures as the cap grows into the 'cup' stage. The gills are then pinkish in colour but quickly become dark brown as the mushrooms flatten out into the more flavoursome 'flats'.

The commercial production of cultivated mushrooms is a highly automated and clinical factory process.

Mushroom growing on a small scale is frequently more difficult because of the problems of preparing a suitable compost and maintaining the correct growing environment. Composting is the most critical factor but a draught-free, dry and even-temperatured growing area is also needed for year round production. Mushrooms develop spasmodically at temperatures below 9°C/48°F and above 20°C/68°F so a constant level within the range of 10°–15°C/50°–60°F should be sought. Sheds, glasshouses, frames, garages and cellars could all be suitable if the necessary environment can be provided. Mushrooms do not have to be grown in the dark but direct sunlight should be avoided since this causes violent temperature fluctuations. You can now buy containers of compost and spawn ready for casing. These are very convenient for home production.

Compost requirements and preparation

The composting process is designed to produce a medium which is ideally suited for growing mushrooms only. The raw material—preferably strawy manure—is inhabited, and could be colonized, by a wide range of organisms but the aerobic breakdown process known as composting must kill most of them and leave a material which has the optimum texture, degradation and nutrient content to produce mushrooms. Ideally the process should begin with horse manure made from wheat straw although other materials may be used. Chemical activators are available which, when watered on to dry wheat straw, initiate a suitable composting process.

On mushroom farms composting takes place in open-ended barns. The manure is built into a long stack about 2 metres (6ft 6in) high and 1.5 metres (5ft) wide. Over two or three weeks the stack is turned, aerated and watered so that fermentation takes place. During composting the stack may be turned four or five times with the decomposing manure being fully mixed on each occasion. The temperature inside the stack frequently reaches 60°–70°C/140°–160°F and ammonia gas is given off along with steam. Greasiness is avoided by a routine application of ground gypsum. By the end of the process the manure is much reduced in volume. The finished compost should have a dark, rich brown colour with a pleasant smell without ammonia. The straw should be non-greasy, short and easily broken. The overall texture must be spongy. It should feel wet but water should not pour out if squeezed.

Small-scale composting must produce similar material. It is more convenient to pile the manure in a pyramid-shaped stack, built on a solid base isolated from the soil so that disease contamination cannot occur. Choose a site well away from the house in order to avoid the ammoniacal smell and, if possible, erect a cover to keep off the wetting rain and drying wind and sun. Turn the stack regularly—every 5 or 6 days—always making sure that the manure is thoroughly moved from top to bottom and from inside to outside. Water any dry compost and break up any solid lumps of strawy material. After about four weeks the compost will be ready for spawning.

In commerce the composing process is followed by a week of peak heating. The temperature of the compost is evenly raised to 60°C/140°F thus ensuring that fermentation is completed and that better yields result. As few amateur growers will have the facilities to peak heat the compost should it be completely prepared in the stack.

Spawning

Mushroom spawn is propagation material and consists of grain or manure on which mushroom mycelium has grown. When composting has finished the final material can either be made into beds—which are built in glasshouses, frames or even outside during the summer—or put into boxes which can then be stacked in a garage, shed or cellar for subsequent growth and cropping. Beds should be 20 to 25cm (8 to 10in) high, flat-topped and approximately 60cm (2ft) wide. Boxes should be of a similar depth and preferably have raised corner posts to allow them to be stacked. Put the

compost loosely into the beds or boxes and then lightly firm the surface before giving a gentle watering.

Do not introduce the spawn into the compost until the temperature falls to 24°C/75°F in the centre of the bed/box. Break the manure spawn into walnut-sized pieces and push them 2 to 3cm (about an inch) down into the compost at a spacing of 25 to 30cm (10 to 12in) apart each way

before firming the compost back round the spawn. Grain spawn is sprinkled on the surface at the rate recommended and gently worked evenly into the top 5 to 7cm (2 to 3in) of the beds/boxes. Spawn running—the spread of mycelium through the compost—can be seen after 7 days and should be complete after 2 weeks.

Casing

The casing layer is the covering which is spread on top of the compost, when spawn-running is complete to a depth of about 5cm (2in). The most easily standardized casing material is a 50:50 mixture of peat and lump chalk or limestone (dust to 0.5cm). Wet the peat thoroughly before mixing but apply the casing when damp, not soaking wet. Casing serves a number of functions which greatly increase productivity. Always keep the layer moist since mushrooms do not develop on a dry surface. A reduction in temperature follows the watering of the casing layer and this stimulates fruiting as will constant dampness which lowers the concentration of soluble salts in the compost.

Crop managment

After casing, keep the temperature at 18°C/65°F. When the pinhead mushrooms appear reduce it to 15°C/60°F. Mushrooms develop best at high humidities but adequate ventilation is also needed. Spray the walls and floors with water if the relative humidity is likely to fall below 70 per cent. Air movement is necessary to remove waste gases and to dry the mushrooms after watering since prolonged dampness increases the disease risk. Apply water as a fine spray so that the casing layer remains moist down as far as the compost which should only be just damp. Watering will have to be increased when cropping begins but it is better to give a little water frequently rather than to overwater the beds or boxes. A number of factors influence the time taken to produce a crop of mushrooms but at

Harvest crops of mushrooms at the 'button' stage to encourage growth

10°C/65°F it will take approximately 3 weeks from casing until the appearance of the first pinhead mushrooms which will then require a further week before they are ready for picking. Development is considerably slower at even slightly lower temperatures. Mushrooms are produced in 'flushes' over a 6 to 7 week period after which more compost must be spawned and brought into cropping.

Harvesting

Twist the mushrooms gently from the surface making sure that all the stalk comes away cleanly. Fill in the holes with fresh casing material to ensure that the crop remains productive over a long period. Remove all damaged mushrooms or broken pieces as they form ideal infection points. Regular picking increases the likelihood of continuous cropping.

When all the mushrooms have been picked from a bed or box remove the spent compost. Attempts to re-use it will almost certainly introduce pests and diseases. It is, however, very useful as a garden conditioner but keep it well away from fresh composting.

Pests and diseases

Pathogens can often cause a marked reduction, or even complete failure, in the growth and cropping of mushrooms. This is particularly true when they are grown on a small scale with little or no experience of the likely problems. Virus diseases cause browning of the mycelium and rotting of the crops. A number of fungal diseases cause distortion and discoloration. Flies and midges are the most important pests. The larvae tunnel in the stalk, cap and gills of the fruiting bodies. Sciarid flies (fungus gnats) and cecid midges (gall gnats) attack at any time but phorid flies (manure flies) are more common in the summer. Maintenance of hygienic pest- and disease-free conditions is more important in mushroom growing than in almost any other type of crop production.

Suitable cultivars

Distinct cultivars are not available but most seedsmen stock a good, reliable strain (race) of the cultivated mushroom.

Left: To prepare suitable compost out of doors, use a structure with a solid floor, open sides to admit air, and a roof to protect the stack of manure from getting wet. Rain will run off the sloping roof which should be 2 m (6 ft) high at the back and 1.5 m (5 ft) at the front

Pack the prepared compost into wooden boxes with corner posts so that they can be stacked one on top of the other.

Right: Put in evenly spaced lumps of spawn about the size of a golf ball and cover with casing material. Moisten the casing and keep it constantly moist.

Far right: 'Button' mushrooms will appear in flushes about 3 or 4 weeks later over a period lasting 6 to 7 weeks. Pick regularly to ensure maximum productivity

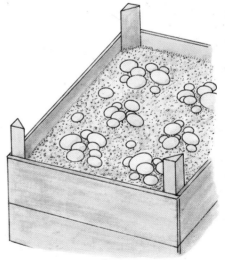

Potatoes

This perennial herb which belongs to the plant family Solanaceae is one of the most important food plants of the world, and is grown for the edible tubers which are formed as swellings on the tips of rhizomes or underground stems. The potato which we grow today—*Solanum tuberosum*—originates from the Andes region of South America where related plants have been grown for food for over 2000 years. The exact route by which the wild potato—*Solanum andigenum*—reached Britain is not known but it is clear that the Spanish explorers brought it to Europe in the 1570s. Contrary to popular legend it seems unlikely that either Sir Francis Drake or Sir Walter Raleigh brought the plant home from the Americas but rather that it came with a traveller from Europe. Whoever was responsible, it is known that the potato had arrived in both Britain and Ireland by the late 1580s. Plant

Right: A typical yield from a single plant of the maincrop potato 'Majestic'

'Epicure' is a first early potato which produces irregular shaped tubers

breeding and selection since those early days have produced the smooth-skinned, shallow-eyed and heavy cropping cultivars that we grow today.

When they were first introduced it was the Irish who began to cultivate potatoes as a staple food crop. It did not become an important part of the Englishman's diet until 150 years later. The Irish potato famine of 1845, caused by a devastating attack of the potato blight fungus, indicated the extent to which working-class people in particular came to depend on potatoes in the mid-nineteenth century.

Since that time the area of potatoes grown in Britain has shown considerable fluctua-

tions—tending to peak at times of national crisis and economic depression. Today there are over 200,000 hectares (500,000 acres) grown for a wide range of outlets. Fresh consumption accounts for the greatest proportion either direct from the field—as with early cultivars—or from store—as with second early or main-crop cultivars. Potatoes are also processed into crisps, flour and dried mashed potato while small, tender tubers are canned whole and large quantities of maincrop cultivars are made into frozen chips. Considerable quantities are also fed to livestock but the proportion of the crop used in this way tends to be influenced by human consumption demands upon the market.

The importance of the potato, as a crop which is primarily grown commercially by large-scale arable farmers, is reflected in the development of modern cultivars. They need to be disease-resistant and able to produce heavy crops of well-shaped, storable tubers which can be mechanically harvested. Cultivars are still classified according to their time of maturity and so first earlies are harvested sometime in the period June to August while the foliage is still green. Second earlies are ready in August or early September with maincrop cultivars being harvested in September/ October and making up the bulk of the stored crop. Potatoes may also be referred to by the colour of the skin and while the

'whites', and to a lesser extent the 'reds', are best known there are also 'blues', 'mauves', 'russets', 'creams' and 'pinks'. The potato is a half-hardy plant, the foliage and the tubers being easily damaged by frost. The exact time of planting in the spring must, therefore, be carefully chosen to ensure that new growth is not retarded. It is also important to lift the tubers before they are frosted in the autumn and to store them under frost-free conditions.

If you are to be self-sufficient for potatoes from your garden you will have to accept that a considerable amount of space will be needed. In the recent past the tendency has been for people to grow their own early crops but, because of their relative cheapness, to buy maincrop supplies as required. Any change from this pattern must be accompanied by a plan which indicates your annual requirement for potatoes—then you can begin to see just how much of your garden will be needed! Self-sufficiency can, of course, bring its own satisfaction—both personal and economic—and we should remember, therefore, that home production of potatoes will allow you to grow a wider range of cultivars, each with its own particular quality and flavour; and that garden cultivation usually gives a higher yield of tubers than farm-scale production—always assuming that you follow the rules.

Soil and fertilizer requirements

To get a good yield of reasonable sized tubers

88

you will need initially to provide your potatoes with sufficient mineral nutrients, a freely drained—yet moisture retentive—growing medium and soil conditions which permit unhindered root growth and tuber development. Many soils will provide these conditions but heavy clays will need their texture lightening by the addition of peat or organic compost and by doing the preparatory cultivations well in advance of planting. This crop does not like very alkaline soils and is one of the few which prefer slightly acid to neutral conditions. Even if your soil is well suited for potatoes you must also choose the correct site in your garden. Avoid shaded areas but consider where you can provide the most protection against frost. Remember that if frost kills off the young foliage in the spring there will be a 2 to 3-week setback to the growing crop while more shoots come up from below ground. If potato cyst eelworm has been a problem recently you must avoid those sites which are infected. Deeply cultivated soils allow roots and rhizomes—and hence tubers—to develop more fully so double dig your potato ground in the

Above: Potatoes may occupy as much as a third of your vegetable garden

Below: The tubers of 'Maris Peer' are resistant to wart disease

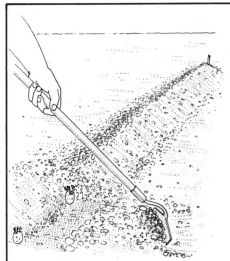

Plant 'chitted' tubers of maincrop varieties 40 cm (16 in) apart in 15-cm (6-in) deep trenches

Use a hoe to cover the rows with a slight mound of earth

autumn. Incorporate organic manure or well-rotted garden compost liberally into the lower spit, using up to 100kg per 10 m² (1¾ cwt per 10 sq yds). Leave the top surface as roughly dug as possible overwinter to allow a natural tilth to develop. In the final preparations before planting, work in a general purpose, well-balanced fertilizer at the rate of 100 to 150g per m² (4 to 6 oz per sq yd). Avoid giving excessive nitrogen or there may be too much vegetative growth and not enough tubers. Apply the fertilizer evenly so that it gradually becomes available to the roots as the plants are earthed up.

'*Chitting' and planting*
Potatoes are propagated vegetatively by tubers saved from the previous season's crop. Tubers with a diameter of 4 to 6cm (1½ to 2½in) are ideal and are called 'seed' potatoes

although, of course, they are not true seeds. When potato plants are infected with virus diseases they produce low yields of poor quality tubers. If these are then used as the propagation material for next year's crop then it, too, will be infected. 'Seed' potatoes are, therefore, grown in areas, such as Scotland, where aphids—which are the carriers of the viruses—are less common. After vigorous inspection the plants are certified as virus-free and you will be well advised always to buy Certified potato 'seed'. You will be able to buy 'seed' from January onwards, but to be certain of delivery, it may be necessary to place an order with your seedsman beforehand.

Initial growth and also final yield of early potatoes are improved if the tubers are started into growth—'chitted' or 'sprouted'

—before planting. Tubers are modified stems and as such have buds or 'eyes' from which growth begins. The tubers have more 'eyes' on the end opposite to the point of attachment to the parent plant. This is called the rose end and tubers for 'chitting' should be placed close together, rose end upwards, in slatted-bottom trays which are then put into a light and frost-free—but unheated—place such as a greenhouse. Only use firm, sound tubers for 'chitting' which can start in late January or early February in order to produce 'seed' with strong, sturdy shoots for planting in March or early April. Some people remove all but two of the shoots from each tuber at planting time. This will certainly allow you to grow larger—yet fewer—potatoes but it is not a very common practice. Second early and maincrop 'seed' is not usually 'chitted'.

The earliest potatoes are likely to come from the earliest plantings but remember the danger of frosts! The time of planting will also depend on the state of the ground but in protected areas of the country, such as the south and west, early and second early crops will be planted sometime in March. In later and more exposed parts you should delay planting these types until the middle of April. Maincrop potatoes should be planted at the end of April. Have some straw ready to scatter over any emerged shoots in the event of a frost forecast.

There are several possible planting methods for potatoes but the easiest is to put the tubers in 15-cm (6-in) deep trenches which have been drawn out with a 15-cm (6-in) wide hoe. Be careful not to knock the shoots of 'chitted' tubers. Rake the soil back over the tubers after planting and leave the surface slightly mounded over each row. Earlies and second earlies are planted 30cm (12in) apart in the rows which are themselves 60cm (2ft) apart, while for maincrop varieties the distances should be 40cm (16in) and 75cm (30in) respectively.

Crop management

When the potato shoots are 15cm (6in) tall they can be ridged up for the first time. Loosen the soil between the rows with a fork and then draw it up around the plants with a hoe so that the sloping ridges meet near the top of the plants. Further ridging should be done at 3-week intervals until the potato foliage is touching. Covering the young stems with soil is beneficial since it encourages rhizome—and hence tuber—development. The soil cultivations, which are done before ridging, greatly help weed control and also improve drainage, particularly on heavy soils. The potato plant is highly responsive to watering in dry seasons especially at certain stages of growth. Early potatoes respond particularly well—producing heavier crops if they are watered once the small tubers are 1 to 2cm ($\frac{1}{2}$ to $\frac{3}{4}$in) in diameter. Watering before this stage can actually reduce the yield. Avoid watering late in the season, once the tuber skin has hardened, since regrowth—and subsequent splitting—is likely to occur.

Keep a close lookout for pests and diseases during the growing season. Aphids (green-fly) cause distortion of the foliage and may spread viruses from infected plants. An equally important pest is potato cyst eelworm which lives in the soil and attacks potato roots forming the characteristic yellow/brown minute cysts. Symptoms on the foliage include yellowing, wilting and, ultimately, death but the confirmatory cysts only form on the roots and it is in these cysts that the eelworms remain for several years in the soil until the next potato crop is planted. Long rotations are obviously needed on infected land. Potato blight is the most important disease causing damage to the foliage and also, as spores are washed into the soil, to the tubers. The tell-tale symptoms are brown fungal blotches on the leaves which spread particularly rapidly in wet, humid conditions. The first signs of attack are usually seen in July and, unless it is controlled, blight can reduce the potential yield by half. Protectant sprays of fungicide should be applied on every occasion—after the beginning of July—that wet, humid conditions last for more than two days. Spray all the foliage and stems thoroughly so that all surfaces are protected.

Hoe between the rows before earthing up

Ridging up plants with a draw hoe

Above: The heavy cropping 'Craigs Royal' bulks quickly for early lifting

Below: 'Pentland Crown' tubers are quite large and of good cooking quality

Harvesting and storage

Earlies, and to a lesser extent second earlies also, are ready to lift when most of the tubers are as large as hen's eggs. The yield of early potatoes increases rapidly through June and July—perhaps by as much as 100g (4 oz) per plant per week—so don't lift the potatoes until you really need them. Maincrop potatoes, harvested in September or October, will be easier to dig if the haulm (foliage) is removed about 3 weeks before. This also reduces the risk of disease spreading from the foliage to the tubers. Carefully dig up the potatoes using a flat tined fork which is less likely to damage the tubers. In warm, dry weather the tubers can be dried before storage. Any diseased or damaged potatoes should, if possible, be used immediately or thrown away. Only healthy tubers can be satisfactorily stored. Potatoes from an average sized garden are best stored in boxes, trays or sacks in a dark, frost-free place. Dark is essential to prevent the tubers developing green areas containing poisonous

'Red King Edward' has the same well-proven features as the white form

alkaloids which make them inedible. Larger quantities of potatoes can be stored in outdoor clamps. For maincrops you should expect 3kg of 'seed' to produce 50kg of crop (7lb produces 1cwt). Inspect the stored tubers monthly. Remove rotting tubers and rub off developing 'sprouts'.

Alternative growing systems

Very early crops of potatoes can be produced by growing plants in containers in a heated greenhouse. Plant two or 3 'chitted' tubers of an early cultivar 7 to 10cm (3 to 4in) deep in a 25 to 30-cm (10 to 12-in) pot containing a fairly rich potting compost. Water the pots well. Keep them in a temperature of 6–7°C/43–45°F at first and then at 10–13°C/50°–55°F. Water and feed as necessary. Harvest the crop when the tubers are large enough.

Another method is to plant—as described for outdoor potatoes—under unheated protection. In frames particularly you will have to cover the glass on frosty nights.

Potatoes can also be grown 'on the flat' without ridging, in which case the most convenient method is to grow them through black polythene. 'Chitted' seed is planted—

exactly as for outdoor early crops—and slightly mounded over. The rows are then completely covered with a sheet of black polythene which is secured by burying the edges in a slit trench. When the shoots appear make a cross-wise slit in the polythene and bring them up into the light. Tubers are formed under the sheet.

Pests and diseases

Aphids, eelworm and potato blight have been discussed already. There are a number of other problems both of the growing plants and the stored tubers. The best known pest—but thankfully the least common in this country—is colorado beetle. If you should ever discover this pest, report it to the police immediately. Blackleg of potatoes is, as the name suggests, a disease which causes blackening of the stem. In June/July the leaves turn yellow and collapse and the typical black stem develops at ground level. Infected tubers should not be stored. Leaf roll and various types of mosaic are the most common virus diseases and are aphid transmitted.

Tubers are often damaged by chewing pests just before lifting when secondary rotting organisms can then attack. Wireworms, millipedes, cutworms and slugs are the main culprits. The three major diseases which attack the skins of tubers are common scab, powdery scab and skin spot. They are unsightly but do not spread during storage. Wart disease causes brown or black outgrowths near the 'eyes' of tubers and some cultivars are particularly susceptible. Various rots can attack potato tubers in store and, unless the infected ones are removed, the diseases spread very quickly. Dry rots enter through wounds, bruises or other diseased areas. Common dry rot and gangrene are the most common forms. Wet rots are more obvious because the infected flesh becomes soft and putrid. The rot caused by blackleg spreads rapidly but the rotten tissue does not smell whereas watery wound rot and bacterial soft rot both cause an evil smelling breakdown.

Suitable cultivars
First earlies

'Arran Pilot' crops and keeps well. 'Epicure': irregular shaped tubers; store well. 'Sutton's Foremost': heavy crops in late July. 'Home Guard': best in moist areas. 'Sharpe's Express': good on medium-heavy land. 'Ulster Chieftain': very early.

Second earlies

'Catriona': purple eyes; crops heavily. 'Craig's Royal': creamy flesh; good in heavy soils. 'Maris Peer': smooth skinned. 'Pentland Dell': good quality tubers.

Maincrops

'Arran Banner': good on poor soils. 'King Edward': excellent results on fertile soil. 'Majestic': crops well; good for chips. 'Golden Wonder': floury flesh; russet skin; bakes well. 'Pentland Crown': vigorous and heavy cropper. 'Desiree': red skin; good quality and high yielding.

Unusual Vegetables

Many vegetables deserve wider attention than they currently receive in Britain. Our climate is perfectly suitable for crops such as kohl rabi, Chinese cabbage, mustard and cress, watercress and Jerusalem artichoke but globe artichoke and cardoon may need some protection while cape gooseberry and soy bean need a really warm, sunny season.

Foreign travel allows people to try out new and exciting flavours in vastly different climates, and they are rightly encouraged to try their hand with some of the vegetables when they get home. Remember that many of the everyday, commonplace vegetables now grown were once unusual or grown for other than culinary purposes when first introduced to Britain. Pest and disease control is often less necessary on these crops because they have not yet been grown sufficiently widely for problems of rotations, pathogen resistance and chemical residues to have arisen.

Kohl rabi
Brassica oleracea var. *gongyloides*

This vegetable is sometimes called the 'turnip-rooted cabbage'. It is a biennial grown as an annual for the swollen stem (not the root) which is produced just above ground level. Leaves are borne on the swollen stem and, after cooking, it has a flavour similar to turnips for which it is a possible substitute.

Soil and fertilizer requirements
Well drained, fertile soils are needed to ensure that the plants grow rapidly. Since it is only in the ground for a relatively short time, kohl rabi can be grown as a catch crop between rows of peas and beans or root crops such as carrots or beetroot.

Plant raising and subsequent growth
Sow seed thinly in 1-cm ($\frac{1}{2}$-in) deep drills taken out 30cm (12in) apart. Sowings should

Above: Kohl rabi 'Purple Vienna' has delicately flavoured white flesh

Below: Pick stems of 'Early White Vienna' when young for the best in flavour

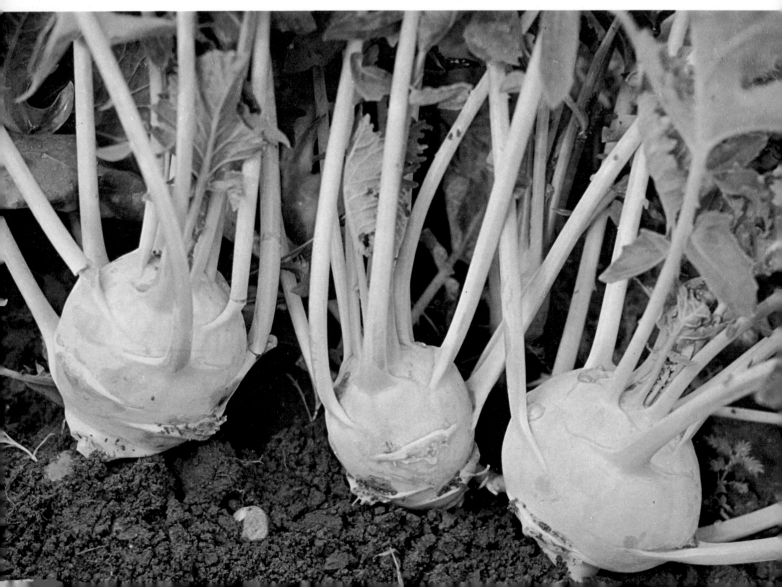

begin in April and continue through the summer until mid-July. Thin the seedlings to 15cm (6in) apart in the rows and grow the plants rapidly to be certain of crisp, tender flesh. The stems will be ready to harvest about 10 to 12 weeks after sowing.

Harvesting

Kohl rabi is ready for harvesting when the stems are about the size of a cricket ball 5 to 7cm (up to 3in) in diameter. Do not allow them to grow larger or the flavour will deteriorate. They will withstand light frosts but are damaged by anything too severe so the season cannot be guaranteed after mid-November. They do not store well.

Suitable cultivars

'Early White Vienna': swollen stems like pale green turnips. 'Early Purple Vienna': white fleshed; more delicately flavoured.

Chinese Cabbage
Brassica cernua

Chinese cabbage, or Pe-Tsai, has more resemblance to a large cos lettuce than to a true cabbage. The crisp, crunchy leaves may be cooked like 'greens' or they may be used in salads. As the name suggests it is also used in a variety of Chinese dishes.

Crop management

This crop is likely to run to seed unless care is taken to choose the correct sowing date. Avoid transplanting and be certain that plants are never short of water.

Sow the seed outside from mid-May onwards for successional cuttings. Drills should be 30 to 45cm (12 to 18in) apart with plants thinned to 30cm (about 12in) apart when large enough. Keep well watered to produce the lush, tender 'hearts' which are ready for cutting from mid-July onwards. Chinese cabbage is not winter hardy in the United Kingdom.

Below: Chinese cabbage is a useful 'dual-purpose' vegetable as good raw as cooked

Suitable cultivars

'Nagaoka 50 days': F1 hybrid; tight, uniform heads. 'Sampan': F1 hybrid; less likely to 'bolt' than other varieties.

Cresses and mustard

This group of cruciferous salad plants contains watercress and land cress—which are grown into the mature state before harvesting—and mustard and cress, which are used as seedlings. The methods of growing the different plants are so dissimilar that they will be considered separately.

Watercress
Nasturtium officinale

This British native plant grows wild in ditches and streams but is also cultivated on a commercial scale. It has a distinctive mustard-like flavour and is eaten raw as a salad vegetable or used for decoration with other dishes. Watercress is a more or less hardy perennial of which two forms are grown. The green-leaved type is easier to establish but is frost susceptible while the bronze or winter watercress is hardier.

Production

The best environment for this plant is in an uncontaminated stream of gently running water. It is important to ensure that sewage or detergent do not pollute the watercourse. Watercress is easily propagated from young shoots—in fact purchased material will frequently develop roots within a few days if stood in a jar of water. Rooted cuttings 10cm (4in) long should be planted into the banks and bottom of the stream at 15-cm (6-in) intervals. Growth will be rapid and cutting should begin after about 6 months of active growth. Watercress can be grown in the absence of running water provided a constantly moist environment is maintained. Choose a shaded site and prepare a trench

Watercress in a stream bed
Stakes support the turves on either side of the stream while clear water runs around the plants

which is 15cm (6in) deep and 40cm (16in) wide and thoroughly soak it before planting rooted cuttings as before. Keep the trench regularly watered to sustain the plants. Never allow the plants to flower as this reduces vegetative growth. Small-scale production is possible in sub-irrigated pots and sunken sinks while winter supplies can be maintained by covering soil or water beds with cloches, polythene tunnels or frames.

American or Land cress
Barbarea verna

An uncommon biennial salad plant which we grow as an annual for the watercress-like leaves. When plants are protected by cloches, frames or polythene tunnels they produce useful supplies of winter cress.

Production

From mid-March onwards sow seed thinly in drills which are 1cm ($\frac{1}{2}$in) deep and 30cm (12in) apart. After emergence thin the plants to 15cm (6in) apart. Sowings made in spring and summer will be ready in 8 to 10 weeks. Protect late summer sowings with cloches or polythene during the winter.

Mustard and cress
Sinapis alba and Lepidium sativum

This should more accurately be called rape and cress since white mustard (*Sinapis alba*) is usually replaced by the greener, longer-standing and better flavoured rape (*Brassica napus*). Curled and plain cress cultivars are available. These annual plants are grown into seedlings which are then cropped at 5cm (2in) long for use in salads and sandwiches. It is possible to have year round production if a minimum temperature of 10°C/50°F can be maintained. There are one or two specialist mustard and cress nurseries which produce all this country's requirements.

Production

Mustard and cress is very easy to grow at home on the windowsill. Cover the bottoms of shallow plastic dishes with blotting paper or kitchen towel and give them a thorough watering. Cress takes between 2 and 3 weeks to reach maturity and requires 3 or 4 days longer than mustard/rape.

Sow the containers of cress first and the companion containers a few days later. Weekly sowings are necessary to ensure continuous supplies. Scatter the seed thickly on the damp pads and keep in the dark—in an airing cupboard or under black polythene—until germination takes place. Then keep the containers in full light and well watered until the seedlings are ready for cutting.

Pests and diseases

None of the cresses are particularly prone to pest and disease attack.

Globe artichoke

Cynara scolymus

This herbaceous perennial, which is more or less winter hardy in Britain, is grown for the young flower heads which are made up of a number of scales with fleshy bases. It is extremely popular in France and large areas are grown in Britanny but, although the plant has been in this country since the fifteenth century, we grow very few. The fleshy receptacle or 'heart' of the flower head is also eaten in the same way as the scales while young leaf stalks can be blanched in the same way as cardoons (q.v.) for use in the autumn.

The globe artichoke is a member of the daisy family. Since it grows to a height of 1.5 metres (5ft) each year it requires a considerable amount of space. It is, however, another dual-purpose plant with ornamental foliage and an attractive flower.

Soil and fertilizer requirements

Like all perennial plants globe artichoke must be grown on well prepared, manured and weed-free land. Complete winter hardiness can only be expected in sheltered districts—hence the importance of the coastal regions of Brittany—and on light, well-drained soils. Some plants will rot during the winter when grown on wet, heavy soils. This is not a long-lived perennial—the productivity falls off after 4 or 5 years—so regular soil improvement is possible. The plants should be top-dressed each spring with 50 to 100g per m² (2 to 4 oz per sq yd) of general purpose fertilizer.

Plant raising and planting

Globe artichokes can be raised from seed but, as with rhubarb, the resultant plants will be unpredictably variable. Vegetative propagation from offsets is the best method of raising new plants. Cut off the 15 to 20-cm (6 to 8-in) long shoots with a sharp knife from selected, true-to-type parent plants either in March or in October. Spring-taken offsets are immediately planted into their final positions at 75-cm (30-in) square spacings but autumn-taken offsets are potted into 9-cm (3½-in) pots and kept in a cold frame until the following spring when they are also planted as indicated. Firm planting and care during establishment are essential. One fifth or a quarter of the globe artichoke bed should be taken up and replaced with young plants each year so a regular propagation programme must be followed.

Crop management

Remove any over-wintered protectant material just as growth begins in the spring and fork in the top-dressing fertilizer. Rapid growth is necessary if tender, succulent 'chokes' are to be produced. Water may be needed in dry years while straw or grass cutting mulches will restrict weed growth. Tidy up the plants by cutting out dead, unwanted material when growth has died down in the autumn. In all but the most sheltered coastal and south-western districts

Above: These young flower heads of globe artichokes are ready for harvesting

Left: Globe artichokes have ornamental foliage and an attractive habit of growth

the plants must be protected with a straw covering during the winter.

Harvesting

Heads will be ready for cutting from mid-summer onwards. Cut the terminal ('king') heads first. Newly planted offsets will often produce a few heads in the first year but productivity should build up in the next three years. The terminal buds will have the largest heads but the later maturing lateral buds are also very tender. Harvesting at an early stage is imperative in order to get the best possible flavour and ensure continued cropping.

Pests and diseases

Few attack this crop.

Suitable cultivars

Named cultivars are not commonly available in Britain but offsets should always be purchased from a reliable nurseryman. 'Gros Camus de Bretagne' and 'Gros Camus d'Angers' are two widely grown and popular French cultivars.

Cardoon

Cynara cardunculus

The cardoon is a close relative of the globe artichoke which it resembles in habit and appearance. It is rarely grown in Britain but Southern European countries consider it a worthwhile vegetable. It is grown for the leaf-stalks and mid-ribs which are blanched in the same way as celery. The culinary uses are the same as celery but the flavour is much more bitter. As cardoon stems are prickly, wear thick gloves when handling them.

Soil and fertilizer requirements

The soil types which are suitable for celery are also satisfactory for cardoons but this crop takes up a great deal more space.

Plant raising and planting

Cardoons are grown in trenches and may either be direct sown in late April or raised under heated protection and transplanted at the end of May. Trenches should be 45cm (18in) wide and 30cm (12in) deep with well-rotted organic manure or compost dug into the bottom. Sow three or four seeds in groups at 50-cm (20-in) intervals down the middle of the trench and later thin out all but one. A more reliable method is to direct sow seeds into 9-cm (3½-in) pots in a heated greenhouse — 13–18°C/55–65°F — during March. Harden off the plants before setting them out in the trench at 50-cm (20-in) intervals in late May.

Crop management

Very little attention is needed during the summer apart from watering if necessary and hoeing out any weeds. Any flower heads which appear during the season should be removed and eaten like globe artichokes. Earthing up begins when the plants are fully grown in mid-September. Cut out any dead or yellow leaves and, during a dry spell, tie up the tops of the plants. Wrap paper around the 'sticks' and earth up in the same way as for celery.

Harvesting

The plants will be blanched in four weeks from earthing up but will be damaged by severe winter frosts. Remove the soil from around the plants as required.

Jerusalem artichoke

Helianthus tuberosus

This hardy perennial which is started afresh each year is more closely related to the Sunflower than to the globe artichoke. It is grown for the underground tubers which are whitish in colour and club-like with knobbly protrusions. They have a delicate flavour—the food material in the tubers is inulin—and are either cooked as a separate vegetable or used in soups and stews.

The plants grow vigorously—2.5 metres (8ft) high in a season is not unusual—and make very good summer screens for un-sightly garden features.

Soil and fertilizer requirements

Jerusalem artichokes can be grown on even the poorest soils. They are likely to produce excessive vegetation if grown on very fertile soils or if heavily manured and fed. Any aspect will suit them but take note of their potential height since by midsummer they will shade the adjacent crops.

Planting and crop management

Save some small tubers from the previous crop as the new propagation material. Plant them in early spring 40cm (16in) apart in rows which are 1 metre (3ft) apart. It is best to plant the tubers with a trowel in 15-cm (6-in) deep holes. The plants will require little attention but in exposed positions support them with posts and wires.

Harvesting

Leave the tubers in the ground over winter and lift as needed. The plant tops will die down in the autumn and the tubers are unlikely to be damaged by frost. Lift even the smallest tubers however, otherwise they will come up again the following year.

Pests and diseases

Very few problems are likely to occur.

Suitable cultivars

There are white and purple-skinned cultivars both of which have white flesh.

Jerusalem artichokes form a useful screen and produce underground tubers

Cape gooseberry

Physalis peruviana

This South American perennial plant is a member of the Potato family and closely related to the ground cherry (*P. pruinosa*) and the tomatillo or jamberry (*P. ixocarpa*). They are all grown for the fruits which are formed within a brown, papery, lantern-like husk. The fruits of Cape gooseberry are 2cm (¾in) in diameter and used in sauces and preserves. Another related species is *Physalis alkekengi*—the familiar Chinese Lantern plant.

Cape gooseberries are marginal plants in the British climate although they should succeed in southern districts. Better results will be obtained if the plants are grown under glass. Sow the seed during March in a temperature of 18–21°C/65–70°F. Prick out the individual seedlings into 20-cm (8-in) pots and grow them, under protection, during the summer in the same way as sweet peppers. In warm seasons the pots may be stood outside on paths or patios where they make a very attractive feature. Harvest the fully ripened fruits in September.

The fruits of Cape gooseberry are used in sauces and preserves

Soybean

Soja max

This is a very important legume which cannot always be successfully grown in Britain because of our variable summers. It is frost susceptible and needs warm, dry weather to produce a reasonable crop of the seeds for which the plants are grown. There are many types available, although, in this country, it is best to grow one of the dwarf cultivars which can be treated exactly like dwarf french beans. Leave the pods to ripen on the plant.

The dried beans are used like haricots but have a higher protein content. They do however, need good weather in late summer or early autumn to dry the seed thoroughly. Soybeans are sometimes used to produce the bean-shoots and rich brown soy sauce is of Chinese cookery fame.

The Herb Garden

Herbs are the oldest known cultivated plants. They have been grown for domestic use probably as long as man has been in existence, first for soothing and healing wounds and sickness, later to give more and better flavour to food and then for their fragrance and cosmetic virtues.

A herb is a plant which is aromatic in one or more of its parts; it may be woody or herbaceous, and it will have one or more of the three properties already mentioned, medicinal, culinary or cosmetic. The Greeks and Romans were great connoisseurs and used herbs profusely for all three purposes; rosemary, lavender and sweet bay were particularly popular. Garlic has an even earlier history, as it is said to have been fed to the slaves who built the Egyptian pyramids. In Britain, herbs were mostly used in medicine, from pre-Roman times, through the Dark Ages to the medieval period, when they were cultivated by the monks, and flourishing herb gardens were maintained on monastery land.

With the accession of the Tudors to the throne, life became more peaceful and the European Renaissance produced fundamental upheavals in thought and outlook. Innovations were tried throughout everyday life as well, and the new plants and foods introduced by explorers suggested experiments with flavourings, and so with herbs. No respectable Elizabethan herb garden had less than 50 different kinds of herbs and they continued to be extremely popular until the late nineteenth century.

From then until the last ten years or so, however, they gradually became less and less popular, in all respects. Today, more highly flavoured food is preferred, and although much modern food is preserved, either tinned, dried, frozen or treated with preservatives, and unavoidably loses some flavour, herbs can augment what remains. There is, too, a swing to 'natural' foods and medicines, as the disadvantages of the synthetically produced kinds become apparent. Herbs are some of the most rewarding plants to grow and a study of them becomes a fascinating hobby when you discover the extraordinary legends and history which are associated with them. They are easily cultivated, and their care will take up little time.

Most newcomers to herb-growing start with the kinds used in cooking, and the big five—parsley, chives, mint, thyme and rosemary—make a good introduction, being particularly easily grown, and amenable to most situations. Somewhere close to the kitchen is the most obvious place, either in a small bed, or in containers; they can even be grown indoors in the kitchen, if there is a window facing the sun, which thyme and rosemary especially appreciate.

If you become really hooked on herb cultivation, you can go in for squirrel-collecting of as many different kinds as possible. Or you can concentrate on one group, such as the culinary, the medicinal, or the fragrant and aromatic. There is the purely botanical herb garden which specializes in the *Labiatae* for instance, a plant family containing a great number of herbs. The *Umbelliferae* is another herbal family, and the Daisy plants (*Compositae*) contribute a good many also.

If you have an eye for the appearance of things, you might like to try laying out a herb garden to your own design. Herbs look best in a formal setting, with clearly defined beds and paths to give precision to their rather fluffy habits of growth. Paving, bricks, flagstones, or gravel are good surfaces for the paths; herbs themselves can also be used to cover the paths, for instance chamomile, or creeping thyme. Sundials, stone seats, and statues all help to enhance the atmosphere of age and antiquity, especially if the herb garden has a stone or brick wall to back it or surround it.

You might like to reproduce the design of the Elizabethan knot garden; authentic patterns are available, and it is possible to grow the herbs the Elizabethans grew, so that the garden is one in which Elizabeth I herself would be at home.

Before you start planting your herbs, look round the garden and decide which part is the most suitable. It is no good relegating them to an odd corner, simply because they are a handy little group of plants which will fill it nicely. Such corners are usually odd because they are dark, dry, wet, too acid, draughty, full of stones or very chalky. Herbs do not ask for a great deal, but if you give them their few requirements, the rewards will be out of all proportion. A good many are Mediterranean natives, so like plenty of sun; for the same reason they are used to growing in well-drained soil in which plant foods are rather on the short side. They prefer shelter from cold winds, and the perennials will often want protection from intense cold in winter. Some do best in moist soils, with some shade. You will find the needs of each specified in the individual descriptions which follow.

A bed or small border close to the house makes life easier for the cook if you are growing culinary kinds; otherwise they can be put wherever the site fulfils the above conditions. As well as forming a garden on their own, they can be perfectly well mixed into an herbaceous border, used as edgings for a mixed border or on the rock garden, or inter-planted with the vegetables. Streamsides and bog gardens are not generally suitable, however, but herbs do lend themselves well to container growing, especially useful if you are short of space. Being portable they can then be put in exactly the right places.

Herbs can be bought as young plants by ordering them from specialist nurseries, or buying in pots from garden centres ready for immediate planting. Some are easily grown from seed and the annuals will need to be grown every year. Wherever you plant, clean up the soil so that it is completely free of weeds. Bindweed, couch-grass and ground-elder are particular pests, because of their tough, extensive persistent roots, but annual weeds growing from seed can be just as much of a nuisance. Incidentally, ground-elder was in fact a much used medicinal herb, for curing gout and rheumatic troubles, brought over by the Romans, and found in every monastery garden.

Get rid of all the large stones unless the soil is heavy; if you have to use a wet soil, mix some coarse sand into it at 3kg per m^2 (7lb per sq yd), and work chalk or gypsum into a clay soil to break it down. Dig the soil in early winter to a spade's depth, and in early spring mix a dressing of rotted garden compost or similar material into the top few inches at 4kg per m^2 (9lb per sq yd).

Choose a day for planting when the soil is moist and rain is forecast, and the weather is mild. Plant firmly and water in; and continue to water regularly if rain does not occur. Make sure that you give the plants enough room upwards and sideways; crowded plants are weak plants. Care through the rest of the spring, summer and autumn will consist of hoeing out any weeds, watering in times of drought, and, with most species, removing the flowers, if you do not want to keep them for seed.

Herbs carry their own built-in resistance to pests and diseases so routine spraying will not be needed, though a few species are afflicted with a particular condition, such as rust on mints, and scale insects infesting sweet bay. Greenfly may attack in hot summers, but they should not be a serious problem if the plants are watered well.

In autumn, the perennials will need cutting back, though some die down underground of their own accord, e.g. chives. In winter cloche or frame protection will probably be necessary for some, and early in spring each year, repeat the light dressing of organic matter.

If you prefer, or are forced, to grow in containers, this is by no means a drawback, but do give them sufficiently large containers. Chives and parsley in particular tend to be crammed into too small pots, and each of these species really needs a 15-cm (6-in) pot if it is to have enough root room and produce a worthwhile top. For most other herbs, 10cm (4in) is the smallest pot size.

Plastic or clay pots, wooden boxes, polystyrene troughs—it does not matter what the container is made of, provided it is not glazed and there are holes for drainage of surplus soil water. The soil in which the plants are grown can be a potting compost of the John Innes type, containing loam, coarse sand and granulated peat in the proportion 7, 3 and 2 respectively with the addition of 112g (4oz) compound fertilizer per bushel of the mixture. For herbs, an extra 2 parts of sand are a good idea, to give them the drainage they like. (In 9 cases out of 10, soil straight out of the garden will not give good results with container-growing, and you will be much more pleased with your plants if you use the proper potting or container compost.)

When you plant, put some pieces of clay pot in the base of the box or clay pot (not plastic pots), add a little compost, and then put the plant centrally on this and fill in firmly with compost round it. Water it in and then do not water again until the surface shows dry, when sufficient water should be given to fill up the 2–4cm ($\frac{3}{4}$–$1\frac{1}{2}$in) space you should have left at the top of the pot when potting. Overwatering is the quickest way to kill herbs in containers, and if in doubt, keep them slightly dry rather than risk overwatering. Repotting is done in spring each year, renewing the compost each time, and dividing the plants if necessary.

Once your herbs are growing well and producing plenty of leaf, you will be able to preserve those that are annual or those which, though perennial, die down in winter. You will then have a supply of flavours for cooking through the year, regardless of the season, and a supply of those herbs used for fragrance, cosmetics and minor ills, but do remember that professional medical advice should be obtained even when a complaint is only suspected of being more than minor.

The part of herbs generally used is the foliage; they contain the maximum of their essential oil just before the majority of the flowers are fully open. Flowers are harvested just before most of them have completely unfolded, and seed is ready when it is about to fall naturally. Choose a warm, dry day and do the gathering in the morning as soon as the dew has dried. Keep each herb

separate, and lay the leaves or flowers in single layers on flat cardboard boxes without lids, or trays of muslin pinned to a wooden framework, or hang them by the stalks in small bunches tied to coat hangers.

Put them in well-ventilated but not draughty, warm, dark places, such as the airing cupboard, clothes-drying cabinet, plate-warming compartment of the stove or a darkened part of the greenhouse—the temperature should be about 21°C (70°F). The plant needs to be dehydrated slowly, gently and evenly, and will take between 7 and 21 days. Leaves should be brittle but not turn to powder when handled; stems should break cleanly—if they bend, they are not quite dry. Roots should be brittle right through. Once they are dry, chop or rub as required, throw away chaff and other unwanted material, and store in airtight, opaque containers, labelling the containers as you fill them.

If you want to increase your herbs, for your own use to renew your stock or to give to friends, this is easily done. Division is a method common to many perennials, for instance the mints, chives, thyme, bergamot, lemon balm, and pot marjoram. Division is usually done in spring, just as the plants are beginning to grow again. The plant is dug up, separated into sections,

which will probably be obvious—don't worry if it means breaking and tearing the roots—and each replanted. Use the outside sections from a clump as these will be the youngest and strongest.

Seed is used for all the annuals, and some of the perennials, generally sown in spring, though some are better if sown as soon as ripe, in late summer. You can sow them broadcast, or in drills (shallow furrows) in a seed-bed, prepared as detailed for vegetables. Take care not to sow more deeply than advised, and sow in April or early May, or even in March if the garden is really sheltered and warm.

Some herbs such as rosemary, lavender and bay, in fact the shrubby herbs, are grown from cuttings and these are taken in summer, using the tip of half-ripe new shoots, about 10cm (4in) long. Make the cut just below a leaf or pair of leaves, strip off the bottom leaves, and put the cuttings in cutting compost, three or four evenly spaced cuttings to a 8.5-cm ($3\frac{1}{2}$-in) pot. Cover with a blown-up clear plastic bag, secured round the pot rim with a rubber band, and put in a warm, shaded place until rooted, and lengthening.

Below: The traditionally designed herb garden at Hall Place in Kent

Angelica
(Angelica archangelica) Umbelliferae

A very tall perennial, up to 2.4m (8ft) tall and 90cm (3ft) wide; it dies after flowering and may only live 3 or 4 years, but is usually cultivated as a biennial. Flowering is July–August. It is native to northern and central Europe and has naturalized in Britain.

The parts mainly used are the leaf and flower stems, gathered in April and May for drying or crystallizing; the leaves can be used for tisanes or for pot-pourri. The oil in the seeds is expressed for adding to Benedictine liqueur. All parts of the plant are aromatic, even the root, with a flavour suggestive of juniper berries.

Angelica was introduced into England in 1568 and is said to have been named after the Archangel Michael; alternatively it may have been named because it blooms on the day of Michael the Archangel, and is therefore a specific against witches, spells and the evil eye.

Cultivation is easy, provided the soil is moist and on the heavy side, and the position lightly shaded. It is hardy. Supports may be needed for the flowering stems; watch for leaf-mining caterpillars and remove affected leaves as soon as seen. Small plants are put in during spring; seed should be sown as soon as ripe in late summer, as it loses its viability quickly. Alternatively, established plants can be allowed to sow themselves.

Balm
(Melissa officinalis) Labiatae

Also known as Lemon Balm and Bee Balm, this is a bushy plant, 75cm (2½ft) tall by 60cm (2ft) wide, perennial but dying down every winter. The creamy white flowers are tiny and appear from June to October. There is a variety with yellow-variegated leaves, less tall, but more ornamental.

The leaves have a strong lemon fragrance when bruised or crushed, though this is less obvious when used in cooking, so you can be generous with the quantities. They make a good substitute for lemon peel and are especially good in milk puddings and summer drinks, and are also very popular for pot-pourri and perfumery. The flowers contain a lot of nectar, hence the attraction for bees.

A native of the Middle East, the leaves were considered to be a certain cure for the bites of venomous beasts and the stings of scorpions. During the eighteenth century it was grown for sale in market gardens round London.

Balm is one of the easiest herbs to grow. Plants are put in in spring, in any reasonable soil, in a sunny or shady place, and increased by division in spring or autumn. Remove the flowers to encourage leaf production.

Basil
(Ocimum basilicum) Labiatae

Sweet basil grows to 60–90cm (2–3ft) tall and 30cm (1ft) wide, and is a tender annual in Britain, though a perennial in its native India. It is bushy, with light green leaves and has tiny white flowers in August. Bush basil, *O. minimum* 15–30cm (6–12in) tall, is good for growing in pots and can be kept through the winter.

The strongly and distinctively flavoured leaves are excellent with tomatoes, sausages, veal, salads and mushrooms using, however, only a very small quantity at a time. They are also used extensively in Italian dishes, and in India for curries. The oil is a constituent of perfume, and medicinally basil is said to be a help in curing headaches and migraine. Sweet basil was introduced in 1573, and it became the custom then, amongst country people, to take a pot as a gift when visiting, rather like the modern fashion of taking flowers for one's hostess. It seems to have been equally disliked and liked since Greek and Roman times; Culpeper (1616–1654) said that: 'This is the herb which all authors are together by the ears about.'

Sow seed in late March in a pot or box and a temperature of 13–16°C (55–60°F); it will germinate in about two weeks. The seed coat turns bright blue when moist. Space the seed well out, and then plant out in early June, disturbing the roots as little as possible, after hardening off. Space the plants 20cm (8in) apart. Otherwise sow thinly outdoors in May, and protect with cloches until frost is unlikely. Be sure to plant in well-drained soil, with shelter from wind and plenty of sun. Take out the stem tips to prevent flowering, and water at midday during hot dry weather. For pot growth in winter, cut the plants down to about 5cm (2in) in early September, and pot in good potting compost.

Bay

(Laurus nobilis) Lauraceae

The bay, or sweet bay as it is also called, forms a shrub-like evergreen tree, 10cm (30ft) or more tall in its native Mediterranean region, but usually about 4.5m (15ft) in sheltered parts of Britain. The leathery leaves are smooth-edged, and small yellow, feathery flowers come in clusters in early May. It withstands clipping well, and is a good plant for formal training, and container cultivation, when it can be trained into a pyramid, or a round-headed standard.

The leaves are used fresh or dried, in casseroles of all kinds; half a leaf is sufficient for the average size casserole because the flavour is strong.

Bay is an ancient plant, its leaves being the ones used for the crowns of the Olympic athletes in the Greek Games. It was also used for crowning poets, hence the term poet laureate, and for many years was used to decorate the home at Christmas, along with other evergreens.

Good soil or compost, drainage and sun are essential, also shelter from cold winds. Bay will die quickly in a wet soil, so be careful when watering in containers. Plant in spring, and protect in bad frosts; clip if required, in spring, or autumn. Watch for brown scale insects on the undersides of the leaves, and on stems, and scrape off if present. Increase by taking short ripe cuttings of new shoots in late summer, giving bottom heat to the pots.

Bergamot

(Monarda didyma) Labiatae

A hardy perennial which dies down to the crown in autumn, it is highly ornamental, producing scarlet flowers in June. Height is 30–60cm (1–2ft) and width 30cm (1ft). From eastern America, it was introduced in 1656 and is also called the Oswego Tea plant.

The leaves are the parts mainly used, and have an aroma of the bergamot orange; they were the main part of the tea made by the American Oswego Indians of Lake Ontario, and are now used for nightcap tisanes on the Continent, as well as for adding to wine, or salads. The flowers can also be dried and used in pot-pourri. Thymol can be obtained from it in useful quantities.

Bergamot was named for Nicolas Monardes, a Spanish botanist of the sixteenth century, and it was used as a substitute for tea at the time of the American Boston Tea Party.

Very moist soils are best, such as near a stream or pond; sun is preferred, though some shade will be accepted. Clumps are prettiest; the flowers of single plants get lost amongst the others in the border. Plant in spring or autumn, mulch with garden compost at these times also, and cut back to tidy in autumn. Bergamot is easily increased by dividing the clumps in spring.

Borage

(Borago officinalis) Boraginaceae

The brilliantly blue flowers of this hardy annual are delightful; they appear from May onwards, and may even be present in a mild winter, as the plant grows from seed very readily at most times of the year. Stems and large leaves are rough and bristly, and the height is 90cm (3ft) tall, width 45cm (1½ft). Its native habitat is uncertain, possibly Aleppo, but it is naturalized in Britain.

Mixed into a summer drink, with lemon, sugar, water and wine, the cucumber-like flavour and fragrance of the leaves make it very refreshing. Borage was formerly much used medicinally, and the flowers were candied, and used for decoration of sweet dishes and cakes.

Borage was still regularly used in salads, or boiled as a pot herb, early in the last century, and according to Pliny and Dioscorides, it was the Nepenthe, made famous by Homer, for bringing absolute forgetfulness when steeped in wine, so perhaps those summer drinks should be treated with respect!

Sow seed outside in spring or autumn. Any soil and site will be suitable; young plants should be thinned to leave at least 30cm (1ft) between them. Spring sowing will produce flowers in June, rather than May. Hard frost will kill the plants, though not the seed.

Caraway

(Carum carvi) Umbelliferae

A native of Europe, Siberia and as far east as the Himalayas, caraway is sometimes found growing wild in southern Britain. It is biennial, 60cm (2ft) high and 30cm (1ft) wide, with needle-like leaves and white flowers in June on a much branched plant. The root is thick, shaped like a miniature parsnip.

Caraway is grown for its strongly flavoured seeds, which are grey-brown when ripe, in late summer. They are used in cakes, bread, cheese and soup, and their oil is expressed for use in Kümmel liqueur. The young leaves have a similar though less strong flavour, and are suitable for soups and salads.

It is one of the oldest flavourings, mention of it having been found in an Egyptian papyrus of 2500 B.C. Its widespread use may have originated with the ancient Arabs, who called it Karawya, and caraway seedcakes were immensely popular in England in Tudor and Elizabethan days.

Cultivation is easy, seed being sown out-doors in April or May in rows 30 cm (1ft) apart, thinning also to 30cm (1ft). A well-drained soil and sunny place are important, particularly as winter wet can kill it. The seeds are gathered in July–August of the following year, as soon as they begin to fall naturally, and dried on trays in the sun or indoors in gentle heat.

Chamomile

(Matricaria recutita, syn *M. chamomilla) Compositae*

There are two kinds of chamomile, this, the true annual chamomile, and the Roman perennial chamomile, *Anthemis nobilis,* used for lawns. Both are strongly aromatic. The true chamomile has white daisy-like flowers from May to October and fine needle-like leaves on a plant about 15cm (6in) tall and about 23cm (9in) wide. It can still be seen at the sides of fields.

It is in regular use on the Continent for chamomile tea, made from the flowers, and drunk after meals to help in digestion and to soothe and settle mild stomach troubles in general. It is an excellent rinse for blonde hair, and also has antiseptic and anti-inflammatory qualities, due to the blue oil which can be distilled from the flowers.

Culpeper said in his Herbal in 1647: 'It is so well known everywhere, that it is but lost time and labour to describe it.' He also said that the Egyptians dedicated it to the sun. It is not mentioned in Gerard's Herbal (1597), rather surprisingly.

Seed can be sown in early spring or autumn, where it is to grow, mixed with sand as it is very fine, preferably when rain is imminent. A sandy soil and sunny position are best. Thin to about 15cm (6in) apart. Flowers will appear eight weeks from sowing, and should be gathered when they are completely open and quite dry.

Chervil

(Anthriscus cerefolium) Umbelliferae

Chervil has a leaf a little like parsley, in clusters 30cm (1ft) wide at the base of the flower stem, which may be 60cm (2ft) tall. Tiny white flowers appear from June–August. It is an annual, from eastern Europe, and naturalized in Britain.

The flavour is mild and quite distinct, reminiscent of aniseed, and the leaves are best used fresh. It is often part of *fines herbes,* and is used for making chervil soup. The leaves wilt quickly and the flavour is soon lost.

It has a long history of use in Britain, having been introduced by the Romans, and then used by the Anglo-Saxons, mainly for its medicinal and blood cleansing qualities. It was an important herb in the Elizabethan garden, and though little used in Britain nowadays, is still very much a part of French cooking.

If chervil is sown where it will be in the summer sun a few weeks after germinating, it will bolt and die quickly especially if dry, so choose a lightly shaded place for a spring sowing. Sow in late August, and again in early spring for continuous succession, where the plants are to grow, as the roots dislike disturbance, and thin to 23cm (9in) apart, cutting off the top growth of the unwanted seedlings. Remove flowers when they appear. Chervil is difficult to dry satisfactorily in the home.

Chives

(Allium schoenoprasum) Alliaceae

For those who find the flavour of onions too strong, chives are a good substitute, the grass-like leaves being delicately reminiscent of onions. They grow wild throughout the northern hemisphere, including Britain and are found in Britain in the north and west on limestone outcrops. Chives grow in perennial clusters, the leaves reaching about 15–20cm (6–8in), though the giant variety grows to 45cm (1½ft) tall; it is much less well-flavoured. Round, pale purple heads of flowers come in June–July. The leaves die down in October and shoot again in February.

The chopped-up leaves give a piquancy to salads and to cooked dishes such as soups, omelettes and sauces, and can be used as a garnish for many dishes. Drying is difficult and needs to be done in comparatively low temperatures.

The Chinese of 3000 B.C. thought highly of chives and they have been in constant use since then by various civilizations. They were introduced to Britain by the Romans as the Rush Leek, from the specific name, *schoinos* (Gr.) rush, and *prason* (Gr.) leek.

Sun or shade and a moistish soil suit them; plant small clusters in spring or autumn, or sow seed in spring, and thin to clumps 20cm (8in) apart when large enough to handle. Remove the flowers when they appear, and divide the clumps when about 12.5cm (5in) wide. Water well in dry weather, and cover with cloches in autumn through the winter. Chives can be grown successfully in pots.

Clary

(Salvia sclarea) Labiatae

Clary is one of the herbs now grown mostly for ornament; it is biennial, 60–90cm (2–3ft) tall, with bluish-white flowers and bracts coloured pale purple or yellowish-white, in August. The variety *turkestanica* has pink-tinged white flowers and stems. It was introduced to Britain from southern Europe in 1562.

Although domestically little used now, the aromatic oil obtained from the leaves is still an ingredient of perfume, and clary has many uses for minor ills. The flowers make a good wine, and the leaves flavour sweet omelettes, jellies and salads.

Gerard, the famous herbalist of the sixteenth century, describes it in detail, and it spread rapidly after its introduction. *Sclarea* is derived from *clarus* (clear) and became Clear Eye, the seeds being used in a decoction which cleared the eyes of small foreign bodies.

Clary is highly aromatic, easily grown from seed sown in spring or early summer, and not particular about position or soil. Thin when large enough to handle to 30cm (1ft) apart. Flowering will occur in the second summer, and the leaves may be used in winter and spring.

Comfrey

(Symphytum officinale) Boraginaceae

Also known as Knitbone, comfrey is a perennial plant, up to 1.2m (4ft) tall, and 45–60cm (1½–2ft) wide, with large hairy leaves 25cm (10in) long, and cream, white, purple or rose-coloured tubular flowers for most of the summer. It is a native of Europe, including Britain. There is a hybrid called *S. x uplandicum*, which has blue flowers, and bristly stems, now naturalized.

Comfrey is thought to have considerable medical properties, the leaves formed into a poultice being external pain relievers; the powdered root is still said to be helpful with bone fractures, and it can also be used with dandelion and chicory root to make coffee, with the same flavour, but without its harmful effects.

During the Middle Ages it was one of the standbys for healing bones and curing boils, ulcers and abscesses.

Being a native, comfrey presents no difficulty in growing, being happy in almost any situation, though better in a little shade. The roots break easily and once in the garden, it should be handled carefully otherwise it will spread rapidly, and be difficult to eradicate. It makes an excellent green manure crop for fruit and vegetables.

Dill

(Anethum graveolens) Umbelliferae

This is the herb given to babies with hiccoughs, in the form of dill-water. The plant is a hardy annual, up to 90cm (3ft) tall and 30cm (1ft) across. The needle-like leaves, and tiny yellow flowers from June–August, make it difficult at first glance to distinguish from fennel.

As well as a digestive use, the seeds when chewed will encourage sleep. Dill vinegar is obtained by soaking the seeds in vinegar for a few days. The aromatic leaves go well with fish, pickled cucumbers, and mildly flavoured vegetables.

Dill is a native of Europe, though in the northern parts is only seen occasionally as a field weed. The name is said to come from an old Norse word, *dilla*, meaning to lull, and in the Middle Ages was used in spells and as a charm against witchcraft.

It is a fragile plant, and seed should be sown where it is to grow, in succession, from April–June. Sun and well-drained soil, with a regular supply of water, are best, the seedlings being thinned to 30cm (1ft) apart. In poor dry soils they become straggly. Stake the plant if the site is windy, and watch for greenfly. Leaves can be used from six weeks after germination, but if for drying, cut the plants down when about 30cm (1ft) high. Seed should be harvested when turning brown and the whole plant purplish in colour. Dill will readily self-sow; keep it away from clumps of fennel, otherwise they will cross-pollinate.

Fennel

(Foeniculum vulgare) Umbelliferae

The herb fennel is grown for its leaves, but vegetable fennel (Florence fennel) for its swollen leaf bases, which form a kind of bulb just above the soil surface. Herb fennel is a hardy perennial, from southern Europe, 60–150m (2–5ft) tall, in clumps 60cm (2ft) wide. The bluish-green needle-like leaves, the sweeter aniseed flavour, and the size of the plant help to distinguish it from dill. Tiny yellow flowers come in July–August, and the cream-coloured taproot is carrot-like. It dies down to soil-level in autumn.

The leaves are much used in fish sauces and fish dishes generally; it helps in the digestion of fish, and grows naturally close to the sea. The seeds when chewed help to overcome hunger—the Greek name for fennel is *marathron*, a 'growing thin', so perhaps they would help in slimming! Fennel goes well with egg recipes, and in dressings for salads.

The Romans, the Anglo-Saxons, and the Elizabethans all made great use of fennel, Pliny giving it 22 separate medicinal uses. In the Middle Ages it was eaten during Lent with salt fish which was almost obligatory at that time. All down the ages it was much used for its effects on the eyes and curing ailments connected with them.

Seed is sown in spring, in sun or shade, and a chalky soil. A warm place will give best results. Thin to 45cm (1½ft) apart and keep the weeds under control, watering well in dry weather. If seed is not required, remove the flower stems as they appear. Staking may be needed. Fennel is highly ornamental and fits well at the back of an herbaceous border.

Garlic

(Allium sativum) Alliaceae

Once only known in Britain as a too-strong flavouring used by the French and Italians, garlic is now regularly added to British food, since it has been found that less will still give an additional piquancy without being overwhelming. It is a member of the onion family, grown for its bulb, which is divided into sections called cloves. The broad grass-like leaves may grow 30–60cm (1–2ft) tall.

Garlic is used in a wide variety of meat and fish dishes. Besides its flavour, it has a good effect on the digestion, and is also valued for having certain bactericidal properties.

It has a long history, reaching back to the building of the Egyptian pyramids. Garlic was used in all parts of Europe from at least 1200 B.C., and English writers from the twelfth century onwards describe it and its uses; Culpeper said that the whole plant was 'of a very strong and offensive smell'.

In Britain, garlic will give best results if planted in early October. Buy garlic bulbs from the greengrocer, the biggest you can, and use the biggest cloves, from the outside of a bulb. Plant each clove so that the tip is 2.5cm (1in) deep. A rich, well-drained soil and a sunny warm position are important. Allow 15cm (6in) between each clove. Shoots will appear from February onwards and a potash feed in mid-July is advisable. Harvest as the leaves turn yellow and die down and then dry thoroughly before storing. Heads of garlic can be hung in strings like onions for use in the kitchen.

Horseradish

(Armoracia rusticana) Cruciferae

The roots of this hardy perennial plant, that go so well with roast beef, can become a terrible invader, so grow it where it can be confined. It is a native plant with long thick white roots, pieces of which when broken off will establish to produce new plants. The 30cm (1ft) long leaves die down in autumn. Small white flowers appear in June.

The grated roots mixed with a cream sauce are used sparingly, because of their hot flavour, with roast meats, certain fish, and as a dip with shellfish. Horseradish has some antibiotic qualities and was once prescribed against scurvy.

In Germany it was used instead of mustard in the Middle Ages, but was not commonly used in Britain until the seventeenth century, when it was mixed with vinegar. The common name means a coarse radish and was intended to distinguish it from ordinary radish.

Plant 7-cm (3-in) long root cuttings in a rich, moist soil in March, 30cm (1ft) apart, just covered with soil. Lift all the plants in autumn, cut and store the larger roots in sand for winter use, and retain the smaller, also in sand, for planting the following spring. This ensures a constant supply of the best quality roots.

Hyssop

(Hyssopus officinalis) Labiatae

A small, shrub-like, perennial plant, evergreen, or semi-evergreen in cold districts, hyssop grows to about 60cm (2ft) and half that width, though much taller if given warmth in winter. Narrow leaves and small blue, pink or white flowers appear from July to September. It is a Mediterranean native.

Hyssop leaves, the part used, have a slightly bitter taste, between rosemary and lavender, and are used in making Chartreuse liqueur. The essential oil is used in perfume making, especially eau-de-Cologne, and the flowers make a good medicinal tea when cut in August. It is little used in the kitchen, and its uses now are mainly medicinal though it can be added sparingly to salads and vegetable dishes. Bees are much attracted by the flowers.

Hyssop was thought to have been brought to Britain by the Romans and is mentioned in some Saxon manuscripts; it was often one of the plants used for edgings to the beds in Elizabethan knot gardens.

Plant in spring or early autumn, preferably in a sandy soil and sun. Increase from cuttings 5cm (2in) long taken in April–May placed in peat/sand, in a cold frame. Pot singly when rooted and plant in autumn. Also sow seed in spring outdoors, thinning to 30cm (1ft) apart. Wet, heavy soils or a cold winter will kill it.

Marjoram

(Origanum majorana) Labiatae

Sweet or knotted marjoram has the best flavoured leaves, and is a half-hardy annual, 20cm (8in) tall, with grey-green foliage, and green balls or 'knots', from which minute pinkish flowers appear from June onwards. Pot marjoram (*O. onites*) is a slightly taller, deciduous perennial, less well-flavoured but hardy, or can be grown in pots during winter to provide fresh leaves. Wild marjoram (*O. vulgare*), or Oregano, grows outdoors in Britain on the downs, as a bush-like, deciduous perennial, to about 30cm (1ft). The leaves have a rather different flavour to the others.

Their spicy characteristic flavour goes particularly well with sausages and pork dishes of all kinds, also poultry and game. The extracted oil helps to soothe bruises and sprains.

All the marjorams can be found in the Mediterranean region, and the Greeks used wild marjoram medicinally a good deal. Officially introduced in Britain in 1573 and 1759, sweet and pot marjoram have been cultivated here ever since.

Sweet marjoram is sown outdoors in mid-May in a sunny sheltered place and thinned to 25cm (10in) apart. Seedlings are slow to grow and warmth and moisture are particularly important to them. Weeds must be kept down in the early stages. Pot marjoram is grown from seed sown in March–April; it is very slow to germinate, and cuttings are a better method of increase, taken in early summer. Division in April is also possible. In late summer it can be cut back hard and lifted about 2 weeks later, potting in a good compost, for winter cultivation. Wild marjoram can be treated as pot marjoram.

Mint

(Mentha spp.*) Labiatae*

There are many kinds of mint, several of which can be used regularly in cooking. Common or garden mint is *M.* x *spicata*, spearmint; *M. suaveolens* (syn *M. rotundifolia*), round-leaved or apple mint; *M.* x *piperita*, peppermint; *M.* x *piperita citrata*, eau-de-Cologne mint, and *M. suaveolens* Variegata, pineapple mint. *M. pulegium* is better known as pennyroyal.

All but pennyroyal are upright plants with comparatively large leaves, to about 30cm (1ft) tall; pennyroyal forms a mat of small leaves on fragile creeping stems, with erect flower stems, and is strongly fragrant of peppermint when walked on.

The various kinds of mint can all be used in cooking, and peppermint is of course well known for its help with digestion. Pineapple mint is good with fruit salads, summer drinks and desserts. Eau-de-Cologne mint has a purplish tinge and is used for potpourri, in airing cupboards and with drinks. Pennyroyal is little used except for lawns, but can be mixed into soups and stuffings. Peppermint is the source of the tea drunk in North Africa, in which dried whole leaves are used.

Mint has been used by man since neolithic times, and is native to Europe, including Britain. Most kinds prefer a moist, slightly heavy soil and a little shade, except pineapple mint which needs well-drained soil, and is killed by cold winters, and pennyroyal, which likes sun. They spread easily and need to be controlled and are very good in window boxes. Increase is by rooted runners planted in spring or autumn. The fungus disease rust can infect them and such plants are best destroyed.

Parsley

(Petroselinum crispum) Umbelliferae

This herb is one of the 'big five', which has continued to be grown and used regularly when most of the others have fallen by the wayside. The moss-curled variety is the most popular, but the flatter, less-curled leaves have more flavour. It is a hardy biennial, with a small white taproot, native of southern Europe, but naturalized in Britain. Height, flowering stem 30–60cm (1–2ft), leaf spread to 23cm (9in). Parsley has its greatest use in cooking, as a general garnish, in sauces, particularly with fish, in sandwiches, salads, bouquet garni and *fines herbes*. Its vitamin C content is comparatively high. Parsley water is apparently good for doing away with freckles.

Its reputation for slow germination is said to be because it goes to the Devil seven times and back before sprouting; it is also said that where parsley germinates quickly the woman rules the household, a saying no doubt coined by an unsuccessful male gardener!

Parsley does best in moist, slightly heavy soils and a shady position. Seed can be sown outdoors from March onwards, but if left until May, will germinate within 10 days because of the increased warmth of the soil. Otherwise it can take 3–5 weeks. A second sowing in early July will provide leaves through the winter, though the first will still have some, less large. Thin to 20cm (8in) apart and water well in dry weather to prevent bolting, and infestation by greenfly. In pots allow one plant to a 15cm (6in) pot, or 6 plants to a 60cm (12ft) long box.

Rosemary

(Rosmarinus officinalis) Labiatae

A strongly aromatic-leaved evergreen shrub, it grows 1.8m (6ft) tall in Nature (the Mediterranean region) and 1.5m (5ft) wide, though much less in Britain. The small, narrow, grey-green leaves and blue flowers in May make it ornamental enough for the border.

The leaves blend particularly well with lamb; it is also good with pork, veal and game, and can be added sparingly to almost any dish. Rosemary is said to have an invigorating and restorative effect; the oil in the leaves is similar to eucalyptus.

The name comes from the Latin *ros*, dew and *maris*, the sea—it grows naturally near the sea. It was formerly much used as decoration at all kinds of ceremonies and festivals, and is another herb whose good health is thought to show that the mistress rules the household.

A warm sunny place, and well-drained average soil are preferred, planting being in mid-spring. Rosemary is amenable to clipping and the upright form, 'Fastigiatus', makes a good hedge. Increase is easy, by 5 to 7.5-cm (2–3-in) cuttings of new shoot tips taken with or without a heel between April and August, placed in sandy compost, and a warm shaded place.

Rue

(Ruta graveolens) Rutaceae

In its blue form, 'Jackman's Blue', this herb
is exceedingly attractive, with its more blue
than green, delicate and elegantly divided
leaves covering a small neat bush, 60cm
(2ft) tall, and as much wide. It is evergreen,
and has small mustard-yellow flowers in
clusters in July and August. The leaves of
the species are grey-green. Southern Europe
is its native home.

The leaves are strongly and rather bitterly
flavoured; their use in sandwiches and
salads should be sparing. The whole plant
has medicinal properties, the main reason
for growing it, and it is one of the oldest
garden plants, having a great deal of history
and many legends attached to it.

The name comes from the Greek *reuo*, to
set free, because it is of help in curing so
many ills; it was thought to help preserve
good sight.

Plant it in a poor dry soil and a sunny
place and it will do well and survive frost
easily. It seeds freely, and may be increased
without difficulty from cuttings. Distance
between plants should be about 45cm (1½ft).

Sage

(Salvia officinalis) Labiatae

The spoon-shaped, deep-green leaves of this
shrubby herb are also ornamental, as rue is,
and there are some varieties which are even
better. 'Tricolor' has leaves marked in
white, purple and pink; 'Icterina' is yellow-
edged, and 'Purpurascens' has a purple
flush all through the leaves and stems. Less
hardy than the species, they still have the
same flavour.

Sage comes from southern Europe and
grows to 60cm (2ft) high and wide. It is
evergreen, with small white or blue-purple
flowers, not often produced.

It has many uses in cooking, especially
with pork dishes, game, and poultry except
chicken, in stuffings, with fat fish and mixed
into cheese spreads. The name comes from
the Latin *salveo*, to save or heal, and the
Romans thought it a veritable cure-all. The
Arabs had a saying 'How can a man die who
has sage in his garden?', and its medicinal
uses are legion.

Sage should be planted in spring in a
light chalky soil and a sunny sheltered place,
never in heavy or wet soil, otherwise winter
rain as well as cold can kill it. It will need
renewing after four or five years, using either
cuttings with a heel taken in late spring and
put in a cold frame, or by layering, which is
also best done in late spring.

Santolina

(Santolina chamaecyparissus) Compositae

Now mostly grown as an ornamental 'ever-
grey' shrub, santolina or lavender cotton has
very finely cut, silvery grey leaves, and yellow 'button' flowers in July–August; it
grows up to 60–90cm (2–3ft) tall and 60cm
(2ft) wide.

The leaves, the part used, smell strongly
and rather unpleasantly when bruised or
rubbed, a little like chamomile. Its medicinal
uses were thought to be for bathing the
eyes, as a stimulant and as an antiseptic,
particularly for bites.

Santolina was introduced in 1596, from
southern Europe, and damp soil is anathema
to it, so supply a well-drained, even stony
place in the sun, and plant in spring. Cuttings
taken in early summer are an easy and
reliable method of increase.

Savory

(Satureja spp.*) Labiatae*

There are two savories, summer and winter (*S. hortensis* and *S. montana*). The summer kind is a hardy annual up to 25cm (10in), with tiny lilac flowers continuing from July to September; it forms a small bush-like plant. Winter savory is perennial, evergreen, shrub-like and a little larger. Both come from southern Europe.

The leaves have a mint-like, slightly bitter flavour and go well with pork recipes, as well as cucumber, salads and beans of all kinds. It is said that leafy shoots, if rubbed on bee or wasp stings, give instant relief.

Although not well known today, savory was formerly used a great deal, and vinegar with chopped savory leaves was used by the Romans as we use mint sauce. In general it took the place of the East Indies spices that are now so often used.

Both forms can be grown from seed sown in April, in sun and a light but rich soil, thinning to about 20cm (8in) apart. Winter savory can also be sown in early autumn, increased from cuttings taken in May, and put in a frame, or divided in spring. Cutting winter savory down near to the crown every spring results in strong new shoots with plenty of leaves in the following season.

Sorrel

(Rumex scutatus) Polygonaceae

The French or Buckler-leaved sorrel is best for use in cooking; it is an herbaceous perennial plant, dying down to ground level in autumn. The leaves are fleshy, light green, and rather rounded; tiny pink-red flowers appear in June–July, but should be removed. It was introduced in 1596, being a native of mountainous areas in southern Europe.

It makes the famous and delicious sorrel soup, so popular in France, with a pleasantly sour flavour; it goes well with salads, and other vegetables, if used in moderation. Sorrel is also said to have considerable medicinal uses, due to the binoxalate of potash which produces its sour flavour.

As with so many herbs, it was formerly widely and regularly used, and is still grown on the Continent. Young plants are put in in spring or autumn, 45cm (18in) apart, giving them a moist, fertile soil such as a well-broken-down clay, to give good leaf size and succulence. Sun is preferred, but they will grow in shade. Since soup recipes recommend 450g (1lb) of leaves at a time, you should allow plenty of room for growing sorrel—a whole row in the kitchen garden will not be too much.

Sweet Cicely

(Myrrhis odorata) Umbelliferae

Sweet cicely is an ornamental perennial which can fit well into an herbaceous border. It has fern-like leaves, and creamy-white heads of flowers in May and June, on 60-cm (2-ft) stems. Eventually it grows much taller. The taproots go down very deeply, so be careful about where it is planted, as it can be difficult to move. Native to Europe, it is naturalized in northern Britain.

The aniseed flavour of the leaves makes it delicious with fruit salads, ordinary salads, in pancakes and summer drinks. The inch-long seeds have the same flavour and are still much used in Germany. The strong fragrance of the whole plant gives it its name, since *Myrrhis* is the Greek for myrrh, which it is thought to resemble.

Easily grown, sweet cicely prefers a moist deep soil and a little shade; it is long-lived, and seeds freely. Plant in spring or autumn.

Tansy

(Chrysanthemum vulgare, syn. *Tanacetum vulgare) Compositae*

Tansy is a herb with a very long history and was much used from Greek times onwards, if not earlier. Native of Europe including Britain, it is a hardy perennial 30–60cm (1–2ft) tall with feathery leaves, yellow button flowers in clusters July–September, and a curious, strong odour, not unpleasant and rather like camphor. It dies down in autumn.

The flowers were and can still be used for tansy tea, being considered a certain cure for colds and rheumatism. A tansy was a popular recipe in the eighteenth century and might consist of eggs, cream, nutmeg, wine, biscuit and tansy juice. Tansy cakes and tansy sauce were also very popular, in Elizabethan times and later. It can take the place of mint in sauce served with lamb and can be used in omelettes and pancakes.

The common name comes from *Athanaton* (immortal), possibly because it lasts so long in flower.

It is easily grown from seed in any soil and situation, and can also be grown by dividing the creeping roots. Plant 30cm (1ft) apart. Take care that it does not become invasive.

Tarragon

(Artemisia dracunculus sativa) Compositae

With a completely distinctive flavour, slightly sweet, the leaf of tarragon should be used in really small quantities otherwise it is overpowering. French tarragon is the one to grow; the Russian variety *A. d. indora* or *A. dracunculoides* is coarse and less well-flavoured. It is a delicately bushy perennial plant, growing to 60–90cm (2–3ft) and 45cm (1½ft) wide, with inconspicuous flowers. It is evergreen.

Tarragon is excellent in casseroles of all kinds, with chicken, fish, tomato dishes and eggs, and for making tarragon vinegar. There are few recipes with which it cannot be used. Its medicinal uses are fewer, though if the root was chewed, it was considered to be consoling for toothache.

The name is indirectly derived from the Latin *dracunculus,* a little dragon; it was thought to cure the poisonous bites and stings of wild creatures.

Well-drained soil is essential; tarragon also prefers sun, and is planted in spring, allowing 60cm (2ft) either way. Shelter from wind is advisable, and protection from winter cold. Increase by division in spring, and transplant every few years, to maintain the flavour. Seed does not set in this country. It can be grown in containers but is not easy.

Thyme

(Thymus spp.*) Labiatae*

Common thyme, *T. vulgaris,* is a small evergreen shrub, 23cm (9in) tall, and up to 30cm (1ft) wide. The tiny grey-green leaves are highly aromatic, and purple flowers appear from June–August. *T.* x *citriodorus* is lemon thyme, with larger leaves strongly lemon-scented, and a rather more trailing habit of growth. It is also a small shrub. *T. herba-barona* is the caraway thyme, low-growing, almost mat-like and aromatic of caraway as well as the normal thyme odour.

Thyme leaves are used in stuffings for savoury dishes, in casseroles and with roast meat, as part of bouquet garni, mixed with cream cheeses, and especially with fatty foods such as pork.

It contains a good deal of thymol, a strong antiseptic, and a meat preservative, hence its use with other herbs when marinating meat. Thymol is said to be used for respiratory infections, and in ointments to ward off mosquitoes and gnats.

A Mediterranean region plant, thyme is best in sun and light soil, planting in spring. It is very easily increased from cuttings of shoot tips in summer, or by pulling the shoots down and covering them with soil, leaving the tips free. Protection from winter cold will be needed. Thyme is a good container plant.

Fruit in your Garden

Apples & Pears

Apples

It can be argued that the apple is the most popular fruit, for it certainly occupies the biggest acreage in the United Kingdom. In discussing the cultivation of this major fruit, those aspects of growing which it has in common with others are dealt with once in detail and referred to again only for the sake of necessary emphasis or where there are important variations. In the same way, basic principles, suitably illustrated by reference to practice, are dealt with in the introductory chapters on soils, planning, pests, equipment, pruning and propagation, but these matters are enlarged upon when dealing with separate fruits if it seems desirable.

Although attempts to produce apples in gardens are usually not really successful, there is no good reason, apart from lack of space, why a constant supply should not be available from August to March, and even beyond. To ensure a proper continuity of supply a range of varieties is necessary, which—so called family-trees apart—calls for at least 12 trees. This in turn suggests either a very large garden or trees that remain small, under control, but are consistently fruitful. This latter state calls for skill and presents the gardener with special problems, but there is no more rewarding aspect of horticulture than directing the growth of trees to fruitful ends. And it can be done, if the right approach is made. The key factors are the choice of rootstocks and varieties, proper pruning and nutrition and the sensible control of the more serious pests and diseases. The keen gardener can see immediately that none of this is insuperable, and the rewards are great.

Site and soil

There is little to be gained by telling the gardener that he must choose a site free from spring frosts, and select a well-drained medium loam for his fruit growing. To the commercial grower these matters are vital, but the gardener has to do his best with the site and soil attached to his house. Within these limits apple trees should be planted in a reasonably sheltered part of the garden, well away from the shade and competition of trees and, assuming the trees are kept in compact form, some added protection from severe frost during the crucial blossoming period should be provided. And, take heart, the heat gained during a sunny spring day in a built-up area is radiated back during the hours of darkness, so urban

Above: Apple blossom brings springtime colour to the fruit garden

gardens are much less likely to suffer spring frost damage than are the open fields of the commercial grower.

The soil in gardens, and especially in new gardens, is often in poor condition, largely because the builders seldom have any respect for the precious top soil.

In summary, soils for really good apple growing have three essential requirements, based upon depth, drainage and texture. Some 45cm (18in) of rooting depth are needed; the trees will not prosper if waterlogged in winter, and the roots—which have to occupy the soil all the year round and cannot run away from unpleasant conditions —must have a proper balance of air and water in their environment. These matters are set out at length in the chapter on *Care of The Soil*. To promote these highly desirable conditions it is a good plan to dig the site thoroughly, breaking up

the sub-soil with a fork, and to work in any rotted compost or farmyard manure or peat which can be obtained, in order to increase rooting depth, assist drainage and improve the structure of the soil. Avoid both shallow, thin soils and stiff waterlogged clays. Between these two extremes much can be done by initial and continuing good husbandry, in other words by toil and sweat, both very good for the majority of us. Do not overlook the question of lime, discussed at length elsewhere. Fortunately apples, and other fruits, do best in a slightly acid soil. In technical terms, if the pH reaction is between 6.2 and 7.2—and most soils come in this category—you have little cause for concern. If it lies markedly below 6.2 or well above 7.2 adjustments will be necessary.

Rootstocks

There are in theory some 28 named or numbered apple rootstocks to choose from. Most of these bear the prefix M, which stands for Malling (pronounced Mawling) the Kentish home of the best-known fruit research station in the world, where most of the investigations into the behaviour of rootstocks has been carried out. Other rootstocks are distinguished by the letters MM, meaning Malling-Merton, signifying joint research work between two bodies. To complicate matters somewhat a further grouping of initials is now with us—EMLA—which means East Malling Long Ashton. Long Ashton is a famous research station near Bristol, and the whole phrase commemorates a most useful piece of joint research work. Briefly, the EMLA rootstocks are re-selected and healthy strains of the earlier M and MM rootstocks. So when a nurseryman offers EMLA M9, for example, he is selling the very best type of M9 rootstock, which is exactly what you want.

Some of the apple rootstocks produce large trees, others produce small trees, and there are all stages in between. For obvious reasons the more vigorous rootstocks, excellent though they are for the commercial gower, are not suitable for the needs of the gardener who has only limited space. Accordingly, the selection for gardeners is, at present, on the following lines. Malling 9 is the most generally suitable. It makes a compact tree, which comes into bearing quickly, but it needs good soil and good treatment if it is to give of the best of which it is capable. It also must be kept staked and securely tied, for even in gardens the tree may blow over or at least be weakened by rocking in the wind.

On either side of M9, in terms of vigour, come M26 and M27. M26 makes a larger tree and should be chosen if the soil is not quite as deep or as fertile as is desirable. On some soils M26 produces trees which lack the normal number of side-shoots and this bare wood effect is a little alarming in young trees, although in later years it may not be noticeable. Even smaller than M9 are the trees grown on M27, the latest in the Malling series. This is a rootstock for the really fertile soils, on which it can be closely planted and still remain compact and fruitful. For my part I choose EMLA M9 for most gardens and EMLA MMIII for really large gardens, knowing that, properly grown, both are excellent.

Varieties

There are many thousands of different varieties and every time some one sows a pip successfully yet another new one is produced, which almost certainly is inferior to those existing. So we are the fortunate heirs to generations of breeding, and can take our choice. But it is not easy, because there are wide differences in the way in which varieties respond to soils, or to good treatment, or to indifferent care, and, of course to climate. Even in the British Isles

Above: 'Cox's Orange Pippin' is an apple of superb quality

Below: Fine-flavoured 'Ashmead's Kernel' is an epicure's apple

there is a sharp gradient in rainfall from west to east, in temperature from north to south, while specially favoured pockets can be found in most parts. Most important is the wide difference in personal taste. Some people like firm, crisp, sharp dessert apples, while others prefer a softer, sweeter, bland flavour and texture. But the gardener has one great advantage over the commercial grower in that he can produce what he likes without worrying about tough skins capable of standing up to rough handling in markets; nor is he concerned with pretty eye-catching skin colours which are attractive to buyers acting on impulse but who may be disappointed when it comes to eating the fruit. Some of the best flavoured apples have rough exteriors. Years ago the Royal Horticultural Society organized a tasting competition. Slices of peeled fruits were offered to the palates of a group of

distinguished judges who had no means of knowing which variety was which. The one selected as the best flavoured was the little-known Ashmead's Kernel, a variety which crops lightly and has an outside which belies the splendid flavour of the flesh. It is never to be found in greengrocers' shops, but there is nothing to stop you growing it in your garden.

The distinction between dessert and culinary varieties is, roughly, that the first group can be eaten raw, when ripe, because the starches have been largely turned to sugars. Cooking apples are by contrast high in acids and are much too sharp to be eaten raw by discerning people, although small boys have been known to devour them with relish. Quality, in terms of flavour, is much more subtle. In dessert apples the development of elusive aromatics which impinge on the nasal passages when the teeth bite into the fruit, plus sugars and a high acid content make for the really well-flavoured apple, such as Cox's Orange Pippin, Ashmead's Kernel, D'Arcy Spice, Ribston Pippin and that apple you ate all those years ago, the name of which you have forgotten but the memory of which remains.

Of cooking varieties, Bramley's Seedling alone retains its firm texture and fine flavour when cooked, while Howgate Wonder and others become soggy messes in the pan. It is worth remembering that Cox's Orange, with its unique combination of sugars and acids, not only eats superbly but also cooks splendidly; Wellington makes excellent mincemeat; Monarch, I am told, is first class for dumplings, and Newton Wonder not only cooks well but, after Christmas, can be eaten raw.

Recommended varieties listed in order of ripening:

Dessert apples	Cooking apples
Scarlet Pimpernel	Grenadier
George Cave	Lane's Prince Albert
Discovery	Bramley's Seedling
Laxton's Epicure	King Edward VII
Worcester Pearmain	
James Grieve	
Laxton's Fortune	
Lord Lambourne	
Egremont Russet	
Cox's Orange Pippin	
Sunset	
Ribston Pippin	
Kidd's Orange Red	
Orlean's Reinette	
Spartan	
Golden Delicious	
Ashmead's Kernel	
Laxton's Superb	
Crispin	
Idared	

Of the dessert varieties ten should be singled out:

Discovery is one of the finds of the century, pomologically speaking, and we can dispense with earlier varieties in favour of waiting for Discovery, in mid-August. It is the first of the apples with any real claims to flavour. It crops heavily, has a bright red and yellow skin and, surprisingly, keeps quite well once picked. It is rather slow coming into bearing, dropping its fruitlets in tantalizing fashion in its early years, but is well worth waiting for patiently.

James Grieve is a gardener's delight. It can be cooked satisfactorily in August and eaten with pleasure in September. It crops without fail every year, frost or no frost, and deserves a medal for good nature. There is no better general purpose pollinating variety than Grieve.

Laxton's Fortune is not an easy apple to grow but is one of the few well-flavoured early to mid-season apples.

Lord Lambourne, like Grieve, is eminently reliable and yet possesses both good flavour and good temper, as well as keeping nicely into November.

Cox is an apple of superb quality. Like all really high quality beings it is difficult. It is prone to mildew, scab and canker and liable to frost damage; but it responds to loving care. In the right hands it crops magnificently and keeps long enough to provide great pleasure at Christmas. However, if previous attempts to grow Cox in your area have failed, plump instead for *Sunset*, which is a sort of poor man's Cox.

Ashmead's Kernel is one for the epicure. If you have any doubts about its cropping, or can't get it, or are short of space, then stick to Cox, or Sunset.

Golden Delicious is very easy to grow, is completely reliable, and possesses an acceptable flavour.

Laxton's Superb is included with some mis-

Right: A young bush tree of the highly coloured and well-flavoured 'Discovery'

Below right: The popular 'Golden Delicious' is a completely reliable variety

Below: 'James Grieve' is a gardener's delight

givings, because it has a tendency to over-crop one year and rest from labour the next. But proper fruit thinning and feeding can overcome this habit of biennial bearing, and its heavy cropping and keeping quality gain it a place.

Idared is included because it can be kept until May but the flavour is not especially distinctive.

Of cooking apples, Bramley's Seedling is much the best, and is particularly suitable for freezing. It makes a bigger tree than our other selections, even on M9, and is susceptible to frost damage. An alternative well worth considering for frosty sites is the little grown but reliable King Edward VII.

New varieties are constantly on offer, but

very few are improvements on existing ones. The Research Stations, however, are engaged in scientific breeding, testing and selecting and East Malling has raised a new Cox type seedling called Suntan, which so far shows promise.

As with rootstocks, improved EMLA strains (clones) of most of the varieties recommended will be available to the amateur as time goes on.

Pollination and Thinning

The otherwise complicated matter of pollination and fertilization would be self-resolving with all these varieties growing in close proximity. The pollen has still to be transferred by flying insects, but it is a safe assumption that bees will be buzzing around in most gardens, carrying the pollen from one compatible variety to another. Good pollination leads to the possibility of over-setting, with the risks of small fruits and the strain of overcropping and exhaustion. Remove surplus fruits in late June and early July, the early varieties being thinned first. The golden rule is to remove the small fruits, and all distorted, diseased, cracked and similar undesirables. Some authorities recommend the removal of the centre fruit in the cluster—the king fruit—but this is not good advice unless you are growing for the show bench.

Space the fruits out so that, roughly, they stand at 10cm to 12cm (4in–5in) apart for eating varieties, and 12cm to 22cm (5in–8in) for Bramley.

Planting

Having prepared the soil, plant the trees in the dormant season, the earlier the better. Ensure that you get the best quality trees by going, if you can, to a specialist nurseryman who grows his own trees. Ordering well in advance is obviously better than hoping for the best in March.

Trees up to three years of age will transplant satisfactorily but one year trees, known as maidens, move most readily. Drive a stout stake in each place beforehand. There is quite a wide specification to choose from, but sweet chestnut posts 1.2m (4ft) long, pointed, with a top diameter of around 5–7cms (2½ins) are about right. Other types of timber can be used satisfactorily but all except sweet chestnut, larch and heart-wood of oak should be treated with preservative, preferably creosote applied under pressure.

Drive each stake in to leave about 75cm (2½ft) still out of the ground. This will be enough to provide support for bush trees and dwarf pyramids, but if you wish to grow the trees as tall pyramids or spindle bushes a taller stake is desirable. Commercial growers of spindle bushes use posts about 2.5m (8ft), leaving 2m (6ft) out of the ground, so that the central leader can be more easily trained. But more about training elsewhere.

Space bush apple trees on M9 rootstock three metres (10ft) apart; dwarf pyramids two metres (6ft 6in), spindle bushes one and a half metres (5ft), while cordons can go as close as 75cm (about 3ft) apart. If, lucky you, you can manage more than one row, then space the rows to give 3 metres (10ft) for all the forms mentioned, both to reduce shading and allow you to attend to spraying, pruning and picking.

Choose a day when the soil is reasonably dry, as far as it ever is in winter, and plant each tree close to its stake. Take out a wide, shallow hole, without loosening the stake, and spread out the roots so that they can

Above: 'Ellison's Orange' looks very attractive trained as an espalier

Right: Apples can also be trained as fans— here, 'Sunset'

make the quickest possible use of the largest amount of ground. Take care to keep the union, the swollen piece on the stem which marks the junction between root stock and variety, at least 10cm (4in) above ground. If you plant the tree deeply with the idea of saving the cost of a stake you will succeed in your intention, but you will grow a very large unfruitful tree instead of the neat compact one you dreamed about, so—take care not to bury the union, because if you

do the inherently vigorous scion will root and the weak system of the rootstock be overpowered. Firm the soil over the roots so that the two are in close contact. If you can lay hands on used potting-soil then a large bucketful to each planting hole will make a world of difference to the growth and establishment of the young tree. Failing that, a shovelful or two of moist peat, worked into the soil, will help.

Tie each tree to the stake, taking care to

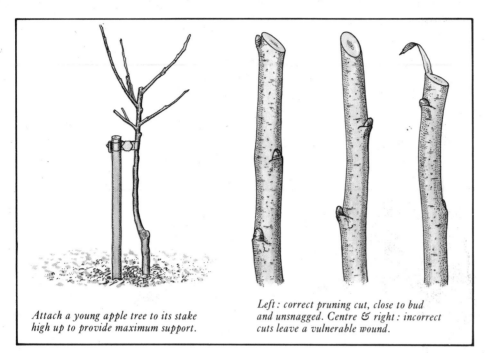

Attach a young apple tree to its stake high up to provide maximum support.

Left: correct pruning cut, close to bud and unsnagged. Centre & right: incorrect cuts leave a vulnerable wound.

needs by the response of the tree. As a generalization a compound fertilizer of the Growmore type with the analysis Nitrogen 7%, Phosphorus 7% and Potassium 7% should be applied each March as an even sprinkling over the surface of the rooting area—which may cover half as much again as the branch spread—at the rate of about half a kilo (1lb) to 8 square metres (10sq yds). If, for any reason, the trees do not respond by growing freely, measured by 50cm (20in) of annual leader extension, then supplement the soil applications with the foliar sprays mentioned in the chapter on *Care of the Soil*. As the trees come into bearing, switch the manuring to a dressing in early September at the same rate, substituting a quick acting nitrate fertilizer. This will, in most cases, assist the tree to lay down blossom buds and thereby increase fruiting productivity and reduce the vegetative growth.

One often sees apple trees growing in

use a broad tie which will not bite into the stem, and allow room for the tree trunk to expand rapidly without being choked. The patent plastic ties on offer are excellent, though not cheap—a little ingenuity with strips cut from plastic bags, or with bicycle tyre inner tubing, may meet the need. Place the tie as high on the stake as possible, for obvious reasons. If you are planting on a really windy site position tree and stake so that the latter is on the side from which the strongest wind is likely, to avoid chafing.

Finish off the job by pruning the maiden tree back to the appropriate height (see page 16) and between planting time and the arrival of spring cover the surface of the ground above the root area with some 5cm (2in) of composted material or farmyard manure to keep in moisture and choke annual weed growth.

Pruning

Thereafter all you have to do to ensure good crops of crisp and delectable fruits is to prune sensibly, feed properly and spray appropriately. Pruning is discussed in a special chapter. If in doubt either leave the tree alone, or carry out the minimum pruning consistent with a common-sense removal of diseased, overcrowded and over-vigorous shoots going in the wrong direction. But pruning is a very satisfactory operation, done properly, and gives the gardener a sense of working with the tree rather than against it, so persevere.

Feeding

Proper feeding is based on the principles set out on page 10. Most fruit trees in gardens are starved, poor things. Basically they should receive not only the annual mulches of manure or compost which all authorities recommend, but also a dressing of a complete fertilizer on all but the most fertile of soils. Fertilizer should never be wasted, and it is easy to apply too much. Gardeners should endeavour by a rough process of trial and error to establish the optimum

Pruning a neglected apple tree. Cut (1) shows partial de-horning. Remove old, worn-out (3) overcrowded and crossing branches (2). Cut back weak extensions (4). Clean root area of weeds (5).

lawns, which is a pleasant sight but is not good practice for trees on M9, because the grass competes seriously with the trees for water and nutrients. If you feel you must grow the trees in the lawn then choose a stronger rootstock, such as MMIII, and increase the manuring levels to compensate for the competition. To repeat, if your soil is very rich, reduce the level of fertilizer application, but since very fertile soils are only occasionally found the chances are that for good results you will have to maintain or exceed the dressings mentioned. But do experiment.

Pests and diseases

The amateur gardener may well have to put up with some pests and some diseases in some years, since it would be expensive and tiresome to spray enough to obtain perfect control.

The major pests, those that occur each year in most areas, include aphids and other sap-sucking plant lice of the same group; leaf-eating caterpillars and codling moth caterpillars, which cause the maggoty fruits around July time.

The most likely diseases are scab and mildew, both caused by microscopic fungi. Scab affects the leaves but the worst damage is to the fruits in the form of unsightly and distorting blackish spots and blotches. Mildew, which is very common, is to be found for the most part on the leaves and shoots, which are crippled by the grey felted fungus. Preventive action can and should be taken against these troubles annually. A suitable small-scale spraying programme, using specifics readily obtainable from sundriesmen and garden centres is:

Timing	Materials	Control
1 Blossom buds showing, but still green	Benlate, and Malathion (or Rogor)	Scab Mildew Aphids Caterpillars
2 Immediately after blossoming	Repeat spray number 1	as 1
3 Fourteen days later	Benlate Karathane	Scab Mildew
4 Third week June	Benlate Karathane Malathion	Scab Mildew Codling moth

Note carefully:

You may not get full control of all pests and diseases by the use of this simple programme, but your trees will be much healthier and your fruits much cleaner.

Always follow carefully the makers' instructions. The spray materials mentioned may well be replaced by better ones, so treat them as examples of the effective but relatively safe chemicals which the sensible gardener can use with confidence.

If you would prefer to follow a less demanding programme, but still control aphids, then use a spray of Rogor immediately flowering has finished; trap the codling moth larvae by means of bands of corrugated cardboard placed around the trunks each July; put up philosophically with leaf-eating caterpillars, scab and mildew, and trust to predators to keep the red spider mites in reasonable bounds.

Harvesting

The varieties recommended will provide a picking sequence, in the order given, starting about 15 August with Discovery (earlier with George Cave and Scarlet Pimpernel), working on steadily to Cox picking around 26 September and finishing with Idared on 15 October. How's that for precision? Naturally, seasons and districts will vary, but the dates given are not likely to be far out. The tree itself signals when picking is due because cutting-off cells begin to form at the junction of the stalk of the fruit and the permanent parts of the tree. If the fruits part readily when raised gently beyond the horizontal then, the time has come. In heavy cropping years it pays to pick over twice or thrice, taking first the outermost fruits with the brightest colour, leaving the remainder to flush and to put on more weight. Always pick ripe fruit with gentleness. The old gardeners used to enjoin the young 'treat 'em as though they were eggs'. Bruised fruit does not keep well.

Storage

Storing apples is always a problem. The

Above: Russet-skinned apples like this 'Egremont Russet' have a special flavour

key factors for good storage life are:
a grow the fruits well,
b pick them with care at the right time
c keep them in a cool, moist, vermin-free place, away from taint.
It is this last requirement which creates most problems. Fortunately polythene is a great help. Apples in polythene bags are kept moist and store very well in most years. Try some in bags, but keep an eye on them, especially if they were on the ripe side when picked. This advice applies to all other methods of storing. Many gardeners have of necessity to use the garage for storing fruit, in which case do not hesitate to water the boxes or trays of fruits occasionally with a watering can fitted with a fine rose. Once a picked apple loses moisture it cannot replace it, so keep the fruits in a humid atmosphere to avoid loss of both weight and flavour.

Look through the stored fruits at regular intervals and bring them out for eating as they ripen.

If mice are troublesome use one of the proprietary baits based on Warfarin or Alphakil at the first sign of their presence, before the mice become addicted to apples in preference to bait.

All being well your household will enjoy home grown apples from August to April. What more can you possibly want?

Pears

It is surprising that pears are not grown more often by amateur gardeners. True, these glorious fruits require warmer and more sheltered conditions than apples, to give of their best, but suitable sites can be found in most gardens. Their lack of popularity may be attributed to the quite mistaken idea that pears make enormous trees which are impossible to tend and pick properly and are slow to come into bearing, to boot. All of which is true of pears on pear rootstocks, but is not true of pears grown on quince.

So let us start with a healthy generalization—a garden without at least one pear tree is incomplete.

Site and soil

Choose the most sheltered site in the garden for growing pear trees, but shade and in particular competition from other trees must be avoided. If necessary, provide the site with added shelter from strong winds by appropriate plantings of, say, flowering shrubs, which will filter the onslaught of the wind without competing with the pears for light and moisture.

The worst effects of the lack of shelter are felt in the spring and autumn. The tender young leaves can be adversely affected by high winds, and pollinating insects do not function well in these conditions. Autumn gales bring the risk of premature dropping, particularly of the large well-grown fruits. Equally, pears should be given the deepest soil available, one which is also well-drained and slightly acid, following the general precepts laid down in the section on apples.

But if the soil falls short of the ideal, and most do, then the gardener can take comfort because pears are very accommodating, and will not fail unless the soil is waterlogged in winter or dries out in summer. They may not give of their magnificent best, but they will not fail. Shallow chalky soils present special difficulties because pears do not like a high lime content and on such soils tend to lack both iron and manganese, producing pale yellow foliage. The notes on lime and liming set out on page 11 are relevant to this point.

Pears can be trained as multiple cordons, fans or espaliers on walls and particularly on those facing south, where the extra warmth and shelter to which the choicer varieties respond is available.

Rootstocks

Most amateurs are confused by the choice of apple rootstocks, but with pears the situation is pleasingly straightforward because in effect there is at present only one suitable rootstock. The history of rootstocks for pears is interesting. In the early years of fruit husbandry pear varieties were grafted on to the root systems of seedling wild pears. The wild pear still grows in the West Midlands, where it makes a very large spectacular tree. Naturally, the cultivated varieties when

grafted on to seedling pears also grew into very large trees, slow to bear and difficult to manage. Some horticultural genius then thought of uniting the pear varieties with the root system of a close relative, the quince, which is much less vigorous in growth.

Pears on quince make small compact trees, which come into bearing in, say, five years after planting. Not all pear varieties unite successfully with the quince tissue. For example, the excellent William's is incompatible. This, and a few others, are propagated by a technique known as double-working, which ensures a strong union of tissue with the advantages of the quince rootstock.

Grafting and budding are usually best left to the specialist nurseryman, but some guidance for the amateur who would like to try his prentice hand is included in the chapter on propagation.

Above: This pear has been successfully trained in espalier form against a wall

Left: The fruits of 'Gorham', here trained as a fan, may be picked from September

Although there are a number of selected clonal quince rootstocks the only one used at present to any extent is that known as Quince A. This gives excellent results, but some of the more vigorous or shy-fruiting varieties require a rootstock with rather less natural vigour. To meet this need the East Malling Research Station has recently re-selected another clone, distinguished as Quince C, and varieties worked on this rootstock should be available for planting by amateur gardeners before long.

It is likely that Quince C will be ideal for gardens, and particularly for the variety Doyenné du Comice, but meanwhile we can with confidence plant trees grown on the well-tried Quince A.

Insist on trees worked on certified rootstocks, and ask for the very best in the form of EMLA quince A or C rootstocks when these become generally available.

Great care should be taken not to plant too deeply. It is essential to keep the union—the swollen piece on the main stem at which the pear variety was grafted (or budded)—well above soil level. If the union is buried then there is a risk that the pear variety will produce its own roots. If this occurs the weaker quince root system will be dominated and the character of the tree will revert back to the undesirable habit of the very vigorous pear. A good guide is to plant the young tree to the soil mark on the stem, which indicates the depth at which the tree was planted in the nursery.

Varieties

Like apples, pear varieties are grouped according to the use to which they are put—dessert varieties for eating raw, cooking varieties, and those used for making that delectable drink, perry. But with pears the position is to an extent simplified in that nearly all dessert varieties can also be cooked, if it is so desired. There are a few varieties, of which Catillac is the main representative, which are useful only for cooking, but for obvious reasons these are now seldom grown.

There are several hundred pear varieties to choose from, but many are best suited to warmer climates than that of the United Kingdom.

A short list of half-a-dozen to cover a long season would include:

William's Bon Chrétien—early September

Merton Pride—late September

Conference—October and November

Doyenné du Comice—November

Packham's Triumph—December

Josephine de Malines—January

William's was raised in Berkshire, but early in life it crossed the Atlantic, where it was re-named Bartlett. It now comes back home each year in tins. It is also imported in the fresh condition from Italy and other Mediterranean countries to compete with the home crop, but there is no reason at all why it should not be grown in our gardens. It has when ripe a melting juicy flesh and a musky flavour. It is excellent for canning and bottling and is said to hold together better than most when frozen. Must be double-worked when grown on Quince.

Merton Pride is a relatively new variety with a short season, but possesses a really outstanding flavour.

Conference is the most reliable of all varieties and if only one tree can be grown then this is the choice, because it will set quite a reasonable crop with its own pollen. Conference is rather too long in shape to be perfect, and the flavour is not in the class of Merton Pride or Comice, but it is very acceptable when ripe. Some people enjoy it while still hard and crunchy.

Doyenné du Comice, usually shortened to Comice, is the best flavoured of all pears, which is saying a lot. It is not easy to grow, but responds to care and affection and is well worth cherishing. It freezes well.

Packham's Triumph is reliable heavy cropping pear of fair quality, which keeps well. *Josephine de Malines* is a juicy late-keeping pear of good flavour, best grown as a bush because of a tendency to carry its fruits at the ends of the shoots.

The six chosen are, of course, only a guide. The experienced gardener may well choose additional varieties; the beginner would make a very good start with the six mentioned. It is a good idea, in any case, to enquire around to find out which varieties appear to do best in a particular district. That chap with the splendid crop will be delighted to answer questions from a keen fellow enthusiast.

Pollination

The selected six varieties will cross-pollinate one another very effectively. Comice always presents a difficulty because it tends to flower late, but there is usually enough overlap between Williams, Conference and Comice to ensure an effective distribution of pollen in the conditions prevailing in most gardens, and in many cases there are other gardens nearby also growing pears.

Below: 'Conference' is the best-known of English pears

Manuring and planting

Prepare the soil thoroughly well in advance by breaking up the sub-soil and incorporating large quantities of farmyard manure or rotted garden compost. Pears may occupy the same piece of ground for thirty years or so and it makes sense to give them a good start.

The pH level should be corrected if below 6, and a fertilizer containing potash and magnesium worked in before planting because these nutrients are slow to move in the soil. Drive in a stake as for an apple tree and arrange the tree in relation to the stake.

Spread out the roots carefully so that they occupy the maximum amount of soil from which to draw water and nutrients, and firm the soil over the roots. If the soil texture is unkind it is wise to use old potting soil as the immediate covering for the roots, to ensure a good start.

Finally, tie the tree to the stake, allowing room for the expansion of the trunk, and spread a thick mulch of rotted garden compost or similar moisture-retaining material over the rooting zone. Mulching material should not be piled around the stem of the young tree because of the risk of mice chewing the bark while resting snugly in the shelter of the mulch.

It should be stressed that the pear responds more than any other fruit to bulky organic matter—if you can get it—in the form of farmyard manure, rotted compost or peat, applied both as incorporated materials on planting and as surface mulches thereafter. The secret of success with pears is to ensure plenty of summer moisture and high levels of nitrogen.

These bulky organic manures will go a long way to provide the required nutrients, but for the very best results they should be supplemented with fertilizers, and many gardeners will have to rely entirely on fertilizers to obtain the best results. The manuring needs can be met by the application in March each year of a general fertilizer, such as Growmore, at 100g per m² (3ozs per sq yd). Once the tree is in full

Below: 'William's' is an early, well-flavoured pear

bearing, say from the eighth year onwards, the application in late August of a quick-acting nitrogenous fertilizer such as nitrate of soda can work wonders in maintaining full cropping without excessive vigour. In cases of poor growth sprays of proprietary foliar feeds, say three at fortnightly intervals beginning at petal fall in mid-May, can be a great help, but they are not necessary as an annual measure on properly manured soil.

If the soil is extraordinarily fertile and the trees are still too vigorous then throw caution to the winds and sow grass seeds to provide a competitive but mown lawn. Both pruning and manuring should be adjusted accordingly, concentrating on summer pruning and the application of late summer nitrogen.

The trees should be planted early in the dormant season, preferably as soon as the leaves have dropped and while the soil is still warm. One-year-old trees are the cheapest, and transplant most readily, but the new gardener may prefer to leave the initial pruning and training to the skilled nurseryman and buy his trees with the heads already formed, usually as open-centre bushes not more than three-years old. If you want special forms, such as the espalier or fan shapes mentioned in the chapter on pruning

and training, ask the nurseryman. The really keen gardener will, however, want to train his own trees, even espaliers, assuming he is young enough, and will start with the unpruned one-year tree or maiden.

Open-centre bush trees should be spaced at about 3m (10ft). Pyramids and spindle bushes can be set closer at 2m (6ft 6in). Espaliers need about 4m (13ft).

All these forms can be planted along the edges of paths, in a gentle curve if necessary, to form an attractive and fruitful boundary between one part of the garden and another.

Pruning and training

Books on fruit growing written in the early years of the twentieth century show pear trees grown in a wide variety of shapes and forms, including vases, goblets, winged pyramids, multiple cordons, fans and espaliers. Any gardener owning healthy trees grown painfully in these forms should cherish them, but the new planter is well advised to restrict his choice to open centre or central-leader bushes, or pyramids, or spindle bushes.

The training of trees in these shapes is described in the separate chapter on pruning and training. If in doubt the best advice is to stick to the most easily managed form, the

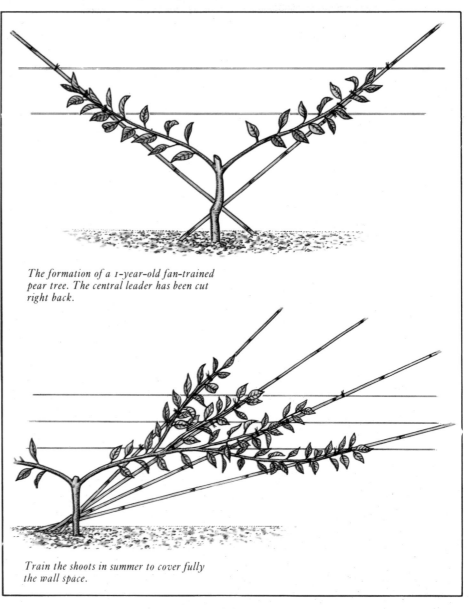

The formation of a 1-year-old fan-trained pear tree. The central leader has been cut right back.

Train the shoots in summer to cover fully the wall space.

open-centre bush tree.

In forming the open centre bush it should be remembered that the pear is neater in its habit than the apple and therefore more branches can be built in. Some varieties, and particularly Conference, tend to form slender branches and the leaders should be pruned for the first eight years or so to ensure that the branches are strong enough to carry heavy crops.

Fruit thinning

In some years, following a frost-free spring, pears may set too many fruits. This is not usually the case but if in July the fruits have begun to turn over and there are still obviously too many remove the surplus to allow the survivors to stand about 15cm (6in) apart. Allowing the trees to carry too large a crop can mean not only small fruits but also the risk of exhaustion affecting next year's crop.

Pests, diseases and birds

It is sad to record that in some districts the most serious pest of pears—and of many another fruit tree and bush—is the bullfinch. Beginning usually at the turn of the year, bullfinches feed voraciously on the buds of a range of trees, and the fruit buds of most varieties of pears are particularly favoured. Oddly, the buds of Comice are not as attractive as those of Conference. The effects of the bud stripping, when severe, are obviously the loss of crop and the not so obvious loss of leaves and growing points, which may adversely affect the general and longer term performance. A special note on bird damage is contained elsewhere and will not be repeated here, other than to point to the essential need to protect the trees in districts where bullfinches are numerous. In some gardens one can see polythene bags which have been slipped over choice maturing fruits in the autumn to protect them against damage by tits and wasps.

The fungus disease known as pear scab can be troublesome in wet districts, and both aphids and the related pear sucker can, in some years, cause serious damage to shoots, leaves and buds.

Two sprayings during the growing season will control these troubles to a satisfactory degree. A start should be made just before the blossoms show colour, and well before they open, using a mixture of malathion and captan (or benlate) and this should be repeated as soon as the last flower has gone.

An extra spray some three weeks later may be necessary if the summer is wet, and especially if Comice and William's, both susceptible to scab, are being grown.

Harvesting

Once pears begin to ripen the process is rapid and difficult to slow down. It is particularly important to pick the early varieties at the right time and to ensure that fruits in store do not mature undetected, because there is nothing more frustrating than to lose precious and hard-won fruits because of the sudden onset of ripening and the rapid decline into that sadly useless condition so

Above: 'Doyenné du Comice' has the finest flavour of all pears

Left: 'Fertility' is a heavy-cropping and reliable variety

appositely described as 'sleepiness'.

The optimum picking date is determined by the variety, the locality and the season. A good guide is to follow the physiological response of the tree. When the appropriate time comes for tree and fruit to part company a layer of cutting-off cells begins to form. If, therefore, near to the anticipated time of picking, the fruits part readily from the tree when lifted gently to the horizontal position, then the time for picking is about to dawn.

Speaking in very general terms, William's is usually ready during the first week of September, Conference about the third week of that month, while the splendid Comice is ready for picking in mid-October. The fruits should be handled carefully to avoid bruising. William's and Merton Pride will not keep for more than a short while after picking, and should be consumed or preserved speedily to avoid wastage. Pears can be frozen but only for use in fruit salads.

Bottling, however, is a very successful method of preserving pears. The remaining varieties in our select list will keep to provide fruit from October to January, if the right conditions are provided.

Storage

The commercial grower controls the temperature, and sometimes the atmosphere, of his store very precisely. Aim to keep the fruits in a cool, moist place, storing them in single layers in trays or similar containers so that the fruits can be inspected readily.

It is well worth experimenting with polythene bags, which provide miniature controlled atmosphere stores and retain moisture. In any case the storage area, be it garden shed or garage, should be kept moist by an occasional damping down with a watering can equipped with a fine rose.

The first signs of ripening are a yellowing of the skin and a softening of the neck. To bring out the full incomparable flavour of the best pears a period of 48 hours or so in a warm living room is often necessary. This is known in the trade as 'conditioning' and should be practised with purchased pears as well as those grown at home.

It is clear that the owner of even a small garden can be independent of shop pears from September to Christmas, and thereby enjoy the unrivalled pleasure of eating a well-grown, beautifully flavoured pear, lovingly produced, with some assistance from nature, by his own endeavours.

Plums & Cherries

trol may be achieved by the introduction of an antagonistic fungus.

Frosty springs we can do little about, short of providing protection by cover, heating or water sprinkling, none of which is easy to provide in gardens.

Site and soil

Plums should be afforded the same considerations as those given to pears and the same preplanting operations used for apples. The only difference is that most of the plums will tolerate heavier, wetter soil than either apples or pears. So if there is a spot in the garden which lies a bit on the wet side

Left: 'Warwickshire Drooper' is a good-natured variety of self-fertile plum

Below: Pyramid-trained plums are very suitable for gardens

The Plum Family

There are at least 14 species of cultivated plums, of varying quality. The species grown in the U.K., *Prunus domestica*, is derived from a natural hybrid between the cherry plum and the sloe. To this mixed genesis we owe the remarkable range of colour, form and flavour.

Plums are divided into the general run of varieties such as Yellow Egg, used in the main for preserving; the dual purpose varieties, such as Victoria, and those varieties which develop a high sugar content and are delicious to eat raw. For convenience we group the latter type under the heading of gages, a term more strictly applied to the greengages and similar varieties. Greengages make a splendid jam, than which there is no better—but the buds of gages are

high on the sweet-toothed bullfinch's list of winter delectables. Damsons stem from a distinct but closely related species. The cultivation details are very similar, so they can be discussed under the same heading as plums.

These delightful fruits, once so easy to grow, are now under a cloud. The problems include increased bird damage, mostly by bullfinches and sparrows; the ancient disease which causes silver leaf; erratic cropping due largely to cold springs, and a new menace caused by a horrid virus disease with the dramatic name of plum pox, or sharka disease, which seriously affects the fruits. Silver leaf continues to elude satisfactory control, although there are some rather slight hopes that one of the new systemic fungicides might succeed where other measures have failed. There is also the intriguing possibility, now being researched, that a biological con-

without being waterlogged, use it for one or two plum trees.

Planting

The form of tree to grow is to some extent governed by the nature of the plant. Many of the popular varieties, including Victoria, possess weak pendulous branches. To keep these branches off the ground it is usual to grow the trees as half-standards, so that the first branch starts at about 1.5m (5ft) from ground level. There are a few strong-branched varieties, such as Czar and Marjorie's Seedling, which can be grown as open-centre bush trees with a short (70cm) leg, but tradition calls for a half-standard tree which, grown on St Julien A rootstock, will give an average branch spread of 4 to 5m (13 to 16ft) across, and which can be planted accordingly.

A half-standard tree must be securely staked to prevent rocking or blowing over.

The best result is achieved by a double-stake and cross-bar, using two posts each 2m (6ft 6in) long. The tree is tied to the cross-bar and padded to prevent chafing.

Plums and gages can also be grown as fan trees against walls, but these rather special sites should be reserved for the choice gages.

Pruning

Pruning is based on rather different principles to those which govern other fruits. For the first four years or so prune the bush or half-standard tree in the winter as for an apple of similar form, with the intention of making sure that the primary branch formation is strong and permanent, and able to carry heavy crops without breaking. Thereafter keep pruning to the very minimum: remove only broken or diseased branches. Do this work in the summer, not the winter, because there is much less likelihood of silver leaf spores invading the wounded tissues during June, July and August. Take care to remove all sucker growths from the roots as they appear.

Branches carrying heavy crops should be temporarily supported to prevent breakage. Use struts, carefully positioned to avoid chafing, or a tall central stake with ties suspended from it as from a maypole. It is seldom necessary to thin plum fruits for garden use, save in exceptional years. In any case the natural drop of young fruits is often severe and alarming, but it is nature's way of shedding the superfluous.

Feeding

The recommendations made for the manuring of pears on p. 118 apply equally to plums, which, conveniently, have similar needs. Plums do, however, differ in their reactions to herbicides, being particularly allergic to simazine.

Harvesting

Plums, ready for picking in September, cannot be stored. Use them as soon as you can: eat them, make jams or bottle the fruits. If in difficulty in a glut period, Victoria can be kept in the refrigerator for a week or two. All good quality fruits can be frozen.

Pests and diseases

Much damage is caused by bullfinches and sparrows, which eat the blossom buds in winter. Reduce damage with black cotton, or spray the trees with one of the temporary deterrents based on Morkit.

Aphids and caterpillars can be readily controlled by spraying with malathion or rogor in accordance with instructions just before blossoming begins. Take great care not to spray open blossoms because of the risk to bees and other welcome visitors. If you miss the right time and there appears the characteristic leaf curling caused by aphids, or the small—later large—holes left by hungry caterpillars, then spray as soon as blossoming has finished.

Silver leaf can be reduced by avoiding the large wounds through which most infections occur. Hence the emphasis on building a strong early branch frame-work and pruning fruiting trees in the summer months. The

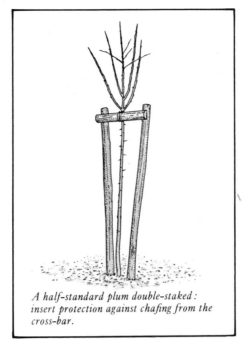

A half-standard plum double-staked: insert protection against chafing from the cross-bar.

'Czar', a very reliable plum, is a cooking variety ready in early August

silvering of the foliage is due to air in the leaf tissues caused by toxins produced by a fungus which may be lower down the branch. The spores of the fungus are not produced from the silvered leaves, so do not be alarmed if you see silver appearing in your or your neighbour's plums—or apples, laurels or even poplars, all of which can be attacked. Occasionally trees which are short of nitrogen are thought to be suffering from silver-leaf because of the pale colour of the leaves. Sometimes the tree or bush manages to control the fungus, the silvering disappears and the plant grows normally. More often, unfortunately, the silvering becomes more pronounced and the branch begins to die. It is sensible to cut out and burn affected branches as soon as they are seen, cutting

well back and dressing the wound with one of the proprietary wound dressings, or at least with a thick layer of white lead paint. But if the whole or the major part of the tree is affected wait to see if natural recovery occurs, taking care to act immediately the branches begin to die. This is crucial, because the fungus enters into its fruiting stage once the tissues die.

At this point purplish bracts appear on the surface issuing vast numbers of dustlike spores to be carried away on the breeze. The original diseased tree, if left alone, will continue to produce spores and menace the neighbourhood for years. Always cut out and burn dead wood from trees affected with silver leaf, and try to persuade your neighbours to do likewise.

Plum pox, or sharka disease, is incurable and can only be prevented by the eradication of all diseased trees. What makes this virus disease particularly difficult to control is that, unusually for fruit tree afflictions, it is carried by aphids. By sucking the sap of diseased trees the aphids may convey the virus particles to healthy trees on which they subsequently feed. The Ministry of Agriculture are working very hard to control this disease. Let us hope they succeed,

The distinctive symptoms of silver leaf disease, which can cause die back

because the fruits from sharka-affected trees are useless.

Rootstocks

There have in recent years been developments in plum growing of great benefit to gardeners. New rootstocks producing small compact trees are now available, and their propagation has been made easier by work at East Malling. Additionally, new systems of training in pyramid form, referred to later, offer hopes of small but fruitful trees.

Nurserymen's catalogues will offer trees on Myrobalan B and Brompton root stocks. Both are excellent, but make big trees needing some 6m (20ft) of space. Choose instead either Pershore or St Julien A. Before long a new series will be available, carrying such intriguing names as Pixy, which is said to be

Above: 'Victoria' still reigns supreme among dessert plums

Left: 'Laxton's Cropper' is a very heavy-bearing variety

very promising for small trees, although the prospect of uniting the majestic Victoria to Pixy seems a trifle undignified.

Varieties

Relatively few of the innumerable varieties available are really suitable for gardens. Any short list, in order of ripening, would include:

River's Early Prolific
Czar
Yellow Egg
Severn Cross
Victoria
Cambridge Gage
Jefferson's Gage
Laxton's Cropper
Warwickshire Drooper
Marjorie's Seedling

To reduce the list to four, consider the following varieties:

Czar is the most reliable of plums, bearing attractive purple fruits in early August. Its only fault is that, like Victoria, it is susceptible to silver-leaf.

Victoria is still much the best of the dual-purpose plums and if there is room for only one tree then this is a clear choice.

Severn Cross is a reliable heavy-cropping jam-making plum of dessert quality.

Marjorie's Seedling, a good-natured, late-ripening purple plum completes the quartet.

The four chosen will cross-pollinate and fertilize each other admirably. An added

qualification for the choice of Victoria as sole representative is that it will set fruit with its own pollen, a quality shared by the other three, but it is thought that in cold springs all plums set better with the aid of cross-pollination.

Damsons are very easy to grow, treated as plums, choosing the variety known variously as the Prune damson, the Shropshire damson or the Westmoreland damson. They all appear to be identical, unless you are fortu-

nate enough to live in Shropshire or Westmoreland, when you use the local name for this hardy fruit. The damson must be tough to grow, as it does, in the Lake District.

Growing Pyramid Plum Trees

Having described the accepted and well tried methods of growing plums let us in conclusion look at a technique which is still relatively new but which shows much promise for gardens. This cautious approach is engendered by the knowledge that it takes a long time to test satisfactorily a new method, and the conservative gardener will quite wisely choose a tried and trusted method rather than the new fangled. Recent work at the Royal Horticultural Society's Garden at Wisley, at East Malling and elsewhere has demonstrated the possibility of growing plums as small trees, closely controlled, either as spindlebushes or, more usually, in the related pyramid form.

The experience obtained suggests that gardeners can with some confidence try

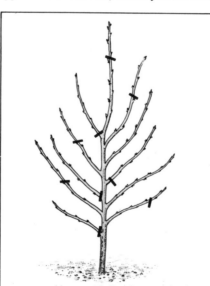

2-year-old pyramid. Retain central axis, removing competing and unnecessary shoots.

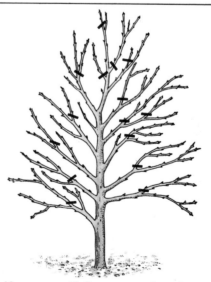

Mature pyramid. Remove upward growing shoots.

this method, which has many advantages. Not only can more varieties be grown in a given area but the trees are much easier to manage and, since there are no large branches to break, silver leaf is less likely to occur.

Until the new pixilated plum rootstocks are available the gardener should choose St Julien A as the rootstock for pyramids, and plant them at 3m (10ft) apart. They need not be in straight lines but can follow a gentle curve, perhaps separating the fruit garden from the flower garden. A stout bamboo cane 3m (10ft) long, to support the central leader, is necessary for the first three years.

The trees should be one-year old at planting. If there are side-shoots (feathers) already present then so much the better. Young plum trees are vigorous, and the maiden tree should be cut back to about 1.5m (5ft) in the April after planting. At the same time any side shoots should be reduced by about half, removing any close to the ground—up to 50cm (20in)—completely, to give a short leg.

During the first summer more primary lateral branches will be produced from the main stem to supplement the original feathers. It is from these, as they develop, that much of the crop will come.

Summer pruning is an essential part of the technique, but the procedure is quite simple. Wait until growth extension has largely ceased, at the end of July, and shorten the ends of the branches, except the central leader, to leave about 20cm (8in). Any side shoots from the branches should be cut back to about 10cm (4in). In each case take care to cut back to a bud pointing downwards, to promote horizontally inclined branch systems, each radiating from the central axis. If necessary young branches can be guided into the right path by securing one end of a length of twine to the centre of the

shoot and the other to the base of the main stem, gently pulling the shoot down towards the horizontal plane. Any really rebellious shoots which insist on growing upright should be cut out at an early stage. This applies especially to shoots in the top half of the pyramid so that narrow, weak angles are avoided and conversely strong wide angled branches are formed.

In subsequent years, this neat and logical pruning continues.

The following April reduce the central leader by two-thirds, which is pretty severe but necessary to keep the stem stout. Prune to a bud on the opposite side to last year's cut. This process of building up the central leader is continued until the tree reaches about 3m (10ft) in height, when an attempt is made to hold it—thus far and no further. Well, not much further, because the tree has other ideas and will continue to grow, and battle is now joined, which the grower must win. Late pruning helps to reduce vigour, so delay the shortening of the leading shoot until May, then shock the tree by shortening the whole leader back to about 2.5cm (1in) of last year's cut. You now have a tree 3m 2.5cm (10ft 1in) tall, which you hack back each May, allowing only a niggardly 2.5cm (1in) increase. If the tree gets really aggressive and insists on growing excessive leader extensions don't hesitate to prune the leading shoot back as part of your summer pruning at the end of July. By these draconian measures you will keep the tree relatively close to the ground.

The side branches are trimmed back each July as before to 20cm (8in) for the terminal shoots and 10cm (4in) for the side shoots. Training plum trees into pyramid forms is in practice a straightforward and enjoyable exercise in applying the principles of plant physiology to a profitable end.

Bullace

Bullace and sloe: what splendid, evocative, home-spun names for fruits that form such an integral part of the countryside. Both are close relatives of the damson and should be grown in similar fashion. The bullace is easy to grow, planted 5m (16ft) apart. It has the advantage of fruiting late, the small, rounded fruits sometimes hanging on the tree in good condition until early November.

The wild bullace has black fruits and is indeed obtainable from nurserymen as Black Bullace, which is simple enough.

The white Bullace is found in several forms, particularly in Essex and East Anglia.

Both black and white kinds are self-fertile, so one tree can be planted on its own.

Sloe

This is our familiar blackthorn, found so frequently in hedges and woods. There seems little point in cultivating it in gardens, unless the owner has a special liking for sloe gin, or a perfectly understandable passion for the damson-like sloe as a preserve.

The tiny white flowers are one of the earlier harbingers of spring, and because of this the crop is all too often affected by spring frost. The point of this is the obvious suggestion that if the sloe was given a sheltered position and a modicum of love in a garden the level of cropping and the quantity of raw material for the home manufacture of sloe gin could be quite astonishing.

Below: The round blackish fruits of sloe have an acid-flavoured flesh and are used for making wine or gin

Below: 'Early Transparent Gage' has a very fine flavour when ripe and is ready for harvest in mid-August

Sweet Cherries

As one who has heaved many a sigh about the references in text books to the growing of sweet cherries in gardens, I would answer that although they may fittingly grow where Julia's lips do smile their proper place is emphatically not in the average suburban garden. At this point it should be made clear that this negative, to be qualified later, applies to the sweet cherry, a giant amongst fruit trees, and not to the relatively diminutive Morello cherry, which is easily accommodated in even a small garden. So we will separate the two, dealing first with the much better known sweet cherry which, like the plum, is a member of the genus *prunus*, this time *Prunus avium*.

The Problems

The difficulty with the sweet cherry is essentially threefold, a trinity of problems concerning size, pollination and bird damage.

The sweet cherry in nature makes a large tree, taking many years to reach the fruiting stage, and until recently horticultural science and craft have not been able effectively to curb its growth. Commercial growers plant their trees as standards, some 13m (say 30ft) apart, on the mysteriously named Malling F 12/1 rootstock. At long last a more dwarfing cherry rootstock, on which the pleasing name Colt has been bestowed, is under trial and looks promising. Hurdle number one may therefore be surmounted.

Pollination is tricky, because the great majority of sweet cherry varieties are not only self-sterile and do not therefore set fruit with their own pollen, but most are in addition cross-incompatible, being so choosy that only selected mates produce a fruitful result. In consequence, the gardener has to plant at least two—and not any old two—varieties, which are mutually compatible even at a distance of 13m. The exception is a new black variety named Stella, as yet relatively untried.

So here again, breeding work promises a breakthrough and in a few years time new varieties grown on Colt rootstock may give us the long awaited compact, early bearing, self-fertile sweet cherry tree. This would also make easier the solution of our third problem, the question of bird damage. In the winter those beautiful buccaneers the bullfinches feed on the hard-won fruit buds, and in summer the trees are favoured by flocks of starlings and other fruit eaters, congregating from several parishes.

The commercial grower deliberately plants his cherry orchards in large blocks so that expensive deterrent measures can be economically applied, but the owner of a couple of isolated trees doesn't really stand a chance.

Site and soil

Some lucky gardeners have the space, and since all are by nature buoyant optimists, there follows a brief summary of sweet cherry growing in the garden.

If you are incredibly fortunate and possess a south-facing wall, and prefer cherries to peaches or gage plums, then it is possible, but difficult, to persuade the sweet cherry to form a fan-shaped tree. Details are given in the chapter on pruning and training. Space them at about 7.5m (24ft) apart, and take particular care to remove any very vigorous shoots growing upwards and outwards, and to tie down others, the aim being to clothe the wall with shoots of weak to moderate vigour as soon as possible. Summer pruning is also a tremendous help in the valiant attempt to control the naturally rampant growth.

But few gardeners have walls to clothe. The rest of us will have to do our best for the present with tall standard trees planted at 13m apart. Choose the best soil you have, in terms of depth, drainage and texture. Although the sweet cherry is distinctly fussy about soil it will also grow satisfactorily on soils which fall somewhat short of the ideal, but will be a dismal failure on badly drained or thin shallow soils.

Tree form and rootstock

Until Colt is available, fully tested, the only suitable rootstock is the vigorous but reliable F 12/1.

The trees are best purchased from a specialist nurseryman as standards, with a stem of 2m (6ft 6in) and the head already formed. It is best to specify 'high-worked' trees, which have the scions inserted on three shoots which form the primary branches. This technique ensures that both the stem and main crotches are formed from F 12/1 tissue, which is resistant to canker.

Stout stakes are necessary in the early years, but can be discarded once the tree is established and growing freely.

The full head should be formed subsequently with the minimum of pruning, removing only those shoots which cross others or are obviously diseased. The recommendations made for the training of plums also apply to sweet cherries.

Varieties

The opportunity for choice is enormous. The colour range is from the pinks and reds to the darker or even black varieties, all mouthwatering and potentially delicious. The red-fruited kinds are best for freezing.

Assuming that there will be no friendly pollen coming from the neighbours' gardens the choice must depend upon not only personal preferences but the vital matter of cross-pollination, which may well mean reference at the point of decision to more detailed tables than are justified here.

The following examples of conjugal association will serve as a guide:

Early Rivers, one of the more easily grown varieties; red, becoming black; can be planted with the later variety with the awkward name of *Bigarreau de Schrecken*, a red to black variety of good quality.

Napoleon Bigarreau, the well known 'Naps', a very productive pink to red variety, some-

what prone to canker, does well planted with *Governor Wood*, a very reliable red-fruited tree which is rather less vigorous than most.

Note well, all these are well established varieties, which may be replaced by new and better ones as yet untried, so the would-be planter should review the position when the time comes to decide.

Manuring

Such a deep rooting subject as the cherry needs little extra nourishment if planted as recommended in good soil. A good mulch will help to get the young tree away. The easiest approach to manuring is to use a complete fertilizer of the Growmore type or equivalent in spring distributed at 100g per m² (3 oz per sq yd) each year on the not-so-good soils, or sulphate of potash on its own at 33g (1 oz) every second year if the tree is obviously in fine fettle.

Pests

Pests and diseases should not be particularly troublesome in the garden, though the commercial grower has to maintain a constant vigil against blackfly, caterpillars, canker, silver leaf, brown rot and birds.

Blackfly, an aphid of enormous breeding capacity, can quickly damage the foliage and the growing points of young shoots. A spray of malathion or similar specific just before the blossoms open will be as effective as the height of the tree permits.

Any branches looking weak or straggly should be removed cleanly, preferably during the summer months.

A tall ladder and an active picker will be needed. The fruits should be picked in dry weather and consumed or preserved forthwith. Ideally they should be allowed to achieve full maturity but the owner can readily be excused if he tries to beat the starlings by making a start as the fruits begin to colour. Another hazard which determines the picking date is fruit splitting, which may occur following rain. The crop potential from two trees is enormous.

The Morello Cherry

The Morello cherry is distinct from the sweet cherry. It stems from a different species, *Prunus cerasus*, which accounts for the difference in stature, habit and flavour. Hybrids between the acid and sweet cherries have given rise to a group known as 'Dukes'. The term Acid or Sour is used to denote the group as a whole. 'Morello' is the one most suitable for gardens.

Soils, sites and forms
The Morello will prosper on soils not ideal for sweet cherries and will put up with the shade of north-facing walls, if need be. It lends itself to wall-training much more readily than does the sweet cherry, but it would be a pity to use any but a north wall for the growing of Morello cherries, since they can be grown so easily as bushes on a short leg.

Rootstocks and spacing
The Morello, so unlike its sweet cousin, actually needs stimulating and needs a vigorous rootstock to keep it going. The clonal selection already mentioned, Malling F 12/1, is the one most widely used.

Above left: 'Merton Glory' is one of the newer varieties of sweet cherry

Left: Sweet cherry 'Napoleon' has long been popularized as 'Naps'

Below: The 'Morello' cherry is easy to grow either as bush or as wall trees

Both wall trees, trained as fans, and bush trees should be spaced at around 5m (16ft) apart, less on the thinner soils. One-year-old trees are particularly suitable and grow away quickly, with the aid of the usual careful planting, staking and mulching. The head of the bush tree should be formed by the shortening of the maiden tree to about 60cm (2ft) to encourage the production of primary branches in the same way as for apples. The detailed formative pruning is outlined in the special chapter on pruning. Once the head has been formed pruning consists merely of the removal of crossing branches and the deliberate cutting back into old wood of, say, three branches each year. This is necessary to ensure that the bush is kept in a compact and fruitful condition. Without this branch shortening the Morello cherry tends to carry most of its fruit on the outer skirts of the tree. Leave the selective branch cutting until May, so that the cut can be made to a newly started shoot.

Manuring
Since they have to carry both a heavy crop and produce the bearing wood for next year at one and the same time, the generous manuring programme suggested for pears is exactly right for Morello cherries. For the same reasons, keep down weeds because competition for moisture and nutrients slows down growth considerably. Irrigation during dry spells is a great help, but not once the fruit starts colouring.

Varieties, pollination and harvesting
This could not be easier, because the Morello cherry, the only one recommended, sets fruit with its own pollen. All that is required is a frost-free flowering period and plenty of bees.

The fruits should be left until ripe, birds and splitting permitting, and then removed by snipping the stalks with a pair of thin-bladed scissors. They can, of course, simply be pulled off in the old-fashioned way but this tends to tear the bark and to let in the nasty fungus disease which causes brown-rot.

Pests and diseases
The main troubles are blackfly, birds, brown-rot and silver leaf. Blackfly should be prevented by the pre-blossom spray recommended for sweet cherries. Birds can be to some extent deterred by glittering strips of foil or plastic and similar scaring devices, or even by netting, which becomes practicable, but messy, with this small tree.

The keen fruit grower, asked what he wants for Christmas, should ask hopefully for a permanent fruit cage.

Brown-rot and silver-leaf are not controlled by spraying, but much can be done by straightforward hygiene, removing rotting fruits and silvered branches when seen.

Uses
It does seem a pity to end a chapter on the doleful subject of pests and diseases, so let us conclude by reminding the reader of the delights of cherry brandy, a great comfort to the weary gardener at the end of the day.

Peaches & Vines

Peaches & nectarines in the garden

The word Nectarine, like Fragaria, is one to cherish. In truth it is not a generic name and denotes only a peach with a smooth skin. Claims have been made that the flavour of nectarines is superior to that of peaches with fuzzy skins, but the evidence for such a sweeping assessment is not strong.

Peaches and nectarines can be regarded for all practical purposes as requiring the same treatment.

Background

Most peaches on sale in the shops are imported, but the peach can be grown successfully in the open in Britain, although the weight of crop tends to fluctuate in relation to the type of weather prevailing at the time of flowering.

The peach is botanically *Prunus persica*, but its origin is from China rather than Persia. When grown in this country it foolishly persists in flowering early, often before the leaves appear. The bleak winds and chilling frosts of early spring then take an inevitable toll. Point number one then: peaches grow superbly well in glasshouses, perform satisfactorily when grown on walls, and tend to behave erratically in the wide open spaces.

The moral is the obvious one, the peach should be given a favourable site for good results. The use of glasshouses for peaches (and vines) is dealt with in a separate chapter; growing against walls and in the open ground will be covered here.

Site and soil

Despite the rather discouraging tone of the opening notes the gardener in the south of England at least should not hesitate to try his hand at peach growing, if he has room.

Windswept sites and obvious frost pockets should be avoided, but shade and competition from nearby trees is equally to be eschewed, no matter how sheltering their embrace.

The soil should be deep, well-drained, yet retentive of summer moisture, a tiresome repetition, but a necessary one because the peach, like the blackcurrant, has the dual task of carrying a crop and replacing the bearing shoots in the same year.

There is still a feeling around that a stone fruit, such as the peach, must have plenty of lime to prosper. It may be a confused linking of calcium and bones which gives

Above: Nectarine 'Pitmaston Orange' has a rich, sugary flavour

Right: Golden peaches and nectarines are the most exotic of summer fruits

rise to this erroneous notion. Those travellers who have seen peach orchards in the limestone areas of Italy will readily appreciate that too much lime locks up iron and manganese in the soil, giving rise to bright yellow rather than green leaves. A soil pH level of around 6.2 is about right. In other words, only markedly acid soils need liming.

One returns to the thought of a south-facing wall as the ideal, knowing that few can follow such advice, or even the less desirable alternatives of west or east facing walls. But some can, and they should.

Paradoxically the more cosy conditions tend to bring about still earlier flowering, and it is wise to equip the peach wall with means of providing quick and temporary protection on frosty nights during the susceptible period. Light hessian, plastic netting and similar materials will provide enough retention of heat to prevent severe damage. The protection should not actually touch the tree and must be removed during the daytime, unless an unusual wind frost

occurs during the daylight hours of spring.

Apart from the risk of frost damage to the delicate flowers and fruitlets the peach is perfectly hardy and needs no winter protection, always allowing for the possibility that a new Ice Age cometh, when we will all need protection.

Rootstocks and varieties

One of the charms of horticulture is the constant exception to the rules.

There are hundreds of peach trees in gardens which have been raised from stones sown by green-fingered gardeners, usually women. All these are brand new varieties, growing on their own roots. In the nature of things very few of these speculative seedlings are improvements on existing tried and named varieties, but many are

126

sufficiently good to warrant a continued life, nourished by their proud foster-parents.

Peach seedlings are used in some parts of the world to provide rootstocks for the cultivated varieties, but performance is apt to be variable and it is best for the amateur to buy his trees on predictable clonal rootstocks. The best, at present, for the amateur is the plum rootstock St Julien A, which produces a small, early bearing, compact tree.

Varieties are numerous and the choice confusing.

Rochester. An American variety, outstanding on open ground. If only one tree can be grown, this is it.

Hale's Early. Rather less robust, but of better quality; a yellow fleshed variety which ripens in late July and is said to freeze well. The even better *Peregrine*, an August variety, is worth trying even in the open.

On walls the choice is wider, including the three varieties already mentioned and the later ripening *Bellegarde*.

Early Rivers and *Elruge* are two nectarines with good records.

Pollination

All but one of the varieties mentioned are, so far as is known, self fertile and can be planted on their own. The exception is Hale's Early, which demands a compatible mate. The real problem is not cross-pollination, but the distribution of the pollen within the flowers. This is normally achieved by insects, but there are not many about when the peach is in flower and the grower of peaches should not hesitate to encourage the spread of pollen by using a tuft of cotton wool as suggested in the chapters on the growing of peaches and strawberries under glass.

Planting

For good results the recommendations made in the earlier reference to the planting of apple trees should be followed carefully. A good start is all important.

Trees on walls on St Julien A should be spaced at 5m (16ft) apart. In the open ground bush trees require the same sort of space, in all directions.

Pruning and training

Trees on walls are usually trained in a fan shape, this being the most efficient way in which to occupy the space. Building up a fan is a fascinating but lengthy process, and many gardeners will prefer to buy a tree in which the initial framework has been formed by the expert nurseryman.

It is best to buy such a tree direct from a specialist rather than a local garden centre which, understandably, obtains from elsewhere the plants for which there is a limited demand.

The dedicated gardener, wishing to train his own fan tree, will buy an unpruned maiden tree and follow the recommendations contained in the chapter on pruning. Similarly the training of an open-centre bush tree to stand in the open garden follows exactly the same principles laid down for the shaping of a bush apple tree.

The pruning of the fan tree in the fruiting stage is quite different from any other fruit yet discussed. The basic principles to adopt are, however, quite straightforward—any very strong shoots growing outwards from

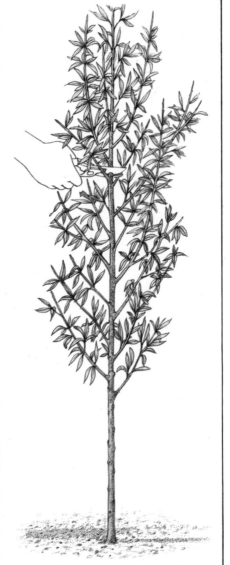

Pruning back a vigorous young peach tree to form an open-centre bush suitable for growing in the open.

the wall, any shoots misguided enough to grow inwards towards the wall, any cankered or broken shoots or branches—all these are removed completely at the end of the growing season.

This leaves for attention the fine tracery of twigs and shoots radiating from the arms of the fan, all neatly tied in to the wire framework.

The peach fruits best on shoots of the previous year's growth. Each shoot carries a mixture of buds: pointed wood buds, rounder blossom buds, and compound units consisting of two fruit buds and one wood bud. The aim is to encourage the production of these shoots in the right places. Once the fruit has been picked the shoot can and should be cut out and a new one tied in its place.

This really is all you need to know, but you can go further and increase the strength of the selected new shoots by removing or pinching-back superfluous ones by the technique of deshooting. It is easy to describe what is involved in this simple operation. Essentially only three growing points are left on each fruiting lateral, *a*) the one at the end, *b*) one at the base chosen to replace the lateral, and *c*) one a little higher up. The last is not really necessary but is left as a belt-and-braces precaution in case disaster befalls the chosen one (and as an added source of sustenance). Either remove all other shoots by finger and thumb, or pinch them back to two leaves if there is a fruit at the joint. Sometimes secondary shoots arise. Pinch these back in turn to one leaf. Similarly the growing point of the extension growth (*a*) can be stopped at five leaves, if time permits, and if no further extension is needed.

At the end of the season prune out with secateurs the laterals which have carried the fruits. Tie in the replacement shoot.

Bush trees have more space in which to operate and do not receive the same detailed attention, apart from the basic operations earlier laid down with regard to overcrowded, crossing, damaged and diseased branches.

Bush peach trees, like Morello cherries, tend to become bare in the centre and fruitful only on the periphery, and each spring should see a deliberate cutting back of say three branches to new shoots.

The pruner should aim at filling all the space with young cropping wood. What could be simpler?

The timing of the pruning is a bit tricky. Prune wall trees in the autumn, after the fruit has been picked. The de-shooting is of course carried out continuously during the summer as the need arises. Bush trees can also be pruned in the autumn, but the shortening of the leggy branches is best left to spring, when the new breaks can be seen more readily.

Manuring

Prepare the soil well before planting, by thorough digging and the incorporation of any available bulky organic matter. Thereafter an annual mulching may suffice for some years, because it is important not to encourage excessive vigour. On the other hand, if the growth of replacement shoots slows down then a dressing in early spring of a compound fertilizer at 100g per m² (3oz per sq yd) is obviously called for.

Trees on walls, and young bush trees, may suffer from lack of water. The thick annual mulch which forms our routine and pious recommendation helps enormously to retain moisture, but wall trees in particular will in most years respond to frequent waterings from mid-May to mid-September, give or take a cloud burst or two, but not during the ripening period because of the risk of fruit splitting.

Fruit thinning

In some years there are too many fruitlets. If all were left the result would be fruits consisting largely of stone, an end clearly to be avoided. Nature plays her part in divesting the tree of the unwanted young, and additional thinning should not be done until the stone is well formed and the fruit likely to stick, if permitted. Even then it is best to play safe by a gradual, staged thinning, beginning in mid-June, when all badly placed fruits—those wedged between shoots, for example—and those marked by abortive caterpillar bites are taken off.

Finally each fruit should stand about 20cm (8in) from its neighbour. In some years no thinning is necessary and indeed there may appear to be no crop, but generally there will be enough.

Harvesting

Peaches ripen at intervals over a period of about six weeks. They should be lifted if possible in the palm of the hand, as opposed to being gripped with the tips of the fingers, given a slight twist, and handled afterwards with appropriate tenderness.

Pests and diseases

The worst trouble is the fungus disease called peach leaf curl, readily recognized by the reddening, curling, crimping and blistering of the leaves. It is not easy to control, but every attempt should be made to stop this crippling disease from getting a hold. New research work suggests the possibility of a spray being developed which will kill the over-wintering fungal mycelium, and stop the disease in its tracks. Meanwhile, at least one spray with a copper or lime sulphur fungicide in early February is necessary. If the tree has been badly attacked the previous summer then a spray should be applied in late autumn, followed by two sprays in spring, one in early February and the other a fortnight later.

A spray with malathion immediately flowering is finished will help to control aphids. The same material is useful during the summer to reduce the undesirable effects of the glasshouse red spider mite, which flourishes on wall trees in warm summers and causes the familiar bronzing of the leaves and premature defoliation.

Above: Peach 'Rochester', though hardy, does best against a wall

Growing grapes in the open garden

Grapes have been successfully grown in Britain since Roman times and the Domesday Book records that 38 vineyards existed in 1088. It is commonly assumed that grapes are difficult to grow in the open and that they will ripen only in favoured sunny summers. This is no longer the case.

South of a line from the Wash to Worcester and taking in the Welsh counties bordering the Bristol Channel, (less so in Pembrokeshire), and the English counties east of Devon, full success can be expected in about seven years out of ten and ripe fruit, albeit of lower quality, in other years. Success does, however, depend on four requirements being met.

Four essential requirements

Firstly, choose a reasonably favourable site in order to achieve a good micro-climate within the 'vineyard'; thus ensure that the site is not unduly shaded from the sun but has some shelter from the wind.

Secondly, select varieties which are early ripening, and which are immune or resistant to mildew. The varieties listed here have been selected to meet these requirements.

Thirdly, the vines must be managed and trained in the manner described below.

Finally, protect the vines from birds well in advance of fruit maturity.

Site

During the growing season vines respond positively to warmth and sunshine; at temperatures below 10°C (50°F) develop-

Below: Grape 'Müller Thurgau' may be used for wine-making or dessert purposes

ment slows markedly. In this connection the majority of modern gardens are, because of their proximity to the house or adjacent trees and hedges, provided with some shelter from wind and shading from direct sunlight for varying parts of the day. Preferably, the site for the mini-vineyard should be exposed to sunlight for most of the day, but if some shelter from wind is available this is likely to prove a positive advantage even if some shading is caused. Shelter which does not unduly shade will help create a micro-climate in which air and soil temperatures are higher because of reduced wind speed. Windbreaks can of course be provided for the vineyard, either in the form of fine mesh netting or as hedges.

Very favourable sites are afforded by brick walls and to a lesser extent by board fences. South facing walls are best, but those with easterly or westerly aspects are not to be despised. On such sites, film plastic sheeting can be rigged up to provide conditions which approximate a lean-to glasshouse. Dessert grapes can be the first choice for prime sites such as these.

Soils and nutrition

The first and most important consideration is that vines grown in the open should not be encouraged to make excessive vegetative growth. If they do, they exhibit a tendency to late ripening and proneness to attack of the fruit bunches by Botrytis (grey mould). Hence deep and fertile soils, such as those that produce lush crops of vegetables, should be manured with care and excessive applications of nitrogen avoided. Vines do, however, benefit from generous applications of nitrogen for the first two years or so of their life.

Almost any type of soil that is adequately drained can be made to grow good vines, given sound management. This applies even to chalk soils, including relatively poor and shallow ones. Sandy, gravelly and loamy soils are usually very suitable. Heavy clays, especially if poorly drained, are the least suitable but even gardeners endowed with such soils should not be deterred. Given care in establishing the young vines – putting a good supply of compost or peat in the planting holes – the vines will eventually grow freely.

One aspect of the nutrition of vines should be emphasized. They are very sensitive to a deficiency of magnesium, which manifests itself in the form of an inter-veinal yellowing of the *older* leaves of the current season's growths. The first symptoms may be expected from midsummer onward and, if severe, will progress to a dessication and premature shedding of the affected older leaves. The symptoms should not be confused with lime-induced iron deficiency – caused by an excess of lime. The symptoms in these cases would be seen in the *youngest* leaves, including the growing point. But the varieties listed later are pretty tolerant of high lime. Curative measures for magnesium deficiency may require the application in early spring of up to 250 g per m^2 (8 oz per sq yd) of agricultural Epsom Salts. On soils prone to the trouble, an annual topping-up of 100–125 g per m^2 (3–8 oz per sq yd) may be required.

Routine manuring should include a constant supply of nitrogen, potash and phosphate, and on markedly acid soils an occasional dressing of lime. If available, applications of well-decayed compost or farmyard manure will be beneficial. Fresh animal dung should not be used.

A compound fertilizer at 250 g per m^2 (8 oz per sq yd) should prove an adequate annual dressing. 'Growmore' fertilizer would be suitable and is best applied in late winter or early spring. Should a need for more nitrogen be indicated by lack of plant vigour and paleness of the foliage, a dressing of sulphate of ammonia or nitro-chalk can be given, either at the time of the main application or during the growing season.

Varieties

The varieties now listed have been selected for their ability to reach maturity even in adverse summers. All are suitable for making wine (Müller Thurgau and Siegerribe may also be used as dessert grapes) and are tolerant of high lime levels, such as occur in chalky soils.

Seyve Villard 5 276 is a hybrid now popularly known as 'Seyvel Blanc'. It is an exceptionally reliable variety both in crop yield and ability to ripen. Its vigour is only average, which makes it easy to manage. It is resistant to mildew and grey mould.

Ripening from the end of September to mid-October, depending on season, it produces a white wine of very fair quality which can be further improved by blending with juice from the Müller Thurgau variety. It is not suitable for dessert.

Müller Thurgau – also known as *Riesling Sylvaner* – is of Swiss origin and is the variety most extensively planted in British commercial vineyards. It is also widely grown in Germany. Unfortunately, it is prone to attack by downy mildew in seasons when the weather is adverse.

A most excellent wine variety, it is also very acceptable for dessert provided the berries are thinned soon after fruit set.

Siegerribe This variety is German in origin. The golden berries are suitable for either dessert or wine, and have a distinct muscat flavour.

Madeleine Angevine This early-ripening, well-flavoured, white grape is suitable for either dessert or wine.

Tereshkova Few black varieties are suitable for dessert when grown in the open in the U.K. but this red variety, sporting a purplish bloom, is early ripening and attractive for dessert. It is of Russian origin, obtained by hybridizing with a Siberian grape.

Siebel 13053—now known as *Cascade*—is proving one of the most prolific and reliable black grapes for wine. Of German origin, it produces large numbers of laterals, which carry a profusion of relatively small bunches. To obtain full yields more fruiting laterals should be retained than for other varieties. Used unblended it produces a red wine of brilliant colour and it is also useful for blending with wine from Baco No. 1.

Baco Because of its rampant vigour this variety is not usually recommended and if planted in a row will require a spacing of at least 3 m (10 ft) and a modified renewal or spur system of training. It will readily cover

Below: The very reliable 'Seyve Villard' grape is only suitable for making wine

a large wall or fence. A prodigious cropper, it will ripen every year provided that it is netted for bird protection and, in cold summers, left to mature on the vine until late October or early November.

Gagarin Blue is a black wine grape from the same Russian source (the Caucasus) as Tereshkova. Some are critical of its large and straggly fruit bunches; many flowers fail to set but the remainder grow to become large berries with a high ratio of pulp to pips. The yield is at or above average and it never fails to ripen by September.

General management

Planting. One-year-old plants establish most successfully, and should be planted in the spring, although this can be done in the autumn. Vines are propagated either from hard wood cuttings or by grafting on to the root system of North American varieties immune to root aphid. Either method is suitable for growing grapes for wine in British gardens. Pot the young plants in a compost such as John Innes No. 1 in 15-cm (6-in) containers. They can then be set out in the open ground quite late in the spring

their permanent positions. This will avoid the risk of damaging the one-year-old canes.

The method of pruning best suited to producing grapes in Britain is the Guyot system, for which the following arrangement of posts and wires has been carefully designed.

Each post should be about 2 m (6 ft) long, driven firmly 50 cm (20 in) into the ground. Intermediate posts should be placed 3 m (10 ft) apart. Posts at the end of long rows will need support in the form of struts.

Four levels of 12 gauge wire are attached to the posts. The first and lowest wire, a single strand, is 45 cm (18 in) above the ground. The second wire, consisting of two strands 2.5 cm (1 in) apart, is set 22 cm (8½ in) above the first. The third wire, again a double strand, is set 30 cm (12 in) above the second. The two strands of the third-level wire are held 30 cm (12 in) apart horizontally by spacer bars attached to the intermediate posts. A final wire of two strands, arranged exactly as the third-level wire, is set 30 cm (12 in) higher than the third, that is 127 cm (5 ft) from the ground.

*Even in an unheated greenhouse
a vine will give excellent results*

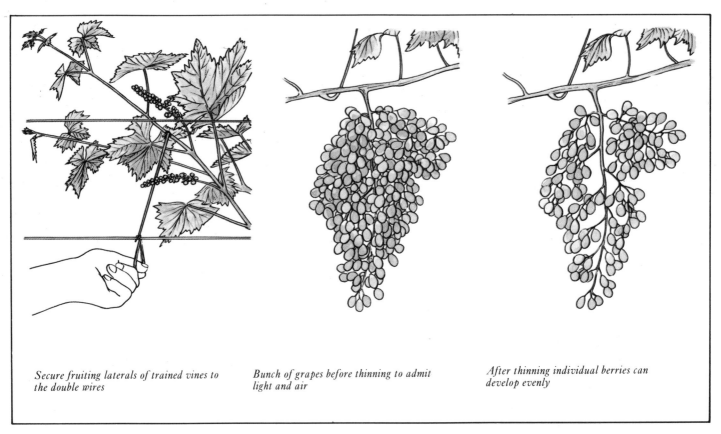

*Secure fruiting laterals of trained vines to
the double wires*

*Bunch of grapes before thinning to admit
light and air*

*After thinning individual berries can
develop evenly*

without check. Alternatively the vines can be purchased already growing in containers.

If you are growing several vines, space them 1.5 m (5 ft) apart, with 2 m (6 ft) between the rows. Very vigorous varieties, such as Baco No. 1, will need more space.

Fill the planting holes with composted vegetation, peat or potting soil. Spring-planted vines will need watering until they are rooting freely.

Staking

While a support system for the vines can be put up any time in the first year, consider doing so before putting the young plants in

The Guyot System of Pruning
The First Year. The aim of the Guyot system is to replace every year those canes which have fruited with young growths produced in the summer.

After planting and before growth begins, cut back each new plant to two or three buds.

Select the strongest shoot which results from the initial pruning, plucking out the remainder, and allow this strong shoot to grow vertically, tying it to a 2 m (6 ft) post.

At the end of the first growing season, prune back the strong single canes of each plant to 60 cm (2 ft) from the ground. No

further work is needed in the first year, save for the erection of the permanent post-and-wire support system described above.
The second year
The object of pruning each young, strong, vertical cane back to 60 cm (2 ft) is to encourage reproduction of three topmost growths close behind the cut. These strong shoots, three to each plant, are grown vertically during year two, supported by slipping them in as they grow between the double strand of wire at the second level.

At the end of the second growing year, tie down two of the three canes horizontally to the lowest wire of the trellis, one to the right and one to the left. Shorten the third, middle cane, severely to three buds from its origin. From this pruned shoot will come a further crop of three new canes.

The third year

This is the harvest year. The horizontal canes trained on the lowest wire will, all being well, produce flowers and fruit. The fruit is carried on laterals – side shoots – produced from almost every bud of the horizontal canes. These laterals will, of course, grow upwards. They are easily broken in the early stages and are therefore secured to the widely spaced double wires of the trellis. The fruiting laterals should be reduced in number to stand some 15 to 20 cm (6 to 8 in) apart. This lateral thinning should be delayed until the flower trusses are visible, so that you can identify and remove barren shoots or those carrying weak trusses and retain only the strongest.

The retained, fruiting, laterals should be stopped by removing the growing tips when they have grown above the top double wire.

A requirement for table grape production

Above: 'Madeleine Angevine' is early-ripening and suitable for dessert or wine

Right: 'Siebel' is a prolific German grape that makes a rich-coloured wine

is that the bunches be thinned. This should be done shortly after fruit set, to increase the size of the individual berries at maturity. For wine, thinning is not necessary.

In contemplating the glories of the fruiting shoots we must not overlook the welfare of the three strong shoots coming from the severely pruned 'third' cane. These strong growths are trained vertically without stopping, unless growth is rampant, in which case each cane can be tied down to the top wire. These three canes are essential to the system, because they provide the source of the replacement of the fruiting wood.

The fourth and subsequent years

At the end of the third year, after harvest, the horizontal canes on the bottom wire are removed, together with all their laterals. In their place two of the three new strong growths are bent down horizontally, one to the right and one to the left, and tied to the lowest wire, to start the whole process of fruiting all over again.

The horizontal canes will frequently be longer than is desirable and should, if necessary, be shortened to allow no more than 15 cm (6 in) of overlap with neighbouring canes on the bottom wire.

The middle cane of the three, held in reserve, is shortened severely, thus providing the cycle of replacement canes. And so on, ad infinitum.

Pests and diseases

The varieties listed, with the possible exception of Müller Thurgau, are not prone to attack by fungal diseases. However, local circumstances, especially those relating to high atmospheric humidity, may cause attacks to occur. If downy mildew (Perenospora) is a problem, take precautions by spraying with a zineb-type fungicide at fortnightly intervals from leaf break to the end of August.

Powdery mildew (Oidium), which if it occurs may cause the berries to split, is controlled by spraying, over the period of time indicated above, with wettable sulphur.

Added protection

By using the Guyot training system the vines can readily be given general protection by means of film plastic fixed so that the plants are enclosed, as long as provision is made for adequate ventilation.

Plastic protection is not usually necessary for wine grapes on reasonably favourable sites, but it can enable less favourable sites to be utilized, including more northerly ones. For dessert grapes, however, it is particularly advantageous and more effective ripening will be achieved in those seasons when warmth is lacking. The choice of varieties given above will survive happily without these measures.

Peaches & Vines under Glass

Growing peaches, nectarines and grapes in a glasshouse is a real luxury, and great fun. Ideally each subject should be grown on its own, as in days of yore, when peach houses and vineries were separate entities in the large private gardens. A possible compromise for the modern gardener is to divide his glasshouse, if large enough, by a partition screen, to provide a distinct compartment in which the rather special conditions governing dormancy, flowering and ripening can be achieved. Even so, it is best to grow one or the other in the same house.

Most of us, however, can only manage one glasshouse to serve all our needs. I have seen cucumbers, orchids, tomatoes, melons, grapes, peaches and flowering pot plants all growing in the same glasshouse, but none of the crops was being well grown. Peaches and vines, however, can be grown with reasonable success in the mixed glasshouse, providing that some basic points of husbandry are observed.

Peaches and nectarines

The earlier chapter on growing peaches in the open contains much that is fundamental to their cultivation under glass. The following is a summary of the main points.

Form of tree

The fan shape is almost universal.

Site and soil

In a normal free-standing structure the tree is best planted in a border, and trained up the span on one side of the house. A lean-to house built on a south-facing wall is ex-

Below: Peach 'Peregrine' is very successful under glass but can be grown in the open

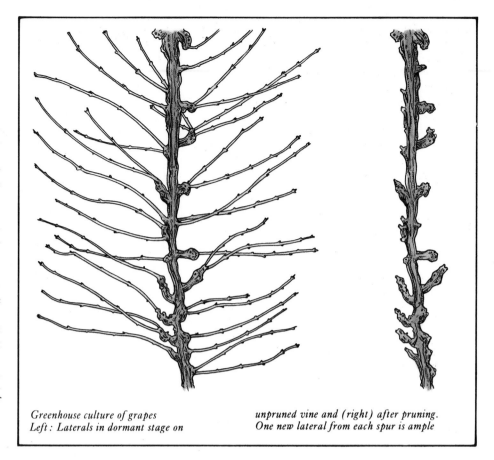

Greenhouse culture of grapes
Left: Laterals in dormant stage on

unpruned vine and (right) after pruning.
One new lateral from each spur is ample

cellent, but in this case, the tree is trained entirely against the wall. Special soil preparations may be necessary to ensure that the roots have a minimum depth of 45 cm (18 in) of well-drained loam and a border width of 60 cm (2 ft).

Rootstock and varieties

St Julien A is an excellent rootstock for peaches. The varieties mentioned in the main chapter are all suitable, but the hardy Rochester is best grown in the open.

Spacing

It is a common and understandable mistake to attempt to grow too many trees in a small space. One good fan tree of the self-fertile Peregrine, for example, will provide more than enough fruits for the average family if given a space of 4 m (13 ft) in which to spread its wings. Hale's Early should not be planted as the sole variety because of pollination uncertainties.

Pruning

The recommendations made in the chapters on training and on peaches grown against walls in the open apply also to trees under glass, except that the time scale is accelerated and the need for pinching, disbudding, de-shooting and fruit thinning is imperative. Great care should be taken to train in the branches necessary to clothe the wall or roof space with precision, to avoid the need to cut out superfluous large branches. The fruits will be large and plump and should be finally spaced at a distance something like 25 cm (10 in) apart.

General cultivation

Manuring and watering are on familiar lines, but many gardeners fail to appreciate how quickly a glasshouse border becomes dry in summer. Dryness at the roots is perhaps the most frequent single cause of failure, because pests such as the glasshouse red spider mite become rampant if the trees are dry, and early leaf-fall results.

The peach is, after all, a hardy subject and during the winter months the night temperature need not be more than 4°C (40°F), and the house should be well-ventilated during daytime save in severe weather. Naturally in a mixed house a compromise will be necessary. Come spring and flowering time the night temperature should be a minimum of 10°C (50°F).

It is essential to hand-pollinate the flowers. As soon as the fruits set, a daily syringing with clear water will go a long way to keep the foliage bright, the fruits swelling and the pests depressed.

Special care must be taken when picking, each fruit being gently lifted in the palm of the hand to avoid bruising.

The really important points are to avoid high temperatures in the dormant season, to keep the borders well watered without being saturated, to syringe frequently, to keep on top of pests and diseases and, above all, to maintain a constant schedule of de-shooting and pinching to keep the trees in a state of controlled fruitfulness.

Grapes

Yet again, the chapter on growing vines out of doors should be read first, since the principles apply equally. While the varieties and the environment are different, much more skill is required. The rewards are, however, very great, since there is nothing in horticulture more thrilling than producing a well-grown crop of glasshouse grapes.

Varieties and propagation

The choice of variety is crucial. The superb high quality muscat grapes, typified by Muscat of Alexandria and Canon Hall Muscat, are difficult to grow and require facilities beyond those at the disposal of most amateur gardeners. Reluctantly, therefore, one is obliged to suggest that even the keenest of amateurs should lower his sights and restrict himself to the easier, but still demanding, varieties of which Black Hamburgh is the most popular. Foster's Seedling, a good natured white grape of fair quality, is an alternative.

The vine is usually grown on its own roots. Propagate by taking 1.5 cm (2 in) hard-wood cuttings, each bearing a single bud, in the dormant period. Place in 7.5 cm (3 in) pots in a warm place.

Soil treatment

Grow glasshouse vines in borders rather than containers. You can either plant the vine immediately outside the glasshouse and train the stem inside, or grow the whole of the plant, roots and all, inside the glasshouse. The latter method has the advantage of giving more control of the total environment, but circumstances may make it necessary to use an outside border. Some excellent grapes have been produced from vines thus planted.

Whichever approach is used it is important that the root-run should not be less than 60 cm (2 ft) deep and 1 m (3 ft) wide. Good drainage is essential, and the border soil should be thoroughly dug and enriched before planting takes place.

Spacing

This will depend on how many main stems, or rods, are to be grown on the one vine. The best results are obtained from single rod or cordon vines, which are spaced 2 m (6 ft 6 ins) apart, to allow the fruit-bearing laterals to develop on either side to 1 m (3 ft) without tangling with the neighbour. One rod of Black Hamburgh, well grown, at the end of the mixed plant glasshouse will meet most purposes.

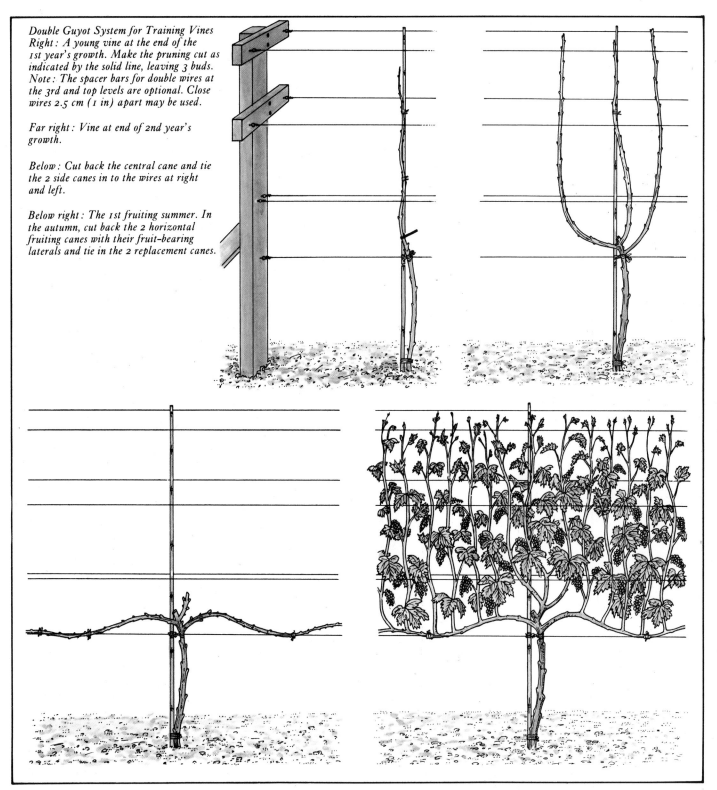

Double Guyot System for Training Vines
Right: A young vine at the end of the 1st year's growth. Make the pruning cut as indicated by the solid line, leaving 3 buds. Note: The spacer bars for double wires at the 3rd and top levels are optional. Close wires 2.5 cm (1 in) apart may be used.

Far right: Vine at end of 2nd year's growth.

Below: Cut back the central cane and tie the 2 side canes in to the wires at right and left.

Below right: The 1st fruiting summer. In the autumn, cut back the 2 horizontal fruiting canes with their fruit-bearing laterals and tie in the 2 replacement canes.

Black Hamburgh is the finest greenhouse grape

Environment

Allow the vine to enter into a dormant state after fruiting and keep the house cool during the winter, the needs of other plant inhabitants permitting. Some of the old school of gardeners used to hose the rod down during frosty periods until encased in ice.

In spring, when growth begins, the minimum temperature may be raised to 7°C (45°F). Bud break can be assisted by syringing with clear water in the mid-morning of fine days.

As growth extends, the night temperature should be raised to a minimum around 10°C (50°F). Much higher temperatures will occur during the summer and a light shading may be required. Regular, as distinct from sporadic, watering is necessary and particularly so with vines grown in indoor borders.

Syringing should continue until the fruits begin to colour, but every effort should be made to ensure that the rods are dry by nightfall. A sharp friendly rap on the rod when the vine is in flower will help to distribute the pollen. Choose a warm period of the day for the rapping session. Varieties other than Black Hamburgh call for rather more complicated procedures.

Pruning

Basically, pruning is very simple, but the timing calls for skill and experience. The fruits are carried on lateral shoots produced annually from spurs on the main rod. The art of growing consists in controlling these laterals. Beginning at the beginning, and assuming that the vine is established, pruning is done immediately after leaf fall, usually in December. It is important not to make major cuts when the rods are active because the sap pressure is such that the vine 'bleeds' from the cut surface.

All the lateral shoots are cut back to two buds. Shorten the extension shoot at the same time, back to two buds if the rod has reached its alloted length, or about halfway back if extension is still permissible.

The result is a rather stunned-looking rod, deprived of all growth save for the knobbly spurs.

When growth starts in spring the young shoots should be reduced to leave two to each spur. This reduction process continues as the need dictates throughout the growing season, so that all energy is concentrated on the two selected shoots. Some of these will tend to grow vertically towards the

glass instead of laterally and it is necessary to pull these down gradually, not suddenly, by an adjustable tie attached to the middle of the shoot at one end and a wire, or the main rod, at the other.

Generally speaking, and assuming that large berries on large bunches is the aim, the bunches should be reduced progressively so that only one well-placed bunch is left on each shoot by say mid June. Even this may be too much for a vine not in the peak of health and vigour; a dozen large bunches per rod is as much as should be asked of a willing vine.

Left to its own devices a lateral will grow on and on; don't let it. Pinch out the growing point two leaves beyond the selected bunch. Sub-laterals should be pinched back to one leaf, to give active leaves without undue competition for light.

Fruit thinning and harvesting

Thinning of the fruits is an unnatural process, but a necessary one if large berries are wanted. The task is best accomplished by the use of a pair of scissors with long narrow blades, known in the trade as 'grape' or 'vine' scissors.

The point of these scissors can be inserted into the heart of the bunch to remove single unwanted grapes. Most attention should be paid to the insides of the bunch, the shoulders needing little thinning. Indeed it helps to lift the shoulder away from the main part of the bunch by means of a tie, to give the swelling berries more room and to admit air to the centre of the bunch. Thinning should be gradual, and carried out in stages. The small berries should be removed first, together with all those in the centre and any damaged or diseased ones.

It is a drastic process, requiring the removal of some two-thirds of the berries. Thinning will be completed by mid-July, and colouring of Black Hamburgh will start a month or so later.

Harvesting can be staged according to use; the berries will keep well on the vines in a buoyant atmosphere, but you must trim out any over-ripe or rotting berries.

Miscellany

After harvest the vines are kept as cool as conditions permit, but the border must not be allowed to become really dry even in the dormant period.

Pests, diseases and disorders naturally abound on such a choice subject, but all are within control. The most likely disease is powdery mildew, controlled by spraying with dinocap in spring as a preventive measure. A further precaution is not to allow the foliage to become overcrowded.

Manuring is on the familiar lines laid down with such emphasis at various points in this book. A summer fillip is a great help in June when the vine is under strain. This can take the form of a quick-acting nitrogenous fertilizer, a favourite being dried blood.

Above: A luscious crop of apricots in full bearing

The Apricot

The apricot, *Prunus armeniaca*, comes from China, but has been grown and cherished in England since the sixteenth century. Jane Austen mentions the variety Moorpark, which is still grown, in *Mansfield Park*.

Site and soil

In many ways the cultivation of the apricot is similar to that of the peach, except it is even more susceptible to spring frost and is best confined to walls, where protection can be provided.

The soil preparations and subsequent treatment again resemble those for the peach with particular emphasis on the need for moisture retention and the irrigation of trees grown against walls.

Training and pruning

The apricot differs from the peach in that the fruit is carried not only on the young shoots but also on spurs. There must therefore be a possibility that the apricot could be grown as a closely pruned, pyramid type tree in the same way as plums, although it is traditionally trained as a fan. Clearly there is scope here for experiment.

The most suitable rootstock is St Julien A, although here again we lack the benefit of sustained trials.

A spacing of about 6m (19ft 6in) should be allowed for fan trees.

Detailed pruning and de-shooting is essential for the best results. Spurs can be encouraged to form, where there is space, by the judicious shortening of selected side-shoots in July.

Varieties

The well tried Moorpark is the safest choice. There is additionally an earlier variety, New Large Early, which fruits in July, and in more northerly districts the variety Hemskerke is more reliable than Moorpark. All of these varieties are self-fertile.

Pests and diseases

The apricot is surprisingly resistant to the more serious manifestations of pest and disease but is subject to a sudden death of branches, due it is thought more to adverse soil conditions than to specific pathogens.

Any dead branches should be cut out immediately and the wounds painted.

Quinces

Most gardeners know the quince mainly as an admirable rootstock for its near relative the pear, but it is also worth growing, in the bigger garden, as a fruiting subject in its own right. The large yellow fruits are too sharp for direct consumption but make an excellent preserve or jelly, or they can be used to add piquancy to stewed apples or pears.

Yet another close relation is the well-known 'japonica', awkwardly known botanically as *Chaenomeles japonica*, grown for its bright red flowers but which also produces fruits that can be turned into jelly. Even more striking from the fruiting aspect is *C. cathayensis Wilsonii*, the huge fruits of which can also be transformed into jelly by the thrifty. But the real, epicurean flavour comes from the true quince, *Cydonia oblonga*.

Varieties are few in number, the most popular being the one prosaically called 'Pear-shaped'. Another, not so easy to recall but well recommended variety is Bereczki, a name which in itself should guarantee an extra zing to the flavour.

Sites and soils

The quince, although perfectly hardy, only fruits freely and regularly when given some shelter. Another essential requirement is summer moisture, so the shelter provided must not come from the competition of nearby thirsty trees. Quinces may be planted near water.

Below: It is well worth growing a quince if you have space in your garden

Planting as such is straightforward, but should be followed by mulching and appropriate shallow cultivations or the use of herbicides to prevent strong weed growth.

Each quince tree will require a space of about 3m (10ft) on either side. Sometimes, under good conditions, a small tree is formed but usually the quince is grown as a loose bush.

Propagation, pruning and pollination

Unlike other tree fruits quince is grown on its own roots, so there is none of the fuss and bother of choosing a rootstock, and budding or grafting thereon.

If you know of a quince tree growing and fruiting well in your district then do not hesitate to ask the owner for a rooted sucker, to be dug up carefully during the winter, or alternatively ask for a few hard wood cuttings, taken in the manner of black currants.

Pruning consists essentially of the removal of any obviously overcrowded, damaged, diseased or over-vigorous and therefore unproductive branches, together with the periodic removal of any unwanted sucker growths. In other words, a commonsense tidying up process during the winter is all that is necessary.

All varieties will set fruit with their own pollen, so only one tree need be grown, which is enough to meet most requirements.

Picking and storage

Leave the fruits on the tree until late autumn. Store in a cool but frostproof shed or garage, and pick over for use in the kitchen as they ripen. Freeze only unblemished fruits. The maturing fruits give off a pronounced aroma, which can be picked up by apples and pears stored nearby. It may well be thought that a quince-flavoured apple has acquired an added quality, but on the whole it is best to keep the stronger-scented quince away from other fruits in store. Storage conditions should be as recommended for apples.

Crabs

At first glance it looks a bit odd to include a crab apple as a provider of fruit in the garden, and as a source of crab apple jelly, but a rather special case can be made for the planting of those delightful members of the Malus family which combine free-flowering with a profusion of edible fruits.

The best of many fruiting Crabs is the variety 'John Downie'. The mass of white flowers precedes bright orange and red fruits, quite large, which make excellent jelly. Even more striking is the awkwardly styled *Malus niedzwetzkyana*, which carries a riot of red flowers in spring and an autumn crop of large, reddish-purple apples with an attractive bloom.

It is worth mentioning the claims of the cultivated apple as a decorative plant, and in particular the large-flowered cooking apple 'Arthur Turner'. It is so easy to overlook the obvious.

Above: The fruits of the medlar are eaten only when over-ripe

Medlars

Mespilus germanica is really a member of the group to which the apple and pear belong, and should be regarded as an attractive and easily grown apple, with a difference. It is usually grafted on to a rootstock of seedling mespilus, or quince or even hawthorn, and requires a space of some 5m (15ft). It looks well as a specimen tree, when the autumn colour can be best appreciated.

The difference lies in the fruits, which are left on the tree until the risk of frost occurs, when they are gathered and stored in single layers in a cool place, with the eyes placed downwards. At this stage the fruits are still hard and useless but once picked a process of ripening, nicely known as 'bletting', sets in. When the medlar is not only ripe, but positively overripe, the gastric juices of the connoisseur begin to flow. It is not to everyone's taste.

Over the years selections of improved varieties have been made and named. Since the whole object is to obtain good flavour either Nottingham or Royal should be chosen in preference to those varieties which possess other qualities, such as fruit size or heavy cropping.

Mulberries

Morus nigra is a slow growing tree of considerable distinction. Although easily propagated by cuttings the mulberry is best planted from a container.

Although occasionally found on walls it is more usually grown as a small but stately tree on a lawn. A distance of 7m (23ft) from its nearest neighbour is required, ultimately. It should be encouraged to grow freely when young by dint of mulching and watering. Once it comes into bearing it requires little attention, other than the gathering of the fruits. These tend to fall to the ground quickly, and a plastic sheet helps to keep them intact and reduce the general messiness. The owner usually shares the crop with the birds, using what he can rescue of the dark red, pleasantly acid fruits, for dessert, tarts or wine.

The type species, the black mulberry, is the one usually grown for fruiting.

Figs

Ficus carica is another tree of enormous antiquity, originating from warmer climates than our own. In more spacious days fig trees were grown in glass-houses. Nowadays some excellent specimens can be found outside, usually as fan trees against a south wall or occasionally growing as a bush in a sheltered site. The handsome foliage alone justifies planting, but it can also be persuaded to fruit on short young shoots, providing these have not been cut by frost or lost by unskilled pruning. The soil should not be too rich, or the shoots will be soft and susceptible to frost damage. Figs were once grown in restricted borders to reduce vigour.

Paradoxically, it is important to ensure that wall trees in particular do not suffer from drought from May to August. A fan-trained tree requires a spacing of 5m (16ft). Pruning consists essentially of the removal of excessively strong, misplaced and overcrowded shoots, either as they form or at the end of the summer, and the tying-in where necessary of young growths for next year's fruiting. Protection against severe winter frost is always desirable. At the end of the winter a further pruning may be necessary to cut out any damaged shoots. The fruit is allowed to ripen fully on the tree.

The most popular variety for growing outdoors is Brown Turkey, which is offered also under a shower of synonyms. A well-flavoured lighter variety is White Marseilles.

Troubles

All plants, alas, are liable to be attacked by pests and diseases, but figs, mulberries and medlars are more robust than most. The medlar is most likely to need assistance; troubles and specifics alike are mentioned under apples and pears.

Left: Young figs on the tree

Currants & Gooseberries

Black Currants

The currant family is so prolific in its response to love and care, so rich in flavour and goodness, so capable of preservation, that no garden of reasonable size should be without bushes of at least black currants and, where possible, red currants as well, since they serve a quite distinct purpose. The fruits have nothing to do with the currants of the currant and sultana group, which are really small dried grapes from foreign parts.

Black currants, although closely related to the red currant in belonging to the genus *Ribes*, produce their fruits rather differently so are best treated separately from their red and white brethren. So we begin with the black currant, *Ribes nigrum*. The sad truth is that many black currants in gardens are disease ridden parasites which should be grubbed immediately.

Below: Black currant 'Perfection'

Site and soil

These delectable fruits give of their best if planted in rich, deep soil, well-supplied with summer moisture. If your soil is light and hungry don't despair, but give the black currants all the compost, lawn clippings and summer water you can spare or lug around. The site should be open, but not windswept, because black currants will not thrive if subjected to the shade and competition of trees or the constant buffeting of high winds. They will, if looked after, prosper for ten years or so, sometimes much longer, so choose a site where they can remain without becoming a nuisance. The best fruit is produced on young shoots, those grown in the previous summer. A good bush will have a golden brown look about it in the winter sunshine because the bark of the young wood is lighter in colour than the older stems, which take on a dull, dark tinge. The strongest young shoots come direct from the root system, or as side branches low down in the bush. Accordingly black currants are grown as stools, rather than bushes on a leg, which is what nature intended in the first place, and it is always pleasant to follow the natural bent. The black currant bush is then expected to do two jobs each year: on the one hand to produce a crop of fruit, and at the same time grow a crop of strong young shoots. This is asking a lot, but the good gardener will ensure that the essential needs are supplied by a combination of sensible pruning, lavish manuring, appropriate watering and adequate pest and disease control.

Propagation

Black currants are very easily propagated by hard-wood cuttings, taken in late October ideally, but the source of the cutting is of vital importance. The bushes may suffer from two particularly nasty disorders, known variously as big bud mite and reversion. More about these troubles in their proper place, but it is vital to start off without them. So don't accept cuttings from your friendly neighbour with the worn-out bushes. The Ministry of Agriculture, Fisheries & Food run a scheme under which stocks of black currant bushes are inspected in the nursery and given certificates if they appear to be healthy. All good nurserymen are certified, so to speak, and should be patronized. Choose young wood about as thick as the standard ball-point pen for the cutting. Discard the unripened tip of the shoot and cut the middle portion into lengths of 25cm (10in), pruning close to a bud at either end. Put the prepared cuttings into nicely tilled, well-prepared soil in the open ground with-

Below: 'Wellington Triple X' is a reliable variety of black currant

out delay, burying each so that only two buds or thereabouts are showing, and that is it. You can feel disappointed if less than nine out of ten root. The normal spacing for cuttings in gardens is 20cm (8in) apart, the intention being to lift the rooted cuttings some thirteen months later and plant them in their final positions. But if you know exactly where the final position will be, and the ground is free, you can save a year by rooting the cuttings where they are to spend the next decade, plus. In this case put three cuttings in each site, forming a little triangle, each cutting 20cm (8in) apart. You will then have three bushes growing together, but they won't mind, and the results will come so much quicker from the composite stool.

The bush, or clump, will require between 1.25m (4ft) and 1.50m (5ft) of space, according to the fertility of the soil and the variety chosen. The neat growing Baldwin for example will be content with the closer planting, whereas the vigorous Wellington Triple X will need more space. Allow the bushes to touch and intermingle at the edges, so that space is properly occupied; in other words a row of mature black currant bushes should form a sort of controlled hedge.

Above: 'Baldwin' is the most highly recommended black currant variety

Planting and Pruning

Most gardeners will in the first place purchase bushes, rather than cuttings. Specify one-year or at the most two-year bushes and order only half the number of bushes you need, making sure that they are from certified stock, unpruned and freshly lifted. Avoid the horrors occasionally to be seen on sale, typified by ancient bushes with little new wood, carrying obvious signs of big bud mite, with exposed roots gasping for moisture in the cold wind. A good one-year-old will have a minimum of three strong basal shoots each at least 0.5m (19in) in length, and a vigorous, hairy root system. Spread the roots out in the planting hole as widely as they will go, using fine soil or potting compost (if either is available) to cover the roots, and firm well with your feet.

Immediately after planting black currants cut back all shoots to 5 cm (2 in). (Use the pruned shoots for cuttings.)

In winter, prune established plants by removing one-third of the old wood.

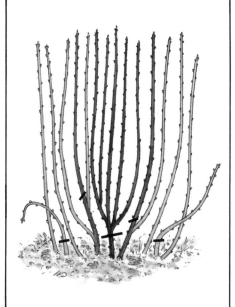

Neglected bushes will respond to removal of all old wood, and any broken, diseased or overcrowded branches.

And now, using secateurs, cut down each shoot close to the ground, leaving behind not more than five centimetres (2 inches). This drastic decapitation is essential if you are to have strong basal shoots next year from these transplanted bushes. If you don't prune hard on planting the poor bushes will try to carry fruit the following summer, and will be stunted for life. However, all is not lost because you can now take the pruned shoots, prepare cuttings from them as earlier described and place three in each of the remaining sites. There should be little difference in the outward appearance of the two types of bush twelve months hence, when there will be no need to prune either sort, because there is no transplanting shock to overcome, and only strong young shoots are present, all ready to carry the first crop in the succeeding summer.

Thereafter the pruning procedure is straightforward. Each winter prune out completely about one-third of the old dark coloured wood, leaving behind and untouched as much as you can of the young wood. In the early years much of this young wood will come direct from the root system as suckers, but as the bush develops new growth will break from the older wood, so the bushes reach maturity with a mixture of older wood and dependent young shoots.

Common sense will tell you to prune out at this same winter pruning any broken, diseased, overcrowded or weeping branches, whether they are young or old.

Feeding

Pruning is one way of stimulating the production of young wood, but the best approach is to feed the bushes properly. No apology is needed for stressing once again the importance of proper manuring as the basis for growing really heavy crops of black currants year after year. Briefly, the essentials are ample water and nitrogen, based on a proper balance of the other essential nutrients. So it's back to the emphasis on bulky organic manures, plus appropriate fertilizers, having ensured that the pH level of the soil is, as far as possible, around 6.2.

Gardeners have for the most part to assume average conditions, since they cannot readily obtain soil analyses in the way commercial growers do. So, as a generalization, apply a general fertilizer containing nitrogen, phosphorous and potassium in the proportions of 7 per cent of each, at the rate of 100g per m² (3oz per sq yd), applied in early March and evenly distributed over what is thought to be the rooting area, roughly half as much again as the branch spread.

If the new wood is produced in plenty, then reduce the amount of fertilizer by half, or even omit the general spring dressing occasionally and substitute a mid-August dressing of, say, nitro-chalk or nitram, or similar quick acting nitrogenous fertilizer. Control the invasion of weeds by applying a mulch.

Pests and diseases

One could prepare a terrifying list of pests and diseases which sometimes attack black currants, but there are three which are dominant and must be mentioned: reversion, bug bud and aphids.

Reversion is a virus disease, seen as changes in the leaf shape, from the normal deeply lobed outline to a narrow leaf resembling an oak leaf or, in extreme cases, a nettle. The change in leaf shape in itself doesn't matter, but it is an external symptom of an incurable internal condition which seriously reduces cropping. Infected bushes should be grubbed and burned. The control is two-fold—make a clean start and then prevent the entry and build-up of the carrier, our second menace, the big bud mite, sometimes called the black currant gall mite. This creature is too small to be seen without magnification. Myriads of them spend most of their life tucked away inside the bud, causing the normal long and narrow bud to swell and become grossly rotund. Badly affected buds die, which is bad enough, but worse still is the risk that the mites have earlier been feeding on a bush affected with reversion, which they then transmit to your precious bushes. If the mites have not been in contact with the virus before drifting on to newly opened buds in the spring no reversion results, but the two troubles go together all too frequently. The important point is to make a clean start with certified stock, and then spray the bushes each spring, just before the first blossom opens. The commercial grower has access to new and powerful specifics, but the amateur must rest content with the old fashioned but safer material called lime-sulphur, used at a strength of 2 per cent. The timing is important, because the mites are external for a short period only, before they enter new buds. Swollen buds should be picked off when seen in the winter, and burned.

The remaining pest is the aphid, or green fly, which, with thousands of companions, sucks the sap in the spring in particular, distorting leaves and crippling shoots. There are two distinct and alternative approaches to control. One possibility is to spray the bushes thoroughly with a tar-oil wash on a calm day in the dormant season, after pruning, to kill the overwintering eggs. Tar oil smells of carbolic, and thus, as a bonus, gives the distinct impression of doing good.

A somewhat easier, and on the whole a more effective way, is to spray with a systemic insecticide just before blossoming, when the eggs have hatched but feeding and breeding have not commenced. A suitable material is the one known technically as dimethoate, and sold most commonly as Rogor.

Varieties

There are many good varieties available. A longish list would include the following. Those marked * are particularly good for freezing.

Mendip Cross
Wellington Triple X, sometimes rendered
    as Wellington XXX*
Seabrook's Black
Westwick Choice*
Baldwin's Black*

Top of the list is Baldwin, because of its neat habit and high vitamin C content. It must be grown well on good soil. A less demanding alternative would be Wellington Triple X, untidy of habit, but reliable.

All the varieties chosen will set fruit with their own pollen, but bumble bees or other flower visitants are necessary to distribute the pollen and avoid the erratic spacing of berries, a condition known as 'running-off'. Black currants should be picked when dry. As they colour, pick over the bushes several times as necessary. Leave them until fully ripe, when they will taste much better than shop bought fruits.

Black currants cannot be stored in a fresh condition, but are unsurpassed as a preserved fruit. Whether frozen, bottled, jammed or syruped, that unique flavour is available all the year round. Finally, a cassis drink, made of the juice and a dry white wine, is superb refreshment on a hot day.

Red & white currants

Red currants are much easier to grow than black currants, and it is surprising therefore that they are not to be found more often in gardens. Two further recommendations are that they can be grown in a restricted space, and if necessary on a north-facing wall. The greatest disadvantage is their year-round popularity with marauding birds. The flavour is not so generally popular, partly because people are not familiar with it except in the form of red currant jelly served with mutton, but there is scope for the adventurous cook.

The white currant is largely a curiosity to be grown by the experimenting gardener.

Soil requirements and feeding

The soil requirements for the red currant are the basic ones discussed in the chapter on apples: good preparation for a long-lived plant and the avoidance of wet, poorly drained sites. The red currant needs potassium rather than nitrogen, although a

Below: 'Red Lake' is a heavy-cropping American red currant

be produced from the main branches. Prune back any laterals not needed for new leaders to encourage the formation of fruiting spurs. In the winter, prune the leaders by about one third, and at the same time shorten the side shoots to 2.5cm (1in) or so. Sub-laterals will be produced in subsequent years from the original cut-back shoots, and these too should be trimmed back to 2.5cm (1in).

If you decide to buy in bushes rather than raise your own then there is much to be said for two-year-old bushes with the head already partly formed in the nursery.

The ideal red currant bush sits neatly on a short stem, and carries eight radiating branches from each of which bright pink clusters of fruit hang each summer, clothing each branch from top to bottom.

Although not essential, summer pruning of the laterals carried by the fruiting bush is a great aid to neatness and fruitfulness. Cut back the side shoots as soon as the first fruits begin to colour. As this is only an intermediate stage, the length of the cut shoot does not greatly matter, but aim at 10cm (4in) or thereabouts, knowing that you will cut the laterals back to 2.5cm (1in) in the winter. Summer pruning improves the colouring of the fruit and allows easier access for picking.

Alas, accessibility will be of as much delight to the birds as to the gardener. They attack the fruits in summer and buds in winter, so year round deterrents will be needed. Netting, cotton threads, strips of glittering foil, stuffed cats, baleful but moribund owls—all can be brought to bear in attempts to persuade our feathered foes to feed somewhere else. It is best to prune in early November and protect the bushes, unless you are lucky enough to be in a district free of fruit-bud-devouring birds.

Suitable sites

It is feasible to grow these rigidly trained red currants against fences or walls as fans, or multiple or single cordons. The latter can be grown, suitably staked, as a tall edging or boundary to paths, each cordon close to its neighbour—say 50cm (20in) apart. They are good natured enough to put up with north-facing sites, if the soil is well-prepared and watering and manuring not neglected.

Varieties

Laxton's No. 1 is excellent, and so are some of the north American types, particularly Red Lake, both of which are suitable for freezing. The variety of white currant usually grown is known as White Dutch.

Pests and other troubles

Red currants are relatively trouble-free, but aphids can make an awful mess of a bush. Prevent this disaster by applying either a winter tar oil or the early spring systemic spray recommended for black currants. The red currant is so fruitful, rarely seen in shops and yet deliciously versatile in cooking, that it well justifies a place in any garden.

balanced diet founded on plenty of incorporated organic matter remains necessary. Follow the advice given for black currants in the use of fertilizers, with the addition that potash supplies should be ensured from the start. Before planting, incorporate sulphate of potash into the soil at the rate of 3of per m² (1oz per sq yd). Do *not* use muriate of potash for red currants.

Propagation and pruning

The strict precautions regarding the choice of propagation material stressed in the case of black currants are not so necessary for the red species, *Ribes rubrum*. Another important difference is that the fruit is carried in the main on short spurs formed in clusters close to the older wood. Accordingly most red currants are grown not as stools but as bushes, each on a short stem or leg.

Propagation is by hard-wood cuttings of the new growth taken in November, each cutting pruned close to buds top and bottom, ending up with some 30cm (12in) of cutting. Growth is required from the top four buds only, so nick out all the other buds with a sharp knife. Insert the cuttings in the open ground, burying each about half-way. If all goes well you will in a year's time have a small bush with a 10-cm (4-in) leg between ground level and the first of the four strong branches arranged neatly around the central axis, ready for planting in its permanent position. Since these branches are important, give them a little judicious support where it seems appropriate to prevent heavy

branches being blown out by strong winds.

That winter, on planting, prune back each main branch about half-way, cutting to an outward-pointing bud. The aim of this leader pruning is to strengthen the plant, direct its habit of growth, furnish healthy new shoots and increase productivity. Keep up this leader pruning for the next three years or so, choosing suitably placed laterals (side-shoots) to form further main branches to bring the number up to eight or so.

In the first growing season laterals will

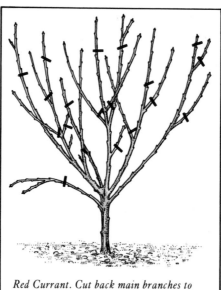

Red Currant. Cut back main branches to strengthen. Cut back sideshoots near junction with main branches.

Gooseberries

An undeserved air of melancholy pervades the gooseberry. Something about the very appearance of the gooseberry bush damps down the fires of enthusiasm. One of the reasons is the apparent lack of colour, because most varieties are picked green for stewing well before they are ripe.

And yet this brother of the currants is a versatile and tasty contributor to our diet, offering the first outdoor fresh fruit of the season as early as May and, in the form of well grown Levellers, or Golden Drops straight from the garden, an epicure's delight. At one time the growing of gooseberries was a

gooseberries, and things have not changed.

Commercial growers in the Fens used to plant gooseberries as an inter-crop amongst apple trees. The idea on planting was to grub the gooseberries as the apple trees grew larger, but such is human frailty that all too often the gooseberry bushes were left in. The surprising thing is how well many of these interplanted gooseberry bushes did under the shade of the taller trees. The Fen soils are, of course, deep and rich in organic matter, and your soil may well be shallow and hungry. The moral is that gooseberries can in some circumstances tolerate some benevolent shade, but that is not the same thing as suggesting they will be happy in the dry and hungry embrace of an old yew.

The second problem governing the form in which the gooseberry is grown is the ever-present risk of mildew. Of the two mildews which attack the gooseberry, the one we are concerned with is the American Gooseberry Mildew, described below. This fungus disease is at its worst on vigorous, rather soft shoots, of the type which grow from the base of the bush as suckers.

So, for these two good reasons most gooseberry bushes are grown in the same way as red currants, that is, as open-centred closely pruned bushes on a short leg, or as single or multiple cordons. It follows that the propagation is by hard wood cuttings taken in the dormant season, with all but the top four buds removed, just as for red

Above: Plump berries of the dessert gooseberry 'Leveller'

Right: 'Careless' is an easily grown and very reliable gooseberry

special cult, with competitions amongst the members of Gooseberry Clubs to produce the heaviest berry. We now can reap a bonus from this passion for bigness, because the varieties which grow quickly can be picked prematurely as early green gooseberries. Since this versatile berry can be stewed, or turned into jam, or eaten raw, or bottled whole, freezes readily and makes a superb wine, of a sort, perhaps we have failed to appreciate what a good return can be had from the garden gooseberry. A colleague once picked 25 kilos from a single bush.

Site and soil

Bushes will last in a fruitful state for even longer than either black or red currants, provided they are looked after, which obviously includes making a good start by the proper preparation of the planting site. Above all, get rid of perennial weeds such as bindweed or bishop's weed (ground elder) or nettles, and reduce the annual weed flora in advance, because hand weeding amongst gooseberry bushes is no joke. Bushes, home raised or purchased, should be planted at 1.50m (5ft) apart, after the recommended preplanting operations have been carried out. Thomas Tusser, that ancient scribe, refers to the value of 'a rotteny mould' for

Grow them in the open sunlight if you can, but try to avoid windswept sites, because gales can easily break the shoots and branches, which function when young on a ball-and-socket junction between the stem and shoot.

In many ways the gooseberry can be grown very successfully on the lines advocated for the red currant, but for rather different reasons. The two main factors influencing the system of training are spines and mildew, an odd combination. Because of the spines it is desirable to regulate the growth of the gooseberry to ensure that your hand can be passed readily through the branches to pick the fruits, and underneath the branches to pull out weeds, without suffering untoward damage. A gooseberry bush grown like a black currant, as a stool with intermingling branches, would make picking and weeding hazardous operations.

currants. But the gooseberry does not root as easily as the red currant, and there is evidence that the removal of the lower buds reduces the rate of rooting. The alternative is to leave all the buds intact, as for black currants, and to form the required leg when transplanting the rooted cutting into its fruiting quarters by pruning away all sucker and lower growths to produce 10cm (4in) of clear stem. Another tip worth following is to plant the gooseberry cuttings in a moist shady place rather than in full sun. The liberal use of thoroughly moistened peat in the rooting zone will markedly enhance the chances of success.

The rooted cuttings may, for reasons which may be linked with the virus diseases which accrue to ancient stock, grow only slowly and are in such case best left for two years in the cutting-bed before transplanting.

If therefore you are, naturally, looking

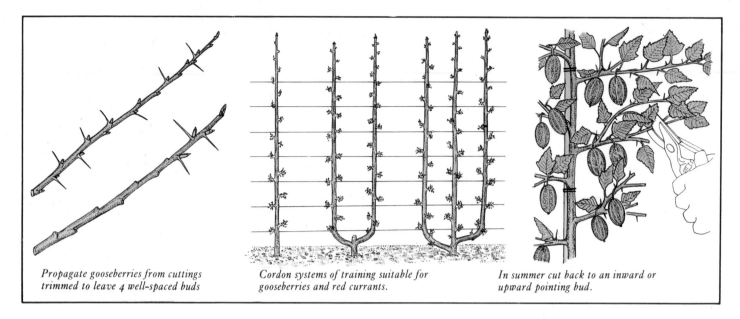

Propagate gooseberries from cuttings trimmed to leave 4 well-spaced buds

Cordon systems of training suitable for gooseberries and red currants.

In summer cut back to an inward or upward pointing bud.

for quick results you should instead buy two-year bushes from a reputable nurseryman. You can always try to increase your stock by cuttings at the same time; the challenge will still be there.

Pruning systems

Prune the leaders as for red currants, but cut back to an inward or upward rather than an outward pointing bud, in an endeavour to prevent the branches from drooping. Equally, as the bush comes into fruiting, contemplate the advantages of the sort of summer pruning recommended for red currants. Spur-pruned gooseberry bushes are easier to pick, and the fruits are larger, although naturally fewer, than is the case with more freely grown bushes, and summer pruning beginning in early July is a useful preliminary to spurring back to about 5cm (2in) in the winter.

Spur-pruning is, therefore, desirable for bushes of large-fruited dessert varieties owned by tidy and logical gardeners, and essential for cordon and similar forms, to which the gooseberry, like the red currant, is especially well-suited.

But the system has its limitations. There is a very annoying condition, known graphically as 'die-back', caused by a fungus, which results in a whole branches collapsing. This can make a mess of all the painstaking attempts to build up a neat framework of carefully trained radiating branches in an open-centre bush. Experience is the best guide here. If die-back is a nuisance, then a freer system of production is clearly called for, and there is no reason, other than the risk of damage from spines and the occurrence of mildew, why gooseberry bushes should not be grown on a system which is a compromise between black and red currants. The gooseberry is very accommodating and will produce crops on the two-year wood just as readily as black currants, or it will crop on natural or induced spurs, or will perform well under both systems, if allowed.

It is desirable still to retain the little leg, to help with weeding, and to prune the leaders to prevent drooping, but some laterals may be left full length where there is room for them. Naturally, you cannot have it all ways. The fruits, although plentiful, will be smaller and picking more hazardous.

Varieties

The choice of the system of pruning and training can be governed to some extent by the variety. For example the excellent Careless grows very well and fruits abundantly if pruned on the more relaxed system, whereas that splendid dessert variety Leveller gives its largest and most attractive fruits if spur pruned.

Varieties abound. If you become affected with the gooseberry growing fever you will want to cover the longest season and the widest range of colours and flavours. The old specialists used to group varieties according to their ripe colours, which pass from green to red and white to yellow and shades in between, and, of course, flavour involves a spectrum from the sharply acid to the luscious sweetness of the dessert varieties. There are, sadly, still many people who have not had the opportunity to taste a really ripe Leveller or Golden Drop, which is a unique and delightful experience. To take expertise further still it is interesting to record that the fruits can be further classified according to skin finish—smooth, downy, rough and hairy—and shape. The berries come round, or oblong, oval or obovate. No doubt in the revived Gooseberry Clubs some one will specify a class for 'yellow, hairy, obovate berries' which is not such fun as a straightforward competition for the heaviest berry.

May Duke. First of the season. Quickly produces small green fruits which should be picked when large enough to handle. Best for stewing.

Careless. Best green gooseberry. May be picked early, when it is best cooked in tarts; midseason, for jam-making, bottling or freezing; late, when the mature medium-large whitish fruits can be eaten raw.

Lancashire Lad, Bedford Red, Whinham's Industry. Red-berried varieties, good flavour, heavy cropping potential.

Leveller. An excellent yellow dessert variety, well worth growing on good soils.

Golden Drop. Yellow dessert berry, sweet and small and of superb quality.

Hybrids between the gooseberry and its near relatives have been bred, and we may yet see a really exciting black, large-fruited, spineless gooseberry of exquisite flavour and high vitamin C content, with enormous cropping potential and resistant to reversion, gall mite and mildew. Of the 400 or so varieties recorded by the Royal Horticultural Society the one producing the largest berries appears to be 'London'. Gavin Brown, in a fascinating article in the R.H.S. Fruit Year Book for 1948, refers to one massive berry weighing '37 pennyweights', which comes to close on 2 ounces or 66 grammes.

Feeding

Manuring should be on the same lines as those recommended for red currants, with emphasis on supplies of potash.

Pests and diseases

Pests include the ubiquitous greenfly, controlled by winter tar oil or spring malathion. There is also the oddly behaved gooseberry sawfly, the larvae of which rapidly defoliate affected bushes. Its appearance is largely unpredictable, so it is best dealt with as soon as noticed by either hand picking or a spray of derris. American Gooseberry Mildew attacks both shoots, which are crippled, and fruits, which are coated with a felt-like and unsightly growth, which can, however, be washed off after picking. This disease should be taken seriously and sprays applied both before and after flowering. Karathane is at present the best and most convenient specific. If the disease gets away despite spraying, then the affected shoots should be pruned off and burned.

And, yet again, birds. Bullfinches love the fruit buds of gooseberries in the winter, and are the cause of those gaunt, deprived branches which are so common. Netting, cottoning and scaring are the usual controls. Where physical protection is not feasible spray the bushes with one of the proprietary washes based on thiram.

Strawberries

In the open garden

Many gardeners are understandably uneasy with Latin names, but no such difficulty arises with the delightful *Fragaria*, 'a pleasing aroma'. The common name is said to come from the Anglo-Saxon and to have no relation to straw, although straw is of course widely used to provide a clean cushion between the ripening berries and the soil.

Our wild strawberry, *Fragaria vesca*, is not the ancestor of the large fruited varieties cultivated in gardens, which arose from crossings between two American species, widely separated in nature. These were brought together almost by chance in Europe. This blessed union, and variants upon it, has resulted in what is probably everybody's favourite fruit. The earlier strawberry was also well-regarded by William Butler (1535–1618) who wrote the often quoted eulogy, 'Doubtless God could have made a better berry, but doubtless God never did'.

Introduction
It is a truism that every garden of reasonable size should have a plot of strawberries. Gooseberries can be picked unripe for stewing in May, but the June strawberry is the first ripe fruit taken from the open ground. With modest protection strawberries can be picked a month earlier, and new late ripening varieties extend the season admirably.

Strawberry jam needs no commendation, but it is difficult to avoid the sigh which accompanies the frozen product. No doubt new techniques will find a way around that problem, indeed they may already be with us or about to burst on the grateful consumer.

The great majority of hardy fruits are borne on the woody stems of trees, bushes, or canes—but the strawberry is a soft herbaceous plant, relatively short lived, which fits in better with the vegetables rather than the fruits. There is much to be said for growing strawberries and similar delicacies attractive to birds within the permanent protection of a fruit cage.

Soil and site
Strawberries grow best on a light to medium soil, one which is well-drained and warms readily in the spring. Heavy, stiff soils can be made more suitable by cultivation and by incorporating plenty of manure and compost, peat and grit. Paradoxically the same recipe, but without the grit, makes the lighter soils even better than they would

Above: It is important to keep strawberries clean as they ripen

otherwise be. The most appetizing berries come from plants whose roots are happily placed in soil rich in manure.

The strawberry flowers early in the season, when there is still the risk of ground frost, to which these ground-hugging plants are particularly susceptible. Accordingly that part of the garden which is warmed by the sun in the daytime and is likely to retain some of the heat through the night is the most suitable.

Clearly this is not a crop for the north

Below: 'Cambridge Vigour' is an early-ripening strawberry

facing border, neither will it prosper in the shade of trees. There is no reason, though, why strawberries should not be used as a short-lived intercrop to fill in the ground between newly planted apple trees, say. True, both the application of sprays and protection from birds then become a bit complicated, but gardening tends to consist of a series of sensible compromises.

Propagation and planting
Strawberries are propagated, or propagate themselves, by means of runners. Their cultivation is complicated by the fact that strawberries are very prone to a number of virus diseases, most of them spread by aphids. The Research Stations have devised ways of removing the viruses, treating a few plants at a time.

These healthy strawberry plants are used purely for propagation, and are grown in isolated conditions, as free as possible from both virus and aphids. Ministry of Agriculture officers inspect the strawberry plant nurseries and, if appropriate, issue certificates of health to the growers who, at a later stage, offer the progeny of the original mother plants for sale.

It follows that it is very sensible for the gardener to start with healthy material and, conversely, it is unwise to use runners from dubious sources, such as a neighbour's allotment. However, it also makes economic sense for the gardener to propagate in the

first year from plants bought in as certified stock, as long as the mother plants remain healthy, a state demonstrated by vigorous growth, leaves free from yellowing and distortion and, of course, ample cropping.

The best results are obtained by directing chosen early runners into small pots half buried and filled with John Innes potting compost or an equivalent mixture. With judicious watering these runners will be

of healthy runners, plants them at 80cm (30in) apart, and allows enough runners to form within the row to give the full complement of plants. This method will not give the best results as far as quick cropping is concerned.

The distance between the rows is governed by the methods used to control weeds. If the scale of operations is large enough to warrant a rotary cultivator or similar machine then

choose a site as free as possible from perennial weeds. Gardeners' nightmares are often caused by the thought of couch grass or bindweed romping in the strawberry beds.

Finally, on planting, care must be taken not to bury the crown of the plant, which is liable to rot if submerged.

Feeding

Unlike most of the woody fruiting plants the strawberry does not respond favourably to applications of nitrogenous fertilizers. Indeed the result is sometimes to make the plant too vigorous, at the expense of fruiting and the risk of increased disease.

A dressing before planting of sulphate of potash at 17g per m^2 ($\frac{1}{2}$oz per sq yd) and bone meal—to supply phosphate—at 100g per m^2 (3oz per sq yd) will, as a supplement to the bulky organic material, keep the plants going for the normal three fruiting years. If the plants look tired after the second crop then apply in early spring a complete fertilizer of the Growmore type at 100g per m^2 (3oz per sq yd).

Watering may be necessary in dry springs to help plump up the rapidly growing berries, but it is best not to water, if conditions permit, after the first fruits begin to colour. A well-prepared bed will retain moisture.

Care before fruiting

If there is a warning of frost when the plants are in flower it is worthwhile covering the beds or rows overnight with a loose layer of straw or other temporary protection, removing the cover the following morning. Straw, or black polythene, is useful also in providing a clean barrier between the ripening fruits and the soil, but this particular form of protection should not be placed in position until after mid-May, when the danger of frost has in most years departed, because the risk of frost damage is increased if the earth's radiating warmth is prevented from reaching the flowers.

Plant strawberry plants carefully to avoid burying the crown.

Root runners in summer by pegging down in buried pots of moist prepared compost.

ready for severance and planting in a new site in August. Thus treated the crowns will be big enough to fruit the following June, nine months after planting, which isn't bad going.

If the bought-in plants are vigorous, pot-raised runners planted in good conditions before mid-September then all will be well. If the less expensive open ground runners are used they may not be available until the late autumn or winter. In this case, or even if for some reason you are not able to plant until the spring, the blossoms should be removed during the first summer, as they appear on the young plants. This act of self-denial will pay dividends the following year, when the properly established crowns will produce numerous large and luscious fruits, a process which will continue for a total of three or four years or more.

Apart from the exceptional case earlier suggested of limited propagation from plants known to be healthy, runners should be regarded as a drain on the energies of precious plants, and should be cut off as soon as formed, unless you have deliberately left room for new runners to fill out the plantation. The best results are obtained from plants set out at about 40cm (15in) apart, and all subsequent runners removed. The plants enlarge by the multiplication of crowns, and the space is rapidly fully occupied. In these expensive times, however, it is understandable if the gardener buys in half the quantity

the rows must be spaced accordingly, probably about 1m (39in) apart. If weed control is to be achieved by hand pulling—which is much the best method—or by a combination of pulling, hoeing and the use of herbicides, then it is a good idea to plant four rows, each 40cm (15in) apart, to form an old-fashioned strawberry bed. Service paths 1m (39in) wide should be left between each bed so that you can readily lean over to pick fruit or pull out weeds. This is the most effective use of space. It is of prime importance to

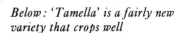
Below: 'Tamella' is a fairly new variety that crops well

Care after fruiting

Once the crop has been gained it is important to assist the plants to lay down next year's flower buds. Accordingly, immediately—which probably means the first convenient weekend after—fruit picking is over, any netting should be removed, the bed thoroughly weeded, all surplus runners removed and the old, worn out foliage clipped back with the garden shears, taking care not to cut into the crowns. It is as well to rake off and burn the debris. Some text books talk about burning on the spot instead of cutting, but this is a tricky business best avoided.

Lifespan of strawberry beds

The normal sequence is thus: the first (maiden) crop produces the largest individual berries, and they are the first to ripen. In the second year comes the heaviest crop, often a mixture of medium sized berries from the older plants and large berries from any maiden runners that have been allowed to root. By the third year a degree of exhaustion is setting in and the berries tend to be small, but splendid for jam making. Generally speaking three cropping years is enough, from which it follows that the keen strawberry grower will plant a new bed each year, to replace the grubbed piece. If you are fortunate enough to have plants that are obviously healthy and full of cropping potential, then let them go on for a fourth or even a fifth year.

Varieties

Because of the virus problem and the continued efforts of plant breeders, both in the U.K. and abroad, we are constantly being offered new varieties, but not everything new is an improvement on the old.

The gardener should put flavour high on his list of requirements, unlike the commercial grower who has to think also of such factors as crop weight and market qualities. Ask any gardener who was growing before the last war for his views on really well-flavoured strawberries and he will inevitably start with Sir Joseph Paxton, with us no longer, and Royal Sovereign, which is still available. It is best to grow Royal Sovereign, if this is the choice, as the sole variety, because it is sensitive to viruses often carried cheerfully by other more robust varieties.

A certified stock of Royal Sovereign takes a lot of beating as an early, well flavoured variety, but if you have a large family of non-discriminating consumers for whom to provide then choose instead from the following heavier cropping and worth-growing varieties, arranged roughly in order of ripening. Those marked * are best for freezing.

Cambridge Rival*
Cambridge Vigour*
Grandee
Cambridge Favourite
Tamella
Redgauntlet
Talisman
Cambridge Late Pine

Those mentioned are the major varieties. They are all very good but, who knows, even better ones may be on their way.

There are other types, for example the so-called perpetual or remontant varieties, of which Gento, Sans Rivale and Triomphe are typical. These are useful in extending the season into the autumn. The early flowers should be removed to encourage late fruiting. The plants must be kept well nourished so they can cope with the strain of summer.

Quite distinct is the alpine strawberry, represented by the variety Baron Solemacher, which produces small berries of excellent flavour over a long period. The berries are so small that it takes quite a long time to pick enough to satisfy the cook, but they are delicious in trifles and fruit salads.

Pests and diseases

The best remedy against the troubles to which strawberries are sensitive is to start with healthy plants and constantly to renew the beds. In many gardens the worst pests are birds, which attack the ripening fruits with gusto. The use of scaring devices helps to move these pests on to the next door garden, temporarily, but only complete netting provides a really satisfactory answer. A fruit cage is the best solution.

Slugs can be a nuisance, and particularly so if all the good advice about using muck and compost has been faithfully followed. The scattering of a proprietary slug bait based on methiocarb or related substances over the soil in April will reduce the risk of damage by these pests.

Greenflies (aphids) are messy debilitators and spreaders of virus diseases. A spray of malathion during the second half of April will get rid of the worst of likely attacks.

The most frequently encountered fungus disease is grey mould, an apt name for the species of botrytis which causes the fruits to rot. It is particularly rampant in a wet summer. Three sprays with benlate (benomyl), one when the first flowers open and the other two at ten-day intervals, afford adequate but not complete protection in very wet years.

Any plant which is obviously stunted, wilted and unhappy is best put out of its misery quickly, consigning it to the flames if you are allowed to light bonfires in your district.

Extending the Season

This accommodating and good natured plant can be gently persuaded to flower and fruit before and after its normal time. Early fruits can be obtained by providing some protection from the worst of the weather in the early spring, and by enhancing the environment by the trapping of sun heat and, perhaps, adding some artificial heat. At the other end of the season fruits can be produced in the autumn by the use of those varieties, such as Redgauntlet, which have the ability to form a second crop under favourable circumstances, or those which possess the knack of continued flowering, thus producing rather small crops over a long period rather than concentrating all their energies in maturing a large June crop. Thus, with ingenuity, strawberry fruits can be picked from the garden from May to October.

Outdoor planting—Cloches and tunnels

The most straightforward approach is to cover outdoor plants with glass cloches—an odd misnomer, since they are not always bell shaped—or with continuous plastic film in the form of a low structure or tunnel. The uses and management of cloches, frames and tunnels are discussed in the chapter on protected cultivations; here we deal specifically with strawberries.

The best results are obtained from maiden plants set out in August from pots or similar containers. These plants, duly watered, will form plump crowns for the following year's

Below: Plastic tunnels provide excellent protection for early strawberries

fruiting. If planting is delayed, or the soil not ideal, then it is sensible to increase the number of fruiting crowns by planting at a closer spacing than that recommended earlier. For example, the maiden plants can be set initially at say 20cm (8in) apart, and thinned out to stand at 40cm (16in) after picking the first crop. This is not necessary with good plants, put in early on good soil, which will occupy the space of 40cm profitably.

The standard barn cloche, with side walls and a width of about 65cm (26in) is admirable. There are a number of proprietary glass and plastic cloches on offer, but a height of around 30cm (12in) and a width of not less than 60cm (24in) are desirable for both cloches and tunnels.

Nothing is gained by covering the plants too early, and it is as well to wait until a calm day towards the end of February.

As the plants come into flower, ventilation should be given during the day, both to prevent the temperature from reaching excessive heights and to admit pollinating insects.

Ventilation can be achieved by removing the ends, or by removing every fifth cloche, closing the gaps when the sun goes off the row. Polythene tunnels are ventilated by raising the film on one side.

Watering and pest and disease control follow normal lines, but on an earlier time scale and with a keener awareness. The plants must not be allowed to become dry, nor must botrytis be left unchecked.

Once fruiting is finished all protection should be removed, the foliage trimmed back, weeds pulled out, and surplus runners and plants removed. The once maiden bed then enters into a sedate and matronly second year of productivity.

Royal Sovereign and Cambridge Premier are particularly useful varieties for this gentle forwarding technique. Some gardeners have also used the main cropping Redgauntlet,

and report picking a good second autumn crop as a bonus.

The fruiting of the so-called perpetual varieties can be extended into the late autumn by placing cloches over the plants in September.

Strawberries in containers

It is quite possible to grow strawberries on patios, or in window boxes or on sunny balconies, or roofs, by the use of conventional containers, or barrels, or the newer tower pots and similar developments.

Good drainage and a John Innes or similar potting compost are essential. In this case annual planting with new maiden plants is necessary for the best results. The sad response obtained by many would-be balcony gardeners can usually be traced to poor drainage, indifferent compost, containers of insufficient size, lack of water, neglect of feeding or failure to control pests and diseases. Proper attention to these minor difficulties will give excellent results on strawberry plants grown in containers.

Forcing in glasshouses

Gardeners fortunate enough to own a glasshouse will be able easily to satisfy a passion for out-of-season strawberries. Superb displays of forced strawberries in pots were exhibited for several years at Chelsea Show by the Waterperry School of Horticulture.

The variety used was exclusively certified Royal Sovereign. Newer varieties will obviously come along, and may be superior, but for the time being the amateur should stay with a good stock of Sovereign for this type of forcing.

The key points can be summarized as follows:

Pot raised plants should be obtained from a specialist grower, preferably in late July. These plants should be grown on without check in 15cm (6in) pots in good compost in a sunny position, and kept well-watered. At the end of November they are allowed to enter into a semi-dormant condition, prefer-

ably stacking the pots on their sides against a wall. This period of cool dormancy is important.

After Christmas the plants are gently re-started into growth in a cold glasshouse, aiming at a minimum night temperature of 4°C (39°F).

By the end of January growth should be obvious: watering and syringing can be increased on sunny days and the temperature raised slightly. When flowers begin to show the minimum night temperature should be increased to 10°C (50°F).

In normal years bold flowers should be open towards the end of March. Pollinating insects are scarce at this time of the year, so the keen gardener can perform the functions of the bee himself, to make sure, using a tuft of cotton-wool, or a rabbit's tail at the end of a short cane. The idea is to move the pollen around within the flowers so that the 'pips' or achenes on the outside are fertilized and the 'fruit' swells evenly and rapidly. Bees work best in sunny periods in the middle of the day, a policy it is wise to imitate.

As the first petals fall the watering should be increased, the plants fed and the night temperature increased to a minimum of 13°C (55°F). Plants which have been kept well-watered, but not excessively so, will produce large, good-flavoured fruits, while those that have become dry during this crucial period will respond with mildewed leaves and small woody fruits.

It is a good idea to support the swelling fruits in the forks of twigs inserted in the pot at strategic spacings.

The need for precise temperature control is difficult to maintain in the case of the mixed population glasshouse run by most amateur gardeners, and obviously some compromise may be called for, but the aim should be to grow the plants slowly at the beginning and then steam-up somewhat once the flowers open. A harvest of large, ripe, fragrant fruits in April should be the good gardener's ample reward.

Raise the sides of polythene tunnels for pollination, watering and picking.

Standard barn glass cloches are placed end-to-end to form a continuous row.

Cane Fruits

Raspberries

There has been a great upsurge of interest in raspberry growing in gardens, due in large measure to the ease with which this excellent fruit can be frozen. There are other reasons also, including the high cost of purchased raspberries, even on a pick-your-own basis, and the advent of new and heavy cropping varieties.

One considerable advantage the raspberry has over all hardy fruits except the strawberry is the ability to come into full bearing quickly, assuming the plants are well-grown. Well-grown implies good manuring, adequate water supplies, and the early removal

and, other things being equal, it is better to plant in the thin shade of protective trees or shrubs than to expose the canes to the fierce blast of the unfiltered wind. The fruit is carried on side-shoots which are very readily severed from their origins by a summer's gale, and with the shattered shoots go all hopes of a crop. So, plant in shelter, if you can, without going to extremes. Above all else, plant the canes in a relatively weed-free part of the garden. The raspberry cannot compete successfully with strong growing weeds. Weeds will appear, of course, and should be pulled up at an early stage, or destroyed by gentle, shallow hoeing, taking care not to cultivate deeply at any time after planting.

Propagation

Propagation is relatively easy, because all that is necessary is to dig up suckers, or spawn, in the autumn and plant these rooted canes. There are one or two problems. The raspberry sometimes suffers from virus diseases, and once these are in the plant a cure is beyond all but the lavishly equipped laboratory. Secondly, and of lesser importance, new raspberry seedlings often appear at the base of the fruiting canes. It is therefore best only to propagate your own raspberries if the plantation from which you obtain the suckers is of riotous, fecund and uniform vigour. There is an excellent certification scheme used by nurserymen, and this is much the safest bet for the

Above: Raspberry 'Glen Clova' and (right) 'Malling Delight'

of weeds, necessary to allow the plants both to fruit and renew their entire aerial system each summer.

Soil and site

The wild raspberry—*Rubus idaeus*—grows in the British Isles, so this native is well suited to our climate, and particularly to the wetter and cooler parts of the island. The crops in Scotland are much heavier than those obtained in the drier south-east, which points clearly to the need for good soil preparations, and in particular to the desirability of ensuring a constant supply of moisture during the growing season.

It is of equal importance to avoid waterlogging in the winter months because the fine fibrous roots of the raspberry are very susceptible to bad drainage, which can lead to the death of canes. The raspberry will tolerate a reasonable amount of moist shade

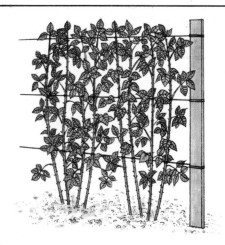

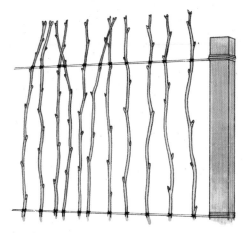

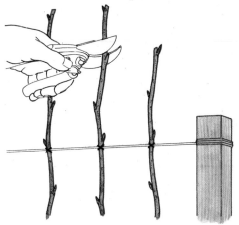

Support system for raspberries. Place wires at 2 m, 1.2 m and 60 cm (6 ft, 4 ft, 2 ft).

In the autumn tie in new canes to the supporting wires at each level after cutting old canes right back

In spring, prune back the unripened tips

beginner. It is so important to make a good start that the point is worth repeating even in the form of negatives. Never use suckers from weakly growing plantations with sparse new canes carrying light-coloured foliage. Even if free, they are much too expensive.

Varieties

Varieties are numerous and mostly new. Whereas the Cox's Orange Pippin dates from 1825, and other popular apples are even older, there are few raspberry varieties available today which were extant even thirty years ago. The change is partly due to the depredations of virus diseases, but even more to the splendid work of Research Stations who saw the need for new varieties, and who with great patience and skill bred the new and greatly improved kinds that we now have. Gardeners are incredibly fortunate in the spin-off they enjoy from research which is carried out essentially on behalf of the commercial grower. The selection of varieties is not easy, but any modern nurseryman's list is likely to include the following. Those marked * are best for freezing.

Malling Exploit*
Malling Promise
Lloyd George
Malling Delight
Malling Jewel*
Malling Orion
Glen Clova*
Malling Admiral
Norfolk Giant

The latest report from one research station shows that over seven thousand new seedlings were grown-on in 1975. If only one of these is an improvement on what we already have then we will have benefited. An example of the possibilities in scientific breeding lies in a brief reference in the report to one of the new late ripening varieties, named Malling Leo, which outcropped the excellent established variety Norfolk Giant by a magnificent 60 per cent in the preliminary trials. My choice of three to cover the season would be:

Malling Promise, a well-tried, heavy-cropping early variety.

Malling Jewel, one from the same stable but rather later and of good freezing quality. If I had room for one variety only this would be my choice.

Norfolk Giant, a late variety which always crops well. If Malling Leo lives up to its early promise then it will be the natural successor to Norfolk Giant, but we won't know its real value for some years.

So far we have been considering the main summer fruiting varieties, those which produce their fruits on last year's canes. It is surprising that the autumn fruiting varieties are not grown more widely. These fruit on the current year's canes and prolong the season, although the crop is not as heavy as that produced by the summer fruiting kinds. Of the two varieties listed, Zeva and September, the latter is to be preferred. If you like to be different there are also yellow, summer fruiting, raspberries of which the one most frequently encountered is Yellow Antwerp.

Planting

The planting of both summer and autumn fruiting varieties is best done during the late autumn, in early November for preference. The soil at that time is still warm enough for re-rooting to take place, and plants to become established before the strain of the following growing season commences.

If late autumn planting is not feasible then any time up to the middle of March is still possible, but the earlier the better. Cover the roots with the most friable of the soil which was dug from the planting hole or, even better, with used potting soil. Spread the roots out, plant shallowly when the soil is reasonably dry, make the ground firm, and all will be well.

Space the plants 60cm (2ft) apart and, if you can manage more than one row, allow some 2m (6ft 6in) between the rows. Finish with a good mulching of the surface, although this can be deferred until growth begins, if more convenient.

Pruning

Pruning begins on planting, and follows the same principle applied to newly planted black currant bushes, in that the aim is to prevent the formation of fruit (on summer fruiting varieties) in the first year. Instead all the energy of the new plant, which after all has only a limited root system, is directed to the production of new roots and new canes. Accordingly, cut each newly planted cane back to about 25cm (10in) above ground level. Unlike black currant prunings the cut shoots cannot be used as cuttings from which to produce new plants, because the raspberry, like so many members of the genus *Rubus*, has a perennial rootstock which produces only biennial stems. In other words the stems die after fruiting, to be replaced by new stems growing directly from the roots.

Pruning is therefore simple, because in a way the plants are naturally self pruning. To improve on nature, not only cut out completely the fruited canes but also reduce their numbers during the growing season. This is done by pulling out the weak surplus suckers, wearing a protective glove. The idea is to leave behind strong young canes at about 10cm (4in) apart. At the end of the season prune out the decrepit old and tie in the triumphant young. In fact pruning can be done at any time once fruiting is over, and in some years the young cane appears to be all the better for the early removal of the previous generation.

One further act of pruning remains. In early March the tip of each cane is trimmed back to a uniform height. The purpose is to encourage the fruiting laterals to break and at the same time to remove a source of rather weak laterals at the end of the shoots. It is wise to prune the tips in spring rather than winter so allowance can be made thereby for dying-back following a hard winter. There is room for experiment here, in that the tradition with the older varieties is to cut back to about 1.75m (6ft) but the new, more vigorous ones need not be trimmed so severely, indeed it is wasteful to do so. If

During the growing season pull out by hand unwanted suckers.

the canes are really vigorous then the lightly pruned tips can be bent over and secured to the top wire in a series of loops. Naturally, varieties that fruit in autumn (September) are cut down to ground level each winter, so that a new crop of canes is produced and fruit carried in the same season.

Supports

In many gardens the canes are left to support each other as best they can, with moderate results. There is no doubt that if you are looking for heavy and regular cropping combined with neatness and long life, the raspberries should be grown against posts and wire. Use stout posts, with end struts. Space each post about 3m (10ft) apart, and standing 2m (6ft 6in) out of the ground. Three wires are stapled to the posts, one at the top, the bottom one 60cm (2ft) from the ground and the other mid-way between the two. It is possible to contrive simpler and less expensive supports, but none so satisfying. There is no reason, however, why raspberries should not be grown in clumps rather than rows, each clump being supported by a single post. Whichever system is used take care to prevent the suckers straying away from the parent plant.

Feeding

It is tiresome but necessary to repeat that the best results follow on the incorporation of large quantities of farmyard manure or composted vegetation or other moisture-retaining bulky organic matter before planting. This foundation should be supplemented by an application of sulphate of potash to the soil at 25g per m² (1oz per sq yd), and the whole status maintained subsequently by an annual mulching of whatever compost is available, including lawn clippings. Thereafter be guided by the performance of the plants. Raspberries respond to supplies of potassium and on soils which tend to be low in potash the dressing mentioned above may be necessary as an annual rite of spring. If growth generally is unsatisfactory, despite the liberal use of bulky organic materials, then apply a general compound fertilizer in the spring. Growmore at 100g per m² (3oz per sq yd) is about right. More concentrated compounds should be used at lesser rates according to analysis.

Pests and problems

On really heavy clay soils that tend to lie wet it is possible to overdo the mulch to the extent of excluding air from the soil and bringing about soil stagnation and the death of canes. But such soils will not need mulching in any case, save in drought years. Another risk, worth taking, is that mulching sometimes encourages a tiny pest called cane midge, which feeds just below the rind of the cane and allows disease to enter. Carry on mulching, if you can, and deal with midge if it occurs.

Much more troublesome than cane-midge is the loathsome raspberry beetle, which gives rise to maggoty fruits. Dust the fruitlets with derris or spray with malathion as soon as the first pink fruits are seen. Aphids also can be a nuisance, but are easily dealt with by spraying with malathion or other suitable aphicide as soon as the colonies appear. The most difficult of the fungus diseases is called cane-spot, but this is at its worst on loganberries.

Blackberries

Every autumn the remaining hedgerows in the countryside are studded with family groups busily engaged in picking wild blackberries. A large proportion of the fruit is devoured on the spot and the rest is whisked home for stewing with apples; freezing or making into jam or jelly. Such is the popularity of our native fruit. But all ardent blackberryers will testify that what with hedgerow clearances, the relentless advance of the urban sprawl and losses due to careless stubble burning—to say nothing of drought—one has to travel much further now to fill baskets than used to be the case.

The answer is to grow blackberries in the garden. The blackberry is very accommodating and tolerant of adverse site and soil

Above: 'Bedford Giant' produces very large sweet fruits

conditions, and can therefore be used to turn the rough corners of the garden, if any there be, to profit. An excellent crop has been gathered each year in one large and somewhat neglected garden from a wire fence used once to confine chickens, and that with no attention whatsoever beyond picking and the minimum of pruning to keep the rods within reasonable bounds. The cultivated varieties tend to lack the sharpness and bite of their wild cousins but are well worth the space and effort required.

Soil and site

Although the blackberry will grow and crop on poor soil and in shady positions, it will only give of its bountiful best if offered well prepared soil, plenty of summer moisture

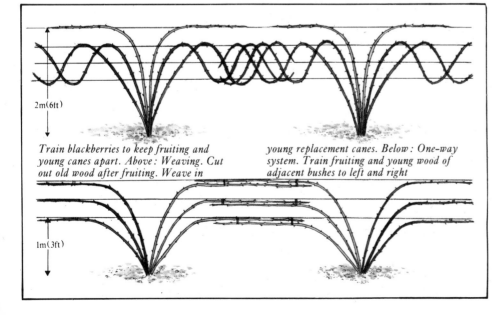

2m(6ft)

Train blackberries to keep fruiting and young canes apart. Above: Weaving. Cut out old wood after fruiting. Weave in

young replacement canes. Below: One-way system. Train fruiting and young wood of adjacent bushes to left and right

1m(3ft)

and an open site. In other words, the recommendations for soil, site and manuring made earlier for the raspberry will suit the blackberry splendidly, but if really necessary it will still crop satisfactorily where the raspberry would be a dismal failure.

Propagation

We all know how the blackberry is propagated in the wild because it is obvious that those big clumps extend outwards partly by new seedlings, but even more by a process of natural layering. This is accomplished as the young canes arch over under their own weight, causing the tips to come into contact with the ground. These tips become covered with debris, which allows them to root and at the same time to produce another aerial rod which stretches outwards to new territory in a series of arching loops.

If the gardener wishes to increase his stock all he has to do is to copy nature. The tip of a selected young cane is buried shallowly in July or thereabouts, securing the parent cane to ensure that the tip is properly anchored. It helps if a couple of handfuls of used potting compost are placed around the buried tip, and rooting is accelerated if the tip is kept moist. During the next winter or spring the new emergent rooted shoot can be detached, lifted and planted to carry on an independent existence.

Blackberries can also be readily propagated on a large scale by single bud cuttings, but that technique calls for special facilities and need not concern the average gardener.

Planting

Spread out the roots of the new plant—home raised or purchased—so that they occupy as large a feeding zone as possible, the soil firmed and the surface mulched in accordance with basic good practice and principles. Each newly planted blackberry must then be shortened back to about 30cm (1ft). The plants should be given plenty of room. The very vigorous varieties, such as Himalaya Giant, will need about 4.5m (15ft) while the more refined types such as the Parsley-leafed will manage with 3m (10ft).

Training and pruning

The gardener, like the modern parent of young children, has the choice of allowing the canes to scramble around in a free-for-all fashion, or to adopt the stern alternative of insisting on a bit of discipline. There are situations where nature can be left to herself, more or less, but the best results are beyond all doubt obtained from formal training. One system, which gives excellent results, allows the fruiting rods to be kept separate from the rampant young cane, which makes for an easier life for the owner. It also enables a greater length of fruiting cane to be utilized because of the manner in which the rods are trained in a weaving and looping pattern on the bottom three wires. This operation calls for thick gloves and old clothes, combined with calm weather and a mild winter's day. The young cane is tied in as it develops during the summer, guided into the central V-shaped space and then along the top wire. After fruiting, the old rods are cut out and the new cane tied in on the bottom wire.

If the prospect of battling with the thorny canes any more than absolutely necessary proves daunting, the one-way training system has much to commend it. Here, after the young cane is tied into its fruiting quarters, no further handling is required. Obviously this system does not use the space as effectively as the first one.

The pruning of blackberries has, in a way, already been implied from the descriptions of training. Most varieties have biennial stems, which die after fruiting and are then replaced by the young canes, but the fruiting rods of some of the more vigorous varieties are perennial. It is useful to know this, because if there are not enough young canes produced in a particular year the old rods can be retained for another season. All that is necessary, apart from any repositioning required, is to prune the laterals which carried the fruits back to 2.5cm (1in).

In its growth habit the blackberry resembles a rambling rose, which suggests that it could be trained vertically.

Varieties

A walk in the country in spring quickly reveals that even the wild blackberry comes from a very mixed family. Botanically, the blackberry is *Rubus fruticosus*, but the type has mutated into a number of sub-species,

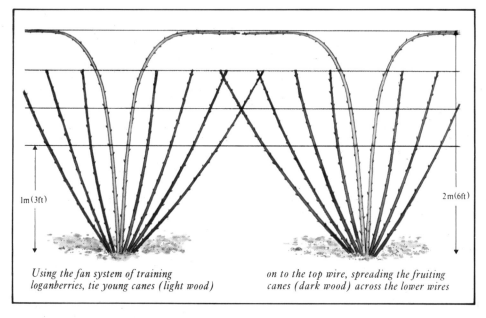

1m(3ft)

2m(6ft)

Using the fan system of training loganberries, tie young canes (light wood)   *on to the top wire, spreading the fruiting canes (dark wood) across the lower wires*

including the nicely named *Rubus laciniatus*, the cut-leafed or parsley-leafed species. Some authorities suggest that the very vigorous Himalaya Giant comes from *Rubus procerus*. Additionally, new scientific breeding has produced new varieties to add to the range. With this background it is not surprising that there is a wide choice available.

The commercial producers grow the vigorous varieties because they crop most heavily, so if you have the space it makes some sense to grow Himalaya Giant, Bedford Giant or John Innes. All those mentioned will freeze satisfactorily. Be warned, however, that vigorous really does mean

Far left: Blackberries can make a useful dividing screen in the garden

Left: Berries of the thornless variety 'Oregon' are easier to harvest

vigorous, and they are heavily armed with thorns. More manageable, because it is relatively dainty, is the parsley-leafed variety. There is a thornless clone, which is understandably popular. All in all the variety most amateurs will be happiest with is the one offered as Oregon Thornless.

Pests and diseases

Always plant healthy looking plants, never start with weak, sickly canes, and particularly so if the stem is scarred and cankered.

Having made a good start with healthy plants in well-prepared soil in a good site there is not much to go wrong, save for the troubles which come in from your neighbours' gardens and against which it is sensible to take at least minimum precautions. A spray of malathion (or rogor) should be applied as soon as aphids are seen, taking care to observe the manufacturer's instructions. The raspberry beetle is best controlled by a derris spray applied in the late evening as the first flowers open.

If pests and diseases are kept at bay and the plants are properly nourished they should last in a heavy cropping state indefinitely and provide a pleasant investment.

Loganberries

How often can you buy fresh loganberries in the shops? Even pick-your-own and farm-gate-sale loganberries are difficult to find, and yet fresh loganberries offer a special flavour which for most of us can only be experienced if we grow our own. Any surplus from the garden is readily preserved against the dark days ahead, so why not grow at least a few in the garden? They are quite easy to grow, provided a few rules are observed, although it is fair to say that the loganberry is not as accommodating as its close relatives the raspberry and blackberry.

Origins and varieties

The loganberry gets its name from the gardener who first spotted this particular natural hybrid in his garden in 1881, Judge J. H. Logan, of Santa Cruz, California. Botanists believe that it is a cross between a raspberry and another *Rubus*, the American dewberry.

Below: A thornless variety of loganberry makes pruning and training simpler

Largely because of its hybrid origin there are few true varieties as such. There are a number of selections which have been made from time to time when keen-eyed growers or research workers have selected vegetative changes which appear to be improvements on the original. The new clones, as the resulting families are called, are issued under special identifying numbers, such as LY59, and a thornless sport known as L654. There are many inferior variants, including seedlings, and it is wise to buy in plants from a reputable source. This is particularly important because the loganberry is specially prone both to virus diseases and to a nasty fungus disease called cane spot, which is carried over from year to year on affected plants. Home propagation is not therefore recommended.

Planting and training

The same general rules apply as for blackberries, which see, except that loganberries are much less vigorous and can be planted as close as 2.5m (about 8ft) apart.

Because of cane spot disease it is essential to train loganberries in such a manner that the young canes are either above or to one side of the fruiting canes. This is because if the fungus is present on the older wood the spores could be carried in rain drops on to the young and innocent new growth below.

The fan system of training shown meets the need, but care should be taken to maintain a wide central area through which the young cane is trained initially.

Pruning is simplicity itself, consisting of the complete removal of the fruited wood and the training in its place of the young cane.

As an alternative the one way system shown in diagram 2 in the chapter on blackberries keeps the canes in their separate age groups and avoids double handling but at the expense of unoccupied training space.

Gloves should be worn when handling loganberry canes. It is when pruning that the value of the thornless clone is particularly appreciated.

Troubles

Cane spot is the major nuisance. The fungus causes damage to the stems, in the main. The early purple spots later become rough cankers which affect the functioning of the plant. Other parasites may invade and as a result the cane often dies. Two sprays are desirable, one just before the first flowers open and the second as soon as flowering is over. Of the fungicides at present readily available to the gardener Bordeaux mixture is the most suitable.

The same beetle that sometimes attacks other members of the *Rubus* family and causes maggots to appear in the fruits can also be troublesome with loganberries. Derris, dusted on at the end of flowering and repeated when the first colour shows, will go a long way to prevent this disconcerting pest.

Crown gall sometimes occurs at ground level if the planting site is waterlogged or the roots damaged.

Unusual berried fruits

The genus *Rubus* intercrosses readily, with the result that we have a large number of hybrids worth mentioning, and some are even worth growing by the adventurous. They are all good fun, but only a few succeed in being sufficiently distinct from their progenitors to warrant garden space where this is limited.

From a long catalogue a short list worth considering includes the Boysenberry, the Low Berry, the Veitchberry and the Wineberry, with secondary mention for the Laxton Berry, the Phenomenal Berry, the Youngberry and the King's Acre Berry. All are attractive, but this chapter includes notes on only the first four.

The Boysenberry

This is popular in the U.S.A. and is said to stem from very mixed parentage. The large reddish-black fruits possess a rather special flavour. It grows vigorously and should be treated as a blackberry and planted at 4m (12ft) apart. A thornless form has appeared and is now on sale; one nurseryman claims that each plant of this clone can yield up to 5kg (10lb) of fruit.

All authorities unite in stressing that the Boysenberry resists drought well, so this could well be the right plant for a garden in a dry area where the soil is thin.

The Low Berry

Not very much is known about the Low Berry, another American hybrid, but it has interesting antecedents and eminent authorities are on record in its favour. The Judge Logan earlier mentioned as the raiser of the excellent hybrid which bears his name also raised the Low Berry by crossing 'a blackberry' with *Rubus vitifolius*. He obviously led a busy life. The fruits are jet black, large and long (5cm (2in)) with a flavour similar to a good blackberry but rather sweeter than a loganberry. It is sometimes called the Mammoth Berry. It is vigorous, when happy, producing canes up to 5m (16ft 6in) long, and so should be given the sort of space allotted to the more rampant blackberries.

One reason why such an interesting subject has not become more popular may be related to its uncertain hardiness. Whether it is worth devoting wall space to the Low Berry must be a matter for personal judgment, but it is a possibility worth considering by those fond of good quality berries.

The Veitchberry

This fills a gap in the berry season, coming as it does in July, when the large, sweet, purplish-red berries are welcome.

It is a home-raised cross between a raspberry and a blackberry, the vigorous canes taking after the latter. It should be cultivated on the same lines as the blackberry, and valued alike for the earliness and the size of the mulberry-like fruits.

The Wineberry

A species in its own right—*Rubus phoenicolasius*—which deserves consideration as a decorative subject quite apart from its fruits. It comes from Japan, but is perversely occasionally called the Chinese Blackberry, which is a double-barrelled misnomer, because the fruits are in fact yellow turning through orange to red, and the habit is more like the raspberry.

The canes grow some 2m (6ft 6in) in length and are covered with soft reddish bristles, the whole being aesthetically pleasing. The small, round fruits are pleasant enough, without being ecstatically delicious. Its place in the select list is earned by its ornamental appearance.

Other Unusual Berries

Although the following are not cane fruits, they are best dealt with here.

The Worcesterberry

Opinion is sharply divided on the merits of this interesting plant, a member of the family *Ribes*. It has been regarded with favour for many years by gardeners keen on unusual plants such as a cross between a blackcurrant and a gooseberry. And that is exactly what it looks like—a gooseberry bearing small black berries which make a passable preserve. Cold science regards it as a form of the species *Ribes divaricatum*, producing poorly flavoured berries.

Above: The wineberry is a decorative addition to the fruit garden

Left: Fruits of the boysenberry, whose canes can grow up to 2·5m (8ft) long

The Blueberry

Do rhododendrons flourish in your district? If so, your soil should be just right for blueberry growing.

A relative of the cranberry, the blueberry has assumed new importance in recent years and a number of experimental plantations have been laid down to satisfy a demand, stemming from the experiences of visitors to the U.S.A., where several different types are grown commercially.

Like other *Vaccinium* species the blueberry requires an acid soil for success. It forms a bush which requires little attention beyond a periodic cutting back of branches and the removal of overcrowded shoots.

The kinds being tried in the U.K. are of the 'highbush' type, which can reach 2m (6ft 6in) in height and spread, and more. The berries are ready in the late summer and are used in particular in tarts and preserves.

The varieties Bluecrop and Herbert, and particularly Bluecrop, have cropped well in trials; both are said to possess good flavour and to freeze well.

The Cranberry

This berry has a special attraction for those with North American connections, since the species known as *Oxycoccus macrocarpus* is cultivated there for market and the fruit consumed in tarts and jellies.

Our own wild cranberry does not appear to have found its way into many gardens, although it should thrive, like its larger fruited American cousin, in lime-free, damp soils, where it can be left to look after itself, apart from an occasional sorting out of old and tangled growths.

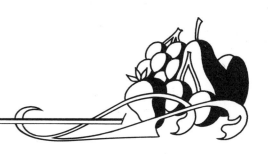

Nuts

The range of the nut-bearing crops which can be grown in our gardens is very wide in size—from hazel to walnut—but limited in variety.

The Walnut

This splendid tree well repays planting but the limit is set by the size a well-grown tree can reach. The Walnut—*Juglans regia*—is susceptible to spring frost, which may affect the tender young growths. A good, well-drained soil is necessary for the best results. Many of the older trees to be seen were raised from seeds which, as always, have given rise to a variety of forms. This problem has now been recognized and as a result selected varieties are propagated by grafting on to seedling walnut rootstocks.

Some 14m (45ft) is required for a mature walnut tree, which, whether it fruits profusely or not, will provide pleasure to all who see it, and yield splendid timber at the end. Although flowers of both sexes are present on the one tree the pollen has to be distributed and there are sometimes discrepancies in the time of flowering, with the result that cropping may be erratic. It follows that a mixture of varieties is likely to give the best results, which means more trees, which require more space, which . . . The old adage about beating dogs, wives and walnuts is best forgotten.

The French variety Franquette, the American Lieb Mayette and the English Leeds Castle and Patching are the ones generally grown, the two latter being particularly favoured for pickling.

Tentative attempts are being made to induce early fruiting and small compact trees, but we must wait and see.

Cobnut and Filbert

Although distinct, cobnuts and filberts are treated in similar fashion in gardens, where they are usually relegated to the outskirts of the garden to form screens, and then left to their own devices. But since the nuts flower very early this exposure may result in poor cropping. Both cobnuts and filberts respond to detailed cultivation. A start should be made with plants at 5m (16ft) apart. The newly planted bushes should be cut back to 45cm (18in) to stimulate strong shoots to form the main branches of an open centre bush. These branches should in turn be pruned each year by about one-third, according to strength, with the purpose of causing the fruit-bearing laterals to break from some 12 main branches, each about 2m (6ft 6in) tall.

An old practice is the snapping by hand of long side shoots in August to leave roughly 12cm (5in) behind and the broken piece still attached at the end. This technique is known as 'brutting'. The principle is identical with that behind the summer pruning of apples and pears, but there is less likelihood of secondary growth occurring. The brutted shoots are pruned back to some 5cm (2in) in early spring. Suckers are removed on sight.

My memory suggests that we used to sing something about 'gathering nuts in May',

Below: Spread cobnuts out to dry for a few days before storing

Left: Immature fruits of the walnut, a tree that will enhance any garden

which seems odd. (Perhaps it should be 'nuts *and* may', the latter being haws.) These particular nuts are not ready until late September, when they are shared with the squirrels.

The varieties most usually grown are Kentish Cob, Cosford Cob and the White and Red Filberts.

The Gardener's Year

January

Fruit
Any pruning of fruit trees and bushes not yet done can be undertaken. Planting can continue but wait until the soil is reasonably dry. Check on fruit still in store.

Bullfinches start feeding in earnest on fruit buds early in the new year; encourage them to feed elsewhere.

Vegetables
Plan your cropping programme for the year. Place seed and potato orders. Continue with winter digging and manuring. Apply lime if needed. Examine stored vegetables.

Sow—Heated protection—early summer cauliflowers; bulb onions; spring maturing lettuce and maincrop tomatoes—all for subsequent transplanting.

Cold protection—radishes and early carrots.

Indoors—make weekly sowings of mustard and cress (continue throughout the year).

February

Fruit
At the end of the month remove the tips of young raspberry canes to encourage strong fruit bearing laterals. Spray against peach leaf curl—later may be too late.

Vegetables
Box up potato 'seed' tubers for chitting. Examine stored vegetables. Finish winter digging. Top dress over-wintered crops when growth re-starts.

Sow—Heated protection—early summer cabbage; early leeks; tomatoes for cold houses; peppers and aubergines for heated houses; dwarf French beans in pots.

Cold protection—early peas; early summer turnips.

Outside—bulb onions (late in month); radish and salad onions (successional sowings through the spring and summer will give continuity).

Plant—Under protection—spring maturing lettuce under cold protection; early tomatoes in heated structures.

Outside—shallots and garlic as early as possible.

March

Fruit
Cover early strawberries with cloches. Pruning and planting of fruit trees should be completed. Applications of fertilizer and mulches to fruit crops should be completed by mid-month.

Vegetables
Break down winter digging to produce sowing/planting tilths as needed. Hoe over-wintered crops when the soil begins to dry.

Sow—Heated protection—heated house cucumbers and melons; early Brussels sprouts; celery and celeriac; outdoor tomatoes; cardoons; cape gooseberries and New Zealand spinach—all for transplanting.

Cold protection—Brussels sprouts; dwarf French beans.

Outside—maincrop leeks; Brussels sprouts and summer/autumn cauliflower (which can be sown successionally until the end of May)—all for transplanting. Broad beans; early carrots (until late April); peas (successional crops); parsnips; summer turnips; summer spinach (successionally until the end of June); summer corn salad.

Plant—Under protection—maincrop tomatoes in heated houses.

Outside—early lettuce; sea-kale (root cuttings or divided crowns); onion sets; globe artichokes; early summer cauliflower (end of month); rhubarb crowns.

July

Fruit
Apple fruits should be thinned, if the set is bountiful. Summer pruning of apples and pears can begin. The strawberry bed, now looking bedraggled, should be trimmed.

The young stems of the cane fruits will need guiding in the way they should grow.

Vegetables
Hoe, feed and water as needed; thin out drilled crops; tie in tomatoes; blanch Florence fennel.

Sow—Outside—peas (for an autumn crop); dwarf French beans (for an autumn crop); winter spinach (successional sowings until late September); plain leaved kale; parsley; winter radish; winter turnip (until mid-August); spring cabbage (for transplanting).

Plant—Outside—winter cauliflower; curly kale.

August

Fruit
The apple harvest begins with 'George Cave' and 'Discovery'. Prune the earlier plums as soon as the crop is picked. Plant pot-raised strawberry runners for fruiting next June.

Black currants, raspberries and peaches can all be pruned once the fruit has been picked.

Vegetables
Water and feed as necessary; hoe between crops; bend over onion tops; stop outdoor tomato plants; earth up celery and leeks; thin late sown beetroot and kales; blanch early sowings of endive (continue into the early autumn).

Sow—Cold protection—winter lettuce for transplanting.

Outside—spring greens; carrots (for autumn use); winter endive; over-wintered bulb onions; winter corn salad; over-wintered salad onions.

September

Fruit
Harvest apples and pears. Take keeping varieties into store in the early morning before the temperature rises.

Vegetables
Lift and dry bulb onions; hoe and water as required; remove and compost or burn all debris; earth up cardoons.

Sow—Cold protection—early summer cauliflower for planting next spring.

Outside—over-wintered lettuce for early summer cutting.

Plant—Under protection—autumn tomatoes in heated houses and winter lettuce in cold glasshouses or frames.

Outside—spring cabbage.

April

Fruit
Apply crucial sprays against the pests and diseases of apples, pears, plums, black currants and strawberries.

Vegetables
Stake early peas, hoe as needed, clear away debris from winter brassica crops.

Sow—Heated protection—frame melons; early runner beans; early sweet corn and cold house/frame cucumbers.

Cold protection—calabrese for transplanting; runner beans.

Outside—asparagus; purple/white sprouting broccoli; summer/autumn cabbage; savoys; red cabbage; winter cauliflower—all for transplanting. Globe beet and outdoor lettuce (both successively until early August); salsify; scorzonera; Florence fennel; silverskin onions; dwarf French beans; soy beans; leaf beets; maincrop carrots and kohl rabi (both successively until mid-July).

Plant—under protection—heated house cucumbers and melons; cold house tomatoes; heated and cold house peppers.

Outside—early summer cabbage; asparagus crowns; early potatoes (beginning of month); Jerusalem artichokes; glasshouse raised bulb onions; maincrop potatoes (end of month).

May

Fruit
Frost is still possible until the end of the month so that adventurous fruit crops should be protected on clear nights.

Over-vigorous fruit trees—and only the over-vigorous—may be bark-ringed. The leaders of established pyramid plums may be removed with the same intention of providing a check to excessive vigour.

Vegetables
Stake peas and beans; earth up early potatoes; hoe as needed; build up compost heap; thin out seedlings where necessary (beetroot, carrots, turnips, lettuce, parsnips); top dress early summer crops.

Sow—Heated protection—marrows: courgettes; pumpkins; squashes and ridge cucumbers—all for transplanting.

Outside—winter cabbage and curly kale for transplanting.

Asparagus; peas; maincrop runner beans; early endive; chicory; sweet corn, Chinese cabbage (successional sowings); maincrop long beet; marrows/courgettes/pumpkins/squashes (all *in situ* at the end of the month).

Plant—Under protection—aubergines and cape gooseberries in heated protection; cold house/frame cucumbers and frame melons.

Outside—Brussels sprouts (until mid-June); early leeks, runner beans and sweet corn; marrows/courgettes; tomatoes (all after the last frost); cardoons; New Zealand spinach; summer and autumn cauliflower (planted successionally).

June

Fruit
Fruits should be swelling nicely and early gooseberries and strawberries ready for picking. The latter should be strawed down early in the month to keep the fruits clean.

The first, tentative, thinning of overcrowded peaches and plums may be necessary; but apples are best left unthinned until next month, except for early cooking varieties.

Vegetables
Hoe crops regularly; water as required; top dress if necessary; thin out drilled crops; earth up potatoes; stake runner beans.

Sow—Heated protection—autumn tomatoes at the end of the month.

Outside—swedes.

Plant—Outside—celery and celeriac; ridge cucumbers; calabrese; purple/white/perennial broccoli; summer/autumn cabbage; savoys; red cabbage; maincrop leeks.

October

Fruit
Cuttings of black currants, red currants and gooseberries can be taken and inserted while the ground is still warm.

Strawberry runners can still be planted but should not be allowed to fruit next year.

New stakes and ties for fruit trees may be required in readiness for the winter's gales.

Order new trees, canes and bushes for delivery in November.

Vegetables
Hoe between and tidy perennial and over-wintered crops; earth up celery and winter cauliflowers; blanch winter endive (successionally); remove all debris; collect and store canes/stakes; generally clean up garden; order manure.

Sow—Cold protection—spring-maturing lettuce for transplanting.

November

Fruit
Tree leaves should be consigned to the compost heap or to a special heap to rot down for leaf mould.

This is the best month for the planting of all fruits except strawberries.

Winter pruning can begin. Do not hurry; wait until the leaves have fallen so that next year's fruit buds can be seen clearly.

Vegetables
Dig areas which are clear; continue with clearing up; give final earthing up of celery; begin to force chicory; lift rhubarb roots in preparation for shed forcing.

Sow—Outside—broad beans.

Plant—Under protection—spring-maturing lettuce in cold houses or frames.

Outside—rhubarb crowns (or in March).

December

Fruit
In the fruit garden planting and pruning will occupy the week-ends. Apples, pears, quinces, medlars and nuts will now come from store; preserved raspberries, strawberries, plums and the like will come from freezer and larder.

Vegetables
Continue with digging; examine stored vegetables; clean and maintain all tools and equipment; begin to force rhubarb and seakale.

Sow—Heated protection—early tomatoes for February planting.

In the Kitchen

Freezing, Preserving and Cooking.

Preserving Techniques

Freezing

Freezing is the most up-to-date and simplest way of preserving both cooked and uncooked foods, and the one that best retains their original flavour, texture, appearance and nutritional value. In the freezer food is stored at $-18°C$ ($0°F$) or lower. Ideally, garden produce should be prepared and put into the freezer immediately it is picked but if delay is unavoidable it should be kept in cool conditions; wrapped or covered and stored in the refrigerator is best. Pick when young and small and in perfect condition.

Packaging material

Packaging material must be strong to prevent damage, moisture-proof to keep in liquids and prevent others entering, vapour-proof to prevent the transfer of flavours or aromas, to prevent dehydration and to stop oxidation, which spoils the colour and breaks down nutriments, non-toxic so they do not support growth of bacteria or moulds, and must not become dry or brittle in the cold of the freezer.

Starting with the cheapest the following are suitable:

Polythene bags Minimum thickness is 120 gauge but 150–250 gauge are stronger, better for longer storage and easier to re-use.

Plastic cling film Special freezer film is easy to mould round any shape to exclude air. Thinner film can be used to wrap several items to be overwrapped together.

'Boil-in' food bags in which food can be frozen and then dropped into boiling water to reheat.

Aluminium foil Used much as plastic film with a freezer grade for extra protection. Do not wrap acid fruits in such a way that they are in contact with aluminium foil.

Rigid containers in a wide range of shapes and materials including foil, waxed cardboard and plastic, some with their own covers and others to be covered by plastic film or foil.

It is always important to exclude as much air as possible. With bags gather neck close to food, insert a straw into bag and suck out air until bag forms round contents. Remove straw and fasten with tie. In containers 1–2.5cm ($\frac{1}{2}$–1in) headroom should be left especially when there is liquid, as this expands as it freezes. Extra space can be filled with crumpled plastic film.

Labelling should be done before freezing and should record the kind of food and variety, quantity or weight, date, and notes for thawing and cooking or reheating.

Quantities which can be frozen at one time

Refer to the instruction book supplied with the freezer. The usual recommendation is a tenth of total capacity in each 24 hours. For example, each cubic foot (0.028cu m) holds approx. 11kg (25lb) of food; a 4 cubic foot (0.113cu m) freezer will hold approx. 45 kg (100lb) so freeze only up to 4.5kg (10lb).

Freezing Vegetables

General notes

1. Prepare according to kind by peeling, scraping, trimming, etc.
2. Blanch all vegetables except where specified. Put 450g (1lb) only of prepared vegetable into a wire basket or cheesecloth bag or nylon wine straining bag. Lower into pan containing 3.4–4.5 litre (6–8 pints) of rapidly boiling water over full heat.

Always choose the right packaging material for successful freezing

Time from moment water returns to boil. Small vegetables or those cut into small pieces need less blanching time than larger ones.

3. Cool. Transfer immediately to large basin of very cold water with plenty of ice in it. Cool for same time as blanching. Drain well.

4. Freezing. Pack into containers and freeze or open freeze first. To open freeze spread out in single layer on a tray and put in freezer. When frozen transfer the pieces, each separate from the next, to the chosen container.

5. Freezing Temperatures. Two to three hours before putting in food, turn to setting manufacturer recommends. This is the coldest setting and time must be allowed for freezer temperature to reduce. The low temperature will form small ice crystals in the food; large ones puncture cell walls spoiling flavour and texture.

Is blanching necessary?

The blanching process retards the action of enzymes—chemical substances naturally present in food—which cause undesirable changes in odour, colour, flavour, texture and food value especially in the presence of atmospheric oxygen. Freezing alone only reduces their activity to a very slow rate. Vegetables not blanched must be used quickly or flavour and texture are affected. They also take longer to cook before serving.

Storage time All vegetables can be kept frozen for up to 12

Right: One of the most rewarding advantages of freezer-owning is summer vegetables all year round

months.

Cooking frozen vegetables All vegetables, except corn on the cob, should be cooked without thawing.

a) Drop into boiling salted water 1cm (½in) deep, and allow only ½–¾ time allowed for fresh vegetables.

b) *Purees*—Melt a little butter in a double saucepan or basin standing in pan of boiling water. Add puree, cover and heat.

Can all vegetables be frozen? Ones with high water content, such as many salads, become an unusable pulp when thawed. There is little point in freezing cabbages which are available fresh all through the year or some of the root vegetables, if you have good outdoor storage for them.

Special Instructions

Artichokes, Globe Trim stalks level with bases. Cut off coarse outer leaves, trim off tips of other leaves and soak 1 hour, with lemon juice added. Blanch, up to six at a time, with lemon juice added, for 7 minutes. Cook completely if to be served cold, and remove choke before freezing.

Artichokes, Jerusalem Best frozen as purée. Use as basis for soup or mix with potatoes.

Asparagus Cut into lengths to fit containers. Grade according to thickness. Blanch 2–4 minutes, according to thickness.

Aubergines Trim off ends. Cut into 1cm (½in) slices. Blanch 4 minutes.

Beans, Broad Shell. Blanch 2–3 minutes.

Beans, French Top and tail; leave whole. Blanch 2 minutes.

Beans, Runner Top and tail; remove strings. Cut into thick chunks. Blanch 2 minutes.

Beetroot Use only small ones. Cook completely and skin. Under 5cm (2in) diameter, freeze whole. Others slice or dice.

Brussels Sprouts Remove discoloured leaves and trim stalk. Blanch 2 minutes if small, 3 minutes if medium.

Calabrese and Broccoli Cut into uniform lengths. Remove large leaves and trim stems to not more than 2.5cm (1in) thick. Blanch 3 minutes.

Carrots Top and tail; scrape. If small, leave whole and blanch 5 minutes. If larger, slice or dice; blanch 3 minutes.

Cauliflower Use unopened flower heads and divide into florets. Add lemon juice to water; blanch 3–5 minutes, depending on size.

Celeriac Best frozen as purée. Can also be cut into slices and blanched 6 minutes.

Celery Cannot be eaten raw after freezing but useful as flavouring for soups, stews, etc. Cut into 5cm (2in) lengths; blanch 3 minutes.

Chicory Cannot be eaten raw after freezing. Blanch 2 minutes in water with lemon juice, or braise before freezing.

Corn-on-the-Cob Husk and remove silk. Blanch 4–6 minutes according to size.

Corn Kernels Husk and remove silk; blanch 4 minutes, cool quickly, then cut downwards to remove kernels.

Chard Remove tough stems and shred. Blanch 2–3 minutes.

Courgettes Top and tail. Cut into 1cm (½in) slices; blanch 1–2 minutes. Can also be cooked in butter until tender. Add herbs on reheating.

Fennel Cut bulbous base into slices lengthwise or crosswise. Blanch 3 minutes

Peas, Garden Shell; blanch 1 minute.

Peas, Mangetout and Sugar Peas including Asparagus Peas Trim ends and remove any strings. Blanch 2 minutes.

Kale Remove tough stems and shred. Blanch 2–3 minutes.

Kohlrabi Use only when young and tender. Trim, wash and peel. Blanch small ones, whole, 3 minutes or larger ones, diced, 2 minutes.

Leeks Trim off roots and tops of green parts. Wash very well to remove all soil. Cut larger ones into slices. Blanch 2–4 minutes, according to thickness.

Marrow Cut small, young ones into 1cm (½in) thick slices; blanch 3 minutes. If to be fried there is no need to thaw first. Large ones are not worth freezing.

Mushrooms Wash and dry. Do not peel. Open freeze—can be sliced first. Can also sauté in butter until almost tender.

Onions Available throughout year so little point in freezing except to save time later. Peel, slice and blanch 1 minute.

Onions, Tiny Peel and blanch 3 minutes. After thawing can be added to sauces (white, tomato, etc.) to serve as vegetable or in stock to add to stews.

Parsnips Use only small ones as larger ones may be woody. Peel, cut into strips or dice; blanch 3 minutes. Also freeze as a purée.

Pepper, Red and Green Cut out stems, cut into halves downwards and remove seeds and white pith. Leave in halves for stuffing later or slice. Blanch halves 3 minutes, slices 2 minutes.

Potatoes Scrape small, new potatoes and boil until almost cooked. (To serve—cook in boiling water about 5 minutes; toss in butter with mint or parsley.) *Potatoes, Chips* Fry until almost cooked, but not coloured, then freeze. *Potatoes, Croquettes* Coat and fry. *Potatoes, Mashed* As Duchesse potatoes or part of plated meal. *Potatoes, Jacket* Bake, cut into halves, mix pulp with filling ingredients and return to shell. *Potatoes, Roast* Cook in usual way and drain.

Pumpkin Cook until tender and mash. Add extra flavourings when using as pie filling or for soup.

Salsify and Scorzonera Scrub; blanch 2 minutes. Remove skins while warm and cut into 5cm (2in) lengths.

Spinach Remove stems and wash very well. Blanch 2 minutes or cook without liquid. Drain, press out excess fluid and chop.

Swedes and Turnips Peel, cube and blanch 2 minutes or cook and purée.

Tomatoes Really a fruit so no need to blanch. Frozen whole they can be used for frying. Can be stewed or made into juice or peeled and frozen whole for adding to stews.

Vegetable Purées Can be used in soups or served as a vegetable. Small portions can be used for baby food.

Mixed Vegetables and Stew Packs For these, prepare each vegetable according to kind before mixing.

Freezing Herbs

Pick just before flowering, when they are at their best. Wash and dry, then freeze in one of the following ways:

1. Pack sprigs into polythene bags. Thaw before use if whole leaves are wanted or crumble frozen ones to save chopping.

2. Chop leaves and pack into ice cube compartments. Fill up with water and freeze. Store in polythene bags. Thaw in a small sieve or add cubes to soups, sauces and stews.

3. Chop, mix into butter and freeze as herb butter.

Freezing Fruits

General Notes

Just ripe, perfect fruit, frozen quickly after picking is the best. Wash only if really necessary, then freeze in one of the following ways:

1. *Dry pack* i.e. without sugar or syrup. For berries and currants and for unprepared fruit to be used later for jam making. Can be open frozen.

2. *Sugar pack* Carefully mix fruit with enough sugar to sweeten; usually 100–125g (4oz) per ½kg (1lb) fruit. The fruit can be sliced or lightly crushed.

3. *Syrup pack* Syrup can contain 225–450g (½–1lb) sugar to 600ml (1 pint) water. Use when cold. 750mg ascorbic acid tablet or powder (from chemist) dissolved in a little cold water and added to 600ml (1 pint) syrup helps prevent discoloration. Immerse prepared fruit in syrup and, if necessary, use crumpled waxed or greaseproof paper to keep fruit under syrup.

Right : Freeze surplus quantities of pears (and plums) in heavy harvest years

4. *As purée* Purée raw or cooked fruit and freeze in small quantities to use in mousses, icecreams and sauces.

5. *Fruit juices* The juice from oranges, grapefruit, lemons and limes, alone or mixed, sweetened or not, freezes well.

Fruit can also be frozen in tarts, pies and flans, in puddings, as icecream, sorbet and sauces.

Storage time All fruits can be kept frozen for up to 1 year.

Special instructions

Apples To prevent discoloration, drop into salted water, 1 × 5ml spoon (1tsp) salt to 1 litre (2 pints) water, after peeling and coring. Freeze as *purée* or as *apple sauce*. For *pie filling* blanch in water with lemon juice added for 2 minutes. Drain and dry. Pack into correct amounts for pie or tart. Add sugar if wished. *Baked apples* Stuff and bake in usual way. Cook completely to serve cold; slightly undercook if to be reheated. Can also be frozen in syrup which can be flavoured with lemon, orange, ginger, etc.

Apricots Remove stones. If fully ripe, add to syrup; if a little under-ripe, stew first, and if really soft, make into purée.

Blackberries Use when fully ripe. Use methods 1, 2, 3 or 4.

Blueberries, bilberries, cranberries, whortleberries Use methods 1, 2, 3 or 4. Sometimes advisable to soften skins by putting in colander over boiling water for 1 minute.

Cherries Remove stones. Use methods 1, 2 or 3. Make sure sour varieties are not over-sweetened.

Citrus fruits: oranges, lemons, grapefruits and limes. Wash, dry and wrap to use later to make marmalade or orange or lemon curd. Also dry pack slices, and strips of peel, to add to drinks. Use method 2 for segments or slices, and method 3 for segments or slices of small, peeled whole oranges. Also freeze juice and skins for grating (while still frozen) or cleaned shells for stuffing with icecream or sorbet.

Damsons, Greengages and Plums Method 1 for up to 3 months only, to use for jam, or methods 2 and 3. If a little under-ripe, stew in usual way.

Figs Wash and remove stems. Handle carefully. Wrap each in plastic film, then store in boxes. Use also method 3.

Gooseberries Top and tail. Method 1 for pies and puddings and jam making, method 3 (but stew fruit in syrup), and method 4.

Grapes Wash well and dry. Seedless ones can be frozen whole (others remove seeds) or may be peeled. Can freeze bunches by method 1 for about 3 weeks for table decorations.

Melon Use when fully ripe and cut flesh into dice or balls. Methods 2 and 3.

Peaches and Nectarines Cover with boiling water 1 minute, then remove skins and stone. Slice if wished. Use method 3.

Pears Those with delicate flavour often lose it during freezing, but they can be added to fruit salads. Peel, core and, if wished, slice. Drop immediately into syrup and poach until soft.

Pomegranates Cut into halves and take out juice sacs. Use method 3. Good in fruit salads.

Raspberries and Loganberries Methods 1 and 2 are best but method 3 can be used.

Strawberries are usually disappointing. Use method 1 for later use in jams and purées, method 2 (best to halve or slice the fruit), or method 3 (keeping amount of syrup to a minimum).

Rhubarb Use method 2 and pack into amounts for pies, or method 4.

Jam making from frozen fruit See under Jams.

Thawing frozen fruit The best method is to thaw slowly in a refrigerator and use just before completely thawed.

Freeze in quantities for your own family needs, or in small quantities. Use two or more packs when entertaining.

Freezing prepared dishes

The same general principles apply when freezing made-up dishes as when freezing home-grown vegetables and fruits. These are that the food should be as fresh as possible, it must be packed for the freezer in the correct materials, and the freezer must be turned to the lowest setting 2–3 hours before the food is put in. In addition the following points are important.

1. There is a saving in time and fuel in making-up double, triple or more quantities of a dish at one time; serve one and freeze the rest.

2. Made-up dishes to be frozen and later served hot should be undercooked by 15–20 minutes as the cooking will be finished during the heating-up period.

3. Cooked food should be cooled as quickly as possible and must not be put into the freezer until cold.

4. So that ovenproof dishes can be used time after time, line them, before cooking, with aluminium foil. Freeze in the foil lined dish, when frozen remove food with foil, overwrap, label and return to freezer. Return dish to cupboard and, later, reheat the food in the original dish.

6. It is a matter of personal preference whether fruit or vegetable pies and tarts are frozen before or after cooking.

7. Avoid freezing dishes containing large quantities of garlic or herbs, except for just a short period, as their flavours tend to become stronger or musty during storage. Extra flavourings can be added when heating through.

8. Sauces may tend to separate during reheating. Beating will usually correct this but is not always possible in a made-up dish. Thickening with cornflour instead of flour will help.

9. Save freezer space by cooking soups in just enough liquid to stop the vegetables burning. Add rest of liquid on reheating, having noted the amount required on the label.

10. Complete main courses, including vegetables, assembled on foil plates, some specially shaped, and covered with foil can provide a meal quickly. Do not include green leaf vegetables. When possible, toss vegetables in a little butter before freezing.

11. When small quantities of vegetables are left at the end of a meal, freeze them and later add to well-flavoured stock to make a vegetable soup.

12. If you are not sure whether or not your favourite recipes can be frozen, freeze a small amount and reheat after one or two weeks. See if the flavour has changed and if the consistency remains satisfactory.

Thawing Made-Up Dishes

Most fruit and vegetable dishes can be reheated without thawing. If it is to be heated in the oven put the frozen food in before the heat is turned on and use a moderate heat. If food is to be browned, either increase oven heat when food is hot or finish under a hot grill. If to be heated on the top of the stove, use a strong pan with a tightly fitting lid and heat very, very gently to begin with and then increase the heat a little.

When time is available or when the food is to be served cold it is safer to thaw in the refrigerator rather than in the kitchen; as a rough guide leave in refrigerator overnight.

Bottling

Bottling is a way of preserving fruit, usually in syrup. Heat is necessary to render the enzymes in the fruit inactive and to kill the yeasts and moulds naturally present on fruit. The bottles must be tested to ensure a seal has been formed to prevent

Five methods of bottling fruit

Fruit	1 pint water	Method 1	Method 2	Method 3	Method 4	Method 5
Berries	225–450g (½lb–1lb)	74°C (165°F) maintained	74°C (165°F) maintained			
Currants	450g (1lb)	10 minutes	2 minutes	1 minute	44–55 minutes	30–40 minutes
Gooseberries	225g					
Rhubarb	(½lb)					
Apple—slices	To taste	74°C (165°F) 10 minutes	74°C (165°F) 2 minutes	1 minute	—	30–40 minutes
Cherries—dark	100–125g	82°C (180°F)	82°C (180°F)	1 minute	55–70 minutes	40–50 minutes
Damsons						
Plums—dark	(4oz)	15 minutes	10 minutes			
Apricots	225g (½lb)	82°C (180°F)	82°C (180°F)			
Cherries—white	100–125g	15 minutes	10 minutes	1 minute	—	40–50 minutes
Greengages	(4oz)					
Plums—light						
Grapefruit	100–125g					
Lemons	(4oz)					
Oranges						
Apple—pulp	To taste					
Nectarines	225g	82°C (180°F)	82°C (180°F)			
Peaches	(½lb)	15 minutes	20 minutes	3–4 minutes	—	50–60 minutes
Figs	100–125g	88°C (190°F)	88°C (190°F)			
Pears	(4oz)	30 minutes	40 minutes	5 minutes	—	60–70 minutes
Tomatoes—whole						
Tomatoes—solid	—	88°C (190°F) 40 minutes	88°C (190°F) 50 minutes	15 minutes	—	70–80 minutes

*Time is for ½–1kg (1–2lb) bottles. Allow an extra 5 minutes (Method 5:10 minutes) per 1½–2kg (3–4lb) bottles

further yeasts and moulds entering.

Vegetables must not be home bottled but tomatoes, actually a fruit, can be.

Equipment

Bottles, rubber rings and lids The ½kg and 1kg (1lb and 2lb) sizes are the most convenient ones but larger ones up to 4kg (8 pint) are available.

Where rubber rings are used to form the seal between the top of the bottle and the lid they should be stretched a little to ensure they return to their original size; if not, discard them. Use rings only once.

Screw tops The bottles are covered with metal lids fitted with rubber gaskets or glass lids with separate rubber rings. Over these are adjusted metal screw tops, which are fitted loosely during processing but are then tightened to press lids firmly to bottles.

Clip tops Metal tops and rubber rings are kept firmly in place by a spring clip which fits on to the top and grips the sides of the bottle. Steam and heated air can force their way from the bottle but air cannot enter.

Testing Before use, examine tops of bottles and lids to make sure there is no chip or crack to prevent a seal.

Preparation Wash well, rinse with boiling water and drain bottles and lids but do not dry. Soak rubber rings in cold water for 10 minutes and dip into boiling water just before fitting.

General notes

As is the case with all preserving methods, fruit should be as perfect as possible and slightly under- rather than over-ripe. Prepare each fruit as for stewing and, if liked, remove stones. This leaves more space for fruit and during storage stones may alter flavour a little.

Syrup Fruit bottled in sugar syrup has the best flavour but golden syrup and honey can replace sugar. It can be bottled in water (a sweetener can be added). Dissolve sugar in water and boil 1 minute. If to be used cold, use only half the water and add chilled water or ice to bring to correct strength.

Tomatoes Tomatoes are best peeled. Small ones can be left whole and processed in brine, but tomatoes of any size, halved or quartered, can be packed so tightly that salt and sugar can be added without space for liquid. Allow 1 × 5ml spoon (1tsp) salt and 2 × 5ml spoons (2tsps) sugar to each.

Packing Fruit shrinks a little in the heat so pack as tightly as possible. A slender piece of wood, such as a chopstick, can be used to position the fruit. Add the liquid (except in method 4), then tap bottle on several thicknesses of cloth to remove air bubbles. It may be better to do this a little at a time. Proceed according to method chosen.

Thermometer A thermometer is really essential for method 1 and useful in method 2. If you buy a sugar thermometer it can also be used when making jams and jellies, checking fat temperatures, sweet making, etc.

Five methods of bottling fruit

The first two methods give a good appearance and use little fuel but usually only a few bottles can be processed at a time. In a pressure cooker time is saved but it is easy to overcook and shrink the fruit. Oven bottling uses more fuel and temperatures often vary between ovens but often more can be processed at one time.

Method 1 Slow heating in water Pour in enough *cold* syrup or water almost to fill the bottle and to cover the fruit. Adjust clips or put screw tops on loosely. Use pan deep enough for bottles to be completely covered with cold water when standing on a false bottom of a wire rack, slats of wood or a thick cloth. They must not touch the bottom of the pan and should be separated from each other with folded newspaper. Cover with the lid or a board. Heat the water very slowly, testing with a thermometer, so that after 1 hour it has reached only 54°C/130°F, and after a further ½ hour the temperature given on the chart. Maintain for time given and then remove bottles: ladle out water until the bottles can be lifted with oven gloves, or use bottling tongs. Put bottles,

one at a time, on to a wooden surface, to prevent cracking, and tighten screw tops at once. Leave clip tops. After 24 hours, test for seal (see below).

Method 2 Quick heating in water Differs from method 1 in the following ways: 1) Warm the bottles before filling. 2) Use hot syrup or water at 60°C/140°F. 3) Fill the pan with warm water at 38°C/100°F. 4) Heat to simmering point 88°C/190°F in 25–30 minutes. Simmer for time given on chart and proceed as method 1.

Method 3 In a pressure cooker Pour 2.5cm (1in) water into the cooker, put in the rack and bring to the boil. Use warm bottles and fill with *boiling* liquid. Put on lids and tops; loosen screw tops by a quarter turn. Put on cooker lid with vent open, heat until steam escapes, close vent, bring pressure to 5lb then reduce heat and maintain at 5lb for time given on chart. Remove cooker from heat, leave 10 minutes then open. Proceed as method 1.

Method 4 Bottling in a slow oven Preheat oven to 130°C/250°F, Gas Mark ½. Stand bottles on strong cardboard or a baking tray lined with 4 thicknesses of newspaper; do not let bottles touch. Fill with fruit but do not add liquid or put lids on. Put into oven leaving space for heat to circulate round jars. Heat for time given on chart, then remove one at a time, fill to overflowing with boiling syrup or water. Cover with rubber ring, warmed lid and screw or clip top. If fruit shrinks a great deal use fruit from one jar to fill up the others before adding liquid. Proceed as method 1.

Method 5 Bottling in a moderate oven Preheat oven to 150°C/300°F, Gas Mark 2. Add fruit and boiling syrup or water to bottles and put on rubber rings and lids (not screw or clip tops). Otherwise proceed as method 4. Process for time given on chart. Remove from oven, one at a time, putting screw or clips on immediately.

To Test for a Seal Leave 24 hours. Remove screw or clip tops. Grip lids with fingers and try to lift bottles. If the lid stays firm a vacuum has been created and the jar can be labelled with name of fruit, strength of syrup and date, and stored in a cool, dry place.

If lid comes away from bottle either reprocess at once or just use as stewed fruit. Re-examine bottle and lid for chips or cracks and, if necessary, change rubber ring. Never process for a third time.

Storage Time The fruit is safe to use as long as the seal remains intact but it is best to use within 1–3 years. After that the texture of the fruit may alter.

Jams and Jellies

Rows of brightly-coloured jams and jellies, with a rich fruity flavour and which keep well, are the expected rewards for the jam maker's efforts. But as fruits vary from season to season even the most experienced can have the occasional failure unless the reason for each step is understood and simple tests made.

Jam

Fruit Slightly under-ripe, freshly gathered fruit is best. Over-ripe fruit will have lost some of its pectin. Wash fruit just before using; remove stalks and leaves and, if liked, remove stones.

Pectin is a natural gum-like substance present in varying degrees in fruit which, when the fruit is boiled with sugar, is capable of forming a jelly. Pectin is only released when acid is also present. Fruits containing both pectin and acid, such as cooking apples, currants, damsons, gooseberries and some plums, make a well-setting jam; others, including apricots, blackberries, greengages, loganberries and raspberries have medium-setting properties and often acid is added. Cherries, pears, rhubarb and some strawberries produce a poor set. Add 2 × 15ml spoons (2tbsps)

lemon juice to each 2kg (4lb) fruit at the beginning of cooking
to correct acid deficiency. Commercially made pectin, or
fruit rich in pectin such as apple, can be added to fruits with
little pectin.

Pan Use a large, thick pan of aluminium, stainless steel or
unchipped enamel.

Cooking fruit Cooking is done slowly to soften the skins and
extract the pectin. Water is added only to prevent the fruit
burning and soft fruits usually do not require water. Simmer
until fruit is reduced to a pulp.

Test for pectin Put 1 × 5ml spoon (1tsp) of the liquid from the
fruit into a small glass. When cool add 1 × 15ml spoon (1tbsp)
methylated spirit. Shake gently and leave 1 minute. A jelly-like
lump indicates plenty of pectin, two or three less firm ones means
less pectin and many tiny ones show little pectin.

Sugar Use preserving, lump or granulated sugar which dissolves
more quickly if warmed in slow oven. Use ¾kg (1½lb) sugar to
each ½kg (1lb) fruit for a good clot, ½kg (1lb) for medium pectin.
Where there is little pectin add commercial pectin as given on
pack and treat as good clot.

After adding the sugar, stir to dissolve, then bring to boil over full
heat and cook rapidly. Stir occasionally until a set is reached
(3–20 minutes, according to kind).

Test for set Quickest and most reliable is to use a sugar
thermometer. Stand it in hot water, then stir jam and put
thermometer into centre making sure bulb does not touch base
of pan. 104°C/220°F shows setting point has been reached.
Another method is to put 1 × 5ml spoon (1tsp) jam on to a cold
saucer, allow to cool, then push with finger. If cooked enough,
surface should have set and will wrinkle. Remove from heat at
each test.

Potting jam Remove from heat and remove any scum. Pour at
once into clean, heated jars and fill to brim. Wipe neck of jar, if
necessary, press waxed discs, wax side down, on to surface of
jam and finish with a transparent cellulose or parchment cover.
Label and date when cold and store in a cool, dry, dark, well
ventilated place.

If fruit contains whole fruit, such as strawberries with
commercial pectin, or for whole fruit jam, cool in pan until a
skin forms. Stir gently, then pour into jars. This should spread
fruit evenly.

Whole fruit jam Layer ½kg (1lb) fruit with ½kg (1lb) sugar, cover
and leave 24 hours. Transfer to pan, add lemon juice if needed,
bring slowly to boil, stirring carefully until sugar dissolves, and
cook rapidly to set point.

Jam yield If 2½kg (5lb) jam is obtained for each 1½kg (3lb) sugar
used, the jam should have a good set and keep well.

Jam from frozen fruits As some pectin is lost during storage, use
10% more fruit than usual. Put frozen fruit in pan with a little
water and heat very gently until juice runs. Proceed as above.

Jelly

As the pulp is discarded choose fruit with a strong flavour such
as blackberries, damsons, redcurrants, quince or well-flavoured
crabapples. Some, such as sloes, mulberries, cranberries,
elderberries, bilberries, whortleberries, etc., set better when
mixed with apple.

Wash fruit, remove any unsound part but do not bother to
stalk currants or peel or core apples. Cut up large fruit. Put into
a pan with 150ml (¼ pint) water to ½kg (1lb) berries and up to
450ml (¾ pint) for hard fruits. Simmer slowly ¾–1 hour until
fruit is very soft. Test for pectin. If poor, cook further to
evaporate excess water.

Strain the pulp through a jelly bag of felt or flannel, scalded by
pouring boiling water through it. Attach by its cotton loops to
legs of upturned kitchen chair or stool. (Or use several
thicknesses of butter muslin or calico in same way.) Put large
basin underneath, then pour in contents of pan gently and leave
until juice has run through. *Do not* squeeze bag or jelly will
cloud.

If pectin test gave very firm clot recook pulp with half
original amount of water and strain. Mix with first liquid.

Adding sugar Measure juice, return to pan and bring to boil.
Add 350–550g (¾–1¼lb) sugar to 600ml (1 pint) juice, adding
most sugar to a firm pectin clot. Finish as for jam but boiling
time to a set is likely to be 10–15 minutes. Jelly is usually set in
small jars.

Herb jellies Using apple or crabapple jelly recipe as basis, cook
the fruit with sprigs of the herb. For a stronger flavour add the
herb, chopped, just before setting point is reached.

Marmalade

The basic principles for making marmalade are the same as those
employed for jam, but instead of sweet fruits, the citrus fruits—
oranges, lemons, grapefruits and limes—are used, either singly
or in varying combinations. Originally marmalade was made only
with quince (whence, from the Latin *marmelo*, comes its lovely
name) but it is more often associated with bitter Seville oranges.
More recently sweet oranges and mixtures of oranges have
become popular. Another new idea is to add a little brandy,
Scotch whisky or ginger wine to the recipe. The peel of citrus
fruits requires longer cooking than the skins of fruit used for
jam, so extra water is added. The main sources of pectin are the
pips and white pith. The pith can be included in the marmalade
to give a more bitter taste.

Preparation Wash fruit very well, cut into halves and squeeze out
juice. Put juice into large basin and pips into smaller one.
Remove pulp, chop finely and add to juice. If pith is not to be
left in marmalade separate from peel, chop and add to pips.
Shred peel finely and add to juice. If pith remains in marmalade
it is quicker to slice by special machine, or mince. Use 1.7 litres
(3 pints) water to ½kg (1lb) fruit. Cover pips with water and add
rest to peel. There is no need to soak the pips overnight.

Cooking peel Tie pips and pith in muslin. Add with their water to
contents of other basin in large pan. Boil until peel is soft and
original bulk reduced to half (1½–3 hours). *Or* cook in a pressure
cooker for ½–1 hour using only half the water. It is best to test
for pectin and if the clot is not firm then add juice of 1 lemon to
each ½kg (1lb) fruit and boil before testing again. Then remove
bag of pips, squeezing out as much liquid as possible.

Adding sugar Add 3kg (6lb) sugar to 1½kg (3lb) fruit. Stir until
sugar is dissolved, bring to boil and boil rapidly to setting point
(up to 20 minutes).

Test for set, pot and cover as for jam.

Marmalade from frozen fruit As for jam. Use 10% extra fruit to
allow for loss of pectin.

Jelly Marmalade

Follow the general marmalade instructions except:
1) Mix juice, pulp, pith and pips. Finely shred peel and tie in muslin.
2) Remove bag of peel after 1 hour to avoid overcooking.
3) When soft, pour through jelly bag.
4) Add ½kg (1lb) sugar to each 600ml (1 pint) liquid.
5) Add peel shreds when marmalade comes to boil again.

Fresh Apricot Jam

Metric	Imperial
1½kg fresh apricots, halved and stoned	3lb fresh apricots, halved and stoned
300ml water	½ pint water
1½kg sugar	3lb sugar

A delicious jam to be used on special occasions. Put into small jars.
Put the apricots into a pan with the water and simmer until fruit is soft. Test for pectin. Add sugar, stir until dissolved and boil until setting point is reached. Meanwhile crack some of the stones, remove kernels; dip these into boiling water and split in half. Add to jam with the sugar to give delicate vanilla flavour. Follow jam-making instructions.
Makes about 2½kg (5lb) jam

Fruit Salad Jam

Metric	Imperial
¼kg red plums, stoned	½lb red plums, stoned
½kg cooking apples, peeled, cored and chopped	1lb cooking apples, peeled, cored and chopped
¾kg pears, peeled, cored and chopped	1½lb pears, peeled, cored and chopped
300ml water	½ pint water
1¼kg sugar	2½lb sugar

Put the plums, apples and pears into a pan with the water for about ½ hour or until fruit is tender. Test for pectin. Add sugar, stir until dissolved. Follow jam-making instructions.
Makes about 2¼kg (4½lb) jam

Gooseberry and Elderflower Jam

Metric	Imperial
1kg green gooseberries	2lb green gooseberries
600ml water	1 pint water
3–4 heads elderflower, tied in muslin	3–4 heads elderflower, tied in muslin
1½kg sugar	3lb sugar

The elderflowers give a delicious muscatel flavour to this jam and the amount used can be varied to suit personal taste.
Top, tail and wash gooseberries, put into a pan with the water and elderflowers and simmer until fruit is soft. Test for pectin and if a good clot is not obtained, continue cooking to evaporate some of water, then test again. Remove elderflowers and add sugar. Follow jam-making instructions.
Note Gooseberry jam tends to turn red if boiled for any length of time after sugar is added. To keep it green make sure there is adequate pectin concentration before adding the sugar and so keep down boiling time.
Makes about 2½kg (5lb) jam

Quince Jam

Metric	Imperial
1kg quinces, peeled, cored and chopped	2lb quinces, peeled, cored and chopped
1 litre water	2 pints water
Juice of 1 lemon	Juice of 1 lemon
1½kg sugar	3lb sugar

Put the quinces into a saucepan. Add the water and lemon juice and simmer until the fruit is soft. If necessary, add a little more water. Test for pectin. Add sugar. Follow jam-making instructions.
Makes about 2½kg (5lb) jam

Black Currant Jelly

Metric	Imperial
1kg black currants	2lb black currants
1 litre water	1¾ pints water
Sugar	Sugar

A good preserve, this also makes a delicious winter drink if 2–3 × 15ml spoons (2–3tbsps) are dissolved in 600ml (1 pint) boiling water.
Wash black currants, put into a pan with the water and simmer until the fruit can be mashed to a pulp with a wooden spoon. Test for pectin. Pour through a jelly bag. If test gave a very firm clot, cook again with about 600ml (1 pint) more water. Measure pulp and add 550g (1¼lb) sugar to each 600ml (1 pint) juice. Follow jelly-making instructions.
Makes about 2½kg (5lb) jelly

Rosemary Jelly

Metric	Imperial
1kg apples, windfall, cooking or crab	2lb apples, windfall, cooking or crab
900ml water	1½ pints water
3–4 good sprigs of rosemary	3–4 good sprigs of rosemary
Sugar	Sugar

For an interesting change from red currant jelly, serve this with lamb. When lamb chops have been grilled, spread rosemary jelly on top and return to grill for 1 to 2 minutes longer.
Wash and cut up apples, discarding any bruised parts. Put into pan with water and rosemary and simmer until fruit can be mashed with a wooden spoon. Test for pectin. Pour through a jelly bag, measure juice and add ½kg (1lb) sugar to each 600ml (1 pint) juice. Follow jelly-making instructions. Other herbs can be used in the same way. A few drops of green food colouring can be added to improve the appearance of the jelly.

Lemon Shred Jelly

Metric	Imperial
12 lemons	12 lemons
3.6 litres water	6 pints water
Sugar	Sugar

A clear lemon jelly is one of the most attractive you can make at home
Follow directions for making jelly marmalade, but add ¾kg (1½lb) sugar to each 600ml (1 pint) liquid because lemons are so rich in pectin and acid.

Grapefruit Marmalade

Metric	Imperial
1kg grapefruit	2lb grapefruit
2 lemons	2 lemons
4 litres water	7 pints water
Approx. 2kg sugar	Approx. 4lb sugar

Follow directions for making marmalade.

Pickles and Chutneys

Both vegetables and fruits, and often a mixture of the two, can be made into pickles and chutneys. So wide is the possible variety, especially of chutneys, that completely individual ones can be devised.

Pickled Vegetables
Choose young, freshly picked specimens. There are two essential ingredients:

Salt to draw out water from the vegetables and toughen them slightly. If this is not done the water will dilute the vinegar and the pickle will not keep. Salt is best for very high water content vegetables such as cucumber and marrow. For a more gentle action the vegetables can be completely immersed (weigh down with a plate) in a brine of ¼kg (½lb) salt in 2.3 litres (4 pints) water. Beetroot are not salted or brined.

Vinegar Use *bottled* white, malt, cider or wine vinegar, not the less strong draught. Ready-spiced vinegar can be bought or simply made by boiling 2.3 litres (4 pints) vinegar with 50–100g (2–4oz) mixed pickling spice, tied in muslin, and 1 × 15ml spoon (1tbsp) salt together for 5 minutes. Strain when cold. Mixed pickling spice is equal quantities of stick cinnamon, allspice, cloves, mace and a few peppercorns, but can be varied by adding root ginger (crushed), chilli seeds, etc.

Never use powdered spices which cloud the vinegar. Use vinegar cold for crisp pickles such as cauliflower, cabbage, cucumber, onions, red cabbage, etc. For a clear pickle, use white vinegar and strain through muslin after spicing. Sugar can be added when a less sharp flavour is preferred, e.g. with beetroot and red cabbage.

Pans Use aluminium, unchipped enamel or stainless steel pans. *Do not* use copper, brass or iron as they react with and flavour the vinegar.

Jars and covers Any type of jar can be used providing it can be fitted with a cover of glass, plastic or plastic-coated metal. Vinegar must not come into contact with a metal covering and if jam-pot covers or greaseproof paper are used the vinegar will evaporate and so expose some of the vegetables which will discolour.

General method for making Trim, peel, if appropriate, and cut into even-sized pieces. Either place in brine or in layers in a non-metal bowl with a good sprinkling of salt between the layers. Leave 12–48 hours, then rinse in cold water and drain very well. Pack into clean jars leaving 2.5cm (1in) above them so they can be completely covered with spiced vinegar. Cover and store in a cool, dry place.

Pickled Fruits
Apples, damsons, peaches, pears, plums, etc. and green tomatoes can all be pickled but are not salted first. Instead they are simmered in spiced vinegar until tender. Add 1 or 2 bay leaves and thinly peeled rind of 1 lemon to the spiced vinegar recipe above. Sugar (according to the type of fruit) is dissolved in the strained vinegar before the fruit is added, the pan is covered and the fruit is simmered until slightly undercooked. Then the fruit is packed into jars and the vinegar boiled until syrupy and poured over the fruit.
Whole fruits should be pricked several times with a large sterilized needle before cooking to avoid shrinkage.

Chutney
Chutney gets its name from a Hindi word, and is of course a prominent feature in Indian meals. In English cookery chutneys are most often served as accompaniments to cold roast meats, poultry and game, where their rich appearance is as decorative as their flavour is apt. A spoonful of good chutney can make all the difference to a sauce or casserole.

A wide variety of fruits and vegetables can be used for making chutney. Fruits most generally used are apples, gooseberries, plums and rhubarb, but apricots, blackberries, damsons, peaches, etc. can be used. Onions are included in most chutney recipes and garlic, red or green tomatoes, oranges, celery, red and green peppers, dried fruits such as dates, seedless raisins and sultanas, flavourings of ground spices (if using whole spices, double amount, bruise, tie in muslin and remove before potting), mustard, grated orange and lemon rind, cayenne pepper and crystallized ginger are among the possibles. Dark sugar should be used for dark chutneys and long slow cooking after addition of sugar helps to darken. To keep chutneys light in colour, use granulated sugar and cook basic ingredients very well before adding it. The basic ingredients are often minced but a different texture can be achieved by leaving some in larger pieces. The preserving agents are the vinegar, salt and spices. Pot and cover as given for pickles. Allow to mature at least 3 months before eating.

Apple and Blackberry Chutney

Metric	Imperial
1½kg blackberries	3lb blackberries
1 litre vinegar	2 pints vinegar
2½kg cooking apples, peeled, cored and sliced	5lb cooking apples, peeled, cored and sliced
1kg onions skinned and minced	2lb onions, skinned and minced
50g ground ginger	2oz ground ginger
25g dry mustard	1oz mustard
2 × 5ml spoons cayenne pepper	2tsps cayenne pepper
Grated rind of ½ lemon	Grated rind of ½ lemon
1kg sugar	2lb sugar
25g salt	1oz salt

The pips must be sieved from the blackberries so cook first on their own before mixing with the other ingredients.
Apples make a very good basis for chutneys whether alone or in combination with other fruits such as bananas or pears, or with fruiting vegetables such as tomatoes and green or red peppers. Depending on the second ingredient the amount of sugar can be varied or even omitted if a very tart flavour is desired
Cook blackberries in about half the vinegar until really soft. Rub through a sieve. Put into pan with remaining ingredients and simmer until thick.
Makes about 3kg (6lb) chutney

Damson or Plum Chutney

Metric	Imperial
2kg damsons	4lb damsons
½kg onions, chopped	1lb onions, chopped
600ml vinegar	1 pint vinegar
25g salt	1oz salt
5g ground cinnamon	¼oz ground cinnamon
15g fresh root ginger, bruised	½oz fresh root ginger, bruised
5g whole allspice	¼oz whole allspice
225g sugar	8oz sugar

Damsons make a very good dark chutney.
Put all ingredients into a pan and simmer until dark and thick.

Tomato Chutney

Metric	Imperial
1kg green tomatoes, skinned and chopped	2lb green tomatoes, skinned and chopped
½kg red tomatoes, skinned and chopped	1lb red tomatoes, skinned and chopped
¼kg apples, peeled, cored and finely chopped	½lb apples, peeled, cored and finely chopped
¼kg onions, finely chopped	½lb onions, finely chopped
600ml vinegar	1 pint vinegar
2 × 5ml spoons salt	2tsps salt
175g brown sugar	6oz brown sugar
25g mixed pickling spice	1oz mixed pickling spice

Put the tomatoes, apples and onions into a pan with the vinegar, salt, sugar and the spice, tied in muslin, and simmer until tender and thick.

Piccalilli

Metric	Imperial
1kg marrow, peeled, seeded and cubed	2lb marrow, peeled, seeded and cubed
¼kg young runner beans, cut into pieces	½lb young runner beans, cut into pieces
½kg green tomatoes, skinned	1lb green tomatoes, skinned
1 large cauliflower in florets	1 large cauliflower, in florets
1kg small pickling onions, peeled	2lb small pickling onions, peeled
1.8 litre white vinegar	3 pints white vinegar
40g dry mustard	1½oz dry mustard
25g ground ginger	1oz ground ginger
20g turmeric	¾oz turmeric
100–225g sugar, optional	4–8oz sugar, optional
20g flour	¾oz flour

Sometimes called mustard pickles. The vegetables in this pickle are softened by cooking; use any assortment of vegetables, such as given here.

Put alternate layers of vegetables and kitchen salt in a bowl and leave 24 hours. Drain. Simmer in the vinegar for 10–15 minutes or until the vegetables are tender but not mashed. Drain and pack into jars retaining vinegar. Add mustard, ginger and turmeric, mixed with a little vinegar, to reserved liquid (with the sugar if used). Simmer about 10 minutes. Mix flour with a little vinegar to make a smooth paste. Stir into the spiced vinegar and boil for 5 minutes. Pour carefully on to vegetables in jars, tapping jars on a cloth from time to time to remove air bubbles. Cover (see page 166).

Pickled Onions

Use small, even-sized onions. Peel (under water to stop tears), using a stainless steel knife. Soak in brine for 24–48 hours, then pack into jars. Cover with *cold* spiced vinegar for crisp onions, *boiling* vinegar for softer ones.

Red Cabbage Pickle

Choose cabbages with a good colour and discard any discoloured outer leaves. Wash well and shred. Arrange alternate layers of cabbage and kitchen salt in a bowl using about 50g (2oz) salt to each ½kg (1lb) cabbage. Leave 24 hours and then drain thoroughly. Pack into jars and cover with spiced vinegar. For a more mellow pickle, dissolve quantity sugar in the vinegar. Use after 1 week. After about 3 months the cabbage tends to lose its crispness.

Pickled Walnuts

Walnuts must be pickled before the end of June, before the shells begin to form at the end opposite the stalk. Prick with a needle or silver fork. (This stains the fingers badly so wear rubber gloves.) Discard any in which a shell can be felt. Cover with brine (¼kg (½lb)) salt in 2.4l (4pts) water), leave 5 days, change brine and soak a further 7 days. Drain well, then spread out on flat dishes and leave until they have turned black all over. Pack into jars and cover with spiced vinegar. Use after about 4 weeks.

Herb Vinegar

Make these vinegars at the height of summer when herbs are young and the heat of the sun helps extract their flavour. Use them to add subtle flavours to food, especially salad dressings.

Pack freshly gathered leaves into a glass jar and fill up with red or white wine vinegar, distilled white vinegar or cider vinegar. Cork tightly and stand on a sunny shelf for 2 weeks. Strain into a bottle, cork tightly again and use within 3–4 months.

Use basil, chervil, chives, lemon thyme, marjoram, mint, parsley, rosemary, sage, tarragon, thyme, etc. or a mixture of herbs. Three or four crushed cloves of garlic can be used in the same way.

Herb Oils

Like the vinegars these are used to add extra, subtle flavours to food. Put 3 or 4 sprigs of fresh herbs into a 600ml (1 pint) bottle of oil, close tightly and leave until the oil is flavoured. This should take 2–4 weeks and the oil is best used within 3–4 months either in making dressings for salads or cooking vegetables.

Use the same herbs as suggested for vinegars.

Salting

Nowadays, little salting is done because other methods preserve the flavour of food better but *Salted Beans* are still popular. The correct proportion of ½kg (1lb) salt to each 1½kg (3lb) of fresh young beans is very important. Less salt will not preserve them and with more the flavour is spoiled. Top and tail beans and string if necessary. Leave French beans whole and cut runner beans into thick chunks. In an earthenware crock or large glass jar, layer beans and salt alternately, beginning and ending with salt. They *must* be pressed down very firmly. Leave about 4 days until they shrink. Add more beans and salt and continue until jar remains full. Cover with a moisture-proof covering and use within 1 year.

To use Remove some of beans, wash very well and soak in warm water for 2 hours to remove brine. Cook in usual way.

Drying

Once one of the main ways of preserving vegetables and fruits, it is rarely used now except for herbs and edible leaves, such as blackberry and raspberry which are simple to dry. Gather when young and small, on a dry day and before they have been in strong sunlight. For small-leaved herbs such as thyme, wash, drain and, when dry, tie into small bundles, protect from dust with muslin and hang to dry in a warm place. Strip larger leaves from stems, tie in muslin and dip into boiling water for 1 minute. Drain and spread out on a wire (cooling) tray covered with washed muslin. Place in a cool oven, leaving door slightly ajar, at 43–54°C/110–130°F, Gas Mark ¼, for about 1 hour or until dry and crisp. Crush with rolling pin and store in small jars with tightly fitting lids to prevent loss of flavour.

Soups & Hors-d'Oeuvre

Tomato Concertinas

Metric	Imperial
4 large tomatoes	4 large tomatoes
10–12 fresh basil leaves, chopped	10–12 fresh basil leaves, chopped
4 hard-boiled eggs, sliced	4 hard-boiled eggs, sliced
4 × 15ml spoons mayonnaise	4tbsps mayonnaise
2 spring onions or small piece onion, chopped	2 spring onions or small piece onion, chopped
Salt and pepper	Salt and pepper
16 strips green pepper	16 strips green pepper
½ cucumber, thinly sliced	½ cucumber, thinly sliced
Chervil sprigs	Chervil sprigs

This is a simple but unusual first course.
Put the tomatoes on small plates with the stalk ends down. Cut through centre almost to the base and make two similar cuts at each side of this first one. Put a little of the basil in each cut. Chill tomatoes. Just before serving put a slice of egg in each cut. Chop up rest of eggs and add to the mayonnaise with onions and seasoning. Put a line of this over the top of each tomato and decorate with the pepper strips. Surround each tomato with cucumber slices and chervil sprigs.
Serves 4

Potted Mushrooms*

Metric	Imperial
75g butter	3oz butter
½kg mushrooms, chopped	1lb mushrooms, chopped
1 × 5ml spoon dried thyme	1tsp dried thyme
Salt and freshly ground black pepper	Salt and freshly ground black pepper

A very old recipe, this is well worth reviving.
Melt 25g (1oz) of the butter in a saucepan, add the mushrooms, thyme and seasoning, and cook very slowly, covered, for 10 minutes. Using a slotted spoon, lift out the mushrooms and chop as finely as possible. Meanwhile, reduce the liquid in the pan by boiling without a lid until only 2–3 × 15ml spoons (2–3tbsps) remain. Mix in the mushrooms and check for seasoning. Pack tightly into 4 small (ramekin) dishes and smooth the top. When the mushrooms are cold, melt remaining butter, skim the surface and pour into each dish to cover the mushrooms completely. When set, cover with cling film, store in the refrigerator and eat within 4 days.
To freeze Wrap in cling film and then in freezer foil. Use within 3 months.
To thaw Thaw in the refrigerator for 3–4 hours.
Serves 4

Crispy Fried Vegetables with Garlic Mayonnaise

Metric	Imperial
½kg vegetables, see below	1lb vegetables, see below
Batter:	*Batter:*
2 eggs, separated	2 eggs, separated
300ml pale ale	½ pint pale ale
25g butter, melted	1oz butter, melted
175g flour	6oz flour
Salt and pepper	Salt and pepper
1 × 5ml spoon dry mustard	1tsp dry mustard
Garlic mayonnaise:	*Garlic mayonnaise:*
150ml mayonnaise	¼ pint mayonnaise
2 × 15ml spoons double cream	2tbsps double cream
2 cloves garlic, crushed	2 cloves garlic, crushed
1 × 15ml spoon dried mixed herbs	1tbsp dried mixed herbs
Salt and pepper	Salt and pepper

Try this unusual starter for a formal meal.
A variety of vegetables can be used for this recipe, including aubergine, celeriac, courgettes, cauliflower florets, Jerusalem artichokes, fennel, mushrooms, parsnip, etc. Courgettes and mushrooms are used raw; the others are steamed or boiled until half cooked. Cut into pieces the size of medium mushrooms.

To make the batter, mix egg yolks and ale together, add butter and beat until smooth. Gradually beat in the flour and seasoning. Whisk egg whites until very stiff, then fold into the batter.

Mix all the ingredients together for the mayonnaise and spoon into a serving dish.

Dip each piece of vegetable into the batter, making sure it is completely coated, and fry in hot deep fat at 180–190°C/350–375°F until golden brown and crisp. Drain on absorbent paper and serve at once with the mayonnaise.
Serves 4–6

* indicates suitability for freezing

Crispy fried vegetables and potted mushrooms

German Vegetable Soup*

Metric	Imperial
40g butter	1½oz butter
1 small onion, chopped	1 small onion, chopped
4 large carrots, peeled and thinly sliced	4 large carrots, peeled and thinly sliced
½ turnip or swede, peeled and diced	½ turnip or swede, peeled and diced
2–3 stalks celery, sliced	2–3 stalks celery, sliced
2 potatoes, peeled and diced	2 potatoes, peeled and diced
1 medium leek, sliced	1 medium leek, sliced
1 litre beef stock	2 pints beef stock
Salt and pepper	Salt and pepper
6 × 15ml spoons peas, fresh or frozen	6tbsps peas, fresh or frozen
6 × 15ml spoons corn kernels, fresh or frozen	6tbsps corn kernels, fresh or frozen
½ small cabbage, shredded	½ small cabbage, shredded
Approx. 175g cooked beetroot, diced, fresh or frozen	Approx. 6oz cooked beetroot, diced, fresh or frozen
125g sliced frankfurters or browned and sliced bratwurst	4oz sliced frankfurters or browned and sliced bratwurst

This is a thick, hearty, colourful vegetable soup which is almost a meal on its own, especially when served with rye bread.

Melt the butter, add prepared onion, carrots, turnip or swede, celery, potatoes and leek and toss until butter is absorbed. Add the stock and seasoning and simmer 20 minutes. Add peas, corn kernels and cabbage and simmer a further 15 minutes. Add beetroot and sausages, heat a further 5 minutes only and then serve.

To freeze See page 178. Add cabbage, beetroot and frankfurters on reheating.

Serves 6

Stuffed Globe Artichokes*

Metric	Imperial
4 large artichokes	4 large artichokes
225g cooked ham, finely minced	½lb cooked ham, finely minced
1 clove garlic, crushed, optional	1 clove garlic, crushed, optional
1 onion, chopped and lightly fried	1 onion, chopped and lightly fried
50g fresh breadcrumbs	2oz fresh breadcrumbs
1 × 1.25ml spoon dried herbs	¼tsp dried herbs
Salt and pepper	Salt and pepper
1 egg yolk	1 egg yolk
White wine or cider	White wine or cider
150ml tomato juice	¼ pint tomato juice

Use large artichokes for stuffing.

Trim off the rough, lower leaves and cut off the stalk as close as possible to the flower so the artichoke will stand upright. Trim off tops of other leaves with scissors. Put into a pan of boiling, salted water and simmer 10–15 minutes, according to size. Drain and plunge into cold water. When cool enough to handle cut into halves and remove the chokes (i.e. hairy centre reached by separating the central leaves of the artichokes). Make stuffing by mixing the ham, garlic, onion, breadcrumbs, herbs and seasoning, adding the egg yolk and enough wine or cider to moisten. Put in the place of the chokes. Tie each artichoke into shape with string and stand in a greased dish just large enough to hold them. Mix the tomato juice with an equal quantity of wine or cider and pour over. Cover with a lid or foil and bake at 180°C/350°F, Gas Mark 4 for about 45 minutes or until tender. Serve hot.

To freeze Reduce cooking time to 30 minutes, cool quickly and freeze in a rigid container.

To serve Thaw overnight in the refrigerator or transfer to original dish, put into a cold oven and reheat for about 30 minutes at temperature given above.

Serves 4

Grilled Grapefruit Medley

Metric	Imperial
2 grapefruit	2 grapefruit
50g brown sugar	2oz brown sugar
4 × 5ml spoons brandy	4tsps brandy
15g butter	½oz butter
50g sultanas	2oz sultanas
25g crystallized or glacé cherries, halved	1oz crystallized or glacé cherries, halved
1 × 1.25ml spoon ground cinnamon	¼tsp ground cinnamon

An excellent first course, serve this on a cold day.

Cut the grapefruit into halves, remove cores and loosen segments. Sprinkle with half the sugar and the brandy. Put under a hot grill until the brandy flares. At the same time heat the remaining ingredients together in a small pan. As the flames die down put each grapefruit half into a fruit dish and pile the dried fruit mixture on top. Serve at once.

Serves 4

German vegetable soup and grilled grapefruit medley

Scotch Broth*

Metric	Imperial
1kg silverside	2lb silverside
1 litre cold water	2 pints cold water
Salt and pepper	Salt and pepper
25g barley, washed	1oz barley, washed
1 turnip, peeled and diced	1 turnip, peeled and diced
1 leek, diced	1 leek, diced
1 large onion, diced	1 large onion, diced
3 large carrots, peeled and quartered	3 large carrots, peeled and quartered
1 small swede or turnip, peeled and quartered	1 small swede or turnip, peeled and quartered
2–3 stalks celery, cut into 2cm lengths	2–3 stalks celery, cut into 1in lengths
Chopped parsley	Chopped parsley

Many countries have soups similar to this, in which meat for the main course is simmered in water with vegetables. In this version the vegetables to be served hot with the meat (except potatoes) are cooked in the liquid as well as the ones which are part of the broth.
Put the meat, water, seasoning and barley into a pan, bring to the boil and skim. Add the diced vegetables, cover and simmer for 2 hours. Add the remaining vegetables and simmer a further hour. Lift the meat and larger pieces of vegetable on to a heated dish and serve as the main course. Leave remaining vegetables in the liquid and serve as broth, sprinkling with chopped parsley. If liked, a small amount of shredded cabbage can be added for the last ½ hour. Neck of mutton can be used instead of silverside.
To freeze See general note on page 178.
Serves 4–5

Vegetarian Pâté

Metric	Imperial
3 small carrots, peeled and grated	3 small carrots, peeled and grated
1 very small onion, grated	1 very small onion, grated
1 small green pepper, seeded and chopped	1 small green pepper, seeded and chopped
50g small mushrooms, chopped	2oz small mushrooms, chopped
50g chopped nuts	2oz chopped nuts
1 inner stalk celery and its leaves, chopped	1 inner stalk celery and its leaves, chopped
Small piece firm turnip, peeled and grated	Small piece of firm turnip, peeled and grated
Grated rind of 1 small orange	Grated rind of 1 small orange
Salt and pepper	Salt and pepper
1 × 5ml spoon Worcestershire sauce	1tsp Worcestershire sauce
Good pinch cayenne pepper	Good pinch cayenne pepper
15g powdered unflavoured gelatine	½oz powdered unflavoured gelatine
3 × 15ml spoons orange juice	3tbsps orange juice

A colourful pâté, this has an interesting orange flavour.
Mix together the carrots, onion, green pepper, mushrooms, nuts, celery, turnip and orange rind. Season with salt, pepper, sauce and cayenne pepper. Dissolve the gelatine in the orange juice and mix in. Divide between 4 small lightly oiled dishes. Turn out when set and serve with hot buttered toast.
Serves 4

Fruits Vinaigrette*

Metric	Imperial
Vinaigrette:	Vinaigrette:
1 × 5ml spoon caster sugar	1tsp caster sugar
Salt and freshly ground black pepper	Salt and freshly ground black pepper
Good pinch dry mustard or 1 × 1.25ml spoon prepared French mustard	Good pinch dry mustard or ¼tsp prepared French mustard
1 × 15ml spoon wine vinegar	1tbsp wine vinegar
3–4 × 15ml spoons olive oil	3–4tbsps olive oil
1 × 15ml spoon chopped fresh herbs, see method	1tbsp chopped fresh herbs, see method

Fruit: In summer and autumn choose from fresh pears, peaches, plums and melons. Oranges and grapefruit are available throughout the year and so are grapes, which are best mixed with other fruits. The fruits chosen should be as near ripe perfection as possible. Frozen fruit can be used and is best thawed in the refrigerator and dressed while still very cold. Drain if necessary.

Use either one type of fruit or a mixture for this very refreshing first course.
Put sugar, salt, pepper, mustard and vinegar into a basin and mix with a wooden spoon until sugar dissolves. Add the oil, a little at a time, until well blended. (Herb oils and/or vinegars can be used (see page 167).) Stir in the herbs. These can be fresh or frozen. Use mint, parsley or chervil, chives, thyme, tarragon, marjoram and basil, using either just one herb or a mixture of two or three. Have the dressing ready before preparing the fruit.
Preparation Pears and peaches should be peeled and the cores or stones discarded; cut melon into balls or cubes; cut oranges and grapefruit into sections or slices after peeling, and grapes peel and seed. For fruit salad cut fruit into smaller pieces. Add immediately to the dressing to prevent discoloration. Serve in small glasses or, as appropriate, orange or grapefruit shells with herb bread (see page 228).
To freeze Pack into rigid polythene containers. Cover, seal and freeze.
To serve Thaw overnight in a refrigerator or at room temperature for 3–4 hours. Stir carefully before serving.
Serves 4

Summer Vegetable Soup

Metric	Imperial
600ml yogurt	1 pint yogurt
½ large cucumber, coarsely grated	½ large cucumber, coarsely grated
2 tomatoes, skinned, seeded and chopped	2 tomatoes, skinned, seeded and chopped
1 medium carrot, peeled and grated	1 medium carrot, peeled and grated
50g peas, fresh or frozen, cooked	2oz peas, fresh or frozen, cooked
2–3 spring onions, chopped	2–3 spring onions, chopped
2 × 15ml spoons finely chopped mint	2tbsps finely chopped mint
5 × 15ml spoons single cream	5tbsps single cream
Salt and freshly ground white pepper	Salt and freshly ground white pepper
Approx. 300ml strong, fat-free, chicken stock	Approx. ½ pint strong, fat-free chicken stock
Garnish:	Garnish:
Hard-boiled egg, finely chopped	Hard-boiled egg, finely chopped
Spring onion curls	Spring onion curls

Yogurt gives a sharp flavour to this soup which is very refreshing in hot weather.

Mix all the ingredients in the order given, adding enough stock to give the consistency of thick cream. Chill well. Serve in individual dishes, garnishing each with a little chopped hard-boiled egg and one or two spring onion curls. This soup will not freeze.

Serves 4

Cauliflower Soup*

Metric	Imperial
1 medium to large cauliflower	1 medium to large cauliflower
15g butter	½oz butter
600ml chicken or veal stock	1 pint chicken or veal stock
Salt and white pepper	Salt and white pepper
15g cornflour	½oz cornflour
150ml milk	¼ pint milk
1 egg yolk	1 egg yolk
3 × 15ml spoons single cream	3tbsps single cream
Garnish:	Garnish:
Flaked browned almonds	Flaked browned almonds
Chopped chives	Chopped chives

This soup has a delicate flavour and so is an ideal start to a fairly elaborate meal.

Break the cauliflower into florets, wash and drain well. Melt the butter, add cauliflower and toss to absorb the butter without browning. Add stock and seasoning, cover and simmer for 20 minutes. Remove one floret and divide into very small sprigs. Put contents of pan into blender and liquidize until smooth. Return to the rinsed pan and heat. Mix the cornflour to a smooth paste with the milk and add to the soup. Bring to the boil and boil, stirring, for 3 minutes. Mix egg yolk and cream, add to the soup and heat, without boiling, to cook the egg. Adjust the seasoning and add the retained sprigs. Garnish each bowl of soup with a few flaked almonds and with chopped chives.

To freeze See general note on page 178.

Serves 4

Pears with Tarragon and Cream*

Metric	Imperial
2 ripe pears	2 ripe pears
1 egg	1 egg
2 × 15ml spoons tarragon vinegar	2tbsps tarragon vinegar
2 × 5ml spoons caster sugar	2tsps caster sugar
3 × 15ml spoons whipped cream	3tbsps whipped cream
Lettuce leaves	Lettuce leaves
Paprika	Paprika

Serve this first course when you have pears completely ripe but not over-ripe. The tarragon and cream dressing can be frozen ready to add to the pears.

Chill the pears in the refrigerator for 1 hour or longer. Put the egg, vinegar and sugar into a small pan and mix well. Put over a low heat and stir, without boiling, until the mixture thickens. Stand the pan in cold water to cool quickly and stir occasionally. When quite cold, fold in the cream. Just before serving, peel, halve and core the pears. Put each half, cut side down, on a crisp lettuce leaf. Coat at once with the dressing, sprinkle a little paprika on top and serve.

To freeze dressing As this is the smallest amount which can be made at one time some will be left over. Put into a very small container, seal and freeze.

To use Thaw at room temperature for 1–2 hours.

Serves 4

Jerusalem Artichoke Soup*

Metric	Imperial
450g Jerusalem artichokes	1lb Jerusalem artichokes
25g butter	1oz butter
1 onion, chopped	1 onion, chopped
600ml chicken or veal stock	1 pint chicken or veal stock
Salt and white pepper	Salt and white pepper
15g cornflour	½oz cornflour
150ml milk	¼ pint milk
150ml single cream	¼ pint single cream
Garnish:	Garnish:
Fried croûtons of bread	Fried croûtons of bread

This rather delicately flavoured soup is ideal as the first course of a dinner.

Prepare the artichokes by peeling as thinly as possible, cutting into pieces and putting each at once into cold water with a little lemon juice or vinegar added, to preserve the colour. Melt the butter and toss prepared artichokes and onion until the fat is absorbed, but do not allow the vegetables to colour. Add the stock and seasoning, bring to the boil and simmer for about 45 minutes until the vegetables are soft. Put into blender or rub through a non-metal sieve. Return to the rinsed pan with the cornflour mixed until dissolved with the milk. Bring to the boil, simmer and stir for 3 minutes. Remove from heat, cool a fraction and then stir in cream. Garnish each bowl with a few fried croûtons of bread or serve them separately.

To freeze See general note on page 178.

Serves 4–5

Mushrooms à la Grecque*

Metric	Imperial
300ml water	½ pint water
1 small onion, chopped	1 small onion, chopped
2 × 15ml spoons olive oil	2tbsps olive oil
1 × 5ml spoon tomato purée	1tsp tomato purée
Salt and pepper	Salt and pepper
Bouquet garni	Bouquet garni
Juice of ½ lemon	Juice of ½ lemon
350g small button mushrooms	¾lb small button mushrooms
Garnish:	Garnish:
Chopped parsley	Chopped parsley
Lemon wedges	Lemon wedges

A savoury way of serving mushrooms or other vegetables as a first course, this can be prepared well in advance.

Put the water, onion, oil, purée, seasoning, herbs and lemon juice into a pan and simmer 5 minutes. Trim off ends of mushroom stalks and wipe mushrooms with a damp cloth. Add to liquid and simmer 10 minutes. Remove with a slotted spoon. Boil liquid rapidly until it is reduced to 3–4 × 15ml spoons (3–4tbsps), removing herbs when about half the liquid remains. Pour over mushrooms and chill. Just before serving, sprinkle lavishly with chopped parsley and add a lemon wedge to each serving.

To freeze Put into a rigid container, ungarnished, seal and freeze.

To serve Thaw 6 hours, or longer, in the refrigerator and garnish before serving.

Alternative vegetables: artichoke hearts, aubergine, celery, chicory, cucumber, fennel, leeks, small onions, pepper quarters. Prepare in the same way, simmering, if necessary for a longer time, until the vegetables are cooked.

Serves 4–5

Tomato and Mint Soup*

Metric	Imperial
25g butter	1oz butter
1 carrot, peeled and cubed	1 carrot, peeled and cubed
1 onion, chopped	1 onion, chopped
3 stalks celery, chopped	3 stalks of celery, chopped
50g bacon pieces, chopped	2oz bacon pieces, chopped
Few bacon rinds	Few bacon rinds
¾kg tomatoes, chopped	1½lb tomatoes, chopped
750ml stock	1¼ pints stock
Salt and pepper	Salt and pepper
1–2 × 5ml spoons sugar, or to taste	1–2tsps sugar, or to taste
2 × 15ml spoons chopped fresh mint	2tbsps chopped fresh mint
15g cornflour	½oz cornflour
150ml milk	¼ pint milk
Garnish:	Garnish:
A few mint leaves	A few mint leaves

A very good soup for the vegetable gardener, this can be made when tomatoes and mint are at their best together.

Melt the butter and toss in the prepared carrot, onion, celery and bacon until butter is absorbed. Add bacon rinds and tomatoes. Cook 2 minutes, then add stock, seasoning, sugar and mint. (The amount of sugar will depend upon the tomatoes so add some at this stage and taste for sweetness later.) Cover and simmer for 45 minutes. Rub through a sieve (more flavour is obtained if the soup is put into the blender first). Return to rinsed pan, add cornflour mixed to a smooth paste with milk and boil, stirring, for 3 minutes. Test for seasoning. Garnish each bowl of soup with 2 or 3 mint leaves. It can also be served cold adding also a little soured cream.

To freeze See general note on page 178.

Serves 4–5

Nineteenth-century Poacher's Broth*

Metric	Imperial
1 large rabbit	1 large rabbit
Small piece salt pork	Small piece salt pork
1.8 litres cold water	3 pints cold water
2 onions, roughly chopped	2 onions, roughly chopped
Pepper	Pepper
225g potatoes, peeled and diced	½lb potatoes, peeled and diced
225g kale, finely shredded	½lb kale, finely shredded
Garnish:	Garnish:
1 medium onion, sliced and pushed out into rings	1 medium onion, sliced and pushed out into rings

The ingredients for this broth are readily available to the vegetable gardener, except, of course, the rabbit. If this proves difficult, substitute boiling fowl.

Cut the rabbit into serving portions, put into a pan with the salt pork, cover with cold water and bring to the boil. Discard this water, add the measured cold water, onions and pepper. Bring to the boil and simmer 1½ hours. Remove rabbit and salt pork. Add the potatoes and kale. Cook a further 20–30 minutes. Meanwhile, reserve the meaty joints of hind legs and back of rabbit for a later meal, remove meat from the other joints, cut into dice and add to the broth with the lean meat from the pork, also diced. Serve hot with 2 or 3 raw onion rings in each dish.

To freeze See general note below.

Serves 8

Individual Spinach Soufflés

Metric	Imperial
15g butter	½oz butter
15g flour	½oz flour
125g spinach purée	4oz spinach purée
3 × 15ml spoons single cream	3tbsps single cream
Salt, pepper and grated nutmeg	Salt, pepper and grated nutmeg
50g grated cheese	2oz grated cheese
2 eggs, separated	2 eggs, separated

This is an elegant starter for an evening meal.

Melt the butter, stir in the flour and cook for a few minutes. Add the spinach purée (which must be well drained and quite dry) and, when blended, the cream and seasonings. Cook and stir carefully for a few minutes until very thick, then remove from heat. Stir in the cheese and then the yolks, one at a time. Whisk egg whites until very stiff and fold in with a metal spoon. Divide between 4 individual, greased soufflé dishes and bake at 200°C/400°F, Gas Mark 6 for 15–20 minutes until well-risen and set. Serve at once.

Serves 4

Sweetcorn Chowder*

Metric	Imperial
50g streaky bacon, diced	2oz streaky bacon, diced
½ small onion, diced	½ small onion, diced
3 potatoes, peeled and cubed	3 potatoes, peeled and cubed
300ml boiling water	½ pint boiling water
Salt and pepper	Salt and pepper
450g corn kernels, fresh or frozen	1lb corn kernels, fresh or frozen
15g cornflour	½oz cornflour
900ml milk	1½ pints milk
Garnish:	Garnish:
Cooked peas	Cooked peas

Chowder is a thick soup usually containing either salt pork or bacon and potatoes. It can be described as a 'meal soup' if small pieces of meat or fish are added.

Fry the bacon in a strong pan and, as the fat runs, add onion and fry about 5 minutes without browning. Add prepared potatoes, water and seasoning, cover and cook for 15 minutes. Add corn and cook a further 5 minutes. Mix the cornflour to a smooth paste with some of the milk and add to chowder with remaining milk. Bring to the boil and cook and stir for 5 minutes. Serve hot garnished with peas.

To freeze See general note below.

Serves 4–5

General Notes on Freezing Soups

With freezer space usually at a premium it is an advantage to freeze soups in a condensed form whenever possible. This is done by following the recipe but adding only enough measured stock or water barely to cover the vegetables and any other ingredients such as meat. If given in the recipe, put through the blender or rub through a sieve. *Do not add cornflour or egg yolk for thickening.* Freeze in smallest possible container, marking plainly the amount of liquid still to be added and the thickening needed.

To reheat Put frozen soup into a pan with the extra liquid and heat. When all is melted, finish as given in the recipe.

Main Course Dishes

Turnips and Gammon

Metric
¾kg new turnips, peeled and
    cut into 1cm cubes
15g butter
350–450g thick slice of
    gammon cut into 1cm cubes
Freshly ground black pepper
2 × 15ml spoons chopped
    parsley
2–3 × 15ml spoons single
    cream or top-of-the-milk
Garnish:
Mushrooms and small
    tomatoes, grilled or baked

Imperial
1½lb new turnips, peeled and
    cut into ½in cubes
½oz butter
¾–1lb thick slice of gammon,
    cut into 1in cubes
Freshly ground black pepper
2 tbsps chopped parsley
2–3tbsps single cream or
    top-of-the-milk
Garnish:
Mushrooms and small
    tomatoes, grilled or baked

A deceptively simple dish, this is absolutely delicious to eat, especially when you can dig up the turnips just before you want them.
Boil the prepared turnips in salted water for 10–15 minutes or until just cooked, then drain. Meanwhile, melt the butter and fry the gammon dice slowly until cooked, then add the turnip and pepper and toss carefully together for 5 minutes. Stir in the parsley and cream, reheat and pile into the centre of a heated serving dish. Surround with the mushrooms and tomatoes.
Serves 4

Cabbage and Sausage Casserole

Metric
3 rashers streaky bacon,
    rinded and chopped
1 medium onion, chopped
½ large cooking apple, peeled,
    cored and chopped
450–575g savoy cabbage,
    shredded
450g pork sausages (8)
Garnish:
Small potatoes
Parsley or other herb butter

Imperial
3 rashers streaky bacon
    rinded and chopped
1 medium onion, chopped
½ large cooking apple, peeled,
    cored and chopped
1–1¼lb savoy cabbage,
    shredded
1lb pork sausages (8)
Garnish:
Small potatoes
Parsley or other herb butter

Try this very good way of making an inexpensive but tasty dish from cabbage during the winter months.
Fry the bacon until the fat begins to flow and then add and fry the onion and the apple. Wash and drain prepared cabbage, add to pan and cook about 5 minutes. Transfer to an oblong baking dish. Fry the sausages for about 3 minutes to start them cooking, then put on the cabbage, and cook at 200°C/400°F, Gas Mark 6 for 30 minutes.

Cook the potatoes in the usual way, drain, toss in parsley or other herb butter and arrange round the sausages.
Serves 4–6

Mediterranean-style Veal Chops*

Metric
25g butter
1 × 15ml spoon oil
4 veal chops
Salt and freshly ground black
    pepper
350g mushrooms, sliced
2 large green or red peppers,
    seeded and sliced
350g tomatoes, skinned and
    sliced
1 × 15ml spoon chopped fresh
    basil
1 × 5ml spoon sugar
300ml chicken stock or water

Imperial
1oz butter
1tbsp oil
4 veal chops
Salt and freshly ground black
    pepper
¾lb mushrooms, sliced
2 large green or red peppers,
    seeded and sliced
¾lb tomatoes, skinned and
    sliced
1tbsp chopped fresh basil
1tsp sugar
½ pint chicken stock or water

Melt the butter and oil together and fry the chops, quickly, until browned on both sides; season and remove from pan. Fry the prepared mushrooms and peppers until soft, add the tomatoes, seasoning, basil, sugar and stock or water. Boil for 3 minutes. Return chops to the pan and simmer, uncovered, for about 30 minutes. The sauce should be very thick. Arrange the chops on a heated dish with the sauce and garnish with lemon wedges.
To freeze Cool quickly after 20 minutes simmering, pack into rigid containers, seal, label and freeze.
To serve Thaw overnight in a refrigerator or put, unthawed, into a strong pan and heat slowly until thawed. Simmer for 10 minutes and serve as above.
Serves 4

Mediterranean-style veal chops with a potato border

Chakchouka

Metric
2 × 15ml spoons olive oil
2 medium onions, sliced
4 medium green peppers,
   seeded and sliced
Salt and pepper
Good pinch cayenne pepper
1 × 1.25ml spoon chilli powder
2 or 4 small to medium
   tomatoes, halved
4–8 eggs

Imperial
2tbsps olive oil
2 medium onions, sliced
4 medium green peppers,
   seeded and sliced
Salt and pepper
Good pinch cayenne pepper
¼tsp chilli powder
2 or 4 small to medium
   tomatoes, halved
4–8 eggs

Chakchouka is the North African name for a vegetable dish which, in one form or another, is popular in all the Arab countries surrounding the Mediterranean.

Heat the oil, stir in the prepared onions and peppers and cook slowly in a covered pan until cooked. Season with salt, pepper, cayenne and chilli powder. Put the tomato halves on to the vegetables, put on the lid and cook for a further 3 minutes. The tomato halves should remain unbroken.

Divide the onions and peppers between 4 individual dishes and make a hollow in each. Put the tomato halves on the edges. Break one or two eggs per person into the hollows, season the eggs and bake at 200°C/400°F, Gas Mark 6 for 7–10 minutes to set the eggs.

Variations The amount of cayenne and chilli powder can be adjusted to taste. Also, the eggs can be dropped whole into the pan and cooked there or, when partly cooked, the yolks can be broken with a wooden spoon and stirred into the vegetables.

Serves 4

Chicken Divan

Metric
50g butter
25g flour
Salt and pepper
400ml mixed stock and milk
125g grated cheese
1 × 5ml spoon minced or
   grated onion
3 × 15ml spoons dry sherry
125ml whipped double cream,
   optional
450g broccoli, fresh or frozen,
   cooked and drained, or
   calabrese
350–450g cooked chicken
   (or turkey), sliced
Extra 50g grated cheese

Imperial
2oz butter
1oz flour
Salt and pepper
Scant ¾ pint mixed stock and
   milk
4oz grated cheese
1tsp minced or grated onion
3tbsps dry sherry
4floz whipped double cream,
   optional
1lb broccoli, fresh or frozen,
   cooked and drained, or
   calabrese
¾–1lb cooked chicken
   (or turkey), sliced
Extra 2oz grated cheese

This American dish shows a very tasty way of serving left-over cooked chicken (or turkey), again as a hot dish.

Melt the butter in a saucepan. Stir in the flour and cook for 1 minute, then stir in the seasoning and stock and milk. Bring to the boil and simmer, stirring, until thick and smooth. Add the cheese, onion and sherry. Stir in the whipped cream, if used. Put the cooked broccoli into a flameproof dish and coat with half of the sauce. Cover with the chicken slices, the remaining sauce and the extra cheese, in that order. Put under a grill on low heat until the chicken is hot, then turn up heat to brown.

Serves 4

Vegetable and Frankfurter Pie

Metric
225g cooked mixed vegetables
Salt and freshly ground black
   pepper
25g butter or herb butter
225g frankfurters
225g cooked potatoes, sliced
225g tomatoes, skinned and
   sliced
1 × 2.5ml spoon sugar
Puff pastry made from
   250g flour and 65g fat
Beaten egg

Imperial
½lb cooked mixed vegetables
Salt and freshly ground black
   pepper
1oz butter or herb butter
½lb frankfurters
½lb cooked potatoes, sliced
½lb tomatoes, skinned and
   sliced
½tsp sugar
Puff pastry made from
   5oz flour and 2½oz fat
Beaten egg

This in an excellent way of using up left-over cooked vegetables or the remainder of several different frozen vegetable packs.

Put the cooked vegetables into a 700–900ml (1¼–1½ pint) pie dish. Season and add half the butter in small flakes. Cut the frankfurters into halves lengthways and then across (into quarters). Arrange over the vegetables, cover with the potatoes and then the tomatoes. Season, sprinkle with the sugar and the remaining butter in flakes. Roll out the pastry until little larger than the pie dish and cut out a circle following the outside rim of the dish. Moisten pastry or brush with egg and fit on top. Seal, trim and 'knock up' the edges. Make a hole in the centre for steam to escape and decorate with leaves cut from the pastry trimmings. Glaze with the beaten egg and bake for 40 minutes at 200°C/400°F, Gas Mark 6. Serve hot.

Serves 4

Beans and Eggs au Gratin

Metric	Imperial
450g shelled broad beans, fresh or frozen	1lb shelled broad beans, fresh or frozen
2–3 hard-boiled eggs, sliced	2–3 hard-boiled eggs, sliced
40g butter	1½oz butter
40g flour	1½oz flour
400ml creamy milk	¾ pint creamy milk
Salt and cayenne pepper	Salt and cayenne pepper
Topping:	*Topping:*
15g butter	½oz butter
25g fresh breadcrumbs	1oz fresh breadcrumbs
50g grated cheese	2oz grated cheese

A delicious supper or high tea dish, serve this in winter when your frozen broad beans will be doubly welcome.

Cook the beans in salted water until just soft. Drain. Layer the beans and eggs in a baking dish, having beans as top and bottom layers. Make a sauce from the butter, flour and milk, and season with salt and cayenne pepper. Pour over the beans. For the topping, melt the butter and add the breadcrumbs and cheese. When mixed, sprinkle over the sauce. Bake at 220°C/425°F, Gas Mark 7 for 15 minutes or until the topping is browned and crisped.

Variations 1. Use small, whole French beans.

2. Drain 198g (7oz) can tuna, flake and layer with the sliced eggs.

3. Use minced cooked meats or poultry and layer with the eggs.

4. Reserve some egg slices for garnish.

Serves 4–6

Pipérade*

Metric	Imperial
50g butter	2oz butter
1 × 15ml spoon oil	1tbsp oil
125g onions, sliced	4oz onions, sliced
125g red or green peppers, seeded and sliced	4oz red or green peppers, seeded and sliced
2 cloves garlic, crushed	2 cloves garlic, crushed
3 large tomatoes, skinned, seeded and chopped	3 large tomatoes, skinned, seeded and chopped
Salt and pepper	Salt and pepper
4 eggs	4 eggs
2 × 15ml spoons milk	2tbsps milk
Garnish:	*Garnish:*
Parsley, chopped	Parsley, chopped
Toast	Toast
Garlic butter	Garlic butter

A savoury and colourful vegetable and egg dish from the Basque countryside, serve it at luncheon or supper or take it cold on a picnic.

Melt the fats and fry the onions, without colouring, until almost soft. Add peppers and, after 5 minutes, the garlic and tomatoes. Season, and simmer until all ingredients are soft and most of the liquid from the tomatoes has evaporated. Beat eggs, milk and seasoning and scramble lightly, separately. Turn the vegetables on to a heated dish, spread the eggs on top and fork a little of the vegetables into the edges of the egg. Sprinkle with chopped parsley and surround with small triangles of toast spread with garlic butter.

Variations

1. Add grilled rashers of back bacon or gammon for a more substantial dish.

2. Cut the end off a French loaf, remove crumbs and replace with cold piperade, for a picnic dish.

3. Use to stuff tomatoes and serve hot or cold.

To freeze When vegetable ingredients are soft, cool quickly, pack, label and seal.

To serve Thaw overnight in the refrigerator or put, still frozen, into a strong pan over a low heat until thawed. Scramble eggs, etc. as above.

Serves 4

Spinach Luncheon Casserole

Metric	Imperial
1kg spinach, cooked and drained	2lb spinach, cooked and drained
Salt and pepper	Salt and pepper
Juice of ½ lemon	Juice of ½ lemon
125g cooked ham or gammon, chopped	4oz cooked ham or gammon, chopped
25g butter	1oz butter
175g mushrooms	6oz mushrooms
2 eggs	2 eggs
125g grated cheese	4oz grated cheese
2 × 15ml spoons single cream or top-of-the-milk	2tbsps single cream or top-of-the-milk

Like Eggs Florentine, make this dish with fresh spinach as given in the recipe, or with frozen spinach, already chopped.

Season the drained spinach with salt, pepper and lemon juice. Mix in the cooked ham or gammon and put into a greased ovenproof dish. Melt the butter, cook the mushrooms in it and then arrange them on top of the spinach. Beat the eggs with salt and pepper, add the cheese and cream or top-of-the-milk, and pour over the mushrooms. Bake for 25 minutes at 200°C/400°F, Gas Mark 6.

Serves 4

Onions with Sausagemeat*

Metric	Imperial
4 large Spanish-type onions	4 large Spanish-type onions
25g butter	1oz butter
1 × 1.25ml spoon dried mixed herbs or marjoram	¼tsp dried mixed herbs or marjoram
Salt and freshly ground black pepper	Salt and freshly ground black pepper
225g pork sausagemeat	½lb pork sausagemeat
2 × 15ml spoons fresh breadcrumbs	2tbsps fresh breadcrumbs
1 × 15ml spoon Worcestershire sauce	1tbsp Worcestershire sauce
Small whole tomatoes	Small whole tomatoes

Often, when onions are stuffed and baked, the outside layer of onion is overcooked, or the whole onion comes apart. This method prevents such results.

Wash the unskinned onions and, very carefully, trim the root ends so the onions will stand upright but be careful not to remove more than is necessary. Put into a pan of cold water, bring to the boil, reduce the heat and simmer 15 minutes. Drain and rinse in cold water until cool enough to handle. Cut a slice from the top of each onion and discard its brown skin. Remove most of the insides from the onions, leaving a two-layer thickness all round. Chop the removed onion and cook in the butter for a few minutes. Add the herbs, seasoning and sausagemeat. Break up with a fork and fry until the sausagemeat is lightly browned. Add the breadcrumbs and Worcestershire sauce. Use to stuff the onions and pile on top. Any extra should be placed in a greased baking dish. Stand the onions in the dish and bake at 200°C/400°F, Gas Mark 6 for 20 minutes. Garnish with whole small tomatoes baked in the oven at the same time as the onions. The brown skins are easily removed at table.
To freeze Freeze immediately after stuffing.
To serve Thaw in the refrigerator overnight or in the kitchen for 3 hours, then bake as above.
Serves 4

Chicory au Gratin

Metric	Imperial
8 heads of chicory	8 heads of chicory
Lemon juice	Lemon juice
50–125g grated cheese	2–4oz grated cheese
25g butter	1oz butter
25g fresh white breadcrumbs	1oz fresh white breadcrumbs

This can be served when only a light course is required or, with the addition of bacon or gammon, can be made into a more substantial lunch or supper dish.

Trim the chicory and, with a pointed knife, hollow out the hard core at the bottom. Cook in boiling salted water, adding a few drops of lemon juice to keep the chicory white, for 20 minutes. Drain well. Put into a greased flameproof dish and sprinkle with the cheese. Melt the butter, mix in the breadcrumbs and sprinkle on top. Brown under a hot grill or in a hot oven.

To make a more substantial dish put slices of freshly cooked bacon or gammon underneath the chicory or wrap each piece of chicory in a slice of cooked ham before sprinkling with cheese, etc.
Serves 4

Nut and Vegetable Loaf

Metric	Imperial
15g butter or fat	½oz butter or fat
1 small onion, chopped	1 small onion, chopped
1 small carrot, peeled and chopped	1 small carrot, peeled and chopped
1 stalk celery, chopped	1 stalk celery, chopped
2 × 5ml spoons tomato purée	2tsps tomato purée
225g tomatoes, skinned and chopped	½lb tomatoes, skinned and chopped
2 eggs	2 eggs
1 × 5ml spoon dried thyme	1tsp dried thyme
Salt and pepper	Salt and pepper
225g chopped or minced nuts	½lb chopped or minced nuts

Melt the fat and cook prepared onion, carrot and celery until soft, then add the tomato purée and tomatoes and cook for 5 minutes. Put the eggs into a basin with herbs and seasoning; beat well. Stir in the nuts and then the vegetables. Transfer to a greased loaf tin approx. 20 × 11.5cm (8 × 4½in) or ovenproof dish, and bake for 25–30 minutes at 220°C/425°F, Gas Mark 7. Turn out and, if liked, decorate with onion rings and parsley. Serve hot with vegetables and a sauce or gravy, or cold with salad.
Serves 4–6

Stuffed Cauliflower

Metric	Imperial
1 large cauliflower	1 large cauliflower
Filling:	*Filling:*
50g rice	2oz rice
25g butter	1oz butter
1 medium onion, chopped	1 medium onion, chopped
225g minced steak	½lb minced steak
225g tomatoes, skinned and chopped	½lb tomatoes, skinned and chopped
63g tin tomato purée	2¼oz tin tomato purée
Salt, pepper and sugar	Salt, pepper and sugar
1 × 15ml spoon chopped fresh basil	1tbsp chopped fresh basil
Sauce:	*Sauce:*
400ml milk	¾ pint milk
50g mushrooms, sliced	2oz mushrooms, sliced
25g butter	1oz butter
25g flour	1oz flour
Dry mustard	Dry mustard
125g grated cheese	4oz grated cheese

Boil the cauliflower in salted water until *almost* cooked. Boil the rice and drain. Melt the butter, fry the onion and then the meat, breaking it up with a fork. When evenly browned, add tomatoes, tomato purée, salt, pepper, a pinch of sugar and the basil. Simmer 10 minutes, then stir in the rice. Heat the milk and mushrooms together and simmer until the mushrooms are tender. Melt the fat and stir in the flour. Cook, stirring, for 1 minute, then stir in the mustard, seasoning and milk and mushrooms. Bring to the boil and simmer, stirring, until thick. Stir in three-quarters of the cheese.

Put the whole cauliflower into a baking dish and cut downwards, *almost* into four quarters. Put the filling into the cuts, opening them out a little to take it all. Coat each quarter with its share of the sauce, sprinkle with remaining cheese and bake for 20 minutes at 200°C/400°F, Gas Mark 6 to brown lightly.

Serves 4

Eggs Florentine

Metric	Imperial
1kg prepared spinach, cooked and drained	2lb prepared spinach, cooked and drained
25g butter	1oz butter
Salt and pepper	Salt and pepper
A little freshly grated nutmeg	A little freshly grated nutmeg
4–8 eggs, poached	4–8 eggs, poached
Sauce:	*Sauce:*
25g butter	1oz butter
25g flour	1oz flour
300ml milk	½ pint milk
Pinch dry mustard	Pinch dry mustard
75g grated cheese	3oz grated cheese
Little extra cheese	Little extra cheese

This combination of spinach, egg and cheese works very well indeed and is one of the classic spinach dishes.

Chop the spinach finely and drain again. Set aside. To make the cheese sauce: melt butter in pan over low heat, stir in flour and make smooth paste. Cook together for one minute before slowly adding milk, stirring all the time until sauce thickens. Add seasoning, stir in grated cheese until completely melted. Reheat spinach in the butter and add salt, pepper and nutmeg to taste. Divide between four individual dishes, or use one large flameproof dish, and put on 1 or 2 poached eggs for each person. Coat with the cheese sauce, sprinkle a little cheese on top, and brown quickly under a hot grill.

For variety use baked, flaked fish fillets or slices of hot, cooked chicken instead of eggs.

Serves 4

Vegetable and Noodle Casserole

Metric	Imperial
1 × 400g can tomatoes, drained	1 × 14oz can tomatoes, drained
2 stalks celery, chopped	2 stalks celery, chopped
1 medium parsnip, peeled and chopped	1 medium parsnip, peeled and chopped
2 carrots, peeled and sliced	2 carrots, peeled and sliced
1 small swede, peeled and chopped	1 small swede, peeled and chopped
225g courgettes, sliced	½lb courgettes, sliced
1 pepper, seeded and sliced	1 pepper, seeded and sliced
1 bulb fennel, chopped	1 bulb fennel, chopped
1 large onion, sliced	1 large onion, sliced
Bouquet garni of rosemary, lemon thyme, parsley	Bouquet garni of rosemary, lemon thyme, parsley
Salt and pepper	Salt and pepper
2 × 15ml spoons tomato purée	2tbsps tomato purée
150ml dry white wine	¼ pint dry white wine
125g mushrooms	4oz mushrooms
50g noodles	2oz noodles

Put all the vegetables except the mushrooms in a large casserole dish. Add bouquet garni, salt and pepper and tomato purée. Pour in the wine and mix well. Cover with a tight-fitting lid and cook at 180°C/350°F, Gas Mark 4 for 2½ hours. Add the mushrooms after 2 hours. Cook the noodles in boiling salted water as directed on the packet, drain and add to the casserole 5 minutes before serving. Serve hot.

Serves 4

Pissaladière Niçoise

Metric	Imperial
Lightly cooked 20cm flan case of shortcrust pastry made from 200g flour and 90g fat	Lightly cooked 8in flan case of shortcrust pastry made from 7oz flour and 3½oz fat
¾kg onions, chopped	1½lb onions, chopped
4 × 15ml spoons oil	4tbsps oil
1 bouquet garni	1 bouquet garni
Salt and freshly ground black pepper	Salt and freshly ground black pepper
2 cloves garlic, crushed	2 cloves garlic, crushed
Anchovy fillets	Anchovy fillets
Black olives	Black olives

Sometimes a Pissaladière is made in a pastry flan case, as here, and sometimes, like a pizza, on a large round of bread dough.

Put the flan case on to a baking tray. Cook the onions slowly in 3 × 15ml spoons (3tbsps) oil with the herbs, salt and pepper for about 45 minutes. The onions should almost melt and acquire a rich golden colour. Stir in the garlic after about 20 minutes. Transfer to the pastry case and make a lattice pattern on top with the anchovies and olives. Sprinkle the remaining oil on top and bake at 200°C/400°F, Gas Mark 6 for 15 minutes or until really hot.
Serves 4

Potato Rings or Borders

Use these to make a main course look more attractive as well as providing at least part of the vegetables to be served with the meal. Potatoes alone can be used or they can be mixed with a variety of other vegetables—Jerusalem artichokes, cauliflower, carrot, celeriac, kohlrabi, parsnip, swede, turnip—in any proportion from equal quantities to 4 parts potato to 1 part of the other vegetable. The vegetables can be cooked together or separately, and should then be drained well and mashed until smooth. Reheat with a little fat such as butter or bacon fat, and adjust seasoning.

1. Form a border on a heated serving dish and fill with any type of stew, casserole, etc. of fish, meat, poultry or vegetables.
2. Form a shape on part of a large dish and surround with the stew etc. as above.
3. Form a straight strip against which chops can be placed.
4. Form rings as in 1. but on individual plates.

If only potatoes are used then beaten egg (about 1 egg to 1kg (2lb) potatoes) can be mixed in and the mixture used to line the sides and bottom of a 20.5cm (8in) loose-bottomed cake tin which has been greased and sprinkled with browned breadcrumbs. Bake at 220°C/425°F, Gas Mark 7 for about 30 minutes. Then carefully push up the base and slide the shape on to a heated plate. Fill and serve.

The potato mixture can also be made a little softer with the addition of a little more egg and piped into attractive shapes as duchesse potatoes.

Curried Stuffed Marrow

Metric	Imperial
1 × 15ml spoon oil	1tbsp oil
3 medium onions, diced	3 medium onions, diced
1 × 15ml spoon curry powder	1tbsp curry powder
2 × 15ml spoons flour	2tbsps flour
2 eating apples, peeled, cored and diced	2 eating apples, peeled, cored and diced
600ml homemade stock	1 pint homemade stock
2 × 15ml spoons chutney	2tbsps chutney
Salt and pepper	Salt and pepper
450g lamb, cooked and minced	1lb lamb, cooked and minced
1 medium marrow, halved and seeded	1 medium marrow, halved and seeded

Heat the oil in a pan and fry the onions until golden brown. Stir in the curry powder and cook for 2 minutes. Add the flour and cook for a further 2 minutes. Add the apples and gradually stir in the stock, mixing well. Bring to the boil and simmer for a few minutes. Add the chutney, season with salt and pepper, cover and simmer for 30 minutes.

Stir in the minced lamb. Put the mixture into the marrow halves and carefully place the marrow together again. Wrap in foil and place in a baking tin. Cook at 180°C/350°F, Gas Mark 4 for 45 minutes–1 hour until the marrow is tender but not overcooked. Serve sliced.
Serves 4–6

Supper Potato Cakes

Metric	Imperial
900g potatoes, cooked and mashed with 50g butter	2lb potatoes, cooked and mashed with 2oz butter
100g smoked sausage, sliced	4oz smoked sausage, sliced
1 small onion, chopped and fried	1 small onion, chopped and fried
Made mustard	Made mustard
50g cheese, sliced thinly	2oz cheese, sliced thinly
2 eggs, beaten	2 eggs, beaten
Fresh white breadcrumbs	Fresh white breadcrumbs
Deep fat to fry	Deep fat to fry

Form the potatoes into 16 ovals, each about 2·5 × 5cm (1 × 2in) in size. Top 4 with the smoked sausage slices, cover each with another oval and seal the edges. Top another 4 with the onion, spread with a little mustard and cover with the cheese. Cover with remaining ovals and seal edges. Coat all the potato cakes with beaten egg and breadcrumbs. Fry in deep fat until golden brown. Serve hot with Fresh Vegetable Sauce.
Serves 4

Savoury Stuffed Pancakes

Metric
Batter:
125g flour
Pinch of salt
1 egg
300ml mixed milk and water
Oil for frying
To finish:
25g Parmesan cheese, grated

Imperial
Batter:
4oz flour
Pinch of salt
1 egg
½ pint mixed milk and water
Oil for frying
To finish:
1oz Parmesan cheese, grated

Mix the flour and salt together in a bowl, make a well in the centre, drop in the egg, gradually add the liquid and beat well until smooth. Heat the oil in a frying pan, pour off any excess fat, spoon just enough batter into the pan to cover the base thinly, and cook quickly until golden brown underneath. Turn with a palette knife or toss, and cook the other side until golden. Keep the pancakes hot and fill with one of the fillings given below. Fold the pancakes into three, arrange in an ovenproof dish, sprinkle with the Parmesan cheese and cover with foil. Cook for 25–30 minutes at 180 C/350°F, Gas Mark 4, or until the pancakes are hot through. Serve at once.
Serves 4

Chicken, Ham and Mushroom Filling:
50g butter
125g mushrooms, sliced
175g chicken, cooked and chopped
175g cooked ham, minced
300ml double cream, whipped
1 × 5ml spoon chopped fresh savory
1 clove garlic, crushed
Salt and pepper

2oz butter
4oz mushrooms, sliced
6oz chicken, cooked and chopped
6oz cooked ham, minced
½ pint double cream, whipped
1tsp chopped fresh savory
1 clove garlic, crushed
Salt and pepper

Melt the butter in a pan, add the mushrooms and cook for 2 minutes. Remove from heat, stir in the chicken, ham, cream, savory and garlic, and season with salt and pepper. Warm gently, but do not boil.

Spinach Filling:
450g spinach, cooked, drained and finely chopped
Salt and pepper
150ml double cream

1lb spinach, cooked, drained and finely chopped
Salt and pepper
¼ pint double cream

Mix all the ingredients together in a pan and warm gently but do not boil.

Seafood Filling:
125g shelled prawns
2 scallops, diced
125g shelled mussels
150ml dry white wine
Bouquet garni
25g butter
25g flour
150ml milk
Salt and pepper
Fennel tops, chopped

4oz shelled prawns
2 scallops, diced
4oz shelled mussels
¼ pint dry white wine
Bouquet garni
1oz butter
1oz flour
¼ pint milk
Salt and pepper
Fennel tops, chopped

Poach shellfish in the wine with bouquet garni for 5 minutes. Drain, but reserve fish liquor. Remove the bouquet garni. Melt the butter in a pan, stir in the flour and cook for 2 minutes. Gradually add the fish liquor and milk and season with salt and pepper. Add the fennel tops and fish, bring to the boil and cook, stirring, for 2 minutes.

Stuffed Vine or Cabbage Leaves

Metric
25g butter
450g lean minced lamb
2 × 15ml spoons chopped parsley
2 × 15ml spoons chopped mint
4 × 15ml spoons cooked rice
1 onion, grated
1 × 5ml spoon mixed spice
150ml homemade stock
12 vine or cabbage leaves
Sauce:
1 small onion, finely chopped
1 clove garlic, crushed
1 × 15ml spoon oil
450g tomatoes, skinned and chopped
2 × 15ml spoons tomato purée
1 bayleaf
A bouquet garni
Dash of Worcestershire sauce
Salt and pepper
1 glass dry white wine

Imperial
1oz butter
1lb lean minced lamb
2tbsps chopped parsley
2tbsps chopped mint
4tbsps cooked rice
1 onion, grated
1tsp mixed spice
¼ pint homemade stock
12 vine or cabbage leaves
Sauce:
1 small onion, finely chopped
1 clove garlic, crushed
1tbsp oil
1lb tomatoes, skinned and chopped
2tbsps tomato purée
1 bayleaf
A bouquet garni
Dash of Worcestershire sauce
Salt and pepper
1 glass dry white wine

To make the tomato sauce: lightly fry the onion and garlic in the oil until transparent. Stir in the remaining ingredients, slowly bring to the boil, cover and simmer for 1–1½ hours. Remove the bouquet garni before serving.

Melt the butter in a pan, add the meat and cook until lightly browned. Add the parsley, mint, rice, onion, seasoning and mixed spice. Stir in the stock, and cook for 5–10 minutes until the stock is absorbed. Blanch the vine or cabbage leaves by cooking them in boiling water for 2 minutes; drain well. Place each leaf on the working surface, spoon filling in the centre of each leaf and roll up, tucking in the ends to form a neat parcel. Place the rolls close together in an ovenproof dish, and spoon over the tomato sauce to come halfway up the cabbage rolls. Cover with a lid or foil and cook in the centre of the oven at 180°C/350°F, Gas Mark 4, for 45 minutes. Serve the remaining sauce separately.
Serves 4

Spanish Omelette

Metric	Imperial
25g butter	1oz butter
1 clove garlic, crushed	1 clove garlic, crushed
1 small onion, chopped	1 small onion, chopped
1 tomato, skinned and chopped	1 tomato, skinned and chopped
2 potatoes, cooked and diced	2 potatoes, cooked and diced
1 small red pepper, seeded and chopped	1 small red pepper, seeded and chopped
2 × 15ml spoons peas, cooked	2tbsps peas, cooked
1 × 15ml spoon chopped parsley	1tbsp chopped parsley
4 eggs	4 eggs
Salt and pepper	Salt and pepper
Fresh herbs to serve	Fresh herbs to serve

Melt the butter in a large frying pan. Add the garlic and vegetables and cook for a few minutes, stirring. Add the parsley. Whisk the eggs, season well with salt and pepper and pour over vegetables in the pan. Cook slowly, stir once or twice, then leave until eggs almost set. Put pan under a preheated grill to brown. Run a palette knife underneath to loosen the omelette, then slide out on to a serving dish, sprinkle with fresh herbs and serve at once.
Serves 4

Mushroom Risotto

Metric	Imperial
1 onion, sliced	1 onion, sliced
75g butter	3oz butter
225g brown rice	½lb brown rice
150ml dry white wine	¼ pint dry white wine
600ml homemade stock	1 pint homemade stock
225g mushrooms, sliced	½lb mushrooms, sliced
2 × 15ml spoons chopped fresh basil	2tbsps chopped fresh basil
Salt and pepper	Salt and pepper
2–3 × 15ml spoons Parmesan cheese, grated	2–3tbsps Parmesan cheese, grated
To serve:	*To serve:*
350g shelled prawns	¾lb shelled prawns
50g garlic butter	2oz garlic butter

Fry the onion in butter until golden, add the rice and cook for a further 10 minutes. Pour in the wine and allow to bubble briskly until well reduced. Add about a third of the stock, the mushrooms, basil and seasoning. Cook in an open pan over a moderate heat until the liquid has been absorbed. Gradually add the remaining stock and simmer until the rice is just soft, about 25–30 minutes. Turn into a hot serving dish, sprinkle with Parmesan cheese and serve at once with prawns which have been fried in garlic butter until hot.
Serves 4

Stuffed Peppers

Metric	Imperial
4 large red peppers	4 large red peppers
4 × 15ml spoons peas	4tbsps peas
4 × 15ml spoons sweetcorn kernels	4tbsps sweetcorn kernels
125g patna rice, cooked	4oz patna rice, cooked
225g chicken, cooked and diced	½lb chicken, cooked and diced
125g salami, diced	4oz salami, diced
Salt and pepper	Salt and pepper
6 × 15ml spoons French dressing	6tbsps French dressing
1 clove garlic, crushed, optional	1 clove garlic, crushed, optional
1 × 15ml spoon chopped onion	1tbsp chopped onion

Cut the tops off the peppers, scoop out seeds and core. Blanch for 2 minutes, drain and cool. Cook the peas and sweetcorn in boiling salted water for 5–7 minutes. Drain and cool. Combine peas and sweetcorn with the rice; stir in the remaining ingredients. Mix well and pile mixture into the peppers. Allow to stand for at least 1 hour to develop the flavour. Serve lightly chilled with a salad.
Serves 4

Vegetable Lasagne*

Metric	Imperial
10 sheets lasagne pasta	10 sheets lasagne pasta
4 × 15ml spoons oil	4tbsps oil
450g onions, sliced	1lb onions, sliced
450g tomatoes, skinned and sliced	1lb tomatoes, skinned and sliced
450g courgettes, sliced	1lb courgettes, sliced
2 cloves garlic, crushed	2 cloves garlic, crushed
1 × 5ml spoon dried basil	1tsp dried basil
150ml dry white wine	¼ pint dry white wine
Salt and pepper	Salt and pepper
50g butter	2oz butter
50g flour	2oz flour
600ml milk	1 pint milk
2 × 5ml spoons made mustard	2 teaspoons made mustard
175g strong Cheddar cheese, grated	6oz strong Cheddar cheese, grated

Cook the lasagne in boiling salted water with 3 × 15ml spoons (3tbsps) of the oil added to the water. Boil rapidly for 12–15 minutes until the pasta is just tender, drain and cool. Cook the onions, tomatoes and courgettes in the remaining oil, and add the garlic, basil, wine and seasoning. Bring to the boil, cover, and simmer gently for 25 minutes.

Meanwhile, melt the butter in a pan, add the flour and cook for 2 minutes. Gradually add the milk, stirring well, bring to the boil and cook for a further 2 minutes. Add salt, pepper and mustard, stir in the vegetables, and add most of the cheese, reserving a little for the top. Line an ovenproof dish with a third of the pasta, spoon over a third of the sauce, and continue layering, finishing with sauce. Sprinkle over the remaining cheese. Bake at 180°C/350°F, Gas Mark 4 for 25–30 minutes.

To freeze Freeze unbaked. Cover with foil and freeze.

To serve Thaw at room temperature for 6–7 hours then cook as above.

Serves 4

Herb Flan*

Metric	Imperial
Shortcrust pastry made with 175g flour and 75g fat	Shortcrust pastry made with 6oz flour and 3oz fat
25g butter	1oz butter
1 onion, chopped	1 onion, chopped
25g flour	1oz flour
300ml milk	½ pint milk
125g strong Cheddar cheese, grated	4oz strong Cheddar cheese, grated
Salt and pepper	Salt and pepper
2 × 15ml spoons chopped fresh herbs, e.g. basil and marjoram	2tbsps chopped fresh herbs, e.g. basil and marjoram
2 eggs, separated	2 eggs, separated
To garnish:	*To garnish:*
1 tomato, sliced	1 tomato, sliced
Fennel leaves	Fennel leaves

Use the pastry to line a 20cm (8in) flan ring. Bake blind, near the top of the oven, at 220°C/425°F, Gas Mark 7, for 15–20 minutes or until cooked but still pale in colour. Melt the butter and cook onion until transparent; stir in the flour and cook for 2–3 minutes. Gradually add the milk, stirring all the time. Bring to the boil and continue to stir until the sauce thickens. Remove from the heat and stir in the cheese, seasoning and herbs. Add the egg yolks and mix well. Whisk the egg whites until stiff and fold into the sauce. Pour into the pastry case and bake for a further 25–30 minutes until well risen and golden brown. Garnish with sliced tomato and fennel leaves. Serve hot or cold.

To freeze Open freeze and wrap in foil.

To serve Thaw at room temperature for 4–5 hours.

Serves 4–6

Haddock with Fennel and Celery Sauce*

Metric	Imperial
1kg fresh haddock	2lb fresh haddock
65g butter	2½oz butter
Salt and pepper	Salt and pepper
3 stalks celery, chopped	3 stalks celery, chopped
1 small head fennel, chopped	1 small head fennel, chopped
600ml milk	1 pint milk
50g flour	2oz flour
1 × 15ml spoon grated Parmesan cheese	1tbsp grated Parmesan cheese
1 lemon, sliced, to garnish	1 lemon, sliced, to garnish
Fennel leaves, to garnish	Fennel leaves, to garnish

Place the fish in a greased ovenproof dish, dot with 15g (½oz) butter and season with salt and pepper. Put the celery and fennel in a pan of boiling salted water and simmer for 15 minutes. Drain. Spoon the vegetables over the fish, pour over the milk, cover the dish with a lid or foil, and cook at 180°C/350°F, Gas Mark 4 for 12–15 minutes until the fish is just cooked. Drain the liquor from the fish, and reserve. Melt the remaining butter in a pan, stir in the flour and cook for 2 minutes. Gradually stir in the liquor, bring to the boil, and cook, stirring occasionally, for 3 minutes. Pour the sauce over the fish, sprinkle over the Parmesan cheese and return to the oven for about 20 minutes until heated through and bubbling. If the top is not really browned, put the dish under a hot grill for a few minutes. Serve hot, garnished with lemon and fennel.

To freeze Wrap in foil after sprinkling over the cheese, cool quickly and freeze.

To serve Thaw at room temperature for 7–8 hours. Bake for 30 minutes at 180°C/350°F, Gas Mark 4, brown under grill and garnish.

Serves 4

Haddock with fennel and celery sauce and a herb flan

Prawn Stuffed Aubergines

Metric
4 large aubergines
2 × 15ml spoons oil
3 medium onions, sliced
450g tomatoes, skinned and sliced
150ml dry white wine
1 × 15ml spoon tomato purée
1 clove garlic, crushed
Salt and pepper
225g shelled prawns

Imperial
4 large aubergines
2tbsps oil
3 medium onions, sliced
1lb tomatoes, skinned and sliced
¼ pint dry white wine
1tbsp tomato purée
1 clove garlic, crushed
Salt and pepper
½lb shelled prawns

Halve the aubergines lengthways and scoop out the insides to within 6mm (¼in) of the skin. Blanch the shells for 4 minutes, and drain. Heat the oil in a pan, and gently cook the onions until golden brown; add the tomatoes. Chop up the pulp from the aubergines and add to the mixture. Add the wine, tomato purée, garlic and salt and pepper. Simmer, covered, for 25 minutes, then add the prawns. Arrange the aubergine shells in an ovenproof dish, spoon the prawn filling into each shell, cover with a lid or foil, and bake at 200°C/400°F, Gas Mark 6 for about 35–40 minutes or until tender and hot.
Serves 4

Onion and Cheese Bake

Metric
12 slices bread
Approx. 50g softened butter
2 × 15ml spoons oil
3 medium onions, sliced
½kg tomatoes, skinned and sliced
225g Gruyère cheese, grated
Mixed herbs
3 large eggs, beaten
600ml milk
Salt and pepper
225g streaky bacon rashers

Imperial
12 slices bread
Approx. 2oz softened butter
2tbsps oil
3 medium onions, sliced
1lb tomatoes, skinned and sliced
½lb Gruyère cheese, grated
Mixed herbs
3 large eggs, beaten
1 pint milk
Salt and pepper
½lb streaky bacon rashers

Trim the crusts from the bread, spread one side with butter. Use a few slices to line the base of a 1.1 litre (2 pint) ovenproof dish. Heat the oil in a pan, fry the onions until golden brown, cool slightly. Arrange a layer of onions and tomatoes on top of the bread, sprinkle with grated cheese and herbs, place another layer of buttered bread on top. Continue layering, finishing with bread, and top with cheese. Mix the eggs and milk together, season well with salt and pepper, pour over the bread layers. Bake at 180°C/350°F, Gas Mark 4 for 45 minutes to 1 hour, until well risen and golden brown. Roll the bacon rashers into rolls, secure with a cocktail stick. Fry or grill the bacon until cooked and crisp. Serve on top of the onion and cheese bake.
Serves 4

Bacon and Onion Roly Poly

Metric
225g self-raising flour
1 × 5ml spoon baking powder
1 × 2.5ml spoon salt
100g suet
Water to mix
1 × 15ml spoon oil
3 medium onions, sliced
4 rashers bacon, chopped
175g strong Cheddar cheese, grated
1 × 5ml spoon chopped fresh sage
1 beaten egg, to glaze

Imperial
½lb self-raising flour
1tsp baking powder
½tsp salt
4oz suet
Water to mix
1tbsp oil
3 medium onions, sliced
4 rashers bacon, chopped
6oz strong Cheddar cheese, grated
1tsp chopped fresh sage
1 beaten egg, to glaze

Sift the flour, baking powder and salt into a mixing bowl, stir in the suet and add sufficient water to make a fairly stiff dough. Roll into an oblong 30 × 15cm (12 × 6in) on a floured board. Heat the oil in a pan, and fry the onions and bacon until just cooked. Allow to cool and spoon over the pastry. Sprinkle the grated cheese over the onion mixture, and top with sage. Brush the sides of the pastry with beaten egg, roll up into an oblong and seal the ends. Make 4 diagonal cuts in the top of the pastry, put on a baking sheet and bake at 190°C/375°F, Gas Mark 5 for 1 hour or until golden brown.
Serves 4

Onion and Cheese Rarebits

Metric
25g butter
225g strong Cheddar cheese, grated
1 × 5ml spoon dry mustard
2 × 15ml spoons chopped chives
Salt and pepper
3–4 × 15ml spoons brown ale
1 onion, chopped
Freshly toasted bread
Garnish:
Radish roses
Spring onions

Imperial
1oz butter
½lb strong Cheddar cheese, grated
1tsp dry mustard
2tbsps chopped chives
Salt and pepper
3–4tbsps brown ale
1 onion, chopped
Freshly toasted bread
Garnish:
Radish roses
Spring onions

Melt the butter in a shallow saucepan, remove from the heat and stir in the cheese, mustard, chives, seasoning, brown ale and onion. Return to the heat and stir continuously until smooth and creamy, but do not allow to become more than just hot, otherwise the mixture will become stringy. Spread on the hot toast and put under a hot grill until golden and bubbling. Garnish with radish roses and spring onions. Serve at once.
Serves 4–6

Bacon and onion roly poly with onion and cheese rarebits

Salads

Tomato and Vegetable Ring

Metric	Imperial
20g powdered unflavoured gelatine	¾oz powdered unflavoured gelatine
900ml homemade stock	1½ pints homemade stock
2 × 15ml spoons sherry	2tbsps sherry
2 large tomatoes, skinned and sliced	2 large tomatoes, skinned and sliced
½kg cooked and chopped mixed vegetables, e.g. fresh carrots, peas, beans, sweetcorn and celery	1lb cooked and chopped mixed vegetables, e.g. fresh carrots, peas, beans, sweetcorn and celery
1 bunch watercress	1 bunch watercress

Put the gelatine in a basin with 2 × 15ml spoons (2tbsps) water and heat gently over a pan of hot water until melted. Stir into stock and add sherry. Pour 150ml (¼ pint) stock mixture into a 1 litre (2 pint) ring mould and allow to set. Arrange one tomato in the mould, spoon over sufficient stock to cover the slices; allow to set. Repeat the process with the other tomato. Add the mixed vegetables to the remaining stock and carefully pour into the mould. Set in the refrigerator. Dip the mould in hot water for 1–2 seconds, invert mould and turn out onto a serving plate. Fill centre of mould with watercress and serve.
Serves 6–8

Pickled Herrings with Red Cabbage Salad

Metric	Imperial
4 large herrings	4 large herrings
150ml cider vinegar	¼ pint cider vinegar
150ml water	¼ pint water
1 bayleaf	1 bayleaf
6 peppercorns	6 peppercorns
2 cloves	2 cloves
Salt and pepper	Salt and pepper
225g red cabbage, thinly sliced	½lb red cabbage, thinly sliced
1 large eating apple, peeled, cored and diced	1 large eating apple, peeled, cored and diced
2 small onions, sliced	2 small onions, sliced
2 stalks celery, diced	2 stalks celery, diced
Dressing:	*Dressing:*
1 × 15ml spoon Meaux mustard	1tbsp Meaux mustard
150ml double cream	¼ pint double cream
Fennel sprigs to garnish	Fennel sprigs to garnish

Roll herrings from head to tail and secure with a cocktail stick. Place in an ovenproof dish, pour over the cider vinegar and water, add the bayleaf, peppercorns and cloves and season with salt and pepper. Cover with foil or a lid and cook for 40 minutes at 180°C/350°F, Gas Mark 4. Allow to cool, remove herrings and drain well. Mix the cabbage, apple, onions and celery together in a bowl.

To make the dressing: mix the mustard and cream together, season with salt and pepper and stir into the salad ingredients. Pile on to a serving dish and arrange the herrings in a row on top. Garnish with fennel.
Serves 4

Danish Blue Cheese Salad

Metric	Imperial
2 celeriac roots, peeled and grated	2 celeriac roots, peeled and grated
2 large ripe pears, peeled and chopped	2 large ripe pears, peeled and chopped
Juice of ½ lemon	Juice of ½ lemon
1 bunch spring onions, chopped	1 bunch spring onions, chopped
125g stoned dates, chopped	4oz stoned dates, chopped
50g button mushrooms, sliced	2oz button mushrooms, sliced
Salt and pepper	Salt and pepper
50g Danish blue cheese, crumbled	2oz Danish blue cheese, crumbled
150ml double cream	¼ pint double cream
1 endive, separated into leaves	1 endive, separated into leaves
50g salami, sliced and made into cornets	2oz salami, sliced and made into cornets

Mix together the celeriac and pears in a bowl. Sprinkle with the lemon juice. Add the onions, dates and mushrooms and season with salt and pepper. Put the cheese into a basin, mix in the cream, and add to the celeriac mixture. Stir thoroughly. Place the endive leaves on a serving dish and pile salad on top; garnish with the salami cornets.
Serves 4

Pickled herrings with salads of red cabbage and Danish blue cheese

Grapefruit and Grape Salad

Metric	Imperial
4 large grapefruit	4 large grapefruit
125g green grapes	4oz green grapes
50g Brazil nuts, roughly chopped	2oz Brazil nuts, roughly chopped
Dressing:	*Dressing:*
4 × 15ml spoons wine vinegar	4tbsps wine vinegar
6 × 15ml spoons olive oil	6tbsps olive oil
2 × 5ml spoons sugar	2tsps sugar
1 × 5ml spoon dry mustard	1tsp dry mustard
1 × 5ml spoon salt	1tsp salt
3 × 15ml spoons single cream	3tbsps single cream
Mustard and cress	Mustard and cress

Remove skin and pith from the grapefruit. Cut the fruit into segments and put into a bowl. Cut the grapes in half and remove the pips, add these and the nuts to the grapefruit. Put the dressing ingredients in a basin and mix thoroughly. Place the fruit and nuts on a serving dish, spoon dressing over them and garnish with mustard and cress.
Serves 4

Rice and Prawn Medley

Metric	Imperial
125g long grain rice	4oz long grain rice
75g sweetcorn	3oz sweetcorn
125g mushrooms, sliced	4oz mushrooms, sliced
125g green beans, cooked	4oz green beans, cooked
1 small onion, sliced	1 small onion, sliced
125g shelled prawns	4oz shelled prawns
3 small courgettes, sliced	3 small courgettes, sliced
25g butter	1oz butter
Salt and pepper	Salt and pepper
French dressing	French dressing
4 whole prawns with shells	4 whole prawns with shells

Cook the rice in boiling salted water for 12 minutes until just tender. Drain. Put the sweetcorn, mushrooms, beans, onion and peeled prawns in a bowl, add the rice and stir well. Fry the courgettes in butter until lightly coloured, drain on absorbent paper and add to the salad when cool. Season with salt and pepper, toss in French dressing, pile into a serving dish, and garnish with the whole prawns.
Serves 4

Waldorf Salad

Metric	Imperial
450g eating apples	1lb eating apples
Juice of 1 lemon	Juice of 1 lemon
150ml mayonnaise	$\frac{1}{4}$ pint mayonnaise
$\frac{1}{2}$ head celery, chopped	$\frac{1}{2}$ head celery, chopped
15g hazelnuts, chopped	$\frac{1}{2}$oz hazelnuts, chopped
15g walnuts, chopped	$\frac{1}{2}$oz walnuts, chopped
Salt and pepper	Salt and pepper
1 lettuce	1 lettuce
1 × 15ml spoon snipped chives	1tbsp snipped chives

Peel and core the apples, slice one and dice the rest; dip the slices in lemon juice to prevent discoloration. Toss diced apples in the mayonnaise, stir in the celery, hazelnuts and walnuts and season with salt and pepper. Arrange the lettuce on a dish and pile the salad in the centre. Arrange the apple slices on top and sprinkle over with chives.
Serves 4

Curried Chicken Salad

Metric	Imperial
350g cooked chicken	$\frac{3}{4}$lb cooked chicken
1 × 15ml spoon curry powder	1tbsp curry powder
1 clove garlic, crushed	1 clove garlic, crushed
150ml mayonnaise	$\frac{1}{4}$ pint mayonnaise
150ml soured cream	$\frac{1}{4}$ pint soured cream
1 green pepper, seeded and chopped	1 green pepper, seeded and chopped
1 egg, hard-boiled and chopped	1 egg, hard-boiled and chopped
1 × 15ml spoon tomato purée	1tbsp tomato purée
125g mushrooms, sliced	4oz mushrooms, sliced
Salt and pepper	Salt and pepper
Endive	Endive
225g asparagus, cooked	$\frac{1}{2}$lb asparagus, cooked
2 tomatoes, quartered	2 tomatoes, quartered

Cut the chicken into chunks. Put the curry powder in a bowl, add the garlic, mayonnaise and soured cream. Mix well and allow to stand for $\frac{1}{2}$ hour. Stir in the green pepper, hard-boiled egg, tomato purée and mushrooms and season with salt and pepper. Mix in the chicken. Arrange the endive on a dish, pile the chicken salad on top and garnish with asparagus and tomatoes.
Serves 4

Waldorf salad with grapefruit and grape salad

Caesar Salad

Metric	Imperial
225g chicory	½lb chicory
½ small cucumber, sliced	½ small cucumber, sliced
6 radishes, cut into roses	6 radishes, cut into roses
3 slices bread, cubed	3 slices bread, cubed
1 egg, beaten	1 egg, beaten
25g Parmesan cheese, grated	1oz Parmesan cheese, grated
1 × 5ml spoon dry mustard	1tsp dry mustard
1 × 15ml spoon oil	1tbsp oil
25g butter	1oz butter
1 clove garlic, crushed	1 clove garlic, crushed

Arrange the chicory, cucumber and radish roses around the edge of a serving dish. Coat the bread cubes in beaten egg. Mix the Parmesan cheese and dry mustard together and toss the bread cubes in the mixture. Heat the oil and butter in a frying pan. Lightly fry the garlic, then fry the bread cubes until golden brown and crisp. Cool. Pile in the centre of the chicory border and serve at once.
Serves 4

Winter Salad

Metric	Imperial
3 apples, cored and sliced	3 apples, cored and sliced
4 stalks celery, chopped	4 stalks celery, chopped
1 onion, sliced	1 onion, sliced
1 medium beetroot, cooked, peeled and diced	1 medium beetroot, cooked, peeled and diced
Approx. 150ml mayonnaise	Approx. ¼ pint mayonnaise
Salt and pepper	Salt and pepper
1 lettuce	1 lettuce
25g walnuts, chopped	1oz walnuts, chopped
1 × 15ml spoon chopped parsley	1tbsp chopped parsley

Mix the apples, celery, onion and beetroot together, add sufficient mayonnaise to coat, and season well with salt and pepper. Pile on to a bed of lettuce leaves, sprinkle over with walnuts and chopped parsley and serve.
Serves 4

French Bean and Orange Salad

Metric	Imperial
450g French beans	1lb French beans
3 oranges	3 oranges
½ cucumber	½ cucumber
Dressing:	*Dressing:*
150ml mayonnaise	¼ pint mayonnaise
1 × 15ml spoon chopped stuffed olives	1tbsp chopped stuffed olives
1 × 15ml spoon chopped onion	1tbsp chopped onion
1 egg, hard-boiled	1 egg, hard-boiled
1 × 15ml spoon chopped green pepper	1tbsp chopped green pepper
1 × 5ml spoon chopped parsley	1tsp chopped parsley
1 × 5ml spoon tomato purée	1tsp tomato purée

Cook the beans in boiling salted water for 5–7 minutes, until just tender. Remove skin and pith from the oranges and cut into segments. Pile the beans in the centre of a flat dish and arrange the orange segments and sliced cucumber, overlapping each other, round the edge of the beans. Mix all the dressing ingredients together and spoon over the salad just before serving.
Serves 4–6

Christmas Salad

Metric	Imperial
225–350g broad beans, cooked	½–¾lb broad beans, cooked
350g small Brussels sprouts	¾lb small Brussels sprouts
3 stalks celery	3 stalks celery
1 medium onion, chopped	1 medium onion, chopped
50g sultanas	2oz sultanas
50g seedless raisins	2oz seedless raisins
2 grapefruit, or frozen sections	2 grapefruit, or frozen sections
4–5 × 15ml spoons French dressing	4–5tbsps French dressing
1 × 5ml spoon French mustard	1tsp French mustard
25g salted peanuts	1oz salted peanuts
1–2 small tomatoes	1–2 small tomatoes
1 small carrot	1 small carrot

Mix prepared beans and sprouts. Cut celery into 5cm (2in) lengths and then into thin strips. Drop about one-third into iced water to curl and add rest to the beans with the onion. Mix sultanas, raisins and grapefruit sections and add 2 × 15ml spoons (2tbsps) French dressing. Add mustard to remaining dressing and pour over raw vegetables. Chill. Just before serving fold the two mixtures together and spoon on to a serving platter. Sprinkle nuts on top and decorate with tomatoes cut into sections, grated carrot and the curled celery. If liked, bite-sized pieces of turkey, duck, or other cold meats can be folded into the vegetables.
Serves 4

Caesar salad and French bean and orange salad

Red and Green Salad

Metric	Imperial
2 bunches watercress, roughly chopped	2 bunches watercress, roughly chopped
12 spring onions, sliced	12 spring onions, sliced
1 small red pepper, seeded and sliced	1 small red pepper, seeded and sliced
10cm piece cucumber, halved and thinly sliced	4in piece cucumber, halved and thinly sliced
Approx. 2 × 15ml spoons French dressing	Approx. 2tbsps French dressing
6–8 small tomatoes	6–8 small tomatoes

Mix the watercress, onions, red pepper and cucumber together, add the French dressing and toss lightly. Put into a dish. Cut each tomato into 6–8 sections and use, with the skin side uppermost, to decorate the top of the salad.
Serves 6

Italian Pasta Salad

Metric	Imperial
175g pasta shells	6oz pasta shells
225g streaky bacon, chopped	½lb streaky bacon, chopped
175g continental smoked garlic sausage, cut diagonally into 1cm pieces	6oz continental smoked garlic sausage, cut diagonally into ½in pieces
175g black grapes, halved and pipped	6oz black grapes, halved and pipped
125g red pepper, seeded and sliced	4oz red pepper, seeded and sliced
Dressing:	*Dressing:*
125g plain yogurt	4oz plain yogurt
125g double cream	4oz double cream
1 × 15ml spoon chopped fresh mint	1tbsp chopped fresh mint
2 × 5ml spoons lemon juice	2tsps lemon juice
Salt and pepper	Salt and pepper

Cook the pasta in boiling salted water for 9–12 minutes until just tender. Drain. Fry the bacon in its own fat until crispy; drain well. Put the pasta, bacon, garlic sausage, grapes and red pepper in a bowl and mix well.

To make the dressing: put the yogurt, double cream, mint, lemon juice and salt and pepper in a bowl and mix well. Pour over the pasta salad and stir. Pile into a serving dish and allow to stand for ½ hour before serving.
Serves 4

Raw Mushroom and Spinach Salad

Metric	Imperial
125g small, very fresh mushrooms, thinly sliced	4oz small, very fresh mushrooms, thinly sliced
French dressing	French dressing
125g spinach, washed and drained	4oz spinach, washed and drained

Put the mushrooms into a lidded container with 2 × 15ml spoons (2tbsps) French dressing. Shake to coat evenly and refrigerate for at least 2 hours; shake gently from time to time. Just before serving remove thick centre stalks from spinach, slice the green leaves finely and mix with the mushrooms, adding more dressing if required to coat the spinach.
Serves 4

Hot Potato Salad

Metric	Imperial
1 large onion, chopped	1 large onion, chopped
4 × 15ml spoons oil	4tbsps oil
2 × 5ml spoons flour	2tsps flour
2 × 5ml spoons sugar	2tsps sugar
Salt and pepper	Salt and pepper
150ml tarragon vinegar	¼ pint tarragon vinegar
150ml chicken stock	¼ pint chicken stock
½kg potatoes, cooked and sliced	2lb potatoes, cooked and sliced
4 spring onions, chopped	4 spring onions, chopped
½ green pepper, seeded and chopped	½ green pepper, seeded and chopped
4 dill pickles, chopped	4 dill pickles, chopped
1 × 15ml spoon chopped parsley	1tbsp chopped parsley

Fry the onion in the oil until tender but not coloured, stir in the flour and cook for 1 minute. Add the sugar and salt and pepper and gradually stir in the vinegar and stock. Bring to the boil, stirring, and cook for 2 minutes. Stir in the sliced potatoes, spring onions, pepper and pickles. The vegetables should be well coated and heated through. Just before serving sprinkle with the chopped parsley.
Serves 4–6

Raw mushroom and spinach salad with hot potato salad

Salade Niçoise

Metric	Imperial
450g tomatoes, skinned and sliced	1lb tomatoes, skinned and sliced
½ cucumber, sliced	½ cucumber, sliced
Salt and pepper	Salt and pepper
1 × 5ml spoon chopped parsley	1tsp chopped parsley
1 × 5ml spoon chopped fresh basil	1tsp chopped fresh basil
125g French beans, cooked	4oz French beans, cooked
225g can tuna fish, drained	½lb can tuna fish, drained
½ green pepper, seeded and chopped	½ green pepper, seeded and chopped
50g black olives, pitted and chopped	2oz black olives, pitted and chopped
1 clove garlic, crushed	1 clove garlic, crushed
French dressing	French dressing
2 eggs, hard-boiled and quartered	2 eggs, hard-boiled and quartered
8 anchovy fillets	8 anchovy fillets
1 lemon, quartered	1 lemon, quartered

Arrange the tomatoes in layers with the cucumber on a shallow dish. Season with salt and pepper and sprinkle over with herbs. Mix the beans, tuna and pepper together and pile in the centre of the dish; sprinkle with the black olives. Add the garlic to the dressing, and pour over the salad. Arrange the eggs and anchovy fillets attractively on top and garnish with lemon. Allow the salad to stand for about ½ hour before serving to allow the flavours to blend.

Serves 4–6

Strawberry and Walnut Salad

Metric	Imperial
225g asparagus, cooked	½lb asparagus, cooked
450g strawberries, sliced	1lb strawberries, sliced
50g walnuts, cut into halves	2oz walnuts, cut into halves
10cm piece cucumber, sliced	4in piece cucumber, sliced
Dressing:	*Dressing:*
2 egg yolks	2 egg yolks
Salt and pepper	Salt and pepper
150ml olive oil	¼ pint olive oil
2 × 15ml spoons lemon juice	2tbsps lemon juice
1 egg white, stiffly whisked	1 egg white, stiffly whisked

Arrange the asparagus in a circle on a serving platter, to resemble the sun's rays, i.e. pointed ends towards the edge of the dish. Mix the strawberries with the walnuts and cucumber.

To make the dressing: cream the egg yolks and seasoning together. Add the oil drop by drop, stirring all the time until the mayonnaise is thick. Stir in the lemon juice. Just before serving fold in the whisked egg white.

Arrange the strawberry mixture in the centre of the dish and spoon over some of the dressing. Serve the remaining dressing separately.

Serves 4–6

Coleslaw

Metric	Imperial
½ white cabbage, shredded	½ white cabbage, shredded
4 stalks celery, chopped	4 stalks celery, chopped
1 medium onion, chopped	1 medium onion, chopped
4 large carrots, grated	4 large carrots, grated
Salt and pepper	Salt and pepper
4 × 15ml spoons mayonnaise	4tbsps mayonnaise
Few drops lemon juice	Few drops lemon juice
Variations:	*Variations:*
1. ½ small raw cauliflower, sliced	1. ½ small raw cauliflower, sliced
2 red-skinned apples, cored and chopped	2 red-skinned apples, cored and chopped
25g walnuts, chopped	1oz walnuts, chopped
2. 25–50g sultanas	2. 1–2oz sultanas
25–50g raisins	1–2oz raisins
1 × 15ml spoon chopped parsley	1tbsp chopped parsley
2 × 15ml spoons salted peanuts	2tbsps salted peanuts
3. 2 oranges, peeled and cut into segments	3. 2 oranges, peeled and cut into segments
12 dates, stoned and chopped	12 dates, stoned and chopped
50g cobnuts, chopped	2oz cobnuts, chopped

Combine the cabbage, celery and onion together in a large bowl. Stir in the carrots and seasoning. Stir in the mayonnaise and lemon juice making sure all the vegetables are well coated. The salad can be left up to an hour before serving, covered and in a cool place, to absorb the flavour of the dressing. If liked, add any of the three variations. Chopped apple, however, should only be added immediately before serving.

Serves 6–8

Vegetable Side Dishes

Herb and Potato Dumplings

Metric
1½kg potatoes, peeled
2 × 5ml spoons baking powder
1 × 5ml spoon salt
1 × 2.5ml spoon grated nutmeg
50g semolina
75g wheatmeal flour
2 eggs, beaten
2 × 15ml spoons chopped
  fresh mixed herbs: parsley,
  thyme, sage, marjoram
1 small onion, grated
2 slices bread
Oil
125g bacon, chopped

Imperial
3lb potatoes, peeled
2tsps baking powder
1tsp salt
½tsp grated nutmeg
2oz semolina
3oz wheatmeal flour
2 eggs, beaten
2tbsps chopped fresh mixed
  herbs: parsley, thyme, sage,
  marjoram
1 small onion, grated
2 slices bread
Oil
4oz bacon, chopped

Cook the potatoes, sieve and cool. Add the baking powder, salt, nutmeg, semolina, flour, eggs, herbs and onion. Knead to a smooth dough. Remove the crusts from the bread and cut it into cubes. Heat the oil and fry the bread cubes until crisp and golden brown. Flour the hands and make the dough into round dumplings, about the size of a fist. Press a few of the fried croûtons into each dumpling. Put the dumplings into boiling salted water and cook thoroughly for 12–15 minutes. Lightly fry the bacon. Put the dumplings in a serving dish and sprinkle with the bacon pieces. Serve with boiled ham or a pot roast.
Serves 4–6

Brussels Sprouts with Chestnuts

Metric
350g chestnuts
600ml homemade stock
1 stalk celery
1 small onion
1 × 5ml spoon sugar
1 bouquet garni
¾kg Brussels sprouts
50g butter

Imperial
¾lb chestnuts
1 pint homemade stock
1 stalk celery
1 small onion
1tsp sugar
1 bouquet garni
1½lb Brussels sprouts
2oz butter

Put the chestnuts in a pan of cold water and bring to the boil. Drain. Remove both the outside and inside skins. Put the nuts in a pan, cover with the stock and add the celery, onion, sugar and bouquet garni. Bring to the boil, cover, and simmer until the nuts are soft, about 35–40 minutes. Drain, removing the celery, onion and bouquet garni; keep the chestnuts hot. Meanwhile prepare the Brussels sprouts: trim off outer leaves and cut a cross at the base of each stalk. Cook the sprouts in boiling salted water for 10–12 minutes until just soft. Drain, return to the pan, add the chestnuts and butter and toss. Serve hot.
Serves 4–6

Mexican Style Corn

Metric
1 onion, chopped
1 carrot, peeled and cubed
1 stalk celery, chopped
350g sweetcorn kernels, fresh
  or frozen
1 green pepper, seeded and
  sliced
1 red pepper, seeded and
  sliced
1 bayleaf
25g butter
25g flour
150ml milk
Salt and pepper
1 × 5ml spoon chopped fresh
  basil

Imperial
1 onion, chopped
1 carrot, peeled and cubed
1 stalk celery, chopped
¾lb sweetcorn kernels, fresh or
  frozen
1 green pepper, seeded and
  sliced
1 red pepper, seeded and
  sliced
1 bayleaf
1oz butter
1oz flour
¼ pint milk
Salt and pepper
1tsp chopped fresh basil

Put the vegetables in a pan, add the bayleaf, cover with water and bring to the boil. Cover and simmer for 15 minutes. Drain well, but reserve 150ml (¼ pint) water from the vegetables. Melt the butter in a pan, stir in the flour and cook for 2 minutes. Gradually add the vegetable water and the milk, stirring all the time. Bring to the boil, and cook for 2 minutes. Adjust seasoning to taste, stir in the vegetables, pour into a serving dish and serve hot, sprinkled with chopped basil.
Serves 4

Herb and potato dumplings served with ham

Northumberland Pan Haggerty

Metric	Imperial
25–50g dripping	1–2oz dripping
1kg potatoes, peeled and thinly sliced	2lb potatoes, peeled and thinly sliced
½kg onions, thinly sliced	1lb onions, thinly sliced
2 × 15ml spoons chopped parsley	2tbsps chopped parsley
125g Cheddar cheese, grated	4oz Cheddar cheese, grated
Salt and pepper	Salt and pepper

Heat the dripping in a large heavy frying pan and put in the potatoes and onions in alternate layers, separating each layer with a sprinkling of parsley, grated cheese and seasoning. Fry gently until browned, turn over and brown the other side. Cover pan and cook until potatoes are tender.
Serves 4

Pommes Lyonnaise

Metric	Imperial
¾kg potatoes	1½lb potatoes
2 × 15ml spoons oil	2tbsps oil
25g butter	1oz butter
2 large onions, sliced	2 large onions, sliced
Salt and pepper	Salt and pepper
1 × 15ml spoon chopped parsley	1tbsp chopped parsley

Scrub the potatoes and boil them in their skins until nearly tender. Drain, remove the skins and slice. Heat the oil and butter in a heavy based frying pan; fry the potatoes and onions until golden brown and the potatoes crisp. Remove from the heat, sprinkle over the salt and pepper and parsley. Turn into a serving dish and serve at once.
Serves 4

Vegetable Dumplings

Metric	Imperial
100g self-raising flour	4oz self-raising flour
1 × 2.5ml spoon baking powder	½tsp baking powder
50g shredded suet	2oz shredded suet
1 × 2.5ml spoon salt	½tsp salt
1 small carrot, peeled and grated	1 small carrot, peeled and grated
2 × 15ml spoons chopped parsley	2tbsps chopped parsley
Water to mix	Water to mix

Cook and serve with roast meat.
Sift the flour and baking powder into a mixing bowl; stir in the suet and salt. Add the carrot and parsley, and mix in sufficient water to make a stiff dough. Be careful not to add too much water. Flour your hands and form the mixture into small dumplings, about the size of a walnut. Place in a roasting tin round the joint of meat, and cook, turning once, for 15–20 minutes, until well risen and thoroughly cooked, at 180°C/350°F, Gas Mark 4. Serve at once.
Serves 4

Savoury Pumpkin

Metric	Imperial
2 × 15ml spoons oil	2 tbsps oil
1 large onion, sliced	1 large onion, sliced
4 large tomatoes, skinned and sliced	4 large tomatoes, skinned and sliced
225–275g pumpkin, skinned, seeded and sliced	8–10oz pumpkin, skinned, seeded and sliced
1 × 5ml spoon dried basil	1tsp dried basil
Salt and pepper	Salt and pepper

Heat the oil in a pan, add the onion, and cook for 5 minutes. Arrange the tomatoes on top of the onions, and top with the pumpkin. Sprinkle basil between each layer, and season well. Cover and simmer gently for 30 minutes. Serve hot with roast and grilled meats.
Serves 4

Beetroot with Soured Cream and Chives

Metric	Imperial
450g cooked beetroot, peeled and diced	1lb cooked beetroot, peeled and diced
25g butter	1oz butter
Salt and freshly ground black pepper	Salt and freshly ground black pepper
5 × 15ml spoons soured cream	5tbsps soured cream
1–2 × 15ml spoons chopped chives	1–2tbsps chopped chives

Put the beetroot and butter into a pan and heat gently until thoroughly hot. Season with salt and pepper. Push to one side of the pan, pour soured cream into the other and heat. Then mix the two together, sprinkle with the chives and serve at once.
　　If fresh chives are not available, chive butter can be used.
Serves 4–6

Colcannon or Bubble and Squeak

Metric	Imperial
½kg cooked potatoes	1lb cooked potatoes
150–450g cooked cabbage	5oz–1lb cooked cabbage
Salt and freshly ground black pepper	Salt and freshly ground black pepper
50g bacon fat, butter or good dripping	2oz bacon fat, butter or good dripping
Chopped parsley	Chopped parsley

An old recipe which has long been popular just because it is so good, try varying the proportions until you find the one you like best.
Mash the potatoes, chop the cabbage and mix the two together with salt and pepper. Melt the fat in a frying pan, put in the vegetables and form into a large cake about 2.5cm (1in) thick. Cook fairly slowly until the underside is well-browned; cut into half and turn each half carefully. Heat and brown the second side.

Or, if the oven is in use cook the colcannon in it. Melt the fat in the frying pan, add vegetables, heat and stir until the vegetables are hot. Transfer to a greased pie dish or casserole so the cake is about 2.5cm (1in) thick, and bake in a hot oven, 200°C/400°F, Gas Mark 6, for abour ½ hour.

Brussels sprouts or kale can replace all or part of the cabbage.
Serves 4–6

Young Turnips and Mushrooms

Metric	Imperial
450g young turnips, peeled	1lb young turnips, peeled
50g butter or herb butter, e.g. thyme	2oz butter or herb butter, e.g. thyme
1 rasher back bacon, chopped	1 rasher back bacon, chopped
125g mushrooms, trimmed, wiped and sliced	4oz mushrooms, trimmed, wiped and sliced
Salt and freshly ground black pepper	Salt and freshly ground black pepper

You need really young turnips for this dish which is good enough to serve as a separate vegetable course before the main dish.
Cut the prepared turnips into 6mm (¼in) thick slices and boil in salted water for 10 minutes. Drain and keep hot. Meanwhile, melt 40g (1½oz) of the butter and fry the bacon and mushrooms for about 5 minutes. Season. Add the turnip, cover with a lid, and cook gently 5–10 minutes. Lift out turnip slices, arrange on a heated dish, and pour over the mushrooms and bacon. Serve hot with the remaining butter on top.
Serves 4–6

Peas with Mushrooms

Metric	Imperial
Peas, fresh or frozen for 4 people	Peas, fresh or frozen for 4 people
1–2 sprigs fresh rosemary	1–2 sprigs fresh rosemary
1 × 5ml spoon sugar	1tsp sugar
25g butter	1oz butter
Very small onion, chopped	Very small onion, chopped
125g mushrooms, sliced	4oz mushrooms, sliced
Salt and freshly ground black pepper	Salt and freshly ground black pepper
3 × 15ml spoons single cream	3tbsps single cream

Cook the peas in boiling salted water, with the rosemary, until soft. Drain and sprinkle with the sugar. Meanwhile, melt the butter, cook the onion until soft, add mushrooms and seasoning and cook until the mushrooms are tender. Mix with the peas, put into a heated serving dish and trickle the cream over.
Serves 4

Braised Fennel

Metric	Imperial
4 small or 2 large bulbous stems Florentine fennel	4 small or 2 large bulbous stems Florentine fennel
Boiling chicken stock	Boiling chicken stock
25g butter	1oz butter
Salt and freshly ground black pepper	Salt and freshly ground black pepper

Fennel has a strong flavour and goes well with roast meat.
Cut the fennel into halves downwards and wash well. Put into boiling stock to cover, and simmer about 10 minutes. Drain. Put into a casserole, put pats of butter on top, season, cover with a lid and put into the oven underneath the roast for 20–30 minutes, according to size.
Serves 4

Roast lamb with turnips and mushrooms and braised fennel

Red Cabbage Allemande*

Metric
Approx. ½kg red cabbage, trimmed and sliced
1 × 15ml spoon sugar
1 × 5ml spoon salt
2 × 15ml spoons red wine vinegar
25g butter
1 large onion, sliced
1 medium cooking apple, peeled, cored and sliced
300ml beef stock
4 crushed juniper berries
Freshly ground black pepper
1–2 × 15ml spoons redcurrant jelly

Imperial
Approx. 1lb red cabbage, trimmed and sliced
1tbsp sugar
1tsp salt
2tbsps red wine vinegar
1oz butter
1 large onion, sliced
1 medium cooking apple, peeled, cored and sliced
½ pint beef stock
4 crushed juniper berries
Freshly ground black pepper
1–2tbsps redcurrant jelly

This is very good served with the more fatty meats and poultry such as pork, duck and goose.

Put the prepared red cabbage into a large basin. Mix the sugar, salt and vinegar and when sugar and salt are dissolved pour over the cabbage and toss to coat evenly. Leave about ½ hour. Melt the butter, add the onion and apple and toss together until the butter is absorbed. Add the cabbage, beef stock and juniper berries, bring to the boil, cover and simmer for 45 minutes. Remove lid and cook a further 15 minutes or until the cabbage is tender and most of the liquid has evaporated. Add pepper and the redcurrant jelly to taste. Heat and stir until the jelly has dissolved.

To freeze After the 45 minute simmering, cool quickly, transfer to containers, seal, label and freeze.

To serve Put frozen block into a strong pan over low heat, with the lid on until thawed. Then heat in an uncovered pan to evaporate the liquid, and proceed as above.

Serves 4

Carrot Ring

Metric
¾kg carrots, peeled and chopped
3 eggs, separated
Good pinch dry mustard
1 × 15ml spoon grated onion
1 × 5ml spoon paprika
Salt and freshly ground black pepper
50g fresh white breadcrumbs

Imperial
1½lb carrots, peeled and chopped
3 eggs, separated
Good pinch dry mustard
1tbsp grated onion
1tsp paprika
Salt and freshly ground black pepper
2oz fresh white breadcrumbs

Cook the carrots in boiling salted water until tender. Drain and mash. Work in the egg yolks, one at a time, mustard, onion, paprika, seasoning and breadcrumbs. Whisk the egg whites until very stiff and dry and fold into the carrots. Grease a 1.1–1.4 litre (2–2½ pint) ring mould and put a strip of paper in the bottom to help turning out. Put the carrot mixture into the ring mould and stand in a tin of hot water. Cover all with aluminium foil and bake for 30 minutes at 190°C/375°F, Gas Mark 5. Turn out on to a heated dish.

To serve Fill the centre of the ring with some green vegetable such as broccoli, whole or sliced beans, peas, leeks or tiny, cooked mushrooms and onions. *Or*, add chopped poultry or shellfish to mushroom sauce and use to fill the centre.

Serves 4

Chinese Cabbage with Onions and Tomatoes

Metric
1 medium head Chinese cabbage, washed and quartered
50g butter
150ml chicken stock
Salt and freshly ground black pepper
1 medium onion, thinly sliced
1 clove garlic, crushed
125g tomatoes, skinned, seeded and chopped
1 × 5ml spoon mixed dried herbs

Imperial
1 medium head Chinese cabbage, washed and quartered
2oz butter
¼ pint chicken stock
Salt and freshly ground black pepper
1 medium onion, thinly sliced
1 clove garlic, crushed
4oz tomatoes, skinned, seeded and chopped
1tsp mixed dried herbs

This popular vegetable is cooked in the same way as cabbage but it does not have the strong smell often associated with boiled cabbage.

Put the quartered cabbage into boiling, salted water, boil 5 minutes and drain well. Melt 25g (1oz) butter in a pan just big enough to take the cabbage quarters in one layer. Put in the cabbage, stock and seasoning, cover and cook slowly until the cabbage is cooked (10–15 minutes). Meanwhile, melt remaining butter in a pan, add the onion and cook slowly until soft. Add the garlic, tomatoes, herbs and seasoning and cook a further 5 minutes. Strain liquid from cabbage into the tomato mixture and boil rapidly until tomato mixture is a thickish sauce. Put cabbage into a heated dish and pour tomato mixture on top.

Serves 4

Peas Bonne Femme

Metric
3–4 rashers streaky bacon, rinded and chopped
18–24 small white onions, peeled
1 × 15ml spoon flour
450ml chicken stock
Salt and pepper
Peas, fresh or frozen, for 4 people
1 × 15ml spoon melted butter
Chopped parsley

Imperial
3–4 rashers streaky bacon, rinded and chopped
18–24 small white onions, peeled
1tbsp flour
¾ pint chicken stock
Salt and pepper
Peas, fresh or frozen, for 4 people
1tbsp melted butter
Chopped parsley

Peas are one of our most popular vegetables and freeze very well, so this dish can be served at any time.
Put the prepared bacon into a dry, hot frying pan and, as the fat begins to run, put in the onions and fry carefully until they are golden brown. Lift out bacon and onions with a slotted spoon and pour out any fat in excess of 1 × 15ml spoon (1tbsp). Mix flour into retained fat and cook a few minutes. Add stock and seasoning. Heat and stir to make a smooth sauce; simmer 5 minutes. Add bacon and onions and cook a further 5 minutes (if using frozen peas extend this time to 10 minutes). Add peas and cook until tender. Just before serving, stir in the butter, put into a hot serving dish and sprinkle with chopped parsley.
Serves 4

French Beans with Egg and Lemon Sauce

Metric
½kg small whole French beans, fresh or frozen
25g butter
25g flour
300ml chicken stock
Salt and pepper
2 eggs
Juice of 1 large or 2 smaller lemons

Imperial
1lb small whole French beans, fresh or frozen
1oz butter
1oz flour
½ pint chicken stock
Salt and pepper
2 eggs
Juice of 1 large or 2 smaller lemons

This is a delicious way of serving tiny French beans and it looks very attractive. Try it with fish or chicken.
Cook the beans in boiling salted water until tender. Drain and put on to a heated flattish dish. Keep hot. Melt the butter and stir in the flour. Cook for 1 minute, then stir in the stock and seasoning. Bring to the boil and simmer, stirring, until thick and smooth. Beat the eggs until light and frothy, beat in the lemon juice and then stir in 3 tbsps of the sauce, one at a time. Return to pan, heat and stir to cook eggs, but do not boil. Test to see if enough lemon has been added and pour the sauce in a long stripe over the centre of the beans.
Serves 4

Asparagus Polonaise

Metric
Asparagus, fresh or frozen, for 4 people
40g butter
50g fresh white breadcrumbs
Salt and pepper
2 hard-boiled eggs, chopped

Imperial
Asparagus, fresh or frozen, for 4 people
1½oz butter
2oz fresh white breadcrumbs
Salt and pepper
2 hard-boiled eggs, chopped

Polonaise is a popular way of finishing many vegetables. Try this topping with Brussels sprouts, cauliflower, leeks or new potatoes as well.
Cook the asparagus carefully in boiling salted water until tender. Ideally this should be done with the asparagus in a special cage which holds the stalks upright with the green tops out of the water. Drain and arrange on a heated dish. Meanwhile, melt the butter, add the breadcrumbs and fry, carefully, until crisp and golden. Stir in the eggs and seasoning and heat through, then sprinkle over the asparagus.
Serves 4

Creamed Spinach

Metric
½kg spinach
5 × 15ml spoons soured cream
2 × 15ml spoons melted butter
1–2 × 15ml spoons grated horseradish
Salt and pepper
1 × 2.5ml spoon chopped fresh tarragon

Imperial
1lb spinach
5tbsps soured cream
2tbsps melted butter
1–2tbsps grated horseradish
Salt and pepper
½tsp chopped fresh tarragon

Weigh the spinach with the centre stalk removed. Wash it and put into a pan with the water clinging to its leaves, cover and cook 5–10 minutes until soft. Drain well, pressing out as much moisture as possible, and chop. Return to the pan with remaining ingredients and heat while stirring. Serve in a heated dish and, if liked, put a little soured cream on as a decoration or scatter with fried croûtons.
    Frozen spinach can also be used.
Serves 4

French beans with egg and lemon sauce accompany a roast chicken

Kohlrabi in Butter

Metric	Imperial
½kg kohlrabi, peeled and thinly sliced	1lb kohlrabi, peeled and thinly sliced
50g butter	2oz butter
2 × 15ml spoons water	2tbsps water
Salt and pepper	Salt and pepper
Chopped parsley	Chopped parsley

Kohlrabi has a delicate turnip flavour and is best used when young and small.

Put the kohlrabi slices into a pan with the butter, water and seasoning. Bring to the boil, cover with the lid and cook slowly for about 10 minutes until almost tender. Remove the lid and cook a further 5 minutes to evaporate any remaining water. Transfer to a heated dish and sprinkle with the parsley.

Serves 4

Cabbage with Gruyère Cheese

Metric	Imperial
¾–1kg white or savoy cabbage, quartered	1½–2lb white or savoy cabbage, quartered
Bechamel sauce:	*Bechamel sauce:*
300ml milk	½ pint milk
½ small onion	½ small onion
6 white peppercorns	6 white peppercorns
½ bayleaf	½ bayleaf
½ blade mace	½ blade mace
Few sprigs fresh thyme	Few sprigs fresh thyme
15g butter	½oz butter
15g flour	½oz flour
Salt	Salt
125g Gruyère cheese, grated	4oz Gruyère cheese, grated

Drop the prepared cabbage into boiling salted water and simmer 15 minutes. Drain and shred finely.

To make the sauce put the milk, onion, peppercorns, bayleaf, mace and thyme into a pan and simmer 15 minutes. Strain. Melt the butter and stir in the flour. Cook, stirring, for 1 minute. Stir in the strained milk and salt. Bring to the boil and simmer, stirring, until thick and smooth.

Put half the cabbage into a greased baking dish, coat with half the sauce and sprinkle with half the cheese. Repeat the layers. Put into a hot oven, 220°C/425°F, Gas Mark 7 for 20 minutes or until browned. If liked, mix crisply fried breadcrumbs with the cheese to add 'crunch'.

Serves 4

Marrow with Dill

Metric	Imperial
25g butter	1oz butter
2 shallots, chopped	2 shallots, chopped
50g mushrooms, sliced	2oz mushrooms, sliced
450g marrow, peeled, seeded and cubed	1lb marrow, peeled, seeded and cubed
Salt and freshly ground black pepper	Salt and freshly ground black pepper
Chopped fresh dill	Chopped fresh dill

Marrow benefits from the addition of a little extra flavour. It needs no extra liquid in cooking or its flavour will be lost.

Melt the butter and cook the prepared shallots slowly for a few minutes. Add the mushrooms and cook for a further 3 minutes. Add the marrow to the pan with salt and pepper, stir, cover with lid and cook slowly for 15 minutes, stirring once or twice. If the mixture in the pan is too moist, uncover, increase the heat and evaporate some of the liquid. Pour into a heated dish and sprinkle with chopped dill. An alternative garnish is chopped tomato flesh.

Serves 4

Salsify in Cream Sauce

Metric	Imperial
½–¾kg salsify	1–1½lb salsify
Lemon juice	Lemon juice
Cream sauce:	*Cream sauce:*
25g butter	1oz butter
25g flour	1oz flour
450ml mixed milk and cream	¾ pint mixed milk and cream
Salt and pepper	Salt and pepper
225g cooked peas, fresh or frozen	½lb cooked peas, fresh or frozen
1 × 15ml spoon chopped fresh mint	1tbsp chopped fresh mint

Sometimes called 'Poor Man's Asparagus', salsify should be used when young and not too large.

Scrape the salsify and rub with lemon juice to prevent discoloration. Cut into 5cm (2in) lengths, drop into boiling salted water and simmer 20 minutes or until tender. Drain. Meanwhile, melt the butter and stir in the flour. Cook, stirring, for 1 minute. Stir in the milk and cream and seasoning. Bring to the boil and simmer, stirring, until thick and smooth. The proportion of milk to cream depends upon personal taste. Add the salsify and peas to the sauce. Transfer to a heated dish and sprinkle with mint.

Serves 4

Accompaniments

Damson Sauce

Metric	Imperial
2kg damsons	4lb damsons
½kg onions, chopped	1lb onions, chopped
600ml vinegar	1 pint vinegar
25g salt	1oz salt
5g ground cinnamon	¼oz ground cinnamon
15g fresh root ginger, bruised	½oz fresh root ginger, bruised
5g whole allspice	¼oz whole allspice
225g sugar	½lb sugar

Plums can be used instead of damsons in which case the amount of cinnamon must be reduced.
Wash the damsons and put into a pan with the prepared onions, vinegar, salt, cinnamon and the ginger and allspice tied in muslin. Simmer about 45 minutes, stirring from time to time, to break up the flesh of the damsons. Remove spices and rub the pulp through a sieve. Return to the rinsed pan, add the sugar and simmer a further 45 minutes or until sauce is a thick pouring consistency. Pour into heated jars and seal while hot. Allow to mature for 1 to 2 months before using.
Makes about 1½ pints

Horseradish Sauce with Walnuts

Metric	Imperial
2 × 15ml spoons horseradish, freshly grated	2tbsps horseradish, freshly grated
150ml soured cream	¼ pint soured cream
12 walnut halves, finely chopped	12 walnut halves, finely chopped
Salt and pepper	Salt and pepper

A new version of an old favourite to serve with the Sunday roast beef joint. It is also good with cold, pickled mackerel and herrings.
Fold the freshly prepared horseradish into the soured cream with the nuts and seasoning. Taste and add a little more horseradish if necessary.
Makes about 300ml (½ pint) sauce

Pesto or Pistou

Metric	Imperial
50g fresh basil leaves	2oz fresh basil leaves
3 cloves garlic, peeled	3 cloves garlic, peeled
Salt	Salt
125g Gruyère cheese	4oz Gruyère cheese
3 × 15ml spoons olive oil	3tbsps olive oil

A savoury sauce from the areas of the Italian and French Rivieras. Add 1 × 15ml spoon (1tbsp) or more to vegetable soups such as minestrone and to meat sauces served with pasta.
Put the basil, garlic and salt into a mortar and pound together very well. Cut the cheese into very thin strips (with a potato peeler) and add to the mortar alternately with the oil, pounding well between each addition. This should give a creamy sauce which is just a little difficult to pour. If liked, work in 25g (1oz) chopped walnuts.
Makes 4–6 × 15ml spoons (4–5 tbsps) sauce

Tarragon and Lemon Dressing

Metric	Imperial
Grated rind of ½ lemon	Grated rind of ½ lemon
150ml olive oil	¼ pint olive oil
3 × 15ml spoons lemon juice	3tbsps lemon juice
1 × 5ml spoon sugar	1tsp sugar
1 × 5ml spoon chopped fresh tarragon	1tsp chopped fresh tarragon
Salt and pepper	Salt and pepper

This can be used as a dressing for salads to serve with chicken, veal, rabbit, fish and shellfish. It can also be used as a marinade for those meats and fishes.
Mix the lemon rind and oil together with a wooden spoon. Beat in the lemon juice, sugar, tarragon, salt and pepper, in that order.
Makes 225ml (8floz) dressing

Sauces (clockwise): pesto, horseradish, damson, tarragon and lemon dressing

Walnut and Herb Cheese Spread

Metric	Imperial
225g cream cheese	½lb cream cheese
3 × 15ml spoons soured cream	3tbsps soured cream
40g walnuts, finely chopped	1½oz walnuts, finely chopped
2 × 5ml spoons chopped fresh chives	2tsps chopped fresh chives
2 × 5ml spoons chopped fresh tarragon or thyme	2tsps chopped fresh tarragon or thyme
Salt	Salt
Pinch of cayenne pepper	Pinch of cayenne pepper

*A good spread to use in sandwiches and to spread on savoury scones.
Spread thickly on bread it can form a very good base for open sandwiches with a variety of toppings.*

Soften the cream cheese with a wooden spoon and then work in the other ingredients in the order given.

Makes 275g (10oz) spread

Hot Tomato Sauce

Metric	Imperial
1½kg ripe tomatoes	3lb ripe tomatoes
450ml vinegar	¾ pint vinegar
125g onions, chopped	4oz onions, chopped
2 cloves garlic, crushed	2 cloves garlic, crushed
2 dried or 4 fresh chillis	2 dried or 4 fresh chillis
20g salt	¾oz salt
75g granulated sugar	3oz granulated sugar
Pinch of cayenne pepper	Pinch of cayenne pepper
1 medium red pepper, seeded and sliced	1 medium red pepper, seeded and sliced
Very small piece fresh root ginger, bruised	Very small piece fresh root ginger, bruised

*There are three quite definite stages in the making of this sauce:
1) Softening the tomatoes; 2) Cooking with the flavourings;
3) Cooking to thicken the sauce.*

Put the tomatoes into a casserole, cover with the lid and cook at 140°C/275°F, mark 1 for 1½ hours or until very soft. Transfer to a pan, add all the other ingredients, cover with a lid and cook for 1 hour. Remove chillis and ginger and rub through a non-metal sieve. If possible, put through a blender first. Return to the rinsed pan and cook for a further hour or until thick. Pour into heated jars and seal while still hot. Leave for 1–2 months to mature.

Makes about 900ml (1½ pints)

Fresh Vegetable Sauce

Metric	Imperial
½ red or green pepper, seeded and chopped	½ red or green pepper, seeded and chopped
1 very small onion, chopped	1 very small onion, chopped
1 stalk celery, chopped	1 stalk celery, chopped
3 tomatoes, skinned and chopped	3 tomatoes, skinned and chopped
1 sprig of thyme	1 sprig of thyme
2 × 15ml spoons chopped parsley	2tbsps chopped parsley
Salt and pepper	Salt and pepper
1 clove garlic, crushed, optional	1 clove garlic, crushed, optional
Thin strip lemon rind	Thin strip lemon rind

This sauce should be used as soon as possible after preparation. It is good served with bacon and fried eggs, boiled potatoes, braised vegetables and most fried foods.

Put all the ingredients into a blender and blend for 1 minute. Turn out and chill. This sauce can also be made by chopping all the ingredients very, very finely.

Makes 150ml (¼ pint) sauce

Celery, Tomato and Apple Stuffing

Metric	Imperial
25g butter	1oz butter
1 large onion, chopped	1 large onion, chopped
2 stalks celery, chopped	2 stalks celery, chopped
2 large cooking apples, peeled cored and sliced	2 large cooking apples, peeled, cored and sliced
175g fresh breadcrumbs	6oz fresh breadcrumbs
15g caster sugar	½oz caster sugar
1 × 15ml spoon chopped fresh thyme	1tbsp chopped fresh thyme
2 × 5ml spoons chopped parsley	2tsps chopped parsley
Salt and pepper	Salt and pepper
2 large tomatoes, skinned and chopped	2 large tomatoes, skinned and chopped

Use to stuff a duck or boned joint of pork; double the quantities for goose.

Melt the butter and fry the onion and celery until lightly browned. Stir in the prepared apples and cook for 5 minutes. Mix the breadcrumbs, sugar and herbs together; season with salt and pepper. Add the onion mixture and chopped tomatoes and mix well.

(Clockwise): hot tomato sauce, walnut and herb cheese spread, celery, tomato and apple stuffing, fresh vegetable sauce

Grated Carrot Stuffing

Metric
50g fresh white breadcrumbs
50g pork fat, minced
1 small carrot, peeled and
  grated
½ small onion, grated
50g stewed apricots, chopped
1 × 2.5ml spoon ground ginger
Salt and pepper
Approx. 2 × 15ml spoons
  apricot juice

Imperial
2oz fresh white breadcrumbs
2oz pork fat, minced
1 small carrot, peeled and
  grated
½ small onion, grated
2oz stewed apricots, chopped
½tsp ground ginger
Salt and pepper
Approx. 2tbsps apricot juice

A good stuffing for meat, especially for liver or chicken.
Mix all the ingredients together, adding enough apricot juice to moisten the mixture so it will hold together.
Makes 275g (10oz) stuffing

Rouget Sauce*

Metric
225g red currants, washed
225g raspberries, washed
150g caster sugar
2 × 5ml spoons arrowroot
1 × 15ml spoon cold water

Imperial
½lb red currants, washed
½lb raspberries, washed
5oz caster sugar
2tsps arrowroot
1tbsp water

A simple but effective sauce, this can be used in a variety of sweet dishes. It is especially good with icecream and can replace the traditional sauce in peach melba.
Simmer the redcurrants, raspberries and sugar together for 10–12 minutes. Cool a little and then blend until smooth. Return to the rinsed pan with the arrowroot mixed to a smooth paste with the water. Bring to the boil and boil, stirring, for 3 minutes. Allow to cool, stirring from time to time to prevent a skin forming.
To freeze: Pour into small containers, seal and freeze.
To thaw: In the refrigerator for 3–4 hours. Beat before using.
Makes 600ml (1 pint) sauce

Rice, Nut and Carrot Stuffing

Metric
25g butter
50g bacon, rinded and
  chopped
1 large onion, chopped
50g rice, cooked
1 chicken liver, chopped
50g hazelnuts, chopped
2 large carrots, grated
1 × 15ml spoon chopped fresh
  marjoram
Salt and pepper
Beaten egg to bind

Imperial
1oz butter
2oz bacon, rinded and
  chopped
1 large onion, chopped
2oz rice, cooked
1 chicken liver, chopped
2oz hazelnuts, chopped
2 large carrots, grated
1 tbsp chopped fresh
  marjoram
Salt and pepper
Beaten egg to bind

Use with poultry, pork or lamb.
Melt the butter and fry the bacon and onion for 5–7 minutes until lightly browned. Mix in the rice, chicken liver, nuts and carrots together, add the marjoram and season. Use a little beaten egg to bind the ingredients together.
Makes 275g (10oz) stuffing

Fresh Apricot Stuffing

Metric
175g fresh apricots, stoned
100g lamb's liver, lightly fried
75g rice, boiled
1 small onion, grated
2 × 15ml spoons chopped
  parsley
Salt and pepper

Imperial
6oz fresh apricots, stoned
4oz lamb's liver, lightly fried
3oz rice, boiled
1 small onion, grated
2tbsps chopped parsley
Salt and pepper

This stuffing is sufficient for a crown roast of lamb and gives a delicious extra flavour to the meat. It is, of course, good with any cut of lamb.
Chop the apricots and the liver together. Fold in the rice, grated onion, parsley and seasonings. For variation, fresh white breadcrumbs can replace the rice. The amount will depend upon the ripeness of the fruit but start with 75g (3oz).

(Clockwise): grated carrot stuffing, rice and carrot stuffing, rouget sauce

Herb Butters*

Metric	Imperial
125g butter	4oz butter
2–4 × 5ml spoons chopped fresh herbs, or 1–2 × 5ml spoons dried herbs	2–4tsps chopped fresh herbs, or 1–2tsps dried herbs
Lemon juice	Lemon juice

A thin round of flavoured butter adds a delightful touch to many grilled foods. Use to butter the bread for open sandwiches, put on baked jacket potatoes, serve with hot toast, melt small quantities for tossing cooked vegetables, etc.

Allow the butter to soften in a warm kitchen, then cream with a wooden spoon. Gradually beat in the herbs (if using dried ones soak them for ½ hour in a little lemon juice). Cream in a little lemon juice. Form into a roll 2.5–4cm in diameter (1–1½in diameter), wrap in a plastic film and leave 2–4 hours for the flavours to blend. *Or* make into a flat pack and cut into cubes for serving.

To freeze Cut roll into slices and re-form with small pieces of greaseproof paper to separate. Overwrap. Store up to 3 months.

To thaw Separate pieces and leave on a plate for about ½ hour.

Makes 125g (4oz) butter

Herbs to use Experiment with butters made with single herbs or by mixing two or three. Other flavours can be added, e.g. anchovy with parsley, tomato with basil. Garlic butter is good and so is butter containing chopped spring onions, and other herbs may be mixed with these two flavours.

Garlic Bread with Herbs

Metric	Imperial
75g butter	3oz butter
2–4 cloves garlic, crushed	2–4 cloves garlic, crushed
2–4 × 5ml spoons chopped fresh herbs, or 1–2 × 5ml spoons dried herbs	2–4tsps chopped fresh herbs, or 1–2tsps dried herbs
1 loaf French bread	1 loaf French bread

Use butter softened in a warm kitchen. Beat with a wooden spoon, gradually beating in the garlic and herbs. Slice the loaf downwards nearly through and spread each slice with a little butter. Wrap tightly in foil and, if possible, allow to stand for an hour or so before baking. Bake at 200°C/400°F, Gas Mark 6 for 10–15 minutes. Serve hot or cold with appropriate starters or soups.

Serves 4–6

Mayonnaise Verte

Metric	Imperial
50g sorrel	2oz sorrel
25g spinach	1oz spinach
25g parsley or chervil	1oz parsley or chervil
300ml mayonnaise	½ pint mayonnaise

Sorrel is treated in the same way as spinach but it has a slightly bitter flavour, which makes this mayonnaise an excellent one to serve with fish, especially shellfish.

After removing thick stems cook the sorrel, spinach and parsley or chervil into boiling water for about 2 minutes. Strain and squeeze out as much liquid as possible. Chop well and dry in absorbent kitchen paper. Stir into the mayonnaise.

Makes 300ml (½ pint) mayonnaise

Herb Bread

Metric	Imperial
450g wholemeal flour	1lb wholemeal flour
1 × 5ml spoon salt	1tsp salt
2 × 15ml spoons chopped fresh herbs	2tbsps chopped fresh herbs
1 medium onion, chopped and lightly fried, optional	1 medium onion, chopped and lightly fried, optional
Scant 450ml warm water	Scant ¾ pint warm water
2 × 5ml spoons dried yeast	2tsps dried yeast
1 × 5ml spoon sugar	1tsp sugar

Herb breads are delicious served with savoury foods such as a hot, thick vegetable soup for a light mid-day or supper dish. Serve, instead of potatoes, with meat or poultry roasts, casseroles and stews. They are very good with strongly flavoured cheeses.

Sift the flour and salt into a bowl. Mix in the herbs and the onion, if used. Put into a warm place.

Put ¼ pint of the water into a small basin and stir in the yeast and sugar. Leave in a warm place until frothy (about 20 minutes). Pour into the centre of the flour with the remaining water and mix well. Turn out on to a floured board and knead for about 3 minutes. Put into a well-greased loaf tin, put into a plastic bag, seal to exclude draughts and leave in a warm place to rise. When the dough fills the tin, bake at 200°C, 425°F, Gas Mark 7 for 45 minutes.

Makes 1 loaf

Desserts

Loganberry Cheesecake

Metric	Imperial
125g digestive biscuit crumbs	4oz digestive biscuit crumbs
25g demerara sugar	1oz demerara sugar
25g nuts, chopped	1oz nuts, chopped
50g butter, melted	2oz butter, melted
2 eggs, separated	2 eggs, separated
75g sugar	3oz sugar
Pinch of salt	Pinch of salt
225g loganberries	½lb loganberries
15g powdered unflavoured gelatine	½oz powdered unflavoured gelatine
3 × 15ml spoons water	3tbsps water
350g cottage cheese, sieved	¾lb cottage cheese, sieved
150ml double cream, whipped until stiff	¼ pint double cream, whipped until stiff
Extra loganberries	Extra loganberries

Mix the crumbs, demerara sugar, nuts and butter together. Press firmly into the base of a 20cm (8in) spring form or loose-bottomed tin, covered with a circle of foil. Whisk the egg yolks, sugar and salt in a basin over a pan of hot, but not boiling, water until thick and creamy and the whisk leaves a definite trail. Cool, whisking occasionally. Rub the loganberries through a sieve. Dissolve the gelatine in the water. Whisk the egg whites until stiff. Mix the yolks, fruit, gelatine and cottage cheese together and fold in the whites and half the cream. Pour into the prepared tin and smooth over the top. When set, decorate with the reserved cream and decorate with the extra fruit.
Serves 8–10

Plum Slices*

Metric	Imperial
Shortcrust pastry made from 175g flour and 75g fat	Shortcrust pastry made from 6oz flour and 3oz fat
½kg ripe plums, halved and stoned	1lb ripe plums, halved and stoned
2 eggs, separated	2 eggs, separated
65g caster sugar	2½oz caster sugar
50g self-raising flour	2oz self-raising flour
Pinch of salt	Pinch of salt
Vanilla essence	Vanilla essence
Icing sugar	Icing sugar

Use the pastry to line a tin approx. 18cm × 23cm (7in × 9in). Prick the base. Bake blind for 15 minutes at 200°C/400°F, Gas Mark 6, until very lightly browned. Arrange the plum halves on the pastry with the cut sides uppermost. If they are not sweet enough, dip them in sugar first. Whisk the egg whites until very stiff, whisk in the yolks, one at a time, and then the sugar, keeping the mixture as stiff as possible. Fold in the flour, sifted with the salt, and a few drops of vanilla essence. Spread evenly over the plums, and bake for 35–40 minutes, or until the sponge is well risen and golden brown. Turn out on to a wire tray and allow to cool. Sprinkle with icing sugar before serving with cream or custard.
To freeze Wrap in foil or place in a polythene bag, seal, label and freeze.
To serve Place the frozen sponge in a hot oven, 220°C/425°F, Gas Mark 7, for 20 minutes, then reduce temperature to moderate, 180°C/350°F, Gas Mark 4, for a further 15–20 minutes. Serve as above.
Serves 6

Blackberry and Apple Sponge

Metric	Imperial
125g butter	4oz butter
125g caster sugar	4oz caster sugar
2 eggs, beaten	2 eggs, beaten
Few drops vanilla essence	Few drops vanilla essence
175g self-raising flour, sifted	6oz self-raising flour, sifted
450g cooking apples, peeled, cored, sliced and cooked	1lb cooking apples, peeled, cored, sliced and cooked
225g blackberries, cooked	½lb blackberries, cooked
Juice of ½ lemon	Juice of ½ lemon
125g sugar	4oz sugar

Cream the butter and caster sugar together until light and fluffy. Gradually add the beaten eggs and essence, beating well between each addition. Using a metal spoon, fold in the flour. Mix the fruit, lemon juice and sugar together. Put 4 × 15ml spoons (4tbsps) in the bottom of a greased 700g (1½lb) pudding basin. Spoon in the sponge mixture, cover with greased greaseproof paper or foil and secure with string. Steam for 1½ hours. Reheat rest of apple and blackberry mixture and serve with pudding.
Serves 4

Stuffed Apple Jelly

Metric	Imperial
6 small sweet dessert apples	6 small sweet dessert apples
600ml water	1 pint water
50g sugar	2oz sugar
15g angelica, chopped	½oz angelica, chopped
25g glacé cherries, chopped	1oz glacé cherries, chopped
25g nuts, chopped	1oz nuts, chopped
Honey	Honey
Packet of orange or greengage jelly	Packet of orange or greengage jelly
150ml double cream	¼ pint double cream

Peel and core the apples and put at once into the water and sugar at simmering point. Cover the pan and simmer carefully for about 10 minutes, then remove from heat and leave until the apples are soft but still whole. This will take a further 10–15 minutes. Lift out and arrange in serving dish. Mix the angelica, cherries and nuts with a little honey, and use to stuff the apples. Make up the jelly as directed on the packet, using the syrup in which the apples were cooked. When almost set, spoon it over the apples until each is completely coated; pour the rest into the dish. Whisk the cream until stiff and sweeten to taste with a little sugar. Use the cream to decorate the top of the apples.

For a more substantial sweet, put a layer of sponge or plain cake in the bottom of the dish.
Serves 6

Coffee and Walnut Icecream*

Metric	Imperial
150ml milk	¼ pint milk
40g sugar	1½oz sugar
2 egg yolks	2 egg yolks
2 × 5ml spoons powdered coffee, dissolved in 2 × 5ml spoons hot water	2tsps powdered coffee, dissolved in 2tsps hot water
150ml double cream, lightly whipped	¼ pint double cream, lightly whipped
75g walnuts, chopped	3oz walnuts, chopped

Set the freezer or refrigerator at its lowest setting. Heat the milk and sugar together and pour on to the egg yolks, stirring well. Return the mixture to the pan and cook over very gentle heat, stirring all the time until the custard thickens. Strain and add the dissolved coffee. Allow the mixture to cool, then fold in the lightly whipped cream and chopped walnuts. Pour into an ice-cube tray, and freeze. When the icecream is half set, remove from the freezer, turn into a cool bowl, and whisk well. Return to the tray and allow to freeze until set.
Serves 4

Strawberry Sorbet*

Metric	Imperial
225g loaf or granulated sugar	½lb loaf or granulated sugar
600ml water	1 pint water
700g strawberries	1½lb strawberries
2 egg whites	2 egg whites
Food colouring if necessary	Food colouring if necessary

Set the freezer or refrigerator at its lowest setting. Dissolve the sugar in the water, gradually bring to the boil, and boil steadily for 10 minutes, or until the temperature is 104°C/220°F. Allow to cool. Pass the fruit through a sieve, or purée in a blender, make up to 600ml (1 pint) with water, if necessary. Add to the syrup. Pour into an ice tray and half freeze. Remove from freezer and beat well. Fold in the stiffly beaten egg whites. If necessary, stir in a little red food colouring. Return to the tray and continue freezing.
Serves 4–6

Special Fruit Trifle

Metric	Imperial
125g sponge cake	4oz sponge cake
2–3 × 15ml spoons dry white wine	2–3tbsps dry white wine
225g strawberries, fresh or frozen and thawed	½lb strawberries, fresh or frozen, thawed
225g raspberries, fresh or frozen and thawed	½lb raspberries, fresh or frozen, thawed
125g caster sugar	4oz caster sugar
300ml made custard	½ pint made custard
300ml double cream, whipped	½ pint double cream, whipped
75–125g mixed raspberries and strawberries to decorate	3–4oz mixed raspberries and strawberries to decorate

Cut up the sponge cake and use to line the base of a 20cm (8in) glass bowl. Spoon over the wine, ensuring that all the sponge is covered. Allow to stand for 20 minutes. Mix the strawberries, raspberries and sugar together; leave until the sugar is absorbed by the fruit, about 30 minutes. Arrange the fruit on top of the sponge cake. Spoon over the custard. Pipe the whipped cream in rosettes on top, and decorate with the whole strawberries and raspberries.
Serves 4–6

Somerset Flan

Metric
Shortcrust pastry made from
    175g flour and 75g fat
450ml water
140g sugar
½kg cooking apples
2 eggs
25g flour
25g almonds, chopped
Icing sugar

Imperial
Shortcrust pastry made from
    6oz flour and 3oz fat
¾ pint water
5½oz sugar
1lb cooking apples
2 eggs
1oz flour
1oz almonds, chopped
Icing sugar

Use the pastry to line an 18cm (7in) fluted flan ring. Line with greaseproof paper or foil, fill with beans and bake blind for 25 minutes at 200°C/400°F, Gas Mark 6, removing beans and paper after about 15 minutes. Bring the water to the boil and add 75g (3oz) of the sugar. Peel and core the apples, cut into 4, 6 or 8 sections according to size, and drop immediately into the syrup. Cook until soft but not broken, drain and leave until cold. Measure syrup, and if necessary make up to 300ml (½ pint) with hot water. Beat the eggs and remaining sugar together, then beat in flour. Add hot syrup a little at a time, return to the pan, and heat and stir until thick. Arrange apples in flan case and pour egg mixture over. Smooth the top, sprinkle with almonds and cover with icing sugar. Brown under a hot grill, and serve hot or cold, with cream if liked.
Serves 6

Pears in Red Wine*

Metric
225g sugar
5cm cinnamon stick
2 cloves
2 strips orange peel
2 strips lemon peel
½ bottle red wine
6 firm pears
2 × 5ml spoons arrowroot

Imperial
½lb sugar
2in cinnamon stick
2 cloves
2 strips orange peel
2 strips lemon peel
½ bottle red wine
6 firm pears
2tsps arrowroot

Put the sugar, cinnamon, cloves, peel and wine in a pan, and heat slowly; increase heat and boil for 1 minute. Peel the pears, leaving stalks on but removing the 'eye' from the bottom. Place at once in the prepared syrup. Cover pan and poach pears for about 30 minutes until tender. Remove pears from the pan, strain the syrup, check the quantity and if necessary reduce the amount to 300ml (½ pint). Mix the arrowroot with a little water, add to the syrup, and stir until boiling; then cook until quite clear. Arrange the pears in a serving dish and spoon over wine syrup. Serve cold with whipped cream.
To freeze Freeze the pears and sauce together in waxed or plastic containers and cover with a lid or foil.
To serve Thaw at room temperature for 5–6 hours.
Serves 6

Peach and Apple Soufflé*

Metric
700g cooking apples, peeled,
    cored and sliced
9 × 15ml spoons water
4 fresh ripe peaches, skinned
    and stoned
6 eggs, separated
275g caster sugar
2 × 15ml spoons lemon juice
5 × 5ml spoons powdered
    gelatine
2 × 15ml spoons orange
    liqueur
150ml single cream
Few frosted grapes

Imperial
1½lb cooking apples, peeled,
    cored and sliced
9tbsps water
4 fresh ripe peaches, skinned
    and stoned
6 eggs, separated
10oz caster sugar
2tbsps lemon juice
5tsps powdered gelatine
2tbsps orange liqueur
¼ pint single cream
Few frosted grapes

Prepare a 1.4 litre (2½ pint) soufflé dish, by tying a double band of greaseproof paper round the outside of dish, to stand 7.5cm (3in) above the rim. Stew the apples in 6 × 15ml spoons (6tbsps) of the water until soft. Cool. Put the apples and peaches through a sieve or purée in a blender. Place a bowl over a pan of hot water with the egg yolks, sugar and lemon juice; whisk until very thick and creamy. Remove from the heat and whisk until cool. Dissolve the gelatine in the remaining water, in a basin over hot water. Whisk the fruit purée, gelatine and orange liqueur into the egg mixture. Whip the cream and fold into the mixture. Finally, stiffly beat the egg whites and fold in. Turn into the prepared dish and chill until set. Using a knife, remove the paper collar from the soufflé. Decorate with frosted grapes (see page 246).
To freeze Open freeze, undecorated; when frozen put in two polythene bags, one inside the other. Seal and label. Take care that the soufflé does not get squashed.
To serve: Allow 14 hours in the refrigerator or 6–8 hours at room temperature.
Serves 6–8

Greengage Crumble*

Metric	Imperial
700g greengages, stoned	1½lb greengages, stoned
175–200g caster sugar	6–7oz caster sugar
75g butter	3oz butter
175g flour	6oz flour

Arrange the fruit in an ovenproof dish; sprinkle with 75–100g (6–7oz) of the sugar. Rub the fat into the flour until mixture resembles fine breadcrumbs. Stir in the remaining sugar. Sprinkle crumble over the fruit; use a fork to make a pretty decoration. Bake at 200°C/400°F, Gas Mark 6 for 40 minutes or until golden brown.
To freeze Leave unbaked. Cover with foil and freeze.
To serve Bake from frozen at 180°C/350°F, Gas Mark 4 for 1¼–1½ hours, until golden brown and cooked through.
Serves 4

Charlotte Russe

Metric	Imperial
150ml lemon jelly, cool but not set	¼ pint lemon jelly, cool but not set
1 tangerine, skinned and segmented	1 tangerine, skinned and segmented
Candied angelica, cut into leaves	Candied angelica, cut into leaves
22 boudoir sponge biscuits	22 boudoir sponge biscuits
1 egg white, beaten	1 egg white, beaten
15g powdered unflavoured gelatine	½oz powdered unflavoured gelatine
2 × 15ml spoons water	2tbsps water
600ml double cream, lightly whipped	1 pint double cream, lightly whipped
300ml made custard, cooled	½ pint made custard, cooled
2 × 15ml spoons dry white wine	2 tablespoons dry white wine
Rind and juice of 3 lemons	Rind and juice of 3 lemons
50–75g caster sugar	2–3oz caster sugar

Line the base of a 1.1 litre (2 pint) tin with half the jelly, and allow to set. Arrange the tangerine segments and angelica leaves in an attractive pattern on the jelly. Spoon over the remaining jelly, and allow to set. Trim the sponge biscuits, brush them with beaten egg white, and arrange round the sides of the tin. Put the gelatine and water in a basin over a pan of hot water, and dissolve. Mix the whipped cream, custard, wine, juice and rind of lemons together, and stir in the gelatine. Stir in the sugar, and pour the mixture into the prepared tin. Chill until set. Turn out on to a plate and decorate with a red ribbon.
Serves 4–6

Orange and Apricot Mousse*

Metric	Imperial
700g fresh apricots, stoned	1½lb fresh apricots, stoned
150g sugar	5oz sugar
4 × 15ml spoons water	4tbsps water
Grated rind and juice of 2 oranges	Grated rind and juice of 2 oranges
15g powdered unflavoured gelatine	½oz powdered unflavoured gelatine
150ml double cream, whipped	¼ pint double cream, whipped
3 egg whites, stiffly beaten	3 egg whites, stiffly beaten
To decorate:	*To decorate:*
150ml double cream, whipped	¼ pint double cream, whipped
1 nectarine, stoned and sliced	1 nectarine, stoned and sliced

Put the apricots in a pan, add the sugar and half the water, bring to the boil, cover and simmer for 12–15 minutes until the apricots are soft. Cool, put in a blender or rub through a sieve. Mix the purée with the orange rind and juice. Dissolve gelatine in the remaining water in a basin over a pan of hot water and stir into the fruit mixture. Fold in the cream and egg whites. Pour into a serving dish. Chill until set. Decorate with whipped cream, and slices of nectarine.
To freeze Open freeze, then wrap in foil, seal, label and return to the freezer.
To serve Thaw at room temperature for 5–6 hours. Decorate as above after thawing.
Serves 4–6

Yorkshire Apple Tart

Metric	Imperial
Shortcrust pastry made from 275g flour and 150g fat	Shortcrust pastry made from 10oz flour and 5oz fat
350g cooking apples, peeled, cored and sliced	¾lb cooking apples, peeled, cored and sliced
2 × 15ml spoons sugar	2tbsps sugar
1 × 15ml spoon water	1tbsp water
Little milk and sugar to glaze	Little milk and sugar to glaze
125g strong cheese, sliced	4oz strong cheese, sliced

Line a 20cm (8in) flan ring with two-thirds of the pastry. Fill the centre with the apples, add the sugar, and spoon over the water. Cover with the remaining pastry, and seal the edges. Brush the top with a little milk and sprinkle with sugar. Bake at 190°C/375°F, Gas Mark 5, for 20–25 minutes until the crust is firm and lightly browned. Allow to cool. Carefully remove the top crust using a sharp knife. Arrange the cheese on top of the apples. Replace the crust. Return to the oven and bake for a further 10–15 minutes until the cheese has just melted. Serve warm with whipped cream.
Serves 4–6

Rhubarb Fool

Metric
700g rhubarb, trimmed and
  cut into pieces
125–150g sugar, depending
  on taste
150ml made custard
150ml double cream, whipped
To decorate:
150ml double cream, whipped
Chopped nuts

Imperial
1½lb rhubarb, trimmed and
  cut into pieces
4–5oz sugar, depending on
  taste
¼ pint made custard
¼ pint double cream, whipped
To decorate:
¼ pint double cream, whipped
Chopped nuts

Stew the rhubarb in a little water until quite tender, about 10–12 minutes. Add the sugar to taste and cool. Rub the fruit through a sieve or purée in a blender. Stir the custard into the fruit purée. Fold in the whipped cream. Pour into individual dishes or a serving dish. Decorate with whipped cream and nuts and serve with home-made shortbread, sponge fingers, or a favourite sweet biscuit.
Serves 4

Summer Pudding*

Metric
2 × 15ml spoons water
150g sugar
450g red, black and white
  currants, washed and
  stringed
175g plain sponge cake,
  cut in thin slices
Whipped cream

Imperial
2tbsps water
5oz sugar
1lb red, black and white
  currants, washed and
  stringed
6oz plain sponge cake, cut in
  thin slices
Whipped cream

Stir the water and sugar together in a pan, and slowly bring to the boil; boil for 2 minutes. Add prepared fruit and stew gently until it is soft but still retains its shape. Cool. Use two-thirds of the sponge cake to line a 900ml (1½ pint) pudding basin and pour in the fruit and juices. Fill with the remaining sponge cake, cover with a saucer with a weight on top of the pudding and leave overnight in a cool place. Serve with whipped cream.
To freeze Remove saucer, cover with foil and freeze.
To serve Thaw at room temperature for 5–6 hours, turn out and serve with whipped cream.
Serves 4–6

Grape Crème Brûlée

Metric
600ml double cream
1 vanilla pod
6 egg yolks
4 × 15ml spoons caster sugar
225g black or white grapes,
  halved and pipped
25g icing sugar, sifted

Imperial
1 pint double cream
1 vanilla pod
6 egg yolks
4tbsps caster sugar
½lb black or white grapes,
  halved and pipped
1oz icing sugar, sifted

Put the cream and vanilla pod in a double saucepan. Cover and heat gently until just below boiling point. Remove vanilla pod. Mix the egg yolks and sugar together. Pour the cream on to the egg mixture and stir well. Return to the pan and stir until thickened; do not allow to boil. Arrange the grapes in a flameproof dish and strain over the cream and egg mixture. Put the dish into a roasting tin containing water and bake in a slow oven 150°C/300°F, Gas Mark 2 for 1–1½ hours until firm but not coloured. Cool and refrigerate for several hours, or overnight. Heat the grill and dust the top of the brûlée with the icing sugar. Put under the grill for a few seconds until the top is golden brown. Cool thoroughly and serve chilled.
Serves 4–6

Cherries Jubilee

Metric
450g dark red cherries, pitted
300ml water
4–5 × 15ml spoons sugar
2.5cm cinnamon stick
Juice and grated rind of
  ½ orange
2 × 5ml spoons cornflour
4 × 15ml spoons cognac
4 × 15ml spoons cherry
  brandy
Vanilla icecream

Imperial
1lb dark red cherries, pitted
½ pint water
4–5tbsps sugar
1in cinnamon stick
Juice and grated rind of
  ½ orange
2tsps cornflour
4tbsps cognac
4tbsps cherry brandy
Vanilla icecream

Put the cherries in a pan, add the water, bring to the boil and simmer for 2 minutes, until the cherries are tender but still whole. Add the sugar and allow to dissolve. Strain the juice and return to the pan. Add the cinnamon and orange rind. Blend the cornflour with the orange juice; add to the pan. Bring to the boil, stirring, and boil rapidly for 5 minutes, stirring occasionally until the sauce is reduced to a coating consistency. Add the cherries and heat through. Discard cinnamon stick. Heat cognac and cherry brandy and pour over cherries. Ignite, and when the flames have died down pour hot mixture over individual portions of icecream.
Serves 4

Rhubarb fool with cherries jubilee

Orange and Gooseberry Pancakes

Metric	Imperial
125g flour	4oz flour
Pinch of salt	Pinch of salt
1 egg	1 egg
300ml mixed milk and water	½ pint mixed milk and water
450g fresh or frozen and thawed gooseberries	1lb fresh or frozen and thawed gooseberries
Juice and grated rind of 1 orange	Juice and grated rind of 1 orange
75–125g sugar	3–4oz sugar
Lard or oil for frying	Lard or oil for frying

Sift the flour and salt into a bowl and make a well in the centre; break in the egg. Add half the liquid and beat the mixture until smooth. Add the remaining liquid gradually and beat well until mixed and smooth.

To make the filling put the gooseberries, orange juice and rind in a pan, heat gently and simmer 5–7 minutes until the gooseberries are tender but still hold their shape. Stir in sufficient sugar to taste.

Heat a little fat in a frying pan, making sure that all surfaces of the pan are coated; pour off any excess fat. Pour or spoon just enough batter to cover the base of the pan thinly, and cook quickly until golden brown underneath. Turn with a palette knife or toss the pancake and cook the other side until golden. Turn out on to greaseproof paper on a plate, cover and keep hot in the oven. When all the batter is used fill the pancakes with the hot filling, fold into 3 and serve at once, sprinkled generously with sugar. Serve any surplus filling in a jug.
Serves 4

Apricot Shortcake

Metric	Imperial
75g butter	3oz butter
225g self-raising flour	½lb self-raising flour
1 × 1.25ml spoon salt	¼tsp salt
75g sugar	3oz sugar
1 egg, beaten	1 egg, beaten
1–2 × 15ml spoons milk	1–2tbsps milk
350–450g fresh apricots, halved and stoned	¾–1lb fresh apricots, halved and stoned
3–4 × 15ml spoons sugar for filling	3–4tbsps sugar for filling
300ml double cream, whipped	½ pint double cream, whipped

Grease a 20cm (8in) loose-bottomed cake tin. Rub the butter into the flour and salt until the mixture resembles fine breadcrumbs. Stir in the sugar. Add the egg a little at a time until the mixture binds together. If necessary, add a little milk. Carefully knead the mixture on a floured board until smooth. Form into a round and roll out until it measures 20cm (8in) across. Press it into the prepared tin, and refrigerate for 20 minutes. Meanwhile, stew the apricots in their own juice with the sugar for 10–12 minutes until they are just tender, but still hold their shape. Cool. Bake the shortcake at 190°C/375°F, Gas Mark 5, for 20 minutes until golden brown and firm. Cool for 10 minutes, then remove from the tin and cool on a wire tray. When completely cold, carefully split the cake into two layers, using a sharp knife. Spread half the shortcake with half the cream, arrange two-thirds of the apricots on top. Put the second shortcake round on top, and pile on the remaining cream. Decorate with the remainder of the apricots.
Serves 6–8

Strawberries Romanoff

Metric	Imperial
900g fresh strawberries	2lb fresh strawberries
6 × 15ml spoons icing sugar	6tbsps icing sugar
3 × 15ml spoons rum	3tbsps rum
3 × 15ml spoons orange liqueur	3tbsps orange liqueur
300ml double cream	½ pint double cream
3 × 15ml spoons brandy	3tbsps brandy

Hull the strawberries and place in a bowl. Sprinkle with 4 × 15ml spoons (4tbsps) icing sugar, the rum and orange liqueur and mix well. Cover and chill for at least 1 hour. One hour before serving, whip the cream with the remaining sugar and brandy until stiff. Stir into the strawberries, making sure that all the strawberries are coated with cream. Serve chilled.
Serves 6–8

Melon and Grape Jelly

Metric	Imperial
1 melon, halved and seeded	1 melon, halved and seeded
2 sharp eating apples, peeled, cored and sliced	2 sharp eating apples, peeled, cored and sliced
175g black grapes, halved and pipped	6oz black grapes, halved and pipped
Grated rind and juice of 2 limes	Grated rind and juice of 2 limes
15g powdered gelatine	½oz powdered gelatine
2 × 15ml spoons water	2tbsps water
4 × 15ml spoons honey	4tbsps honey

Scoop the melon into balls and mix with the apples and grapes; scoop out the remaining melon flesh and chop roughly. Add the grated rind and juice of limes to the melon balls and apples. Dissolve the gelatine in the water in a basin over a pan of hot water. Stir the gelatine into the fruit mixture and add the honey. Put the chopped melon in the bottom of the melon shells, spoon over the fruit and jelly mixture and put in a cool place to set. Serve cold, cut in slices, with whipped cream if liked.
Serves 4–6

Melon and grape jelly with apricot shortcake

Plum Roly Poly

Metric	Imperial
350g fresh plums, halved and stoned	¾lb fresh plums, halved and stoned
50g caster sugar	2oz caster sugar
8 × 15ml spoons water	8tbsps water
175g self-raising flour	6oz self-raising flour
1 × 1.25ml spoon salt	¼tsp salt
75g shredded suet	3oz shredded suet
Little milk	Little milk

Put the plums in a pan, add the sugar and 2 × 15ml spoons (2tbsps) of the water and heat gently, making sure that the sugar does not burn. Simmer for 5–10 minutes until the plums are tender. Cool. Sift the flour and salt into a bowl, add suet and mix well. Stir in enough of the remaining water to give a light and elastic dough; knead very lightly until smooth. Roll out to 20 × 25cm (8 × 10in). Spread the plums over the pastry leaving a finger's width clear along each edge. Brush the edges with milk and roll the pastry up starting from one short side. Place the roll on greased greaseproof paper and foil and wrap round loosely to allow room for expansion, making sure that the edges are well sealed. Steam the roly poly in a steamer over a pan of rapidly boiling water for 1½–2 hours. When cooked, remove paper and serve hot with custard.
Serves 4–6

Fruit Savarin

Metric	Imperial
25g fresh yeast	1oz fresh yeast
6 × 15ml spoons warm milk	6tbsps warm milk
225g strong flour	½lb strong flour
1 × 2.5ml spoon salt	½tsp salt
25g caster sugar	1oz caster sugar
4 eggs, beaten	4 eggs, beaten
125g butter, softened	4oz butter, softened
Rum syrup:	*Rum syrup:*
4 × 15ml spoons clear honey	4tbsps clear honey
4 × 15ml spoons water	4tbsps water
2–3 × 15ml spoons rum	2–3tbsps rum
For the filling:	*For the filling:*
2 oranges, peeled and segmented	2 oranges, peeled and segmented
2 eating apples, cored and sliced	2 eating apples, cored and sliced
1 pear, peeled, cored and sliced	1 pear, peeled, cored and sliced
50g green grapes, halved and pipped	2oz green grapes, halved and pipped
50g black grapes, halved and pipped	2oz black grapes, halved and pipped
Juice of ½ lemon	Juice of ½ lemon
50g sugar ⎱ made into a syrup by boiling for 5 minutes, then cooled	2oz sugar ⎱ made into a syrup by boiling for 5 minutes, then cooled
150ml water ⎰	¼ pint water ⎰

Lightly grease a savarin tin. Put the yeast, milk and 50g (2oz) of the flour in a bowl and blend until smooth. Allow to stand in a warm place until frothy, about 20 minutes. Add the remaining flour, the salt, sugar, eggs and butter and beat well for 4–5 minutes. Pour into tin and allow to rise in a warm place until it has doubled in size. Bake just above the centre of the oven at 200°C/400°F, Gas Mark 6, for about 40 minutes, or until golden brown and shrinking away from the sides of the tin. Turn out straight away on to a cooling tray and allow to cool. Mix the ingredients for the rum syrup; warm in a pan. Spoon over the savarin. Place on a serving dish. Mix all the fruits together for the filling, stir in the lemon juice and sugar syrup. Just before serving pile the fruit in the centre of the savarin. Serve any remaining fruit separately. Serve with whipped cream.
Serves 4–6

Hazelnut and Chestnut Meringue

Metric	Imperial
450g chestnuts	1lb chestnuts
175g sugar	6oz sugar
2 × 15ml spoons rum	2tbsps rum
150ml double cream, lightly whipped	¼ pint double cream, lightly whipped
5 egg whites	5 egg whites
275g caster sugar	10oz caster sugar
125g hazelnuts, finely chopped	4oz hazelnuts, finely chopped
50g hazelnuts, chopped	2oz hazelnuts, chopped
Chocolate leaves to decorate	Chocolate leaves to decorate

Prepare the chestnuts as for marrons glacés, see page 244, but cook them until tender. Mash with a potato masher, and while still hot stir in the rum and sugar. When cool fold in the cream. Draw a 20cm (8in) circle on a sheet of silicone paper, and place the paper on a baking sheet. Whisk the egg whites until very stiff, then whisk in half the caster sugar, keeping the mixture stiff. Fold in the remaining sugar and the finely chopped hazelnuts. Spread some of the meringue over the circle to form the base of the flan. Using a large star nozzle, pipe the remaining meringue round the edge of the flan to form an edge made of rosettes. Bake towards the bottom of the oven at 130°C/250°F, Gas Mark ¼–½, for 1½–2 hours until firm and just beginning to colour. Allow to cool, remove the paper and place the meringue on a serving dish. Add the chopped hazelnuts to the chestnut mixture, and pile into the centre of the basket. Decorate with chocolate leaves.
Serves 6–8

Hazelnut and chestnut meringue with fruit savarin

Drinks & Candied Fruits

Candying is the process of extracting moisture from fruits and replacing it with the sugar from a syrup in which they are soaked and which is made progressively stronger. The peel from citrus fruits, the stalks of angelica and chestnuts can be preserved in a similar way. During the soaking periods of 24 hours or longer, the moisture from the fruit dilutes the syrup a little. The syrup is then made stronger by adding extra sugar or by evaporating some of the liquid (boiling to get a higher temperature reading) before soaking again. Syrup left after candying can be stored in the refrigerator, diluted with fruit juice or water and used for fruit salad and for stewed fruit or for sweetening drinks.

Candied Fruits

These fruits should be candied when they are fully ripe so that their flavour is at its peak, but while still firm. Small fruit should be chosen in preference to large ones. Prick whole fruits such as plums, greengages, apricots and crabapples with a silver fork (to avoid discoloration), stone cherries and peel and halve peaches and pears, discarding stone or core. *Deal with each type of fruit separately.*

Simmer carefully in water until *just* tender (3–15 minutes), lift out and place in a bowl. Dissolve 175g (6oz) sugar, or half sugar and half glucose, in 300ml (½ pint) of the water in which the fruit was cooked, and pour over the fruit. Leave 24 hours. Drain off the syrup, add 50g (2oz) sugar, dissolve, bring to the boil and pour over the fruit. Repeat this on 5 more successive days.

Then add 75g (3oz) sugar to the syrup, dissolve, add the fruit and simmer 3 minutes. Pour back into bowl and leave 2 days. Repeat with a further 75g (3oz) sugar and leave 4 days. Drain, put on a wire tray and dry in a very cool oven 38–49°C/100–120°F until the surface is no longer sticky. (If your oven cannot be controlled at such a low temperature, heat it to 49°C/120°F, put in the fruit, shut the door, turn off the heat and leave in the cooling oven. This may have to be repeated over several days. A sugar thermometer can be used to check the oven heat.)

A sugar or crystallized finish can be obtained by dipping each piece of fruit into boiling water, draining quickly and then rolling in granulated sugar. If liked, food colouring can be added to the syrup to improve the appearance, especially that of cherries.

Candied fruit should not be stored under airtight conditions or it will go mouldy. Use small boxes of cardboard or wood with waxed paper to line the box and to separate the layers.

Candied Peel

Use well-washed and scrubbed skins of oranges, grapefruit, lemons and limes. Cut fruit into halves, squeeze out juice and remove pulp, or remove peel in quarters. If liked, cut peel into strips about 1cm (½in) wide. *Process each type of fruit separately.* The skins can be frozen until you have enough to make a boiling worthwhile.

Put into a pan, cover with cold water, bring to the boil, simmer 10 minutes and drain. For grapefruit, repeat this process twice more, then simmer until the peel is tender. The other peels also require a total simmering time of about 1 hour. Drain.

Using 450g (1lb) sugar, or half sugar and half glucose, to 600ml (1 pint) water, make a syrup and boil to 104°C/220°F on the sugar thermometer, add peel and leave over the lowest possible heat for a further hour. It is really keeping the syrup hot rather than allowing the temperature to rise more than a very little. Leave covered for 24 hours. Then boil to 107°C/226°F, leave 24 hours, boil to 109°C/228°F and leave 24–48 hours. Reheat, transfer peel to wire trays and dry as candied fruits.

Roll in sugar and store in airtight containers. Some of the thick final syrup can be poured into the hollows of halved or quartered peels and the colour of the peel can be accentuated by adding food colouring to the syrup.

The strips of peel can be served as sweetmeats. They taste even better if the white pith is scraped away after the peel has been simmered until tender.

Candied Angelica

Used to decorate sweet dishes, it is often cut into leaf shapes, or chopped. It can be added to cakes and biscuits.

Pick the stalks early in spring (early May) while young and tender and when the colour is bright. Remove the outer skin by putting into a bowl with 1 × 5ml spoon (1tsp) salt and pouring 600 ml (1 pint) boiling water over. After 15 minutes remove stalks, rinse, add to boiling water and cook gently for 5 minutes or until the skin can be scraped off. Cut into 5–7.5cm (2–3in) lengths.

Dissolve 450g (1lb) sugar, or half sugar and half glucose, in 600ml (1 pint) water, bring to the boil, simmer 5 minutes, pour over the angelica and leave overnight. On each of the next 6 or 7 days, drain off the syrup, bring to the boil, simmer 5 minutes, pour over the angelica and leave 24 hours. By this time the syrup should be as thick as honey. Leave to soak for a further 5 days. Then drain stalks and dry as Candied Fruits. Store in a dry place in airtight bottles. If the colour is pale add a few drops of green food colouring.

Marrons Glacés

Metric	Imperial
1½kg chestnuts	3lb chestnuts
1½kg sugar	3lb sugar
600ml water	1 pint water
Vanilla essence	Vanilla essence
Extra sugar	Extra sugar

Expensive to buy, these sweetmeats are so delicious they are worth spending the time it takes to make them.

Peel the chestnuts by cutting a cross into the top of each one with a sharp knife. Drop a few at a time into boiling water for 5 minutes, or bake in a moderate oven (180°C/350°F or Gas Mark 4). Remove both outer shells and inner skins.

Put peeled chestnuts into a pan with cold water to cover, bring to the boil, then simmer until barely tender. Drain. Dissolve the sugar (or use half sugar and half glucose) in the 600ml (1 pint) water and bring to the boil. Turn off heat, add chestnuts, cover and leave 24 hours. Remove lid, bring to simmering point and simmer 10 minutes. Turn off heat, cover and leave 24 hours. Add 10 drops

Candied fruits with fresh drinks and tisanes

of vanilla essence, bring to simmering point and simmer 10 minutes. Turn off heat, cover and leave 24 hours, then drain, put on to wire trays and leave until no longer sticky. By ensuring the syrup never really boils with the chestnuts in, they are likely to remain whole. However, if some do break up, mould the bits into balls about the size of chestnuts and dry.

Roll each in granulated sugar and wrap in a small piece of foil to prevent it becoming hard. Store in an airtight tin. Homemade marrons glacé should not be stored too long and it is wise to open one or two from time to time to check them.

Makes 1½kg (3lb)

Toffee Apples

Metric	Imperial
Small sweet dessert apples	Small sweet dessert apples
225g sugar	½lb sugar
150ml water	¼ pint water
50g butter	2oz butter
Pinch of cream of tartar	Pinch of cream of tartar
Few drops lemon juice	Few drops lemon juice

Wash and dry apples; remove remains of flowers and the stalks. Push a lollipop, or similar, stick into stalk ends. Put sugar and water into a small, strong, shallow pan, heat slowly and stir until the sugar has dissolved. Add butter and cream of tartar, bring to the boil and boil steadily. If possible, use a sugar thermometer and boil to 138°C/280°F; otherwise, watch carefully and remove from the heat when the syrup is toffee coloured (lightly-browned). Immediately add lemon juice to stop further browning. Quickly dip the apples one at a time into the syrup and turn to coat evenly. Lift out and drain, twisting the apple round and round until the drips stop, then stand on greaseproof paper until set. Use within 24 hours. When the syrup hardens too much to use or if any is left-over it can be diluted with 2 × 15ml spoons (2tbsps) water, stored and reboiled to 138°C/280°F as required.

Makes 4–6 apples

Frosted Grapes

These are used to decorate both savoury and sweet dishes such as baked ham or trifle, icecream dishes, etc.

Use seedless grapes, either white or black, and cut into small clusters. Brush with lightly beaten egg white and then dip into caster sugar to coat evenly. If possible, leave to dry overnight. Mint leaves can be frosted in the same way and used to decorate salads or summer drinks.

Real Lemonade or Orangeade

Metric	Imperial
4 large juicy lemons (or oranges)	4 large juicy lemons (or oranges)
1 litre water	2 pints water
225–450g sugar or honey	½–1lb sugar or honey

Wash the lemons well. Peel off rind, without white pith, put into a pan with the water and sugar and simmer for 20 minutes. Cool a little. Add the juice from the lemons and strain into a lidded container. Chill.

Some of the strips of rind can be used for decoration. If liked, add crushed mint leaves (or other herbs) for last 5 minutes of the simmering time.

Makes 1.5–1.8 litres (2½–3 pints)

246

Fresh Vegetable Cocktail

Metric	Imperial
2 inner stalks celery, with leaves, sliced	2 inner stalks celery, with leaves, sliced
1 medium carrot, peeled and sliced	1 medium carrot, peeled and sliced
5cm piece cucumber, peeled, seeded and sliced	2in piece cucumber, peeled, seeded and sliced
Small piece red or green pepper, sliced	Small piece red or green pepper, sliced
1 spring onion, sliced or small piece of onion	1 spring onion, sliced or small piece of onion
6 large stalks watercress	6 large stalks watercress
450ml tomato or orange juice, fresh or frozen	¾ pint tomato or orange juice, fresh or frozen
Mint or basil leaves or Worcestershire sauce	Mint or basil leaves or Worcestershire sauce
Salt and freshly ground black pepper	Salt and freshly ground black pepper
150ml water and ice cubes	¼ pint water and ice cubes

You need a blender for this recipe.
Put all the vegetables into the blender goblet with enough tomato or orange juice to cover the blades and blend ½ minute. Add mint leaves to orange juice; basil leaves or Worcestershire sauce to tomato juice. Add salt and pepper, the remaining juice and the water and ice cubes. Blend a further ½ minute.

If liked, pour through a fairly open sieve although the roughage in this drink is good for you. Serve as a starter or as a snack. Store in the refrigerator.

Makes 750ml (1¼ pints)

Icecream Soda

Metric	Imperial
225g fruit	½lb fruit
4 × 5ml spoons sugar	4tsps sugar
Approx. 350g vanilla icecream	Approx. 12oz vanilla icecream
Soda water, chilled	Soda water, chilled

Mash soft fruits such as strawberries and chop more firm fruit such as apricots, peaches and plums, with the sugar and mix until the sugar dissolves. Mix in 2 × 15ml spoons (2tbsps) of the icecream. Divide just over half the fruit between 4 tall glasses and put in the remaining icecream. Cover with remaining fruit and fill up with soda water. Serve with drinking straws and long spoons.

Serves 4

Tisanes

These are herbal infusions which are drunk either for their pleasant flavour or, by many people, for medicinal reasons. While commonly served as the first liquid of the day or as a bedtime drink, they are pleasant alternatives to morning coffee and afternoon tea.

Since their delicate flavours are adversely affected by metals, *never* use a metal teapot or metal strainer for tisanes.

Many herbs may be used: dried or fresh leaves of angelica, balm, basil, bergamot*, blackberry, borage, hyssop, lemon thyme, marjoram, all mints, parsley, raspberry, rosemary, sage or thyme.

Put 1 × 5ml spoon (1tsp) per person and 1 × 5ml spoon (1tsp) for the pot into a heated teapot if using dried herbs, or three times that quantity of fresh herbs (bruised to help extract their flavour). Pour on boiling water (milk can be used for bedtime drinks) and allow to infuse 5–10 minutes. Strain. Serve at once or chill, covered, in the refrigerator. Add honey and lemon juice to taste, if wished.

Dried or fresh flowers of camomile, elder and lime can be used in the same way for making teas.

Seeds of caraway and dill are also often used. Bruise them slightly to bring out the flavour, add to boiling water, simmer 5–10 minutes, strain and use. *Bergamot leaves should be simmered, in the same way, for 10 minutes.
Note It is important that the time given for infusing or simmering should not be exceeded or the brew will be bitter. For a stronger brew, increase the amount of herbs used.

Fresh Fruit Crushes
These are made in a blender. Oranges and lemons can be blended with water and sugar or with syrup, but fruits with less flavour need the addition of orange, apple, or other fruit juices. Soda water, tonic water, lemonade, etc. can also be added after blending.

Orange Crush

Metric	Imperial
4 oranges	4 oranges
½ lemon	½ lemon
2–4 × 15ml spoons sugar	2–4tbsps sugar
600ml iced water	1 pint iced water

Put the thinly peeled rind of 2 oranges, the sliced pulp (remove pips) and any juice from the pulp of all the oranges and the ½ lemon into the goblet. Add the sugar and half the water. Blend at high speed for half a minute. Add remaining water and blend 15 seconds. Strain and serve.
Serves 4

Strawberry Crush

Metric	Imperial
175g fresh or frozen strawberries	6oz fresh or frozen strawberries
1–2 × 5ml spoons sugar	1–2tsps sugar
300ml chilled orange juice	½ pint chilled orange juice
Ice cubes	Ice cubes

Put the strawberries into the blender goblet with the sugar and orange juice. Blend ½–1 minute until smooth. Serve with an ice cube in each glass. If preferred, blend strawberries and sugar, divide between the glasses and fill up with chilled soda water or lemonade.
Serves 4

Milk Shakes
These are made in the same way as Fruit Crushes, using fresh or frozen fruit or fruit purées. Use 175–225g (6–8oz) fruit to 600ml (1 pint) chilled milk and sweeten with sugar or sugar syrup if necessary. Use any type of milk including skimmed milk, skimmed milk powder reconstituted, diluted canned milk, etc.

Apricot Milk Shake

Metric	Imperial
225g apricot halves	8oz apricot halves
2 × 15ml spoons sugar syrup	2tbsps sugar syrup
600ml chilled milk	1 pint chilled milk

Put the apricots and syrup into blender goblet with half the milk. Blend until smooth, add remaining milk and blend until frothy.
Serves 4

Yogurt Drinks
The addition of 150ml (¼ pint) milk, or fruit or vegetable juice or purée to a 150g (5floz) carton of plain yogurt makes an excellent 'vitality' drink.

Cucumber and Mint Appetizer

Metric	Imperial
10cm piece cucumber, seeded and chopped	4in piece cucumber, seeded and chopped
1 × 15ml spoon roughly chopped mint leaves	1tbsp roughly chopped mint leaves
150ml chilled milk	¼ pint chilled milk
150ml plain yogurt	¼ pint plain yogurt
Salt and pepper	Salt and pepper

Put the cucumber and mint into the goblet with enough milk to cover the blades; blend about ½ minute at high speed. Add remaining ingredients, blend for a few seconds and serve.
Serves 2

Watercress Vitalizer

Metric	Imperial
¼ bunch watercress, washed	¼ bunch watercress, washed
Very small piece of onion	Very small piece of onion
150ml chilled milk	¼ pint chilled milk
150ml plain yogurt	¼ pint plain yogurt
Salt	Salt

Put the watercress and onion into the goblet with enough milk to cover the blades. Blend about ½ minute at high speed. Add remaining ingredients, blend for a few seconds and serve.
Note To chop very finely in a blender use only enough liquid to just cover the blades.
Serves 2

Mint Julep

Metric	Imperial
8–10 sprigs young mint	8–10 sprigs young mint
1 × 15ml spoon sugar	1tsp sugar
1 × 15ml spoon water	1tbsp water
Crushed ice	Crushed ice
Icing sugar, optional	Icing sugar, optional
Double measure of brandy, whisky, gin or bourbon	Double measure of brandy, whisky, gin or bourbon
Fresh fruit in season	Fresh fruit in season

Crush half the mint and the sugar with a spoon until the sugar dissolves. Add the water and mix until all the mint flavour is extracted. Take a tumbler or a large balloon wineglass, almost fill with crushed ice and push remaining mint in, stalks downwards. If liked, dip the leaves first in icing sugar. Strain the prepared mint mixture into the glass and pour in the spirit. Decorate the top of the ice with small pieces of fruit in season, choosing the most colourful available. Put in a couple of drinking straws and serve. If using brandy add just a dash of rum on top.
Serves 1

Index

248

Index

Acknowledgments

Every writer on the growing of fruit owes a debt to those who
have practised, researched, written and taught before him. In
this country no writer on fruit topics, no matter how
experienced, would wish to avoid acknowledgement to the
East Malling Research Station, the Long Ashton Research
Station and the Royal Horticultural Society. For my part I must
add also the Writtle Agricultural College.

Apart from Institutions, individuals are important, and I have
over forty years benefited by contacts with growers, teaching
colleagues and students, far too many to mention by name, save
that I must acknowledge the help given by my friend
Mr W. T. Pudney, a superb grower of fruit; Mr R. Gardner
(for his invaluable assistance with the problems of vine
cultivation) and my former colleague Mr H. C. Davis.

A. G. Healey

The publishers would like to thank the following organizations and individuals for their kind permission to reproduce the photographs in this
book. In particular special thanks is given to R. H. M. Robinson of the
Harry Smith Horticultural Photographic Collection for his valuable help.
All the horticultural photographs are from this collection except those
listed below:

A-Z Botanical Collection Ltd. 23 left, 47, 85 below, 97, 100 left, centre and
right, 101 centre, 102 right, 106 left and centre, 107 centre and right;
Bernard Alfieri 23 right, 103 left, 110, 143 above, 150 right; Rex Bamber
endpapers, 1, 2-3, 4-5, 61, 93, 108-109, 156-157, 169, 171, 173, 175, 177,
179, 181, 183, 185, 187, 189, 191, 193, 195, 197, 199, 201, 203, 205, 207,
209, 211, 213, 215, 217, 219, 221, 223, 225, 227, 229, 231, 233, 235, 237,
239, 241, 243, 245; Brian Furner 6, 60 right, 83; Iris Hardwick Library
134, 136 below, 146; George E. Hyde 80 below, 153 right; Paul Kemp 158,
159, 161; John Lee 164; John Rigby 20 left and right, 21 above and below,
48 above, 63, 82 above, 89 above.

Illustrations drawn by Rod Sutterby.